Letters Of The Wordsworth Family From 1787 To 1855, Volume 1

Dorothy Wordsworth, William Wordsworth

LETTERS OF
THE WORDSWORTH FAMILY

William Wordsworth

From the statue by Thrupp in Westminster Abbey

LETTERS OF THE
WORDSWORTH FAMILY

FROM 1787 TO 1855

COLLECTED AND EDITED

BY

WILLIAM KNIGHT

IN THREE VOLUMES
VOLUME I

BOSTON AND LONDON
GINN AND COMPANY, PUBLISHERS
1907

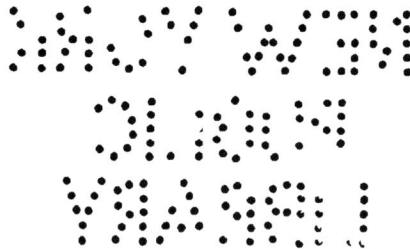

The Athenæum Press
GINN & COMPANY · PRO-
PRIETORS · BOSTON · U.S.A.

THESE VOLUMES
ARE DEDICATED TO
CYNTHIA MORGAN ST. JOHN
OF ITHACA, NEW YORK,
"THE BEST KNOWER" OF WORDSWORTH
IN AMERICA,
AND BUT FOR WHOSE AID
THEY MIGHT NEVER HAVE BEEN
PUBLISHED

PREFACE

No one can regret more than I do the long delay in the publication of these *Letters of the Wordsworth Family*, since the year (1895) in which I undertook, and began in 1896, the preparation of the Poems of Wordsworth for the Eversley edition of the Messrs. Macmillan. It was originally intended that a selection of the poet's Letters should be issued in one or two volumes, after the completion of the *Poems*, the *Prose Works*, and the *Journals of Dorothy Wordsworth*, in the twelve volumes of that edition. For reasons which it is unnecessary to explain, that intention was not carried out, but the collection of Letters was continued and extended. It was limited at first to those of the poet and his sister; but afterwards enlarged by the inclusion of others written by Wordsworth's brother, wife, and daughter, as well as by his sister-in-law Sarah Hutchinson, and his son-in-law Edward Quillinan. As the work progressed, it became increasingly evident that no new "Life" of Wordsworth was needed other than that supplied by the letters of the family. A large part of the *Memoirs* of the poet written by his nephew in 1851, and of my own *Life* published in 1889, as well as of the *Prose Works* (1876), consists of letters; and when these are extracted, and arranged in chronological order — with missing links supplied from other published sources — it is found that the story of Wordsworth's life is told more accurately and vividly than it could be by any indirect narration of it.

It has been the conviction of the present editor for many years that what are called "critical biographies" of great men — however useful they may be — are much inferior in value to the unfolding of the facts of their lives in their own letters. And although Wordsworth disliked the task of penmanship, and was not a great letter-writer, few of his contemporaries, and none of his fellow-poets, revealed themselves more fully than he did through this medium. Not Coleridge, or Southey, or Scott, or Byron, or Landor, or De Quincey, or Shelley — I may add also Tennyson and Browning — have done so to the same extent. Besides, a collection of Wordsworth Family Letters is unique, not only from what it tells us of the writers, but also from the side-lights it casts on the characters of those who are mentioned throughout. Although they belong to a past generation, most of the themes dealt with are of perennial interest. They have not become antiquated to the students of the twentieth century, and posterity may be grateful for their preservation, at least for a time.

It is somewhat curious that Wordsworth had no great interest in the letters written by distinguished men who preceded him, and that he took little trouble in the writing of his own. It is the more remarkable, because his were often so very good when inspiration came to him (as it did in his best poetic work), although he was frequently prolix and repetitive in style. I believe that he scarcely ever took adequate time for the composition of his letters. He never tarried over them, and seldom revised them, while he gave days, and weeks, and months, to the elaboration of some of his shorter poems. He often dashed off his letters without punctuation, and with important words left out. Late in 1839 he wrote to Henry Crabb Robinson : " My mind never took pleasure in throwing itself out after that manner ; and, to say the truth, I think the importance of 'Letters' in modern times much over-rated. If they are good and natural as letters, they will seldom be found interesting to other minds beyond the persons, or the circle, to which they are immediately addressed." The insertion of "not" as the fourth word in the last sentence would make it truer in the opinion of many persons.

As a sample of what he wrote in his more inspired moments, the following — written to Henry Reed at Philadelphia a month later than the above — may be quoted. " I am standing on the brink of that vast ocean I must sail so soon. I must speedily lose sight of the shore, and I could not once have conceived how little I am now troubled by the thought of how long or short a time they who remain on that shore may have a sight of me." And this sentence suggests another, in his long letter written to Lady Beaumont in 1807, on the destiny of his poems, which may be quoted. " It is impossible that any expectations can be lower than mine concerning the immediate effect of this little work[1] upon what is called 'the public.' The things which I have taken, whether from within or without, what have they to do with routs, dinners, morning calls, hurry from door to door, from street to street, on foot or in carriage ? It is an awful truth that there

---

[1] The edition of 1807. — Ed.

neither is, nor can be, any genuine enjoyment of poetry among nineteen out of twenty of those persons who live, or wish to live, in the broad light of the world ; among those who either are, or are striving to make themselves, people of consideration in society. Trouble not yourself about the present reception of my poems. Of what moment is that compared with what I trust is their destiny to console the afflicted, to add sunshine to daylight by making the happy happier, to teach the young and the gracious of every age to see to think and feel, and therefore to become more actively and securely virtuous : this is their office, which I trust they will faithfully perform long after we — that is, all that is mortal of us — have mouldered in our graves."

As a further illustration of Wordsworth at his best as a letter-writer, the following written to Sir George Beaumont may also be quoted. "Theologians may puzzle their heads about dogmas as they will, the Religion of Gratitude cannot mislead us. Of that we are sure, and Gratitude is the handmaid to Hope, and Hope the harbinger of Faith. I look abroad upon Nature. I think of the best part of our Species, I lean upon my Friends, and I meditate upon the Scriptures — especially the Gospel of St. John — and my creed rises up of itself, with the ease of an exhalation, yet a fabric of adamant."

As was almost inevitable at this distance of time, the original manuscript of the Letters in these volumes has, in the vast majority of cases, disappeared. This applies to those published in the *Memoirs* (1851), in the *Prose Works* (1876), in the *Letters of Southey*, the *Memorials of*

De Quincey, and many of those included in the *Life* of Wordsworth which I wrote,—which was issued in 1889,— as well as to the many printed in the *Transactions of the Wordsworth Society*, the letters to Barron Field, Sir William Rowan Hamilton, and others. But those of Dorothy Wordsworth to Jane Pollard (afterwards Mrs. Marshall) and to Mrs. Clarkson survive; while the letters both of William and Dorothy to the Beaumonts at Coleorton existed in 1887, and were then transcribed by me when Lady Beaumont most kindly sent them all to me at St. Andrews. I have tried to obtain a second sight of them — as, through the kindness of those who now own them, I have re-examined all the Pollard ones — but unfortunately they are not now to be found. Those to Mr. Gladstone survive, but very many of those copied by Dr. Grosart have disappeared. It is impossible to give a full list of those which have been recently seen, read, and transcribed by me; or to state where they now are. Many were kindly sent by their owners when requested, and were returned after perusal; but several have changed ownership since then. Copies of others were taken with care, and forwarded to me, when the originals were not sent.

I need hardly say that I found it in many cases more than inexpedient to publish the whole of every letter. Not all of the correspondence — nor the whole of each letter — written by great men is publishable. Purely personal or family matters, and trivial details, must be left out; and sometimes very original and characteristic passages have to be set aside. For example, who would put in print the humorous sentences of Charles Lamb as to the rise of his family through gradations of dignity from the lowest to the highest rung of the ladder? Some critics of the Eversley edition of *The Journals of Dorothy Wordsworth* have written to me objecting that any passages were omitted from them. They little knew what they had the temerity to wish in claiming to read every word of these Diaries, which were not written for publication; none of them — with the possible exception of the record of the *Tour in Scotland* in 1803 — being at first intended to be read beyond the household. Their charm to us now lies in the spontaneity and naturalness, that would never have existed had the eye of others been anticipated. But for that very reason their publication as a whole is undesirable.

All omissions from published letters are indicated in these volumes by points of elision, thus, — . . . . These omissions will explain the occasional want of connection between the sections and paragraphs that are printed.

The abruptness of the commencement and conclusion of some of the letters should also be explained. For a reader to have to peruse the same, or nearly the same, sentence or phrase, repeated hundreds of times, is not only tiresome, but quite useless. It is only when the beginning and the ending of a letter contains something new, or highly characteristic, that it is worthy of quotation. It must also be remembered that the penmanship, neither of Wordsworth nor his sister, was uniformly good; and that it is sometimes quite undecipherable, even by experts. From some familiarity with the autograph MSS. of the others, I may say that it was much worse than Coleridge's, or De Quincey's; while amongst his contemporaries that of Scott was nearly always good, and Southey's uniformly excellent.

I have not retained the punctuation adopted by Wordsworth—sometimes there was none—nor the capital letters, which were both numerous, and very arbitrary. Nor have the archaic spellings — which were equally numerous and arbitrary—been retained. It might have been interesting, from a linguistic point of view, to preserve all the archaisms of spelling and punctuation (even when dashes took the place alike of semicolons, colons, and periods) ; but the Wordsworth family were so arbitrary and casual in their letter-writing — and even careless at times — that it would have been unjust to them, as well as disturbing to their readers, to have done so. Besides, it would have disfigured the pages of these volumes unnecessarily. The titles of Wordsworth's poems, and those of others, have, for distinction's sake, always been italicised instead of being placed within quotation marks ; while the classes, or groups to which they belong, are indicated by the use of quotation marks.

Explanatory footnotes to the letters are numerous, but they have only been inserted when necessary. As the correspondence began one hundred and twenty years ago, and extended over a period of three score years and ten (1787–1860), many of the persons referred to in the course of it — as well as the incidents which took place, and the books and articles mentioned — are of necessity unfamiliar, if not unknown, to the modern reader. Most of these require explanation. A footnote is inserted in reference to each of the correspondents, usually underneath the earliest letter in chronological order, explaining who the correspondent was. Once or twice, however, it has been postponed till a later one is printed; e.g. the explanatory note on Richard Sharp, which should have been inserted on page 181, will be found on page 355 of Volume I.

Several letters. have been accidentally placed out of their chronological order. Most of these will be found in the Appendices to Volume III. Some of them only reached me after the plates of Volumes I and II were cast, and when Volume III was in type. Through the kindness of Mr. Gordon Wordsworth, a grandson and literary representative of the poet, — who himself only discovered them in November, 1906, — a series of letters from both William and Dorothy Wordsworth to Samuel Taylor Coleridge was found amongst the papers of the late Miss Quillinan of Loughrigg Holm. They range from 1799 to 1807. As they concern his grandfather as well as the Wordsworths, they were submitted to, and read by, Mr. Ernest Hartley Coleridge, who was as much impressed as Mr. Wordsworth and I had been by their extreme interest and value, and who cordially agrees to their publication. I have with the consent, and indeed at the suggestion, of Mr. Wordsworth omitted one half of them, as that portion merely repeats what is stated in other letters, or is too minutely domestic. Their discovery makes us all regret that so many others, from which selections might have been made, are now irrecoverable.

I have said that for the serious student of English literature, and for lovers of Wordsworth in particular, the publication of these Letters makes a new and extended Life of him less necessary than it once was. But there is so much fresh material in them, disclosures of character, opinions as to many of the deep questions of the ages, estimates of his predecessors and contemporaries in the poetic hierarchy, etc., that they supply much that may be turned to account by others in the preparation of a new biography. Had I leisure, and were I able to do in reference to them what Mr. Andrew Lang has recently done in reference to the material embodied in Lockhart's *Life of Scott*, I would gladly endeavour to carry out the work of condensation and fresh portraiture. For assuredly the world will wish in days to come new estimates of this poet, based on facts collected from many sources; and I feel that all the work I have done — in many volumes devoted to him — is slight compared with what has yet to be done, and will be done, by others. As I would gladly prepare a new volume of Selections, as a small itinerary manual, — a *vade mecum*, not only to the English Lake District, but to other localities immortalised by the visions of his inward eye, — I would like to condense the story of what he was, and of what he did, within a booklet of one hundred pages. I have material collected for a much larger work, but I fear that I may have to hand it over to others to complete.

It has added greatly to the labour of editing these Letters that so many of them are undated, and have no decipherable postmark; so that the year to which they belong is sometimes a matter of conjecture, and has to be determined by the indirect evidence of their contents or allusions. Unfortunately this has not always been done with accuracy. If I had not had the whole of this work to do — the determination of dates and the tracking of allusions — single-handed, the results might have been more satisfactory. To the knowledge and sagacity of Mr. Gordon Wordsworth I am indebted for the discovery of several *errata*, after the pages had been cast for press. I deeply regret that all the proofs were not revised by him during the years that the volumes have been " in the making," but his suggestions at the eleventh hour have been invaluable.

So far as possible corrections have been made by plate changes in the text, and where — as in the case of a letter inserted out of its proper chronological order — such correction has not been practicable, an explanatory note has been added. The table of contents for each volume and the general index have been prepared for the publishers by Mr. Laurens Maynard.

The portrait of Wordsworth used as a frontispiece to Volume I is from the statue by Frederick Thrupp, in the Baptistery of Westminster Abbey. The frontispiece to Volume II is a picture of Dove Cottage, Grasmere, by John McWhirter, being one of the series of water-colour drawings executed by him for the Edinburgh (Paterson) edition of the works of Wordsworth (1882–1889). The frontispiece to Volume III is a picture of Rydal Mount, from the same series and by the same artist.

W. K.

CONTENTS OF VOLUME I

1797

1798

1799

CONTENTS OF VOLUME I

1809

(See also Letter CLXXXVIII, page 412)

LETTERS OF
THE WORDSWORTH FAMILY

1787

I

Dorothy Wordsworth to Jane Pollard[1]

PENRITH, [1787.]

My dear Jane,

I do not now pass half my time alone. I can bear the ill nature of all my relations, for the affection of my brothers consoles me in all my griefs; but how soon shall I be deprived of this consolation. They are so affectionate. William and Christopher are very clever boys. . . . John, who is to be the sailor, has a most excellent heart. He is not so bright as either William or Christopher, but he has very good common sense, and is very well calculated for the profession he has chosen. Richard (the oldest) is equally affectionate and good, but is far from being as clever as William. I have no doubt of his

---

[1] Jane Pollard, afterwards Mrs. John Marshall of Leeds and Hallstead, was the earliest of Dorothy Wordsworth's girl friends. After Mr. Marshall's death she became the second wife of the first Lord Monteagle of Brandon, grandfather of the present baron, who now possesses Dorothy's letters to her. — Ed.

succeeding in his business, for he is very diligent, and far from being dull. Many a time have W., J., C., and myself shed tears together of the bitterest sorrow. We all of us each day feel more sensibly the loss we sustained when we were deprived of our parents. . . . I was for a whole week kept in expectation of my brothers who staid at school all that time after the vacation began, owing to the ill nature of my uncle, who would not send horses for them, because when they wrote they did not happen to mention them, and only said when they should break up. At last they were sent for, but not till my brother William had hired a horse for himself, and came over. . . . Our fortune will I fear be very small, as Lord Lonsdale will only pay a small part of his debt, which is £4700. My uncle Kit (who is our guardian) having said many disrespectful things of him, and having always espoused the cause of the Duke of Norfolk, has incensed him so much that I fear we shall feel through life the effects of his imprudence. We shall, however, have sufficient to educate my brothers. John, poor fellow, says that he shall have occasion for very little. £200 will be enough to fit him out, and he should wish William to have the rest for his education ; as he has a wish to be a lawyer, if his health will permit, and that will be very expensive. We shall have I believe about £600 a piece, if Lord L. does not pay. It will be very little, but it will be quite enough for my brothers' education ; and, after they are put forward in the world, there is little doubt of their succeeding; and for me, while they live, I shall never want a friend. . . .

Yours affectionately,

D. WORDSWORTH.

II

Dorothy Wordsworth to Jane Pollard

PENRITH, Monday Evening, 10 o'clock, [1787.]

Yesterday morning I parted from the kindest and the most affectionate of brothers. I cannot paint to you my distress at their departure. For a few hours I was absolutely miserable, as a thousand tormenting fears rushed upon me; the approaching winter, the ill-nature of my grandfather and Uncle Chris., the little probability that there is of my soon again seeing my youngest brother, the still less likelihood of my visiting my Halifax friends, in quick succession filled my mind. . . . You know not how forlorn and dull I find myself now that my brothers are gone, neither can you imagine how I enjoyed their company, when I could contrive to be alone with them. If the partial affection of a sister does not greatly magnify all their merits they are charming boys, particularly the three youngest (William, John, and Kit). . . . I often say to myself I have the most affectionate brothers in the world. While I possess them can I ever be entirely miserable? . . . It is indeed mortifying to my brothers and to me that amongst all those who visited at my father's house he had not one real friend. . . . My brother William goes to Cambridge in October. He wishes very much to be a lawyer, if his health will permit; but he is troubled with violent headaches. . . . You must not be surprised if you see him at Halifax in a short time. I think he will not be able to call there on his way to Cambridge, as my uncle William, and a young gentleman who is going to the same college, will accompany him. . . . I have a very pretty collection of books from my brothers,

which they have given me. I will give you a catalogue.
I have the Iliad and Odyssey, Pope's works, Fielding's
works, Hayley's poems, Gil Blas, Dr. Gregory's letters
to his daughters; and my brother Richard intends sending me Shakespeare's plays and the Spectator. I have
also Milton's works, Dr. Goldsmith's poems, &c. . . . I
am determined to do a great deal now both in French and
English. My grandmother sits in the shop in the after-
noons, and by working particularly hard for one hour I
think I may read the next without being discovered. I
rise pretty early in the morning, so I hope in time to have
perused them all. I am at present reading the Iliad, and
like it very much. My brother William read part of it.
. . . I am so little, and wish to appear as girlish as possible; I wear my hair curled about my face in light curls
frizzled at the bottom and turned at the ends. . . .

III

Dorothy Wordsworth to Jane Pollard

[No date. 1787 ?]

. . . I have heard from my brother William since his
arrival at Cambridge. He spent three or four days at
York on the road. . . . John will very likely be off to India
in the spring. . . .

IV

Dorothy Wordsworth to Jane Pollard

[No date. 1787 ?]

[Expresses a longing to go to Halifax to see her friend],
. . . that dear place which I shall ever consider as my

home. . . . We have no father to protect, no mother to guide us. . . . My brother John has set sail for Barbadoes. . . . I hope, poor lad, that he will be successful and happy. He is much delighted with the profession he has chosen. How we are squandered abroad! [She then wishes that her correspondent were her sister, and adds.] How happy we should be! Our fortunes would be very small, but sufficient for us to live comfortably, and on our brothers we would depend for everything. . . .

V

Dorothy Wordsworth to Jane Pollard

Friday, December 7th, [1787.]

. . . Oh! that I could but see you! how happy we should be! I really think that for an hour after our meeting there could nothing pass betwixt us but tears of joy, fits of laughter, and unconnected exclamations. . . . It is now seven months since we parted. We have never been separated so long for these nine years. I shall soon have been here a year; and in two years more I am determined I will come to Halifax, if I cannot sooner; but I hope my uncle is now on the road to preferment. . . . I assure you I am a very skillful architect. I have so many different plans of building our castle, so many contrivances! Do you ever build castles?

When I last wrote I forgot to thank you for those verses you were so kind as to transcribe for me. My brother William was here at the time I got your letter. I told him you had recommended the book to me. He had read it, and admired many of the pieces very much, and promised to get it for me at the book-club, which he did. I was very much pleased with them indeed. The one which you mentioned to me is, I think, very comical. I mean the address to a Louse.[1] There is one to a Mountain Daisy which is very pretty. . . . It is a very fine morning, most likely you are taking a walk up the bank, or in Mr. Cargill's walk. As for me, I never go out but on a Sunday.

VI

Dorothy Wordsworth to Jane Pollard

[PENRITH. No date].

. . . One would imagine that a grandmother would feel for her grandchild all the tenderness of a mother, particularly when that grandchild had no other parent, but there is so little of tenderness in her manner, or of anything affectionate, that while I am in her house I cannot at all consider myself as at home. I feel like a stranger. I was never remarkable for taciturnity, but now I sit for whole hours without saying anything except that I have a shirt to mend, &c. Our only conversation is about *work*, or what sort of a servant such a one's is! What can be more uninteresting than such conversation as this. . . . I often go to the Cowpers, and like Miss D. C. better than ever. I wish my uncle and she would marry.[2] As long as my grandmother lives I must stay with her. . . . I am now writing beside that uncle[3] I so much love. He is a

---

[1] The book containing these verses was Burns's poems, which this letter shows that Wordsworth had read in his seventeenth year. — Ed.

[2] They did so, and Miss Dorothy Cowper was Mrs. Cookson of Windsor. — Ed.

[3] W. Cookson, afterwards rector of Forncett and canon of Windsor. — Ed.

friend to whom next to my aunt I owe the greatest obligations. Every day gives me new proofs of his affection, and every day I like him better than I did before. I am now with him two hours every morning, from nine till eleven. I then read and write French, and learn arithmetic. When I am a good arithmetician I am to learn geography. I sit in his room when we have a fire. He knows I am often pinched for time when I write, so he told me I might do that instead of my French. . . . I had my brother William with me for three weeks. I was very busy during his stay, preparing him for Cambridge. . . .

I have heard from my brother William since his arrival at Cambridge. He spent three or four days at York upon the road. They have sent me word from Whitehaven that they shall fully expect me at Christmas. John and Kit will be there, but I must not go. Poor lads! I shall not see them till next summer, and John will very likely be going off to India in spring. If so, to be sure he will spend a little time here, before his going. . . .

1788

VII

Dorothy Wordsworth to Jane Pollard

NORWICH, December 6, 1788.

[She praises her uncle and aunt Cookson. When it was told her that she was to go with them to Forncett, she was] almost mad with joy. I cried and laughed alternately. It was in a walk with him that it was communicated to me. . . . After the wedding was over [the Cooksons' wedding], we set off on our journey to Newcastle, where we spent a fortnight very agreeably. [Thence to Cambridge] where the buildings, added to the pleasure of seeing my brothers very well and in excellent spirits, delighted me exceedingly. I could scarcely help imagining myself in a different country, when I was walking in the college courts and groves. [Staid only a day in Cambridge, thence to Norwich, and next day to Forncett.] Forncett is a little village, entirely inhabited by farmers, who seem a very decent kind of people. My uncle's house is very comfortable, and the gardens will be charming. I intend to be a great gardener, and to take care of the poultry, which we have in great abundance.

1789

VIII

Dorothy Wordsworth to Jane Pollard

[FORNCETT] January 25, [1789.]

. . . I have leisure to read, work, walk, do as I please. I have every cause to be contented and happy. . . . My brother John, I imagine, sailed for India on Saturday or Sunday in the *Earl of Abergavenny*. William is at Cambridge, Richard at London, and Kit at Hawkshead. How we are squandered abroad. . . . Did I ever tell you that I have got a little school? . . . I have only kept it six months. I have nine scholars. . . . Our hours in winter are, on Sunday mornings, from nine till church time; at noon, from half-past one to three; and at night, from four till half-past five. Those who live near us come to me every Wednesday and Saturday evening. I only instruct them in reading and spelling; and they get off prayers, hymns, and catechism. I have one very bright scholar, some very tolerable, and one or two very bad. I intend in a little time to have a school on a more extensive plan. Mr. Wilberforce[1] has been with us for more than a month. He allows me two guineas a year to distribute in the manner I think best for the poor.

[1] See p. 84. — Ed.

IX

Dorothy Wordsworth to Jane Pollard

Sunday, December 28th, 1789.

. . . We are now happily situated at Forncett, and upon a near view my prospects appear even more delightful than they did upon a more distant one. . . . On Christmas day we went in the morning to one of my uncle's churches, which is only a step or two from the house, and in the afternoon to the other, which is about a mile from us. . . . At present we are reading Hume's History of England. . . . Did I ever tell you that my brother John is gone to Jamaica, and on his return is going to the East Indies. We expect him again in March, or April. One of my amusements is feeding the robin red-breasts. There are at present two in the room, which are gone to rest. You may imagine how tame they are, when I tell you that they hop about the room where we sit, without the least appearance of fear. . . .

1790

X

Dorothy Wordsworth to Jane Pollard

FORNCETT, April 30, 1790.

. . . My brothers, I hope, are all well. I long to have an opportunity of introducing you to my dear William. I am very anxious about him just now, as he will shortly have to provide for himself. Next year he takes his degree. When he will go into Orders I do not know, nor how he will employ himself. He must, when he is three-and-twenty, either go into Orders or take pupils. He will be twenty in April. I do not know whether I mentioned my brother Kit to you. He intends to go to Cambridge. My uncle tells me he is a most amiable youth; and I am told that, for his years, he is a most excellent scholar; and from my own experience I know that he has the best of tempers. . . .

XI

William Wordsworth to Dorothy Wordsworth

Sept. 6, 1790, KESWILL (a small village on the lake of Constance.)

My dear Sister,

My last letter was addressed to you from St. Valier and the Grande Chartreuse. I have, since that period, gone over a very considerable tract of country, and I will give you a sketch of my route as far as relates to mentioning places where I have been, after I have assured you that I am in excellent health and spirits, and have had no reason to complain of the contrary during our whole tour. My spirits have been kept in a perpetual hurry of delight, by the almost uninterrupted succession of sublime and beautiful objects which have passed before my eyes during the course of the last month.

I will endeavour to give you some idea of our route. It will be utterly impossible for me to dwell upon particular scenes, as my paper would be exhausted before I had done with the journey of two or three days. On quitting the Grande Chartreuse, where we remained two days, contemplating, with increased pleasure, its wonderful scenery, we passed through Savoy to Geneva; thence, along the Pays de Vaud side of the lake, to Villeneuve, a small town seated at its head. The lower part of the lake did not afford us a pleasure equal to what might have been expected from its celebrity; this owing partly to its width, and partly to the weather, which was one of those hot gleamy days in which all distant objects are veiled in a species of bright obscurity. But the higher part of the lake made us ample amends: 't is true we had some disagreeable weather, but the banks of the water are infinitely more picturesque, and, as it is much narrower, the landscape suffered proportionally less from that pale steam which before almost entirely hid the opposite shore. From Villeneuve we proceeded up the Rhone to Martigny, where we left our bundles, and struck over the mountains to Chamouny, and visited the glaciers of Savoy. You have undoubtedly heard of these celebrated scenes, but if you have not read about them, any description which I have room to give you must be altogether inadequate.

After passing two days in the environs of Chamouny, we returned to Martigny, and pursued our mount up the Valais, along the Rhine, to Brig. At Brig we quitted the Valais, and passed the Alps at the Simplon, in order to visit part of Italy. The impressions of three hours of our walk among these Alps will never be effaced. From Duomo d'Ossola, a town of Italy which lay in our route, we proceeded to the lake of Locarno, to visit the Boromean Islands, and thence to Como. A more charming path was scarcely ever travelled over. The banks of many of the Italian and Swiss lakes are so steep and rocky, as not to admit of roads; that of Como is partly of this character. A small foot-path is all the communication by land between one village and another, on the side along which we passed, for upwards of thirty miles. We entered upon this path about noon, and, owing to the steepness of the banks, were soon unmolested by the sun, which illuminated the woods, rocks, and villages of the opposite shore. The lake is narrow, and the shadows of the mountains were early thrown across it. It was beautiful to watch them travelling up the side of the hills; for several hours to remark one half of a village covered with shade, and the other bright with the strongest sunshine.

It was with regret that we passed every turn of this charming path, where every new picture was purchased by the loss of another which we should never have been tired of gazing upon. The shores of the lake consist of steeps, covered with large sweeping woods of chestnut, spotted with villages; some clinging from the summits of the advancing rocks, and others hiding themselves within

their recesses. Nor was the surface of the lake less interesting than its shores; half of it glowing with the richest
green and gold, the reflection of the illuminated wood and
path shaded with a soft blue tint. The picture was still
further diversified by the number of sails which stole
lazily by us as we paused in the wood above them. After
all this we had the moon. It was impossible not to contrast that repose, that complacency of spirit, produced by
these lovely scenes, with the sensations I had experienced
two or three days before, in passing the Alps. At the
lake of Como, my mind ran through a thousand dreams
of happiness, which might be enjoyed upon its banks, if
heightened by conversation and the exercise of the social
affections. Among the more awful scenes of the Alps, I
had not a thought of man, or a single created being; my
whole soul was turned to Him who produced the terrible
majesty before me. But I am too particular for the limits
of my paper.

We followed the lake of Como to its head, and thence
proceeded to Chiavenna, where we began to pass a range
of the Alps, which brought us into the country of the
Grisons at Sovozza. From Sovozza we pursued the
valley of Myssen, in which it is situated, to its head;
passed Mount Albula to Hinter Rhine, a small village
near one of the sources of the Rhine. We pursued this
branch of the Rhine downward through the Grisons to
Michenem, where we turned up the other branch of the
same river, following it to Chiamut, a small village near
its source. Here we quitted the Grisons, and entered
Switzerland at the valley of Urseren, and pursued the
course of the Reuss down to Altorf; thence we proceeded,
partly upon the lake, and partly behind the mountains on
its banks, to Lucerne, and thence to Zurich. From Zurich,

along the banks of the lake, we continued our route to Richterschwyl: here we left the lake to visit the famous church and convent of Einsiedeln, and thence to Glaris. But this catalogue must be shockingly tedious. Suffice it to say, that, after passing a day in visiting the romantic valley of Glaris, we proceeded by the lake of Wallenstadt and the canton of Appenzell to the lake of Constance, where this letter was begun nine days ago. From Constance we proceeded along the banks of the Rhine to Schaffhausen, to view the fall of the Rhine there. Magnificent as this fall certainly is, I must confess I was disappointed in it. I had raised my ideas too high.

We followed the Rhine downward about eight leagues from Schaffhausen, where we crossed it, and proceeded by Baden to Lucerne. I am at this present moment (14th September) writing at a small village on the road from Grindelwald to Lauterbrunnen. By consulting your maps, you will find these villages in the south-east part of the canton of Berne, not far from the lakes of Thun and Brientz. After viewing the valley of Lauterbrunnen, we shall have concluded our tour of the more Alpine part of Switzerland. We proceed thence to Berne, and intend, after making two or three small excursions about the lake of Neufchatel, to go to Basle, a town in Switzerland, upon the Rhine, whence we shall, if we find we can afford it, take advantage of the river down to Cologne, and so cross to Ostend, where we shall take the packet to Margate. To-day is the 14th of September; and I hope we shall be in England by the 10th of October.

I have had, during the course of this delightful tour, a great deal of uneasiness from an apprehension of your anxiety on my account. I have thought of you perpetually; and never have my eyes burst upon a scene of particular loveliness but I have almost instantly wished that you could for a moment be transported to the place where I stood to enjoy it. I have been more particularly induced to form those wishes, because the scenes of Switzerland have no resemblance to any I have found in England; consequently it may probably never be in your power to form an idea of them. We are now, as I observed above, upon the point of quitting these most sublime and beautiful parts; and you cannot imagine the melancholy regret which I feel at the idea. I am a perfect enthusiast in my admiration of Nature in all her various forms; and I have looked upon, and as it were conversed with, the objects which this country has presented to my view so long, and with such increasing pleasure, that the idea of parting from them oppresses me with a sadness similar to what I have always felt in quitting a beloved friend.

There is no reason to be surprised at the strong attachment which the Swiss have always shown to their native country. Much of it must undoubtedly have been owing to those charms which have already produced so powerful an effect upon me, and to which the rudest minds cannot possibly be indifferent. Ten thousand times in the course of this tour have I regretted the inability of my memory to retain a more strong impression of the beautiful forms before me; and again and again, in quitting a fortunate station, have I returned to it with the most eager avidity, in the hope of bearing away a more lively picture. At this moment, when many of these landscapes are floating before my mind, I feel a high enjoyment in reflecting that perhaps scarcely a day of my life will pass in which I shall not derive some happiness from these images.

With regard to the manners of the inhabitants of this singular country, the impressions which we have had often occasion to receive have been unfavourable; but it must be remembered that we have had little to do but with inn-keepers, and those corrupted by perpetual intercourse with strangers. Had we been able to speak the language, which is German, and had we time to insinuate ourselves into their cottages, we should probably have had as much occasion to admire the simplicity of their lives as the beauties of their country. My partiality to Switzerland, excited by its natural charms, induces me to hope that the manners of the inhabitants are amiable; but at the same time I cannot help frequently comparing them with those of the French, and, as far as I have had opportunity to observe, they lose very much by the comparison. We not only found the French a much less imposing people, but that politeness diffused through the lowest ranks had an air so engaging that you could scarce attribute it to any other cause than real benevolence. During the time, which was near a month, that we were in France, we had not once to complain of the smallest deficiency of courtesy in any person, much less of any positive rudeness. We had also perpetual occasion to observe that cheerfulness and sprightliness for which the French have always been remarkable.

But I must remind you that we crossed at the time when the whole nation was mad with joy in consequence of the revolution. It was a most interesting period to be in France; and we had many delightful scenes, where the interest of the picture was owing solely to this cause. I was also much pleased with what I saw of the Italians during the short time we were among them. We had several times occasion to observe a softness and elegance which contrasted strongly with the severe austereness of their neighbours on the other side of the Alps. It was with pleasure I observed, at a small inn on the lake of Como, the master of it playing upon his harpsichord, with a large collection of Italian music about him. The outside of the instrument was such that it would not much have graced an English drawing-room; but the tones that he drew from it were by no means contemptible.

But it is time to talk about England. When you write to my brothers, I must beg of you to give my love, and tell them I am sorry it has not been in my power to write to them. Kit will be surprised he has not heard from me, as we were almost upon terms of regular correspondence. I had not heard from Richard for some time before I set out. I did not call upon him when I was in London; not so much because we were determined to hurry through London, but because he, as many of our friends at Cambridge did, would look upon our scheme as mad and impracticable. I expect great pleasure, on my return to Cambridge, in exulting over those of my friends who threatened us with such an accumulation of difficulties as must undoubtedly render it impossible for us to perform the tour.

Every thing, however, has succeeded with us far beyond my most sanguine expectations. We have, it is true, met with little disasters occasionally; but, far from distressing, they rather gave us additional resolution and spirits. We have both enjoyed most excellent health; and we have been so inured to walking, that we are become almost insensible to fatigue. We have several times performed a journey of thirteen leagues over the most mountainous parts of Switzerland without any more weariness than if we had been walking an hour in the groves of Cambridge.

Our appearance is singular; and we have often observed, that, in passing through a village, we have excited a general smile. Our coats, which we had made light on purpose for the journey, are of the same piece; and our manner of carrying our bundles, which is upon our heads, with each an oak stick in our hands, contributes not a little to that general curiosity which we seem to excite.

But I find I have again relapsed into egotism, and must here entreat you, not only to pardon this fault, but also to make allowance for the illegible hand and desultory style of this letter. It has been written, as you will see by its different shades, at many sittings, and is, in fact, the produce of most of the leisure which I have had since it was begun, and is now finally drawing to a conclusion, it being on the 16th of September. I flatter myself still with the hope of seeing you for a fortnight or three weeks, if it be agreeable to my uncle, as there will be no necessity for me to be in Cambridge before the 10th of November. I shall be better able to judge whether I am likely to enjoy this pleasure in about three weeks. I shall probably write to you again before I quit France; if not, most certainly immediately on my landing in England. You will remember me affectionately to my uncle and aunt: as he was acquainted with my giving up all thoughts of a fellowship, he may, perhaps, not be so much displeased at this journey. I should be sorry if I have offended him by it. I hope my little cousin is well. I must now bid you adieu, with assuring you that you are perpetually in my thoughts, and that

I remain,

Most affectionately yours,

W. Wordsworth.

On looking over this letter, I am afraid you will not be able to read half of it. I must again beg you to excuse me.

Miss Wordsworth,
Rev. Wm. Cookson's,
Long Stretton, Norfolk,
L'Angleterre.

XII

Dorothy Wordsworth to Jane Pollard

FORNCETT, October 6th, 1790.

If you have been informed that I have had so dear a friend as my brother William traversing (on foot, with only one companion) the mountains of Switzerland during the whole of this summer, and that he has not yet returned, I flatter myself you will be anxious on my account to hear of his welfare. I received a very long letter from him a week ago, which was begun upon the lake of Constance. . . . I once saw the Miss Martineau you mention at Norwich. Mr. and Mrs. Martineau,[1] her brother and sister, we are very well acquainted with. Last summer we spent two or three days at their house, and had an invitation from them this summer to the musical festival. . . . My school goes on as usual. . . .

[1] They were the father and mother of the late Dr. James Martineau. The Miss Martineau referred to married Mr. Lee of Norwich. — Ed.

XIII

Dorothy Wordsworth to Jane Pollard

December 7th, 1790.

. . . I am living quietly, though very happily, at Forncett, without having been at one ball, one play, one concert. . . . I have a pretty good idea of your feelings on entering the minster at York, by my own when I visited King's College Chapel at Cambridge. . . . Our grandmother has shewn us great kindness, and has promised to give us five hundred pounds (£100 a-piece) the first time she receives her rents. . . . Our several resources are these : the £500 which my grandmother is to give us, £500 which is due on account of my mother's fortune, about £200 which my uncle Kit owes us, and £1000 at present in the hands of our guardians, and about £150 which we are to receive out of the Newbiggin estate, with what may be adjudged as due to us from Lord Lonsdale. My brother Richard has about £100 per annum, and William has received his education, for which a reduction will be made ; so that I hope, unless we are treated in the most unjust manner possible, my three younger brothers and I will have £1000 a-piece, deducting in William's share the expense of his education. . . . John is to go out in the spring in the *Thetis*, East Indiaman. . . . William is to arrive, I hope, by this time at Orleans, where he means to pass the winter for the purpose of learning the French language, which will qualify him for the office of travelling companion to some young gentleman, if he can get recommended. . . . He is at the same time engaged in the study of the Spanish language, and if he settles in England on his return, he will begin the study of the Oriental languages. . . .   We are going to establish a sort of school of industry.   My uncle is at present in treaty about a house for the purpose.   The operations of my little school have been suspended ever since the birth of Christopher. . . .

1791

XIV

Dorothy Wordsworth to Jane Pollard

FORNCETT, May 23rd, 1791.

My brother William is now in Wales, where he intends making a pedestrian tour, along with his old friend and companion Jones, at whose house he is at present staying.[1]

. . . My aunt would tell you that she saw my brothers Richard and William in town. I hope John will arrive there in about a month. We are daily expecting tidings of the *Abergavenny*. I heard from my brother Kit lately. He tells me he has been upon a pedestrian tour amongst the Lakes, with two of his schoolfellows. He is to come to Cambridge next October. . . . The idea of having him so near is, you will imagine, very agreeable to me. I hope we shall see much of each other. He is a most amiable young man. . . . I have been three times at Norwich lately, which is something extraordinary, as we stir little from home. These three journeys produced three visits to the theatre. . . . I rise about six every morning; and, as I have no companion, walk with a book till half-past eight, if the weather permits; if not, I read in the house. Sometimes we walk in the mornings, but

---

[1] Robert Jones of Plas-yn-llan, Denbighshire, fellow-collegian at Cambridge, with whom he made his pedestrian tours on the Continent, and to whom his *Descriptive Sketches* are dedicated. — Ed.

seldom more than half-an-hour, just before dinner. After tea we all walk together till about eight, and I then walk alone, as long as I can, in the garden. I am particularly fond of a moonlight or twilight walk. It is at this time I think most of my absent friends. My brother William was with us six months[1] in the depth of winter. You may recollect that at that time the weather was exceedingly mild. We used to walk every morning about two hours; and every evening we went into the garden, at four or half-past four, and used to pace backwards and forwards till six. Unless you have accustomed yourself to this kind of walking, you will have no idea that it can be pleasant; but I assure you it is most delightful, and if you and I happened to be together in the country (as we probably may), we shall try how you like my plan, if you are not afraid of the evening air. . . .

XV

William Wordsworth to William Mathews[2]

My address is Edward Jones, Esq.
Plas-yn-llan near Ruthin
Denbighshire

Friday, June 17th, [1791.]

Dear Mathews,

For so long a silence it is totally impossible to find any apology, and I am even deprived by it of what I might

---

[1] So it is written, but she must mean weeks, not months. Wordsworth graduated in January, and went to London in February, 1791. — Ed.

[2] A fellow-student at Cambridge. He entered Pembroke College, took his B.A. degree in 1791, and his M.A. in 1794. Wordsworth

otherwise have gained by throwing myself upon your candour and indulgence, as such reliance must appear to
you altogether a matter of necessity and not of choice.
Moralists inform us that whoever meditates any crime *facti
crimen habet*. May not the observation be reversed, and
may not we also say that whoever thinks of, and resolves
to execute, any good intention ought also to have the
merit of the actual performance of it. If I could but
establish this maxim, I should stand in need of no further
apology, for I can with safety assure you, that not many
days have passed over my head since my letter became
due in which I have not resolved to write to you, and
once upwards of two months ago actually took up the
pen but was unfortunately interrupted. But it would be
very idle to consume any more of this sheet prefacing
and prosing in this manner. I shall therefore quit the
subject, by requesting at once that you will grant me that
indulgence which I totally forego claiming as a right, and
only implore as a gift.

You will see by the date of this letter that I am in
Wales, and whether you remember the places of Jones's
residence, or no, will immediately conclude that I am
with him. I quitted London about three weeks ago,
where my time passed in a strange manner; sometimes
whirled about by the vortex of its *strenua inertia*, and
sometimes thrown by the eddy into a corner of the
stream, where I lay in almost motionless indolence.

Think not, however, that I had not many very pleasant
hours; a man must be unfortunate indeed who resides

---

afterward wrote, "This friend of mine was the elder son of Mr.
Mathews, bookseller, near Northumberland House, Strand. He
went to practice as a barrister in the West Indies, and died almost
immediately on his arrival there." — Ed.

four months in Town without some of his time being disposed of in such a manner, as he would forget with reluctance. But I am extremely rude, after having neg-lected your letter so long, to talk so much about myself. I hope if you think it worth while to examine the con-nection of ideas in this letter, that you will find that I have been led naturally to say this much of myself. You will not attribute it merely to politeness if I now make a few enquiries about you, and the manner in which your time passes. I was happy to hear from your letter that you were so agreeably situated in respect to domestic enjoyment, and that your school hours could not be com-plained of as being too much under what may be called a Gothic regulation. How very unreasonable are even those among us who are not totally unphilosophic in wish-ing for the end without undergoing the trouble of the means! I have often [wished], when I have found upon reflection how much of my time has lately passed uncon-nected with reading, that I could perceive in myself a small share of that improvement, which from your neces-sary engagements every day must render you more and more conscious of. All the conclusion that this reflection has ever been able to lead me to is how desirable an attainment would learning be, if the time exacted for it were not so great. Miserable weakness!

Have you heard from Terrot?[1] If not you will not be much surprized to hear from me now that I have never written to him. He passed thro' town without my seeing him, and had near been lost in his passage home. I received [a letter] from him a fortnight after his landing,

---

[1] William Terrot, Berwick-on-Tweed, was fellow-collegian with Wordsworth at St. John's College, Cambridge, from 1787 to 1791. — Ed.

to which I have yet unfortunately [sent] no reply. I am resolved, however, to do away the disgrace this very day. How ridiculous does this resolution, and the necessity of it, make me. I dare say it did not require a twentieth part of the exertion for Regulus (by the bye the story is a lie) to return to Carthage, or for lieutenant Riou to resolve to perish with the *Guardian*.[1]

I have almost exhausted my paper and found I have neither communicated, nor as I intended solicited much information. Under the latter head I purposed to have made many enquiries respecting the acquaintance which you have made with either Men, Women, or Books, since your arrival in Leicestershire; and whether your stock of happiness has upon the whole been upon the increase or the wane. Among other things I wished to have given you some account of the very agreeable manner, in which my time has been spent since I reached Wales, and of a tour which Jones and I intend making through its northern counties; on foot as you will naturally suppose. Of this expedition I hope however to be able to give you some account in my next. I must conclude with assuring you that I shall judge of the perfectness of your forgiveness by the alacrity with which you communicate it. Jones' compliments.

I am, most affectionately yours,

W. WORDSWORTH.

[1] Compare Lieutenant Commander Riou's *Journal of Proceedings on board the Guardian, with a narrative of the Sufferings of the Boat's Crew after they left the ship; particulars of the proceedings in the Guardian till they arrived at the Cape.* — Ed.

XVI

Dorothy Wordsworth to Jane Pollard

FORNCETT, Sunday Morning, June 26, 1791.

. . . I often hear from my brother William, who is now in Wales, where I think he seems so happy that it is probable he will remain there all the summer, or a great part of it. [Referring to her brother Kit she says], his disposition is of the same caste as William's, and his inclinations have taken the same turn, but he is much more likely to make his fortune. He is not so warm as William, but has a most affectionate heart. His abilities, though not so great perhaps as his brother's, may be of more use to him; as he has not fixed his mind upon any particular species of reading, or conceived an aversion to any. He is not fond of Mathematics, but has resolution sufficient to study them, because it will be impossible for him to obtain a fellowship without them. William, you may have heard, lost the chance (indeed the certainty) of a fellowship, by not combating his inclinations. He gave way to his natural dislike to studies so dry as many parts of Mathematics, consequently could not succeed at Cambridge. He reads Italian, Spanish, French, Greek, Latin, and English, but never opens a mathematical book. We promise ourselves much pleasure from reading Italian together at some time. He wishes that I was acquainted with the Italian poets, but how much have I to learn which plain English will teach me. William has a great attachment to poetry; so indeed has Kit, but William particularly; which is not the most likely thing to produce his advancement in the world. His pleasures are chiefly of the imagination. He is never so happy as when in a

beautiful country. Do not think in what I have said
that he reads not at all, for he does read a great deal;
and not only poetry, and other languages he is acquainted
with, but history, &c., &c. Kit has made very good pro-
ficiency in learning, and is certaihly a very clever young
man. He is just seventeen, so that in October '92 we
shall have him at Cambridge. . . . [Tells of riding a good
deal. She had a horse of her uncle's.] The country
about, though not romantic or picturesque, is very pleasing; the surface slowly varied; and we have great plenty
of wood, but a sad want of water. . . . When I last wrote
I told you that our affairs wore a promising aspect; they
are now in a very critical state: our trial is to come on
at the next Carlisle assizes, where we hope the justice of
our cause will carry us through. Lord Lonsdale has
retained all the best counsel, who (except one) are engaged
to serve him upon all occasions, and that one he had just
engaged the moment before my brother went to him. We
have got a very clever man on our side, but as he is young
he will not have much authority. His name is Christian.
He is a friend of my uncle, and knows my brother William
well. I am well acquainted with him, and a very charming man he is. . . . He is professor of common law in
the University of Cambridge.

We have been some time expecting tidings of our brother
John, but have no cause for uneasiness though we hear
nothing of him, as the East India vessels have been
detained in consequence of the expected war with Spain.
My aunt and I are at present pleasing ourselves with the
thought of riding a good deal this summer. . . . ·

I do not think of visiting Halifax till the spring of
1793. By that time I shall be my own mistress. On
coming of age I shall know the amount of my possessions,

and can square my proceedings accordingly. . . . We shall either be very well off in regard to money matters, or left without a farthing. Whatever is the result of this tedious suit I am prepared to meet it. I fear not poverty in my youth, ánd why should I expect it in age, when I have four brothers all of whom have received good education, and are all sincerely attached to me. While I am young I thank God I am not destitute of the means of supporting myself independently. Therefore I can bear the worst with fortitude, and put myself into a situation by which I may procure a livelihood till my brothers are able to assist me. . . .

Yours unalterably,   D. W.

XVII

William Wordsworth to William Mathews

PLAS-YN-LLAN, August 13th, [1791.]

Dear Mathews,

I am extremely concerned to find from your last letter that your share of happiness is so small, and that your time is consumed, and your spirits worn out, in unproductive labour. I should condole with you with greater pleasure, or more properly with less uneasiness, on this misfortune, if I were enabled to point out to you, the method by which your discontent might be allayed. I cannot however think but that your complaints about the diminution of your knowledge must be altogether groundless. Not that I accuse you of a splenetic disposition wilfully fostered by yourself. I think the fatigue which you undergo is a sufficient apology, for that depression of spirits which disposes you to look on the dark side of things. But were you released from this irksome toil, take my word for it, as soon as your spirits became tolerably chearful, you would find that you had been regularly tho' unconsciously advancing. It cannot possibly be otherwise. As to the idea of the decay of your mental powers, you may easily get rid of it, by reading Pope's description of the cave of spleens in the *Rape of the Lock*.[1]

I regret much not having been made acquainted with your wish to have employed your vacation in a pedestrian tour, both on your own account — as it would have contributed greatly to exhilarate your spirits — and on mine, as we should have gained much from the addition of your society. Had I not disgraced myself by deferring to write to you so long, this might easily have been accomplished. Such an excursion would have served like an Aurora Borealis to gild your long Lapland night of melancholy. I know not that you are curious to have any account of our tour. If you are, I must beg you to excuse me from entering into so wide a field, contenting yourself with being informed, that we visited the greater part of North Wales, without having any reason to complain of disappointed expectations.

I wrote to Terrot the very moment after I had concluded my letter to you, and am sorry to say I have not heard from him since. I am fortunately of a disposition to impute this to any other cause than want of regard. Speaking on this subject, I must inform you I was a little disappointed in not finding a letter from you immediately on my return.

You desire me to communicate to you copiously my observations on modern literature, and transmit to you a

[1] See *The Rape of the Lock*, Canto IV, l. 16. " The gloomy cave of spleen." — Ed.

cup replete with the waters of that fountain. You might as well have solicited me to send you an account of the tribes inhabiting the central regions of the African Continent. God knows my incursions into the fields of modern literature — excepting in our own language three volumes of *Tristram Shandy*, and two or three papers of the *Spectator*, half subdued — are absolutely nothing. Were I furnished with a dictionary and a grammar, and other requisites, I might perhaps make an attack upon Italy, an attack valiant; but probably my expedition, like a redoubted one of Caligula's of old, though of another kind, might terminate in gathering shells out of Petrarch, or seaweed from Marino.[1] The truth of the matter is that when in Town I did *little*, and since I came here I have done nothing. A miserable account! However I have not in addition to all this to complain of bad spirits. That would be the devil indeed. I rather think that this gaiety increases with my ignorance, as a spendthrift grows more extravagant, the nearer he approximates to a final dissipation of his property. I was obliged to leave all my books but one or two behind me. I regret much not having brought my Spanish grammar along with me. By peeping into it occasionally I might perhaps have contrived to keep the little Spanish or some part of it, that I was master of. I am prodigiously incensed at those rascal creditors of yours. What do they not deserve? Pains, stripes, imprisonments, &c, &c. If you should happen to write to Terrot shortly, I will thank you for informing him, that I wrote to him some time ago, and wish much to hear from him. It is not impossible that he may not have received my letter, as perhaps it would

[1] Probably H. Marino, author of *Cynthia and Daphne*, translated from the Italian in 1766. — Ed.

go by cross posts. I heard from Greenwood[1] for the first time the very day I received your last. He is in Yorkshire with his father, and writes in high spirits, his letter altogether irregular and fanciful. He seems to me to have much of Yorick in his disposition; at least Yorick, if I am not mistaken, had a deal of the male mad-cap in him, but G. out-madcaps him quite. Adieu, hoping to hear from you soon, and that your letter will bring gladder tidings of yourself. I remain most affectionately yours. Chear up is the word.

W. WORDSWORTH.

XVIII

William Wordsworth to William Mathews

CAMBRIDGE, Sept. 23, [1791.]

My dear Mathews,

I shall not be easy till I think this letter has reached you. I did not receive yours till this very moment. I am much distressed that — indicating as it does a state of mind so much in need of the consolation which friendship can alone impart — that consolation I have been till this very hour unable to administer. Your letter would arrive in Wales not long after I quitted it, on a summons from Mr. Robinson, a gentleman you most likely have heard me speak of, respecting my going into orders, and taking a curacy at Harwich where his interest chiefly lies, which curacy he considered as introductory to the living. I thought it was best to pay my respects to him [in] person, to inform him that I was not of age.[2] Jones

---

[1] Robert H. Greenwood, a school companion at Hawkshead. — Ed.

[2] The age for admission to Anglican orders is twenty-three. When Wordsworth wrote this letter he was only twenty-one. — Ed.

going to Chester just at my departure, and continuing there some time, your letter was not sent after me to Town till his return home, which was not till the 21st instant.   From Town it was sent after me here.   I received it this morning.   I will not employ many words in assuring you of the distress it caused in me to find you so unhappy.   It is evident by the manner in which you address me you are persuaded I am deeply interested in whatever affects your happiness.   Contenting myself with assuring that here you are not mistaken, but that it is probable my regard for you is greater than your diffidence in your power of winning esteem might encourage you to suppose, I shall proceed to make a few observations on your letter, more impelled by a wish to reconcile you to your fortune, than by a hope of succeeding, or the confidence that what I have to say is of much weight.

I imagine it would be altogether an idle labour to attempt to shew that it is possible to be happy in your present situation.   It is much more easy to prevent a dissatisfaction like yours from taking root, than, when it has taken root, to check its vegetation and stop the extravagant stretch of its branches, overshadowing and destroying with their baneful influence, every neighbouring image of chearfulness and comfort.   I take it for granted that you are not likely to continue long in your present employment, but when you leave it how you can put into execution the plan you speak of I cannot perceive.   It is impossible you can ever have your father's consent to a scheme which to a parent at least, if not to every one else, must appear wild even to insanity.   It is an observation to whose truth I have long since consented that small certainties are the bane of great talents.

Convinced as I am of this, I cannot look with much satisfaction on your present situation, yet still I think you ought to be dissuaded from attempting to put in practice the plan you speak of. I do not think you could ever be happy while you were conscious that you were a cause of such sorrow to your parents, as they must undoubtedly be oppressed with; when all that they will know of you is that you are wandering about the world, without perhaps a house to your head. I cannot deny that were I so situated, as to be without relations, to whom I were accountable for my actions, I should perhaps prefer your idea to your present situation, or to vegetating on a paltry curacy. Yet still there is another objection which would have influence upon me which is this. I should not be able to reconcile to my ideas of right, the thought of wandering about a country, without a certainty of being able to maintain myself [MS. torn] being indebted for my existence to those charities of which the acceptance might rob people not half so able to support themselves as myself. It is evident there are a thousand ways in which a person of your education might get his bread, as a recompence for his labour, and while that continues to be the case, for my own part I confess I should be unwilling to accept it on any other conditions. I see many charms in the idea of travelling, much to be enjoyed and much to be learnt, so many that were we in possession of perhaps even less than a hundred a year apiece, which would amply obviate the objection I have just made, and without any relations to whom we were accountable, I would set out with you this moment with all my heart, not entertaining a doubt but that by some means or other we should be soon able to secure ourselves that independence you so ardently pant after, and what is more with minds furnished with such a store of ideas as would enable us to enjoy it. But this is not the case ; therefore, for my own part, I resign the idea. I would wish you to do the same.

What then is to be done? Hope and industry are to be your watchwords and I warrant you their influence will secure you the victory. In order to defend yourself from the necessity of being immured for the future, in such a cell as your present, determine to spare no pains to cultivate the powers of your mind, and you may be certain of being able to support yourself in London. You know there are certain little courts in different parts of London, which are called bags. If you stumble into one of them, there is no advancing, if you wish to proceed on your walk, you must return the way you went in. These bags of Life are what every man of spirit dreads, and ought to dread. Be industrious, and you never need get your head into them, let hope be your walking staff, and your fortune is made. Adieu. God bless you. I shall be impatient to hear from you. Direct to me here. I shall stay here till the University fills. . . .

XIX

Dorothy Wordsworth to Jane Pollard

FORNCETT, 9th October, 1791.

. . . My brother John is arrived in England, and, I am told, is grown a very tall handsome man. . . . Kit is entered at Trinity College, and I hope to see him too by this time next year. William is at Cambridge. I know not when he will go into the North ; probably not so soon as he intended, as he is going to begin a new course of study, which he may perhaps not be able to go on with so well in that part of the world, as I conjecture he may find it difficult to meet with books. He is going, by the advice of my uncle William, to study the Oriental languages. . . .

XX

William Wordsworth to William Mathews

BRIGHTON, Nov. 23, [1791.]

Dear Mathews,

I have been prevented from replying to your letter, by an uncertainty respecting the manner in which I should dispose of myself for the winter, and which I have expected to be determinated every day this month past. I am now on my way to Orleans, where I purpose to pass the winter, and am detained here by adverse winds. I was very happy to hear, that you had given up your travelling scheme, that your father had consented to your changing your situation, and that in consequence your mind was much easier. I approve much of your resolution to stay where you are, till you meet with a more eligible engagement, provided your health does not materially suffer by it. It argues a manly spirit which you will undoubtedly be careful to preserve. I am happy to find that my letter afforded you some consolation. There are few reflections more pleasing than the consciousness that one has contributed in the smallest degree to diminish the anxiety of one's friends. I wrote to Terrot a week ago, requesting that he would not fail to give me a letter at Orleans, as soon as possible. I never have heard from him in answer to the letter I addressed to him from Wales. This I am extremely sorry for. I know not if you have been informed he has lost his second brother in the East Indies. He was shot, though I was told not in an engagement; but I do not know the circumstances. [MS. torn] informed me, who had been staying with Terrot during the summer.

I expect I assure you considerable pleasure from my sojourn on the other side of the water, and some little improvement, which God knows I stand in sufficient need of.

I am doomed to be an idler through my whole life. I have read nothing this age, nor indeed did I ever. Yet with all this I am tolerably happy. Do you think this ought to be a matter of congratulation to me, or no? For my own part I think certainly not. My uncle, the clergyman, proposed to me a short time ago to begin a course of Oriental literature, thinking that that was the best field for a person to distinguish himself in, as a man of letters. To oblige him I consented to pursue the plan upon my return from the continent. But what must I do amongst that immense wilderness, I who have no resolution, and who have not prepared myself for the enterprise by any sort of discipline amongst the Western languages? who know little of Latin, and scarce anything of Greek. A pretty confession for a young gentleman whose whole life ought to have been devoted to study. And thus the world wags. But away with this outrageous egotism. Tell me what you are doing, and what you read. What authors are your favourites, and what number of that venerable body you wish in the Red Sea? I shall be happy to hear from you immediately. My address Mons. W. Wordsworth, Les Trois Empereurs, à Orléans. I am no Frenchman, but I believe that is the way that a letter is addressed in France. I should have deferred this epistle till I had crossed the water, when I might have had an opportunity of giving you something new; had I not imagined you would be surprized at not hearing from me, and had I not had more time on my hands at present than I am likely to have for some time. Adieu.

Yours most affectionately and sincerely,

W. WORDSWORTH.

1792

XXI

Dorothy Wordsworth to Jane Pollard

SOCKBURN, April, [1792?]

. . . You must recollect my friends, the Hutchinsons, my sole companions at Penrith, who removed the tediousness of many an hour, and whose company — in the absence of my brothers — was the only agreeable variety which Penrith afforded. They are settled at Sockburn, six miles from Darlington, perfectly to their satisfaction. They are perfectly independent, and have not a wish ungratified. . . . Their brother has a farm of about £200 rent per annum, and they keep his house. He is uncommonly fond of his sisters. Their house was built by their uncle, who left them the furniture and £1800, which with what they had makes them very comfortable. It is an excellent house, not at all like a farm. It is a grazing estate, watered nearly round by the Tees (a noble river), stocked with sheep. We spend our time very pleasantly, walking, reading, playing at ball in the meadow, in which the house stands "green as an emerald." . . .

XXII

Dorothy Wordsworth to Jane Pollard

FORNCETT, Tuesday, May 6, 1792.

[She speaks of a prospect of going to Windsor in the autumn; but, while pleased to go, she was more pleased with the prospect of her return to the quiet of Forncett. Her brother John had spent four months at Forncett, was now in London, on his way to Cumberland, and intended to sail from Whitehaven for the West Indies.]

I promised to transcribe some of William's compositions. As I made the promise, I will give you a little sonnet; but all the same I charge you, as you value our friendship, not to read or shew it to any one, to your sister or any other person. . . . I take the first that offers. It is only valuable to me because the lane which gave birth to it was the favorite evening walk of my dear William and me.

[She then quotes,

Sweet was the walk along the narrow lane, etc.[1]

and adds]

I have not chosen this sonnet because of any particular beauty it has; it was the first I laid my hands upon.

[1] See *The Poetical Works of William Wordsworth*, Eversley edition, Vol. VIII, p. 215.— Ed.

XXIII

William Wordsworth to William Mathews

BLOIS, May 17th, [1792.]

Dear Mathews,

When I look back on the length of time elapsed since my receipt of your last letter I am overwhelmed by a sense of shame which would deprive me of the courage requisite to finish this sheet did I not build upon that indulgence which always accompanies warm and sincere friendship. Your last reached me just at the moment when I was busy in preparing to quit Orleans, or certainly the sentiments which it breathes had forced from me an immediate answer. Since my arrival day after day and week after week have stolen insensibly over my head with inconceivable rapidity. I am much distressed that you have been so egregiously deceived by Mrs. D. and still more so that those infamous calumnies prevent you from taking upon you an office you are so well qualified to discharge. It gives me still more heartfelt concern to find that this slander has sunk so deep upon your spirits. Even supposing, which is not at all probable, that it should exclude you from the clerical office entirely, you certainly are furnished with talents and acquirements which, if properly made use of, will enable you to get your bread, unshackled by the necessity of professing a particular system of opinions.

You have still the hope that we may be connected in some method of obtaining an independence. I assure you I wish it as much as yourself. Nothing but resolution is necessary. The field of Letters is very extensive, and it is astonishing if we cannot find some little corner, which with a little tillage will produce us enough for the necessities, nay even the comforts of life. Your residence in London gives you if you look abroad, an excellent opportunity of starting something or other. Pray be particular in your answer upon this subject. It is at present my intention to take orders, in the approaching winter or spring. My uncle the clergyman will furnish me with a title. Had it been in my power, I certainly should have wished to defer the moment. But though I may not be resident in London, I need not therefore be prevented from engaging in any literary plan, which may have the appearance of producing a decent harvest. I assure you again and again that nothing but confidence and resolution is necessary. Fluency in writing will tread fast upon the heels of practice, and elegance and strength will not be far behind. I hope you will have the goodness to write to me soon, when you will enlarge upon this head. You say you have many schemes. Submit at least a few of them to my examination. Would it not be possible for you to form an acquaintance with some of the publishing booksellers of London, from whom you might get some hints of what sort of works would be the most likely to answer?

Till within a few days I nourished the pleasing expectation of seeing Jones upon the banks of Loire. But he informs me that at the earnest request of the Bishop of Bangor he has till Michaelmas taken upon [him] the office of usher in a school which the Bishop has just built. You know well that the Welsh Bishops are the sole patrons. This circumstance will connect him with D. Warren,[1] and

[1] The only Welsh Bishop of the name of Warren was John, elected to the see of St. Davids in 1779, transferred to that of Bangor in 1783, and who died in 1800. — Ed.

I hope prepare the way for a snug little Welsh living,
of which our friend is certainly well deserving.   Terrot
some time ago addressed a letter to me at Orleans, promising me that it should soon be followed by another, in
which he represented himself as stickling for preferment
not in the Church or the Army, but in the Custom-house.
'T is all well.   I wish heartily he may succeed.   Let me
entreat you most earnestly to guard against that melancholy, which appears to be making daily inroads upon
your happiness.   Educated as you have been, you ought
to be above despair.   You have the happiness of being
born in a free country, where every road is open, and
where talents and industry are more liberally rewarded
than amongst any other nation of the Universe.

You will naturally expect that writing from a country
agitated by the storms of a Revolution, my letter should
not be confined merely to us, and our friends.   But the
truth is that in London you have perhaps a better opportunity of being informed of the general concerns of
France, than in a petty provincial town in the heart
of the kingdom itself.   The annals of the department [1]
are all with which I have a better opportunity of being
acquainted than you, provided you feel sufficient interest
in informing yourself.   The horrors excited by the relation of the events consequent upon the commencement
of hostilities is general.   Not but that there are men who
felt a gloomy satisfaction from a measure which seemed
to put the patriot army out of a possibility of success.
An ignominious flight, the massacre of their general, a
dance performed with savage joy round his burning body,

---

[1] That is, of *Loir-et-Cher*, in which the town of Blois is situated.
— Ed.

the murder of six prisoners, are events which would have arrested the attention of the reader of the annals of Morocco, or of the most barbarous of savages. The approaching summer will undoubtedly decide the fate of France. It is almost evident that the patriot army, however numerous, will be unable [to] withstand the superior discipline of their enemies. But suppose that the German army is at the gates of Paris, what will be the consequence? It will be impossible to make any material alteration on the Constitution, impossible to reinstate the clergy in their antient guilty splendour, impossible to give an existence to the *noblesse* similar to that it before enjoyed, impossible to add much to the authority of the King:[1] Yet there are in France some [millions?] — I speak without exaggeration — who expect that this will take place.

I shall expect your letter with impatience, though, from my general remissness, | I little deserve | this attention on your part. I shall return to England in the autumn or the beginning of winter. I am not without the expectation of meeting you, a circumstance which be assured would give me the greatest pleasure, as we might then more advantageously than by letter consult upon some literary scheme, a project which I have much at heart. Adieu. I remain my dear Mathews,

Your most affectionate friend,

W. WORDSWORTH.

[1] These sentences may be read in the light of the close of the Franco-German war in 1871. — Ed.

XXIV

Dorothy Wordsworth to Jane Pollard

WINDSOR, October 16, [1792.]

. . . We left Forncett on the last day of July, and arrived at London the following morning. . . . I did not like London at all, and was heartily glad to quit it for Windsor, exactly a week after I had found myself there. . . . I was at the top of Saint Paul's, from whence on a clear day you have a view of the whole city which is most magnificent. I reached Windsor on the 9th of August, and I was charmed with it. When I first set foot upon the terrace I could scarcely persuade myself of the reality of the scene. I fancied myself treading upon fairy ground, and that the country around was brought there by enchantment. The royal family were there. . . . The king stopped to talk with my uncle and aunt, and to play with the children, who — though not acquainted with the new-fangled doctrine of liberty and equality — thought a king's stick as fair game as any other man's, and that princesses were not better than mere cousin Dollys! I think it is impossible to see the king and his family at Windsor, without loving them; even if you eye them with impartiality, and consider them merely as man and woman, not king and princesses. But I am too much of an aristocrat, or what you please to call me, not to reverence him because he is a monarch more than I should were he a private gentleman, and not to see his daughters treated with more respect than ordinary people. I say it is impossible to see them at Windsor without loving them, because at Windsor they are seen unattended by pomp or state, and they are so desirous to please that nothing but ill nature or envy can help [people] being pleased. The king's good temper shews itself in no instance so much as in his affection for children. He was quite delighted with Christopher and Mary. Mary he considers a great beauty, and desired the Duke of York to come to see her. The first time she appeared before him, she had an unbecoming and rather a shabby hat on. We had got her a new one. " Ah," says he, " Mary that's a pretty hat." . . . Do not imagine that I am dazzled by royalty when I say that I do not think I ever saw so handsome a family. The Princess Royal[1] and Princess May[2] are certainly the most beautiful; the former has all the dignity becoming her high rank, with a great deal of grace; the latter has perhaps equal grace, but of a different kind. Hers are the winning graces of sixteen. Perhaps at five and twenty she will not be so fine a woman as her sister. . . . [Describes walks, views, country drives, races, and balls.] My brother William is still in France. We leave Windsor in three weeks. . . .

[1] Married in 1797 to Frederick, King of Würtemberg. — Ed.
[2] Married in 1816 to William Frederick, Duke of Gloucester. — Ed.

1793

XXV

Dorothy Wordsworth to Jane Pollard

FORNCETT, February 16, 1793.

Your letter found me happy in the society of one of my dear brothers. I think I told you that Christopher[1] and I have been separated nearly five years last Christmas. Judge then of my transports at meeting him again. . . . He is like William, with the same traits in his character, but less highly touched. He is not so ardent in any of his pursuits, but is attached to the same ones which have so irresistible an influence over William that they deprive him of the power of chaining his attention to others discordant with his feelings. Christopher is no despicable poet, but he can become a mathematician also. He is not insensible to the beauties of the Greek and Latin classics, or any of the charms of elegant Literature; but he can draw his mind from these fascinating studies to others less alluring. He is steady and sincere in his attachments. William has both these virtues in an eminent degree; and a sort of violence of affection, if I may so term it, which demonstrates itself every moment of the day, when the objects of his affection are present with him, in a thousand almost imperceptible attentions to

---

[1] Afterwards Master of Trinity College, Cambridge. — Ed.

their wishes, in a sort of restless watchfulness which I
know not how to describe, a tenderness that never sleeps,
and at the same time such a delicacy of manners as I have
observed in few men. . . . [Anticipating her brother's
becoming a clergyman, and her living with him, she con-
tinues] I look forward to the happiness of receiving you
in my little parsonage. I hope you will spend at least a
year with me. I have laid the particular scheme of happiness for each season. When I think of winter, I hasten
to furnish our little parlour. I close the shutters, set out
the tea-table, brighten the fire. When our refreshment
is ended, I produce our work, and William brings his book
to our table, and contributes at once to our instruction
and amusement; and, at intervals, we lay aside the book;
and each hazard observations upon what has been read,
without the fear of ridicule or censure. We talk over
past days. We do not sigh for any pleasures beyond our
humble habitation, — "the central place of all our joys."
With such romantic dreams I amuse my fancy during
many an hour which would otherwise pass heavily along;
for kind as are my uncle and aunt, much as I love my
cousins, I cannot help heaving many a sigh at the reflection that I have passed one and twenty years of my life,
and that the first six years only of that time were spent in
the enjoyment of the same pleasures that were enjoyed
by my brothers, and that I was then too young to be sensible of the blessing. We have been endeared to each
other by early misfortune. We in the same moment
lost a father, a mother, a home. We have been equally
deprived of our patrimony. . . . These afflictions have
all contributed to unite us closer by the bonds of affection, notwithstanding we have been compelled to spend
our youth far asunder. "We drag at each remove a

lengthening chain." This idea often strikes me very forcibly. Neither absence, nor distance, nor time, can ever
break the chain that links me to my brothers. . . . By
this time you have doubtless seen my brother Will-iam's
poems.[1] . . . The scenes which he describes have been
viewed with a poet's eye, and are pourtrayed with a poet's
pencil, and the poems contain many passages exquis-itely
beautiful ; but they also contain many faults, the chi-ef of
which is obscurity, and a too frequent use of some particular expressions and uncommon words, for instance
moveless,[2] which he applies in a sense if not new, at least
different from its ordinary one. By moveless, when
applied to the swan, he means that sort of motion which
is smooth, without agitation ; it is a very beautiful epithet,
but ought to have been cautiously used. He ought, at
any rate, only to have hazarded it once, instead of which
it occurs three or four times. The word *viewless* also is
introduced far too often.[3] This, though not so uncommon
a word as the former, ought not to have been made use
of more than once or twice. I regret exceedingly that he
did not submit these works to the inspection of some
friend before their publication, and he also joins with me
in this regret. Their faults are such as a young poet was
most likely to fall into, and least likely to discover ; and
what the suggestions of a friend would easily have made
him see, and at once correct. It is, however, an error
he will never fall into again. . . . My brother Kit and I,
while he was at Forncett, amused ourselves by analysing
every line, and prepared a very bulky criticism, which he
was to transmit to William as soon as he could have added

[1] *An Evening Walk*, and *Descriptive Sketches*.
[2] *An Evening Walk*, ll. 108 and 225 of edition 1793. — Ed.
[3] *Descriptive Sketches*, l. 34. — Ed.

to it the remarks of a Cambridge friend. At the conclu-sion of the *Evening Walk* I think you would be pleased with these lines —

Thus Hope, first pouring, &c.

[She refers to the picture of their small cottage on the horizon of hope, but realises the "dark and broad gulf of time" between.]

There are some very glaring faults, but I hope that you will discover many beauties, which could only have been created by the imagination of a *poet.* . . .

XXVI

Dorothy Wordsworth to Jane Pollard

FORNCETT, [1793.]

The evening is a lovely one, and I have strolled into a neighbouring meadow, where I am enjoying the melody of birds, and the busy sounds of a fine summer's even-ing, while my eye is gratified by a smiling prospect of cultivated fields richly wooded, our own church, and the parsonage house; but oh! how imperfect is my pleasure. I am alone. . . . I hear you pointed out a spot where, if we could erect a little cottage and call it our own, we could be the happiest of human beings. I see my brother [William] fired with the idea of leading his sister to such a retreat as I fancy, ever ready at our call, hastening to assist us in painting. Our parlour is in a moment fur-nished; our garden is adorned by magic; the roses and the honeysuckle spring at our command; the wood behind the house at once lifts its head, furnishing us with a winter shelter and a summer noonday shade. He [her brother W.] is now going upon a tour to the West of England, along with a gentleman who was formerly a schoolfellow,[1] a man of fortune, who is to bear all the expense of the journey, and only requests the favour of William's company, as he is averse to the idea of going alone.

XXVII

Dorothy Wordsworth to Jane Pollard [2]

[No date.]

As William has not the prospect of any immediate employment, I think he cannot pursue a better scheme.[3] [She enlarges on her brother's character and appearance.] He is certainly rather plain.   Otherwise has an extremely thoughtful countenance. . . .   My brother's tour will not be completed till October, at which time they will perhaps make a stand in North Wales, from whence he can very conveniently take a trip to Halifax.   It is more than two years and a half since we last saw each other, and so ardent is our desire for a meeting that we are determined upon procuring to ourselves this happiness, if it were even to be purchased at the price of a journey across the kingdom ; but from North Wales into Yorkshire the distance is nothing.   If therefore my brother does not meet with any employment which is likely to fix him before I go to Halifax, we shall certainly meet there ; but, if he should be engaged, we are determined to see each other at Forncett. . . .   Besides he is impatient to be introduced into our little society at H. . . .   You must know that this

[1] William Calvert. — Ed.
[2] Written at Forncett in the late summer of 1793. — Ed.
[3] Than going with Calvert to the west of England and Wales. — Ed.

favourite brother of mine happens to be no favourite with
any of his near relatives except his brothers, by whom he
is adored; I mean by John and Christopher, for Richard's
disposition and his are totally different. . . . I have not
time to explain to you the prejudices of my two uncles
against my dear William. . . . Though I must confess he
has been somewhat to blame, yet I think excuse might
have been found in his natural disposition.

> In truth he was a strange and wayward wight.
> Fond of each gentle, etc., etc.

That verse of Beattie's *Minstrel* always reminds me of
him; and indeed the whole character of Edwin resembles
much what William was when I first knew him, after my
leaving Halifax.

> And oft he traced the uplands to survey,
> When o'er the sky advanced the kindling dawn,
> The crimson cloud, blue main, and mountain grey,
> And lake dim gleaming on the dusky lawn,
> Far to the west the long long vale withdrawn.

I will transcribe a passage or two from my brother's
letters. The first is from the letter he wrote in answer to
mine, informing him of my certainty of visiting Halifax.
He says " Now, my dearest friend, how much do I wish
that each emotion of pleasure and pain that visits your
heart should excite a similar pleasure or a similar pain
within me by that sympathy which will almost identify
us, when we have stolen to our little cottage. . . . Alas,
my dear sister, how soon must this happiness expire, yet
there are moments worth ages!" . . . In another letter,
in which he informs me of his intention to accept his
friend Calvert's offer, he says " . . . It will be easy for me

to see you at Halifax. Oh, my dear dear sister, with
what rapture shall I again meet you, shall I again wear
out the day in your sight. So eager is my desire to see
you that all obstacles vanish. I see you in a moment
running, or rather flying to my arms." . . .

I have no accomplishment, no one acquirement to
boast, nothing to recommend me but a warm honest affectionate heart. In person I am little altered, my complex-
ion pallid, what you call wishy-washy, which is by the bye
a very expressive word; but what does this signify? I am
your friend. . . . Write, as I have written this letter, at
twenty different sittings or standings, whenever you find
a moment to yourself. . . .

XXVIII

Dorothy Wordsworth to Jane Pollard

FORNCETT, June 16, Sunday Morning, 1793.

I cannot foresee the day of my felicity, the day on
which I am once more to find a home under the same
roof as my brother. All is still obscure and dark.

You remember the enthusiasm with which we used to
be fired, when in the back kitchen, the croft, or in any of
our favourite haunts, we built our little Tower of Joy. . . .
Let us never forget these days. . . . I often hear from
my dear brother William. I am very anxious about him
just now, as he has not yet got an employment. He is
looking out, and wishing for the opportunity of engaging
himself as tutor to some young gentleman, an office for
which he is peculiarly well qualified. . . . I cannot
describe his attention to me. There was no pleasure that
he would not have given up with joy for half an hour's

conversation with me. It was in winter (at Christmas) that he was last at Forncett; and every day, as soon as we rose from dinner, we used to pace the gravel walk in the garden till six o'clock, when we received a summons (which was always welcome) to tea. Nothing but rain or snow prevented our taking this walk. Often have I gone out, when the keenest north wind has been whistling amongst the trees over our heads, and have paced that walk in the garden, which will always be dear to me — from the remembrance of those very long conversations I have had upon it supported by my brother's arm. Ah! I never thought of the cold when he was with me. I am as heretical as yourself in my opinions concerning love and friendship. I am very sure that love will never bind me closer to any human being than friendship binds me to you, my earliest friends, and to William my earliest and my dearest male friend. . . .

XXIX

Dorothy Wordsworth to Jane Pollard

FORNCETT, Aug. 30th, [1793.]

. . . You will certainly see both my brother and myself at Christmas. When William wrote to Mr. Griffith it was his intention to go to Chester, and probably to Manchester, at the latter end of the summer; if so, whether I had been at Halifax or not, he would have paid his friends a visit, but he would also have made a point of seeing me then. His tour was put a stop to by an accident, which might have had fatal consequences. Calvert's horse was not accustomed to draw in a whisky (the carriage in which they travelled), and one day he

dragged them and their vehicle into a ditch, and broke it
to shivers.   Happily neither Mr. C, nor William, were the
worse.   Mr. C mounted his horse and rode into the
North: and William's fine friends, a pair of good legs,
supported him from Salisbury through South Wales.
He is now in the Vale of Clwyd, where he will wait
my arrival at Halifax, and join me there, supposing he
does not enter into some engagement which may interfere with our plans.   He is staying with his friend Jones,
the companion of his Continental Tour, and passes his
time as happily as he could desire. . . .   He says that
"their house is quite a cottage, just such an one as would
suit us," and how sweetly situated in the most delicious of
all vales.   It is nearly three years since my brother and
I parted. [She refers to her brother Richard's kindness
to her.]   Richard and Christopher are both in the North,
John is on his road to the East Indies. . . . [She speaks
of autumn as the sweetest of seasons.]   I grant that the
sensations it excites are not so cheerful as those excited
by the burst of Nature's beauties in the spring months,
yet they are more congenial to my taste.   The melancholy pleasure of walking in a grove or wood, while the
yellow leaves are showering around me, is grateful to my
mind beyond even the exhilarating charms of the budding
trees, while music echoes through the grove. . . .

1794

XXX

William Wordsworth to William Mathews

My address, Mr. Rawson's,
Mill-house, near Halifax
Febry 17.[1]

Dear Mathews,

I am overjoyed to hear from you again and to perceive that your regard for me is undiminished. I quitted Keswick some time since, and have been moving backwards and forwards, which prevented me receiving your very kind letter, as I ought to have done. I am now staying with a gentleman who married a relation of mine, with whom my sister was brought up; my sister is under the same roof with me, and indeed it was to see her that I came into this country. When I received your letter in France informing me of your engagement, and of the prospect of your making a voyage up the Mediterranean, I flattered myself that you would always have reason to look back with pleasure on the time when you undertook that office; and in my letter in answer, (which I dispatched by return of post though you have never received it,) I spoke with great confidence of the probability that this might be a method of securing you an independence. I am sorry to have been disappointed;

---

[1] The postmark shows the year to be 1794. — Ed.

but I find it easy to conceive that with such characters your situation was a most painful one. I approve much of your change of profession; all professions I think are attended with great inconveniences, but that of the priesthood with the most. Tell me on what terms you now study, or how you mean to practise.

You have learned from Myers [1] that, since I had the pleasure of seeing you, I have done nothing and still continue to do nothing. What is to become of me I know not. I cannot bow down my mind to take orders, and as for the law I have neither strength of mind, purse, or constitution, to engage in that pursuit.

It gives me great pleasure to hear you speak in such affectionate terms of our former conversations. Such language adds to the desire which the recollection of those enjoyments inspires me with of repeating them. I am happy to hear that you are master of Spanish and Portuguese. Of Spanish I have read none these three years, and little Italian; but of French I esteem myself a tolerable master. My Italian studies I am going to resume immediately, as it is my intention to instruct my sister in that language.

Have you heard anything of Terrot? where is he, and what doing? If you write to him remember me affectionately to him. I know [not] when I am likely to see you, as I am uncertain when I shall be in London; nor do I think it worth while to take my master's degree next summer. As an honour you know it is nothing, and in a pecuniary light it would be of no use to me; on the contrary, it would cost me a good deal of money. Pray

[1] John Myers, a Westmoreland cousin of Wordsworth, and fellow-collegian at St. John's, Cambridge, 1787-1791. He died in 1821. — Ed.

give my best love to Myers, and in your next, which I shall expect as soon as you have leisure, favour me with his address, and I will write to him. I need not dwell on the pleasure I should have in meeting you, in reading with you the compositions of which you speak, in giving a second birth to [our] former conversations. What rema[rks] do you make on the Portuguese? in what state is knowledge with them? and have the principles of free government any advocate there? or is Liberty a sound, of which they have never heard? Are they so debased by superstition as we are told, or are they improving in anything? I should wish much to hear of those things, and to know what made the most impression upon you, whilst amongst them. Adieu. Pray write to me soon, I regret much having received your letter so late as I did. Be assured that I shall always think of you, with tenderness and affection.

W. WORDSWORTH.

XXXI

Dorothy Wordsworth to Correspondent Unknown [1]

[1794.]

After having enjoyed the company of my brother William at Halifax, we set forward by coach towards Whitehaven, and thence to Kendal. I walked with my brother at my side, from Kendal to Grasmere, eighteen miles, and afterwards from Grasmere to Keswick, fifteen miles, through the most delightful country that was ever seen. We are now at a farm-house, about half a mile from Keswick. When I came, I intended to stay only a few days;

[1] See *Memoirs of William Wordsworth* by Christopher Wordsworth, Vol. I, chap. ix. — Ed.

but the country is so delightful, and, above all, I have so
full an enjoyment of my brother's company, that I have
determined to stay a few weeks longer. After I leave
Windy Brow (this is the name of the farm-house), I shall
proceed to Whitehaven.

XXXII

Dorothy Wordsworth to Jane Pollard

WINDY BROW,[1] NEAR KESWICK, [1794.]

. . . You would hear from my aunt of my wonderful
powers in the way of walking, and of my safe arrival at
Grasmere. At Keswick I still remain. I have been so
much delighted with the people of this house, with its
situation, with the cheapness of living, and above all
with the opportunity which I have of enjoying my brother's
company, that although on my arrival I only talked of
staying a few days, I have already been here above a
fortnight, and intend staying still a few weeks longer, perhaps three or four. You cannot conceive anything more
delightful than the situation of this house. It stands upon
the top of a very steep bank, which rises in a direction
nearly perpendicular from a dashing stream below.

From the window of the room where I write, I have a
prospect of the road winding along the opposite banks of
this river, of a part of the lake of Keswick and the town,
and towering above the town a woody steep of a very considerable height, whose summit is a long range of silver

[1] Windy Brow was a small cottage on the northern bank of the
Greta under Latrigg, now demolished. Mr. Spedding, who owns the
property, has recently revived the old name, and called his modern
house — built at some little distance — Windy Brow. — Ed.

rocks. This is the view from the house; a hundred yards above, it is impossible to describe its grandeur. There is a natural terrace along the side of the mountain, which shelters Windy Brow, whence we command a view of the whole vale of Keswick (the vale of Elysium, as Mr. Gray calls it). This vale is terminated at one end by a huge pile of grand mountains, in whose lap the lovely lake of Derwent is placed; at the other end by the lake of Bassenthwaite, on one side of which Skiddaw towers sublime, and on the other a range of mountains, not of equal size, but of much grandeur; and the middle part of the vale is of beautiful cultivated grounds, interspersed with cottages, and watered by a winding stream which runs between the lakes of Derwent and Bassenthwaite. I have never been more delighted with the manners of any people than of the family under whose roof I am at present. They are the most honest, cleanly, sensible people I ever saw in their rank of life; and I think I may safely affirm, happier than anybody I know. They are contented with a supply of the bare necessaries of life, are active and industrious, and declare with simple frankness, unmixed with ostentation, that they prefer their cottage at Windy Brow to any of the showy edifices in the neighbourhood, and they believe that there is not to be found in the whole vale a happier family than they are. They are fond of reading, and reason not indifferently on what they read. We have a neat parlour to ourselves, which Mr. Calvert has fitted up for his own use, and the lodging-rooms are very comfortable.

Till my brother gets some employment he will lodge here. Mr. Calvert is not now at Windy Brow, as you will suppose. We please ourselves in calculating from our present expenses for how very small a sum we could

live.   We find our own food.   Our breakfast and supper
are of milk, and our dinner chiefly of potatoes, and we
drink no tea.   We have received great civilities from many
very pleasant families, particularly from a Mr. Spedding
of Armathwaite, at whose house you may recollect my
brother was staying before he went to Halifax.   Mr.
Spedding has two daughters, who are in every respect
charming women, and whose acquaintance I am very
desirous of cultivating.   They live in the most delightful
place that ever was beheld.   We have been staying there
three nights, and should have staid longer, if Mrs. Spedding had not been going from home.   She has pressed
me very much to spend some time with them before I
leave the country, which I hope to do.   William is very
intimate with the eldest son, and has always received
great kindness from the family. . . .

XXXIII

Dorothy Wordsworth to Mrs. Crackanthorp [1]

WINDY BROW, April 21, [1794.]

My dear Aunt,

I should have answered your letter immediately after
the receipt of it, if I had not been upon the point of setting forward to Mrs. Spedding's of Armathwaite, where I
have been spending three days.   I am much obliged
to you for the frankness with which you have expressed
your sentiments upon my conduct and am at the same
time extremely sorry that you should think it so severely
to be condemned.   As you have not sufficiently developed

[1] Found at Newbigging, the Crackanthorp's residence, in a box
in an out-house. — Ed.

the reasons of your censure, I have endeavoured to discover them; and I confess no other possible objections against my continuing here a few weeks longer suggest themselves, except the expense, and that you may suppose me to be in an unprotected situation. As to the former of these objections I reply that I drink no tea, that my supper and breakfast are of bread and milk, and my dinner chiefly of potatoes from choice. In answer to the second of these suggestions, namely that I may be supposed to be in an unprotected situation, I affirm that I consider the character and virtues of my brother as a sufficient protection; and besides I am convinced that there is no place in the world in which a good and virtuous young woman would be more likely to continue good and virtuous than under the roof of these honest, worthy, uncorrupted people: so that any guardianship beyond theirs I should think altogether unnecessary. I cannot pass unnoticed that part of your letter in which you speak of my "rambling about the country on foot." So far from considering this as a matter of condemnation, I rather thought it would have given my friends pleasure to hear that I had courage to make use of the strength with which nature has endowed me, when it not only procured me infinitely more pleasure than I should have received from sitting in a post chaise, but was also the means of saving me at least thirty shillings.

In mentioning the inducements which I have to stay at Windy Brow a few weeks longer, it would be unnecessary to speak of the beauty of the country, or the pleasantness of the season. To these are added the society of several of my brother's friends, from whom I have received the most friendly attentions, and above all the society of my brother. I am now twenty-two years of age[1] and such have been the circumstances of my life that I may be said to have enjoyed his company only for a very few months. An opportunity now presents itself of obtaining this satisfaction, an opportunity which I could not see pass from me without unspeakable pain. Besides, I not only derive much pleasure but much improvement from my brother's society. I have regained all the knowledge I had of the French language some years ago, and have added considerably to it. I have now begun Italian, of which I expect to have soon gained a sufficient knowledge to receive much entertainment and advantage from it. I am much obliged to you and my uncle for your kind invitation, which I shall accept with great pleasure on my return from Whitehaven. I have received the kindest civilities from Mrs. Spedding of Armathwaite. She has made me promise that, if it is in my power, I will spend a little time with her. I know of nothing that would make me more happy than to cultivate the acquaintance of the Miss Speddings who are most amiable women. I beg my love to my uncle and the children, and my compliments to Miss Cust.

Believe me, my dear aunt,

Affectionately yours,

D. WORDSWORTH.

[1] She was in her twenty-third year, twenty-two years and four months old. — Ed.

XXXIV

William Wordsworth to William Mathews

WHITEHAVEN, Friday, May 23, [1794.]

Dear Mathews,

I am sorry I did not receive your's of the 11th till yesterday, or I certainly should have answered it sooner. I am very happy to find that your regard for me continues unimpaired, and that you wish so ardently to see me. I assure you it would give me great pleasure to cultivate your friendship in person, but I really cannot on any account venture to London unless upon the certainty of a regular income. Living in London must always be expensive, however frugal you may be. As to the article of eating, that is not much; but dress, and lodging, are *extremely* expensive. But I must do something to maintain myself, even in this country. You mention the possibility of setting on foot a monthly Miscellany from which some emolument might be drawn. I wish, I assure you most heartily, to be engaged in something of that kind; and if you could depend on the talents, and above all the industry of the young man you speak of, I think we three would be quite sufficient with our best exertions to keep alive such a publication. But, as you say, how to set it afloat!

I am so poor that I could not advance anything, and I am afraid you are equally unable to contribute in that way! Perhaps however this might be got over if we could be sure of the patronage of the public. I do not see that my being in the country would have any tendency to diminish the number or deduct from the value of my communications. It would only prevent me from officiating as an editor; and, as you are I suppose both resident in Town, that circumstance would not be of much consequence. I wish much to hear further from you on this head, as I think if we could once raise a work of this kind into any reputation it would really be of consequence to us both. But much is to be attended to before we enter the field. What class of readers ought we to aim at procuring; in what do we, each of us, suppose ourselves the most able, either to entertain or instruct?

Of each other's political sentiments we ought not to be ignorant; and here at the very threshold I solemnly affirm that in no writings of mine will I ever admit of any sentiment which can have the least tendency to induce my readers to suppose that the doctrines which are now enforced by banishment, imprisonment, &c, &c, are other than pregnant with every species of misery. You know perhaps already that I am of that odious class of men called democrats, and of that class I shall for ever continue. In a work like that of which we are speaking, it will be impossible, (and indeed it would render our publication worthless, were we to attempt it,) not to inculcate principles of government and forms of social order of one kind or another. I have therefore thought it proper to say this much in order that if your sentiments — or those of our coadjutor — are dissimilar to mine, we may drop the scheme at once. Besides essays on Morals and Politics, I think I could communicate critical remarks upon Poetry, &c &c, upon the arts of Painting, Gardening, and other subjects of amusement. But I should principally wish our attention to be fixed upon Life and Manners, and to make our publication a vehicle of sound and exalted Morality.

All the periodical Miscellanies that I am acquainted with, except one or two of the Reviews, appear to be written to maintain the existence of prejudice and to disseminate error. To such purposes I have already said I will not prostitute my pen. Besides were we ignorant or wicked enough to be so employed, in our views of pecuniary advantage (from the public at least) we should be disappointed. But on the subject of this scheme I shall be happy to give my ideas at large, as soon as I have received yours, and those of your friend. I repeat it, I think if we are determined to be industrious, we are a sufficient number for any purpose of that kind. I beg therefore I may hear from you immediately, and at great length, explaining your ideas upon our plan. I should also be happy to hear from your friend on the same subject. I am at present nearly quite at leisure, so that with industry I think I can perform my share. I say nearly at leisure, for I am not quite so; as I am correcting and considerably adding to those poems which I published in your absence.[1] It was with great reluctance I huddled up those two little works, and sent them into the world in so imperfect a state. But as I had done nothing by which to distinguish myself at the University, I thought these little things might shew that I could do something. They have been treated with unmerited contempt by some of the periodical publications, and others have spoken in higher terms of them than they deserve. I have another poem written last summer, ready for the press, though I certainly should not publish it unless I hoped to derive from it some pecuniary recompence. As I am speaking on this subject, pray let me request you to have the goodness

---

[1] *An Evening Walk,* and *Descriptive Sketches* (1793). — Ed.

to call on Johnson, my publisher, and ask him if he ever sells any of those poems, and what number he thinks are yet on his hands. This will be doing me a great favor. I ought to have thanked you long since for your account of your plans. I wish you most heartily all the success which you deserve. Pray, in what print are you engaged? · I am yours most affectionately

W. WORDSWORTH.

Do write as soon as possible. My address, R. Wordsworth's, Esq, Whitehaven. This pen and ink are so bad, I can scarce write with them at all.

XXXV

William Wordsworth to William Mathews

WHITEHAVEN, Sunday, June, [1794.]

Dear Mathews,

Your packet of letters, received yesterday night, relieved me from great anxiety. I began to be apprehensive that our intended scheme was falling to the ground, my fears, however, are now done away. This letter I address to you and your friend to whom the satisfaction I have already expressed, will, I have no doubt, be sufficient thanks for his ready compliance with my request. I read the explicit avowal of your political sentiments with great pleasure; any comments which I have to make upon it will be expressed in the best manner by a similar declaration of my own opinions. I disapprove of monarchical and aristocratical governments, however modified. Hereditary distinctions, and privileged orders of every species, I think must necessarily counteract the progress of human improvement:

hence it follows that I am not amongst the admirers of the British Constitution. Now, there are two causes which appear to me to be accomplishing the subversion of this Constitution; first, the infatuation, profligacy, and extravagance of men in power; and secondly, the changes of opinion respecting matters of Government, which within these few years have rapidly taken place in the minds of speculative men.

The operation of the former of these causes I would spare no exertion to diminish, to the latter I would give every additional energy in my power. I conceive that a more excellent system of civil policy might be established amongst us; yet, in my ardour to attain the goal, I do not forget the nature of the ground where the race is to be run. The destruction of those Institutions which I condemn appears to me to be hastening on too rapidly. I recoil from the bare idea of a Revolution; yet, if our conduct with reference both to foreign and domestic policy continues such as it has been for the last two years, how is that dreadful event to be averted? Aware of the difficulty of this, it seems to me that a writer who has the welfare of mankind at heart should call forth his best exertions to convince the people that they can only be preserved from a convulsion by economy in the administration of the public purse, and a gradual and constant reform of those abuses which, if left to themselves, may grow to such a height as to render, even a Revolution desirable. There is a further duty incumbent upon every enlightened friend of mankind. He should let slip no opportunity of explaining and enforcing those general principles of the social order, which are applicable to all times and to all places; he should diffuse by every method a knowledge of those rules of political justice, from which the further any government deviates the more effectually must it defeat the object for which government was ordained. A knowledge of these rules cannot but lead to good; they include an entire preservative from despotism. They will guide the hand of Reform, and if a revolution must afflict us, they alone can mitigate its horrors and establish freedom with tranquility.

After this need I add that I am a determined enemy to every species of violence? I see no connection, but what the obstinacy of pride and ignorance renders necessary, between justice and the sword, between reason and bonds. I deplore the miserable situation of the French; and think we can only be guarded from the same scourge by the undaunted efforts of good men in propagating with unremitting activity those doctrines, which long and severe meditation has taught them are essential to the welfare of mankind. Freedom of inquiry is all that I wish for; let nothing be deemed too sacred for investigation. Rather than restrain the liberty of the press I would suffer the most atrocious doctrines to be recommended: let the field be open and unencumbered, and truth must be victorious. On this subject I think I have said enough, if it be not necessary to add that, when I observe the people should be enlightened upon the subject of politics, I severely condemn all inflammatory addresses to the passions of men, even when it is intended to direct those passions to a good purpose. I know that the multitude walk in darkness. I would put into each man's hand a lantern to guide him, and not have him to set out upon his journey depending for illumination on abortive flashes of lightning, or the coruscations of transitory meteors.

To come now to particulars. I cannot say that the title you have chosen pleases me. It seems too common to attract attention. Do you think any objection can be made to the following " *The Philanthropist, a monthly Miscellany* " ? This title I think would be noticed. It includes everything that can instruct and amuse mankind ; and, if we exert ourselves, I doubt not that we shall be able to satisfy the expectations it will raise. Here let me observe that whatever plans I approve or disapprove I neither wish to be adopted or rejected on the strength of my opinion. As to the choice of matter, and its distribution, I see nothing to object to what you have said upon that subject. I think with you, that each number should open with a topic of general politics. Here it will be proper to give a perspicuous statement of the most important occurrences, not overburthened with trite reflections, yet accompanied with such remarks as may forcibly illustrate the tendency of particular doctrines of government. Next should follow essays upon Morals, and Manners, and Institutions whether social or political. These several departments entirely for such as read for instruction.

Next should come essays partly for instruction and partly for amusement, such as biographical papers exhibiting the characters and opinions of eminent men, particularly those distinguished for their exertions in the cause of liberty, as Turgot, Milton, Sydney, Machiavel, Bucaria, &c. &c. &c. It would perhaps be advisable that these should, as much as possible form a Series, exhibiting the advancement of the human mind in moral knowledge. In this department will be included essays of taste and criticism, and works of imagination and fiction. Next should come a review of those publications which are

particularly characterized by inculcating recommendations of benevolence and philanthropy. Some Poetry
we should have. For this part of our plan we ought to
have no dependence on original communications. The
trash which infests the magazines strongly impresses the
justice of this remark; from new poetical publications of
merit, and such *old* ones as are not generally known, the
pages allotted to verse may generally be filled. Next
come Parliamentary Debates, detailed as you have specified, and such State-Papers as are of importance.

As to our readers, you think that we should endeavour
to obtain as great a variety as possible. You cannot,
however, be ignorant that amongst the partizans of this
war, and of the suspension of the *habeas corpus* act,
amongst the mighty class of selfish alarmists, we cannot
obtain a single friend. We must then look for protection
entirely amongst the dispassionate advocates of liberty
and discussion. These, whether male or female, we
must either amuse or instruct; nor will our end be fully
obtained unless we do both. The clergy of the Church
of England are a body from which periodical publications
derive great patronage: they however will turn from us.
At the Universities of Oxford and Cambridge, amongst
the young men, we shall not look in vain for encouragement. The dissenters, in general, are not rich; but in
every town of any size there are some who would receive a
work like ours with pleasure. I entirely approve of what
you say on the subject of Ireland, and think it very proper
that an agent should be appointed in Dublin to disseminate
the impression. It would be well if either of you have
any friends there, to whom you could write soliciting their
recommendation. Indeed it would be very desirable to
endeavour to have, in each considerable town of Great

Britain and Ireland, a person to introduce the publication into notice. To this purpose, when it is further advanced, I shall exert myself amongst all my friends.

As to coming to Town this step I must at present decline. I have a friend in the country [1] who has offered me a share of his income. It would be using him very ill to run the risk of destroying my usefulness, by precipitating myself into distress and poverty, at the time when he is so ready to support me in a situation wherein I feel I can be of some little service to my fellowmen. Hereafter, if our exertions are sufficient to support us by residing in London, perhaps I may be enabled to prosecute my share of the exertion with greater vigour. While I continue in the country, it will not be easy for me to be of much use, either in the first or last province of the work. In every other I promise my best exertions. I have not been much used to composition of any kind, particularly in prose ; my style therefore may frequently want fluency, and sometimes perhaps perspicuity, but these defects will gradually wear off; an ardent wish to promote the welfare of mankind will preserve me from sinking under them. Both of you appear much engaged. Will it not be necessary to free yourselves from some of those occupations to which your time is at present devoted ? Here you must be the sole judges. As to money, I have not a single sixpence of my own to advance ; but I have several friends who, though not rich, I daresay would be willing to lend me assistance.

The first thing now to be done is, I think, (after establishing a cover correspondence [2]) to communicate to each

[1] Raisley Calvert. — Ed.
[2] By having their folded covers to hold MS. franked for free transmission by post. — Ed.

other a sufficient portion of matter to compose at least two numbers — I mean of general, not temporary matter — which must depend upon circumstances as they occur. I mention this, both because each would be a better judge of his strength, and because such papers may be circulated in manuscript amongst my friends in this part of the world as specimens of the intended work. After this is done, we should then see how much money each of us can raise, what will be the expense of advertising and printing a certain number of copies, and the sale of what number of copies would indemnify us. You have probably both had more experience amongst booksellers than myself, and may be better able to judge how far our publisher may be induced to circulate the work with additional spirit, if he himself participates in the profits. For my part I should wish that if possible it were printed entirely at our own risk, and for our own emolument. But the final decision on all these matters I leave to you. We should by no means *promise* any embellishments; and, as our work will relate rather to moral than natural knowledge, there will not often be occasion for them. I am far from thinking that we should not vary it by occasionally introducing topics of physical science. They should however be as popular, and as generally interesting as we can collect. We should print in the review form.

If you think that by going over to Dublin I could transact any business relative to the publication in a better manner than it could be done by letter, though I have no friends there, I would willingly undertake the voyage, which may be done at any time from this place. Probably I have omitted many things which I ought to have adverted to, you will therefore excuse the little method pursued in the following remarks, which I shall set down as they arise, lest in attempting to arrange them they should slip from my memory. I think it essential that we should not have the least reliance on any accidental assistance; at the same time we should by no means neglect to stir up our friends to favour us with any papers which a wish to add to the stock of general knowledge may induce them to write. Would it not be advisable that each of us should draw up a prospectus of our object and plan, and from the whole may be composed one which we should not delay to submit to the public? Of this prospectus, when finished, the style should be particularly polished and perspicuous.

It would contribute much to render our work interesting, could we have any foreign correspondents informing us of the progress of knowledge in the different metropolises of Europe, and of those new publications, which either attract or merit attention. These writings our knowledge of languages would enable us to peruse, and it would be well to extract from them the parts distinguished by particular excellence. It would be well also if you could procure a perusal of the French monitors; for while we expressed our detestation of the execrable measures pursued in France, we should belie our title if we did not hold up to the approbation of the world such of their regulations and decrees as are dictated by the spirit of Philosophy. We should give also an accurate account of the Polish Revolution, and purify it from those infamous representations which ministerial hirelings have thrown over it. I am not acquainted with the German language, a circumstance which I greatly regret, as the vast tract of country where that tongue is spoken cannot but produce daily performances which ought to be known amongst us. I wish you would answer this letter, as soon as possible ; and at great length. I hope you will be able to procure covers, as in this remote part I cannot at present. You would do well to enclose me one for yourselves fixing the date two or three days after the time when I shall have received yours. I am, with great respect and esteem, your fellow labourer and friend,

W. WORDSWORTH.

XXXVI

William Wordsworth to William Calvert

KESWICK, October 1st, [1794.]

Dear Calvert,

I returned to Keswick last Tuesday having been detained in Lancashire much longer than I expected. I found your brother worse than when I left Keswick, but a good deal better than he had been some weeks before. He is determined to set off for Lisbon, but any person in his state of health must recoil from the idea of going so far alone, particularly into a country of whose language he is ignorant. I have reflected upon this myself, and have been induced to speak with him about the possibility of your giving him as much pecuniary assistance as would enable me to accompany him thither, and stay with him till his health is re-established. I would then return and leave him there. This I think, if possible, you ought to do; you see I speak to you as a friend. But then perhaps your present expenses may render it difficult. Would it not exalt you in your own esteem to retrench a little for so excellent a purpose? Reflecting that his return is uncertain, your brother requests me to inform you that he has drawn out his will, which he means to get executed in London. The purport of his will is to leave you all his property, real and personal, chargeable with a legacy of £600 to me, in case that on enquiry into the state of our affairs in London he should think it advisable to do so. It is at my request that this information is communicated to you, and I have no doubt but that you will do both him and myself the justice to hear this mark of his approbation of me without your good opinion of either of us being at all diminished by it. If you could come over yourself it would be much the best. At all events fail not to write by return of post, as the sooner your brother gets off the better. He will depart immediately after hearing from you.

I am dear Calvert,

Your very affectionate friend,

W. WORDSWORTH.

XXXVII

William Wordsworth to William Mathews

KESWICK, November 7th, 1794.

Dear Mathews,

The more nearly we approached the time fixed for action, the more strongly was I persuaded that we should decline the field. I was not therefore either much sur- prized, or mortified, at the contents of your letter. It is true my distance from Town, unless we were once set forward, could not but be a great obstacle in our way; and at present it is absolutely out of my power to leave this place. My friend, of whom I have spoken to you, has every symptom of a confirmed consumption of the lungs, and I cannot think of quitting him in his present debilitated state. If he should not recover, indeed whatever turn his complaint takes, I am so emboldened by your encouragement that I am determined to throw myself into that mighty gulph which has swallowed up so many, of talents and attainments infinitely superior to my own. One thing however I can boast, and on that one thing I rely, extreme frugality. This must be my main support, my chief *vectigal*. Pray let me have accurate information from you on the subject of your newspaper connection. What is the nature of the service performed by you, and how much of your time does it engross? &c &c. You say a newspaper would be glad of me; do you think you could ensure me employment in that way on terms similar to your own? I mean also in an opposition paper, for really I cannot in conscience and in principle, abet in the smallest degree the measures pursued by the present ministry. They are already so deeply advanced in iniquity that like Macbeth they cannot retreat. When I express myself in this manner I am far from reprobating those whose sentiments on this point differ from my own. I know that many good men were persuaded of the expediency of the present war, and I know also that many persons may think it their duty to support the acting ministry from an idea of thereby supporting the Government, even when they disapprove of most of the present measures.

You will return my best thanks to Burleigh for his obliging letter, and give him to understand, I regret no less than himself my inability to bring about an interview; and that I look forward with eagerness to the time when I may enjoy the pleasures of his conversation.

You speak both of Jones and Myers. The former I have used ill, and want resolution to make an apology. Myers I hope continues a patriot of unabated energy. You would probably see that my brother[1] has been honoured with two college declamation prizes; the second English, and the sole Latin one given. *Ça va*, I mean towards a fellowship, which I hope he will obtain, and I am sure he will merit. He is a lad of talents, and industrious withal. This same industry is a good old Roman quality, and nothing is to be done without it. In colleges this truth is not, at least among the younger part, very generally received. I begin to wish much to be in Town. Cataracts and mountains are good occasional society, but they will not do for constant companions; besides I have not even much of their conversation, and still less of that of my books, as I am so much with my sick friend, and he cannot bear the fatigue of being read to. Nothing indeed but a sense of duty could detain me here under the present circumstances. This is a country for poetry it is true; but the muse is not to be won but by the sacrifice of time, and time I have not to spare.

You inquired after the name of one of my poetical bantlings. Children of this species ought to be named after their characters, and here I am at a loss, as my off-spring seems to have no character at all. I have how-ever christened it by the appellation of Salisbury Plain;[2] though, A night on Salisbury plain, — were it not so insuf-ferably awkward — would better suit the thing itself. Pray let me hear from you as soon as possible, giving me

---

[1] Christopher, afterwards Master of Trinity, Cambridge.— Ed.

[2] The poem first named *The Female Vagrant*, in " Lyrical Bal-lads " (1798); afterwards, and in 1845, *Guilt and Sorrow ; or Inci-dents upon Salisbury Plain.* — Ed.

a just representation of your own employment, not concealing from me any of its disadvantages, and letting me know also what prospect there is of my procuring a similar occupation. I shall wait for your letter in patience.

Believe me, dear Mathews, your very affectionate friend,

W. WORDSWORTH.

1795

XXXVIII

· *William Wordsworth to William Mathews*

[Postmark, PENRITH, Jan. 10, 1795.]

Dear Mathews,

It is a fortnight since I received your letter for which, as you are so much engaged, I am not a little indebted to you. I sat down to reply to it ten days ago, and more than half finished my answer when I was called off, and have not till the present found an opportunity of resuming. I am still much engaged with my sick friend, and sorry am I to add that he worsens daily. I have a most melancholy office of it.

But to other topics. I rejoice with you on the acquittal of the prisoners, and on the same grounds. I cannot say however that I entirely approve of the character of Tooke.[1] He seems to me to be a man much swayed by personal considerations, one who has courted persecution, and that rather from a wish to vex powerful individuals, than to be an instrument of public good. Perhaps I am mistaken; if so, I could wish to have my opinion rectified; such he has appeared to me. I must add that I have not taken up this idea from this last event, for in his share of it I

[1] John Horne Tooke, author of the *Diversions of Purley*, a political pamphleteer and parliamentarian in 1794, tried for high treason but acquitted. — Ed.

see nothing to blame, but from the tenour of his political
conduct previous to that period.   The late occurrencies in
every point of view are interesting to humanity.   They
will abate the insolence and presumption of the aristoc-
racy, by shewing it that neither the violence nor the art
of power can crush even an unfriended individual, though
engaged in the propagation of doctrines confessedly unpal-
atable to privilege; and they will force upon the most
prejudiced this conclusion that there is some reason in
the language of reformers.   Furthermore, they will convince bigoted enemies to our present Constitution that it
contains parts upon which too high a value cannot be
set.   To every class of men occupied in the correction of
abuses it must be an animating reflection that their exertions, so long as they are temperate, will be countenanced
and protected by the good sense of the country.

I will now turn to what more immediately concerns
ourselves.   I sincerely thank you for the exertions you
are ready to make in my behalf.   I certainly mean to
visit London as soon as the case of my friend is determined; and request you would have the goodness to look
out for me some employment in your way.   I must pre-
mise however that I have neither strength of memory,
quickness of penmanship, nor rapidity of composition, to
enable me to report any part of the parliamentary debates.
I am not conscious of any want of ability for translating
from the French or Italian Gazettes; and with two or
three weeks reading I think I could engage for the
Spanish.   You speak of other departments of the paper;
pray how are they in general disposed?   I could furnish
— in the way of paragraph — remarks upon measures and
events as they pass, and now and then an essay upon general Politics.   I should prefer, notwithstanding, confining

myself to the two former employments; at least till I had a little more experience. But I am ignorant of the arrangements of a newspaper, and therefore have to beg you would favour me with a fuller account the first time you have leisure.

There is still a further circumstance which disqualifies me for the office of parliamentary reporter, viz. my being subject to nervous headaches, which invariably attack me when exposed to a heated atmosphere, or to loud noises; and that with such an excess of pain as to deprive me of all recollection. I was aware of the objection drawn from the company one must partly be forced into; but this, when a man has his bread to earn, may be easily surmounted. I saw that Grey[1] and Perry[2] associated very little with the other persons employed in that way. This post however at all events I must decline from the reasons already stated. I should be happy to hear that you could give me grounds to suppose you could find employment for me in any other part of a newspaper, for which you think me qualified. I cannot be detained long by my present occupation, so that you are not likely to give yourself trouble to no purpose. I have now finished with business. I have no news to communicate; and not liking to send you so much blank paper as is now before me, I have paused for a moment to reflect in what way I must fill it up.

[1] Compiler of Debates in the House of Commons. — Ed.

[2] Doubtless James Perry (1755-1821), the newspaper reporter, who first introduced the plan of a succession of reporters, in taking down parliamentary speeches. — Ed.

XXXIX

PENRITH, Jan. 27th, 1795.

I was here interrupted; and have most shamefully neglected, for upwards of a fortnight, a business which was to me an urgent one, viz. the despatching of this letter. I have no apology to make; I have lately undergone much uneasiness of mind; but I have had sufficient *time* on my hands to write a folio volume! I am therefore without excuse. Parliament has now met, and you will have no leisure to attend to me. I am properly punished for my remissness. I am now at Penrith, where I have been some time. My poor friend is barely alive. I shall not stay here any longer than to see him interred; but, as he may linger on for some days, I must request if you can make time to write to me that you would address me at Mrs. Sowerby's, Robin H[ood] Inn, Penrith, Cumberland. Your paper I have heard is out. I have learned nothing further than that it is democratical, and full of advertisements! Perhaps you are allowed a copy of it yourself; if so, you would oblige me highly, very highly, by sending it down to me here, even if it were the day after its publication. I think also I might forward its circulation in this little place. I don't mention this as an inducement for you to comply with my request. I have spoken of it here to an acquaintance, and he says he should like to take it, if it proves a good one. You see things are beginning to turn with respect to the war. Wilberforce[1] and Duncombe are men respected by a very numerous body of people. I have again to request you

---

[1] William Wilberforce (1759–1833). See p. 9. He was, along with Thomas Clarkson, the chief leader of opposition to the slave trade. — Ed.

would excuse my procrastination, and by no means imitate it. Farewell. Believe me, your affectionate friend,

W. WORDSWORTH.

I fear you will be unable to decipher this scrawl. I must learn to write a better hand, before I can earn my bread by my pen.

XL

Dorothy Wordsworth to Jane Pollard, now Mrs. Marshall

MILL-HOUSE, Sept. 2d, 1795.

[She speaks of a visit of Kit's before going up to Cambridge for his final term before graduating, and adds,] He is very like me! It is allowed by every one, and I myself think I never saw a stronger likeness. . . . I am going to live in Dorsetshire. . . . You know the pleasure I have always attached to the idea of home, a blessing which I lost so early. . . . I think I told you that Mr. Montagu had a little boy, who, as you will perceive, could not be very well taken care of, either in his father's chambers, or under the uncertain management of various friends of Mr. M., with whom he has frequently stayed. Lamenting this, he proposed to William to allow him £50 a year for his board, provided I should approve the plan. At the same time William had the offer of a ready furnished house, rent free, with a garden and orchard. A natural daughter of Mr. Tom Myers (a cousin of mine whom I daresay you have heard me mention) is coming over to England by one of the first ships, which is expected in about a month, to be educated. She is, I believe, about

three or four years old, and T. Myers' brother, who has
charge of her, has requested that I should take her under
my care. With these two children, and the produce of
Raisley Calvert's legacy, we shall have an income of at
least £170 or £180 per annum. William finds that he
can get nine per cent for the money upon the best
security. He means to sink half of it upon my life,
which will make me always comfortable and independent. . . . The house belongs to a Mr. Pinney, a very rich
merchant of Bristol. He had given it up to his son to dispose of as he pleased. He has hitherto kept a man and
maid-servant in it; and has now, with his father's approbation offered it to my brother. He is to come occasionally for a few weeks to stay with us, paying for his board.
It is a very good house, and in a pleasant situation. . . .
William is staying at Bristol at present with Mr. Pinney,
and is very much delighted with the whole family, particularly with Mr. Pinney the father. I had heard much of
Mr. Montagu from William. This praise is confirmed by
Kit who says he is beloved and esteemed by all, and a
man of the strictest integrity. The boy will be a great
charge for me, but I am not averse to household employments, and fond of children. . . . William has great hopes
of having a son of Mr. Pinney, about thirteen years of age,
for a pupil. . . . I have great satisfaction in thinking
that William will have such opportunities of studying as
will be advantageous not only to his mind but his purse.
Living in the unsettled way in which he has hitherto lived
in London is altogether unfavourable to mental exertion.
By the bye I must not forget to tell you that he has had
the offer of ten guineas for a work which has not taken
him much time, and half the profits of a second edition
if it should be called for. It is a little sum, but it is

one step. . . . Basil Montagu is yet by no means a spoiled child, notwithstanding the disadvantage under which he has laboured. As for the little girl, I shall feel myself as a mother to her. . . . It is a painful idea that one's existence is of very little use, which I have been always obliged to feel hitherto. . . . I shall be grieved to leave Mill-house; Mr. and Mrs. Rawson have been so very kind to me, and my aunt you know has been my mother. . . . I am determined to work with resolution. . . . It will greatly contribute to my happiness, and place me in such a situation that I shall be doing something. . . . I shall have to join William at Bristol, and proceed thence in a chaise with Basil to Racedown. It is fifty miles. . . .

XLI

William Wordsworth to Francis Wrangham [1]

RACEDOWN COTTAGE, NEAR CREWKERNE, SOMERSET,
Nov. 20th, [1795.]

My dear Wrangham,

I have had a melancholy proof of my procrastinating spirit in having so long deferred writing to you. I have to reproach myself the more with this indolence, as it has probably prevented our finishing the imitation of Juvenal, so as to have it out this season. I am anxious to know whether it has been advanced by your exertions, and to request that, beginning at the verse " Sit tibi sancta cohors comitum" &c, you would favour me with such ideas as may have suggested themselves to you, and parcel out, in such proportions as you approve of, the rest of the poem, to be

---

[1] One of Wordsworth's most intimate friends, afterward the rector of Hummanby, Yorkshire, and a voluminous author. — Ed.

finished by us separately as we can no longer labour at it jointly.

Soon after I left you I completed something like an imitation, though extremely periphrastic, from "Expectata diu tandem provincia" etc. to "spoliatis arma supersunt" &c.[1] I will transcribe it for you, to correct in some future letter. In the mean time, the following verses are at your service, to insert them in the poem, if you think them worth it. There is not a syllable correspondent to them in Juvenal. They were intended to follow after the lines about titles "puissant, gracious," &c.

Ye Kings, in wisdom, sense, and power supreme,
These freaks are worse than any sick man's dream.
To hated worth no Tyrant ere design'd
Malice so subtle, vengeance so refin'd.
Even he, who yoked the living to the dead,
Rivall'd by you, hides the diminish'd head.
Never did Rome herself so set at naught
All plain blunt sense, all subtlety of thought.
Heavens! who sees majesty in George's face?
Or looks at Norfolk and can dream of grace?
What has this blessed earth to do with shame
If Excellence was ever Eden's name?
Must honour still to Lonsdale's tail be bound?
Then execration is an empty sound.
Is Common-sense asleep? has she no wand
From this curst Pharaoh-plague to rid the land?
Then to our Bishop's *reverent* let us fall,
And *worship* Mayors, Tipstaffs, Aldermen and all.
Let Ignorance o'er the monster swarms preside,
Till Egypt sees her antient fame outvied.
The thundering Thurlow, Apis! shall rejoice
In rites once offered to thy bellowing voice.

[1] See *Satire*, viii, ll. 87–124. — Ed.

Insatiate Charlotte's tears, and Charlotte's smile.
. . . the scaly regent of the Nile.
Bishops, of milder Spanish breed, shall boast
The reverence by the fierce Anubis lost.
And 't is their due devotion has been paid
These seven[1] long years to Grenville's onion head.

The two best verses of this extract were given me by Southey, a friend of Coleridge: "Who sees Majesty, &c." He supplied me with another line, which I think worth adopting; we mention Lord Courtnay. Southey's verse is "Whence have I fallen alas! what have I done?" A literal translation of the Courtnay motto, *Ubi lapsus? Quid feci?* Can you manage to add another line to this, and insert it after "forfeit loins"? Let me hear from you soon. You will oblige me by transcribing the part of the imitation in your possession, and still more by transcribing for me any additions of your own. I suppose you were too busy to go on with *The Destruction of Babylon.* I don't think you have much occasion to regret your having been otherwise employed. The subject is certainly not a bad one, but I cannot help thinking your talents might be more happily employed.

You flattered me with a hope that, by your assistance, I might be supplied with the *Morning Chronicle;* have you spoken to the editors about it? If it could be managed, I should be much pleased; as we only see here a provincial weekly paper, and I cannot afford to have the *Chronicle* at my own expense. I have said nothing of Racedown. It is an excellent house, and the country far from unpleasant, but as for society we must manufacture it ourselves. Will you come, and help us?

[1] Five, six, or seven! I do not know how long this luminary has enjoyed the honour of the peerage. — W. W.

We expect Montagu at Christmas, and should be very glad if you could make it convenient to come along with him. If not, at all events we shall hope to see you in the course of next summer. Have you any interest with the booksellers? I have a poem which I should wish to dispose of, provided I could get any thing for it. I recollect reading the first draught of it to you in London. But, since I came to Racedown, I have made alterations and additions so material that it may be looked on almost as another work. Its object is partly to expose the vices of the penal law, and the calamities of war, as they affect individuals.[1] — Adieu,

Your affectionate friend,

W. WORDSWORTH.

Basil is quite well.

XLII

Dorothy Wordsworth to Mrs. Marshall

RACEDOWN, November 30th, [1795.]

. . . I really never more fully intended anything in my life than to write to you very soon after my arrival at Racedown. I certainly had no right to expect to hear from you, till I myself had informed you of my address. . . . We are now surrounded with winter prospects without doors, and within have only winter occupations, books, solitude, and the fireside; yet I may safely say we are never dull. Basil is a charming boy; he affords us perpetual entertainment. Do not suppose from this that we make him our perpetual plaything, far otherwise. I

---

[1] This doubtless refers to *Guilt and Sorrow.*—Ed.

think that is one of the modes of treatment most likely
to ruin a child's temper and character; but I do not
think there is any pleasure more delightful than that
of marking the development of a child's faculties, and
observing his little occupations.

We found everything at Racedown much more complete with respect to household conveniences than I
expected. You may judge of this when I tell you that
we have not had to lay out ten shillings on the house.
We were a whole month without a servant, but now we
have got one of the nicest girls I ever saw; she suits us
exactly, and I have all my domestic concerns so arranged
that everything goes on with the utmost regularity. . . .
We walk about two hours every morning. We have
many very pleasant roads about us; and, what is a great
advantage, they are of a sandy soil, and almost always
dry. We can see the sea if we go 200 yards from the
door; and, at a little distance, have a very extensive view
terminated by the sea, seen through different openings
of the unequal hills. We have not the warmth and luxu-
riance of Devonshire, though there is no want either of
wood or cultivation; but the trees appear to suffer from
the sea-blasts. We have hills which — seen from a distance — almost take the character of mountains; some
cultivated nearly to their summits, others in a wild state,
covered with furze and broom. These delight me the
most, as they remind me of our native wilds.

Our common parlour is the prettiest little room that
can be, with very good furniture, a huge [box?] on each
side the fire, a marble chimney-piece, with stove, and
an oil cloth for the floor. The other parlour is rather
larger, has a good carpet, has sideboards in the recesses
on each side of the fire, and has upon the whole a better

appearance, but we do not like it half so well as our little breakfast room. I have had only one great disappointment since we came, and that is about the little girl. I lament it the more, as I am sure if her father knew all the circumstances, he would wish her to be placed under our care. Mr. Montagu intended being with us a month ago, but we have not seen him yet. I have the satisfaction of thinking that he will see great improvements in Basil. [She mentions that they were seven miles from Crewkerne, and at nearly equal distance from Axminster, Bridport, and Lyme.]

XLIII

William Wordsworth to Francis Wrangham

[1795.]

My dear Wrangham,

Your letter was very acceptable. I have done wrong in not replying to it sooner; if precedents would excuse me I would follow Mr. Pitt's rule, and take them from my own conduct; you also might furnish me with some additional store. As to your promoting my interest in the way of pupils, upon a review of my own attainments I think there is so little that I am able to teach that this scheme may be suffered to fly quietly away to the paradise of fools. Your verses are good, but having lost my Juvenal I cannot compare them with the original. There is one weak line "Urged by avarices," &c; and "murderers shall *die*," after "whips racks & torture," sounds weak.

If your poems[1] are published I should have liked to have had a copy. I have been employed lately in

---

[1] *Poems; containing the Restoration of the Jews; a Seaton Prize Poem, with many Translations*, by Francis Wrangham, 1795. — Ed.

writing a tragedy [1] — the first draught of which is nearly finished. Let me hear from you very soon and I do promise — not a Godwynian, Montaguian, Lincolnian, promise — that I will become a prompt correspondent. This letter will do as well as a collection of rebuses and enigmas.

As I suppose patience is a topic upon which you occasionally harangue from the pulpit, I recommend it to you to put this letter in your pocket next Sunday, and collect your parishioners under the reading desk, or under the old yews in the Church yard, if more convenient, and (giving it to them) set your arms akimbo, and contemplate its open Christian operation upon their tempers. God bless you. Adieu.

W. WORDSWORTH.

Basil is well.

I was going to conclude, but I have found another piece of blank paper. On the other side you will find, or Have found, something about a promise to [be] faithful in writing to you. This I repeat, in spite of Mr. Pitt's additional duty. The copy of the poem you will contrive to frank; else, ten to one, I shall not be able to release it from the post office. I have lately been living upon air, and the essence of carrots, cabbages, turnips, and other esculent vegetables, — not excluding parsley, the produce of my garden.

The Verses [2] will do. Pray let me hear from you soon, with a fresh supply, and the whole copy. What I have sent you is some of it sad stuff, but there is enough to cut out.

[1] *The Borderers.* — Ed.
[2] The " Imitation of Juvenal." — Ed.

Your poems,[1] What is become of them?   It is no disgrace to a man in the moon not to know what is doing here below, and then I do not think the worse of this because I have not heard of them, for we have neither magazine, review, nor any new publication whatever.

[The following lines are included in this letter to Wrangham, and are presumably part of the "Imitation of Juvenal," with which they were both occupied. — Ed.]

> So patient Senates quibble by the hour
> And prove with endless puns a monarch's power,
> Or whet his kingly faculties to chase
> Legions of devils through a key-hole's space.
> What arts had better claim with wrath to warm
> A Pym's brave heart, or stir a Hampden's arm?
> But why for . . . make a distant age
> Or spend upon the dead the muse's rage?
> The nation's hope shall shew the present time
> As rich in folly as the past in crime.
> Do arts like these a royal mind evince?
> Are these the studies that beseem a prince?
> Wedged in with blacklegs at a boxer's show
> To shout with transport o'er a knock-down blow,
> Mid knots of grooms the council of his state
> To scheme and counter-scheme for purse and plate.
> Thy ancient honours when shalt thou resume?
> Oh! shame! is this thy service boastful plume?
> Go, modern Prince, at Henry's tomb proclaim
> Thy rival triumphs, thy Newmarket fame.
> There hang thy trophies; bid the jockey's vest,
> The whip, the cap, and spurs, thy praise attest;
> And let that heir of Glory's endless day
> Edward, the flower of chivalry, survey
> (Fit token of thy reverence and love)
> The boxer's armour, the dishonoured *Glove*.

.   .   .   .

[1] See note, p. 92. — Ed.

[I have either lost, or mislaid, my Juvenal ; therefore I cannot quote his words. What follows about Cicero might be parallelized by some lines about Andrew Marvel and Arpinas Alias *i.e.* another Yorkshireman, by Captain Cooke, but most successfully by Drake.[1] This you will at once perceive. The Decii may perhaps do as follows.]

When Calais heard (while Famine and Disease
To stern Plantagenet resigned her keys)
That victims yet were wanting to assuage
A baffled conqueror's deeply searching rage,
Six which themselves must single from a train,
All brothers, long endeared by kindred pain,
Who then through rows of weeping comrades went,
And self-devoted sought the monarch's tent,
Six simple burghers — To the rope that tied

. . . .

What wonder? on my soul 't would split a tub
To see the arch grimace of Marquis Scrub,
Nor safe the petticoats of dames that hear
The box resound on Viscount Buffo's ear.
But here 's a thought which well our mirth may cross
That Smithfield should sustain so vast a loss,
That spite of the defrauded Kitchen's prayers
Scrub lives a genuine Marquess above stairs,
And they who feed with this Patrician wit
Mirth that to aching ribs will not submit
Good honest souls ! — if right my judgment lies
Though very happy are not very wise
Unless resolved in mercy to the law
Their legislative licence to withdraw
And on a frugal plan without more words.

. . . .

But whence yon swarm that loads the western bridge,
Crams through the arch, and bellies o'er the ridge?

[1] See Preface to this volume. — Ed.

His Grace's watermen in open race
Are called to try their prowess with his Grace.
Could aught but envy now his pride rebuke?
The cry is six to one upon the Duke.
If Stephen's distanced, onward see him strive
Slap-dash, tail foremost, as his arms shall drive.
With shouts the *assembled* people rend the skies
His Grace and his protection win the prize.
Now, Norfolk set thy heralds to their tools,
Marshal forth-with a pair of oars in gules.
Though yet the star *some hearts* at court may charm
The nobler badge shall glitter on *his arm*.
Enough on these inferiour things.
A single word on Kings, and sons of Kings,
Were Kings a free born work, a people's choice.
Would More or Henry boast the general voice?
What fool, besotted as we are by names,
Could pause between a Raleigh and a James?
How did Buchanan waste the Sage's lore!
Not virtuous Seneca on Nero more.
A leprous stain! ere half his thread was spun
Ripe for the block that might have spared his son,
For never did the uxorious martyr seek
Food for sick passion in a minion's cheek,
But whence this gall, this lengthened face of woe?
We were no saints at twenty, be it so;
Yet happy they who in life's later scene
Need only blush for what they once have been,
Who pushed by thoughtless youth to deeds of shame
Mid such bad daring sought a coward's name.
I grant that not in parents' hearts alone
A stripling's years may for his faults atone,
So would I plead for York; but long disgrace
And Moore and Partridge stare me in the face.
Alas! 't was other cause than lack of years
That moistened Dunkirk's sands with blood and tears,

Else had Morality beheld her line
With Guards and Uhlans run along the Rhine,
Religion hailed her creeds by war restored,
And Truth had blest the logic of his sword.

.   .   .   .

Were such your servant Percy! (be it tried
Between ourselves! The noble laid aside),
Now would you be content with bare release
From such a desperate breaker of the peace?
Your friend the country-Justice scarce would fail
To give a hint of whips and the cart's tail,
Or should you even stop short of Woolwich docks
Would less suffice than Bridewell and the stocks?
But ye who make our manners laws, and hence
Self judged, can with such discipline dispense,
And at your will what in a groom were base
Shall stick new splendour on his gartered Grace.
The theme is fruitful; nor can sorrow find
Shame of such dye, but worse remains behind.
My Lord can muster (all but honour spent)
From his wife's Faro-bank a decent rent,
The glittering rabble housed to . . and swear
Swindle and rob, is no informer there.
Or is the painted staffs avenging host
By sixpenny sedition-shops engrossed,
Or rather skulking for the common weal
Round fire-side treason-parties *en famille?*
How throngs the crowd to yon theatric school
To see an English lord enact a fool
Your, vassal necks how poor the garter's pride!
Plebeian hands the . . . mace have wrenched
From sovereigns deep in pedigree intrenched.
Let grandeur tell thee whither now is flown
The brightest jewel of a George's throne.
Blush Pride to see a farmer's wife produce
The first of genuine kings, a king for use,

The bastard gave some favorite stocks of peers
Patents of manhood for eight hundred years.
Eight hundred years uncalled to other tasks
Butlers have simply broached their Lordships casks,
My Lady ne'er approached a thing so coarse
As Tom, but when he helped her to her horse
A Norman Robber then, &c &c.

1796

XLIV

Dorothy Wordsworth to Mrs. Marshall

RACEDOWN, [end of Jan. or beginning of Feb. 1796.]

. . . We have not seen Mr. Montagu, which disappointed us a good deal. . . . The Pinneys have been with us five weeks, one week at Christmas, and a month since. They left us yesterday. We all enjoyed ourselves very much. They seemed to relish the pleasures of our fireside in the evening, and the excursion of the morning. They are very amiable young men, particularly the elder. He is two and twenty, has a charming countenance, and the sweetest temper I ever observed. He has travelled a good deal in the way of education, been at one of the great schools, and at Oxford, has always had plenty of money to spend. This instead of having spoiled him, or made him conceited, has wrought the pleasantest effects. He is well informed, has an uncommonly good heart, and is very agreeable in conversation. He has no profession. His brother has been brought up a merchant. . . . We have read a good deal while they were with us (for they are fond of reading) but we have not gone on with our usual regularity. When the weather was fine, they were out generally all the morning, walking sometimes. Then, I went with them frequently, riding sometimes, hunting, coursing, cleaving wood — a very desirable employment, and what all housekeepers would do well to recommend to the young men of their household in such a cold country as this, for it produces warmth both within and without doors. We have had snow upon the ground this week past. Had we not seen this sight we should have been almost unconscious that we had lived one winter in the country. We have had the mildest weather I ever remember; till within the last week we have never wished for a larger fire than prudent people might think themselves authorized to burn in a country where coals are so expensive. . . .

I have not spoken of Basil yet. He is my perpetual pleasure, quite metamorphosed from a shivering half-starved plant to a lusty blooming fearless boy. He dreads neither cold nor rain. He has played frequently for an hour or two without appearing sensible that the rain was pouring down upon him, or the wind blowing about him. I have had a melancholy letter from Mary Hutchinson: I fear that Margaret is dead before this time. She was then attending her at Sockburn, without the least hope of her recovery. Last year at this time we were all together, and little supposed that any of us was so near death. Our life affords little incident for letters. We had our neighbors to dine, while our friends (the Pinneys) were with us. This was what we called a grand rout! and very dull it was, except for the entertainment of talking about it before and after. William is going to publish a poem.[1] The Pinneys have taken it to the booksellers. I am studying my Italian very hard. I am now reading the *Fool of Quality* which amuses me exceedingly. Within the last month I have read *Tristram*

---

[1] Possibly *Guilt and Sorrow* in its first form, *The Female Vagrant;* but more probably the tragedy of *The Borderers.* —Ed.

Shandy, Brydone's *Sicily and Malta*, and Moore's *Travels in France*. I have also read lately Madame Roland's *Mémoirs*, and some other French things. . . .

XLV

William Wordsworth to Francis Wrangham

RACEDOWN, March 7, [1796.]

My dear Wrangham,

Your letter had long been looked for. The agreeable intelligence it contained respecting your good fortune (I believe among the Antients good fortune was reckoned among the first of a man's merits — as being a proof, perhaps, of his being under the special care of the Gods, — and therefore the expression is not to be objected to), the intelligence then of your good fortune made me quite forget that there was any occasion to apologize for your *inveterate* silence. I sincerely congratulate you on your late induction,[1] as it must set you entirely above the necessity of engaging in any employment unsuited to your taste and pleasures. I am glad to hear of your projected volume;[2] and hope you will not suffer your *promotion* to interfere with the advancement of your literary reputation, or to rob your friends and the public of the pleasure to be derived from the pieces you are possessed of. I shall be happy to communicate any observations which may suggest themselves to me on perusal of your MS. I assure you I do not mean to

[1] To the rectory of Hummanby, Yorkshire. — Ed.
[2] Wrangham was the author of many works. This may refer to his *Thirteen Practical Sermons* (1800), or his poem *The Holy Land* (1800). — Ed.

drop the Juvenal scheme; on the contrary I am determined to bring it to a speedy conclusion. With this view I have this morning sketched out ideas to run parallel with the last forty lines beginning at "Quis Catalina tuis natalibus," and mean to compose them forthwith. We have had the two Pinneys[1] with us, John for a month. They left us yesterday, and as I now feel a return of literary appetite I mean to take a smack of satire by way of sandwich. My next letter then will probably contain the passage, for your strictures. If you could find leisure you would oblige me by employing an hour on some part of the work, as there is more of it than I wish to execute. I am afraid you have neglected to make application for the newspapers; they would be a great amusement to us in the depth of our present solitude. I have been engaged an hour and a half this morning in hewing wood and rooting up hedges, and I think it no bad employment to feel "the penalty of Adam" in this way. Some of our friends have not been so lucky, witness poor Montagu. You are now a rich man; and, of course, like every sensible rich man, will occasionally turn your thoughts towards travel, foreign, or domestic. Devonshire and Cornwall have many attractions. If they should be powerful enough to lead you this way, you will not pass us by. I have some thoughts of exploring the country westward of us, in the course of next summer, but in an humble evangelical way: to wit, *à pied.* As there are no large cities *that* road, I shall not have much occasion to shake the dust off my

---

[1] Mr. Pinney was a Bristol merchant who owned Racedown, and gave it to his son. The son offered it to Wordsworth rent free, on the sole condition that he should occasionally go down, and stay for a few weeks. — Ed.

feet, in sign of indignation or abhorrence. On other accounts however it will be necessary to perform that operation.

I mean to publish a volume. Could you engage to get rid for me of a dozen copies or more among your numerous acquaintance? The damages — to use a Lancashire phrase — will be four or five shillings per copy. I do not mean to put forth a formal subscription; but could wish, upon my acquaintances and *their* acquaintances, to quarter so many as would ensure me from positive loss; further, this adventurer wisheth not. Adieu — your affectionate friend,

W. WORDSWORTH.

Basil is quite well, *quant au physique, mais pour le moral il-y-a bien à craindre.* Among other things he lies like a little devil. Adieu.

[Dorothy writes.]

. . . William has had a letter from France since we came here. Annette [1] mentions having dispatched half a dozen, none of which he has received. . . . With respect to letters we are more independent than most people, as William is so good a walker, and I too have walked over twice to Crewkerne — the distance is seven miles — to make purchases; and what is more we turned out of our way three miles, in one of our walks thither, to see a house of Lord Powletts' and a very fine view; we were amply repaid for our trouble. If you want to find our situation out, look on your maps for Crewkerne, Chard, Axminster, Bridport and Lime. We are nearly equi-distant from all these places. A little brook, which runs at the distance of one field from us, divides us from Devonshire.

[1] See *Poetical Works*, Vol. II, p. 335, note *. — Ed.

This country abounds in apples. In some of our walks we go through orchards without any other enclosure or security than as a common field. When I spoke of the sea I forgot to tell you that my brother saw the West India fleet sailing in all its glory, before the storm had made such dreadful ravages. The peasants are miserably poor: their cottages are shapeless structures of wood and clay: indeed they are not at all beyond what might be expected in savage life. . . .

XLVI

Dorothy Wordsworth to Mrs. Marshall

RACEDOWN, March 19, [1796.]

. . . The dreams of our ardent imaginations have not proved shadowy. You seem to be as happy as youthful expectation and enthusiastic hope ever prompted us to feel that you might be in the society of one whom you have so long loved. I dare say, you have not forgotten our walks in the wood at the side of the Rawson's house. You must remember how happy we were in the hopes of those comforts which are now within your reach, and how we looked back with melancholy pleasure upon those other enjoyments which can never return, of which the first and chiefest was that of wandering wild together. . . . [She refers to Mrs. Marshall's infant boy, and says] You ask to be informed of our system respecting Basil. It is a very simple one; so simple that, in this age of systems, you will hardly be likely to follow it. We teach him nothing at present, but what he learns from the evidence of his senses. He has an insatiable curiosity, which we are always careful to satisfy to the best of our ability. He is directed to everything he sees, the sky, the fields, trees, shrubs, corn, the making of tools, carts, &c., &c., &c. He knows his letters, but we have not attempted any further step in the path of *book-learning*. Our grand study has been to make him happy, in which we have not been altogether disappointed. He is certainly the most contented child I ever saw, the least disposed to be fretful. At first when he came he was extremely petted from indulgence and weakness of body, and perpetually disposed to cry. Upon these occasions (perhaps this may be of use to you) we used to tell him that, if he chose to cry, he must go into a certain room where he could not be heard ; and *stay* till he chose to be quiet, because the noise was unpleasant to us. At first his visits were very long, but he always came out again perfectly good-humoured. He found that this rule was never departed from, and when he found this fretful disposition coming on, he would say, "Auntie, I think I'm going to cry," and retire till the fit was over. He has now entirely conquered the disposition. I dare say it is three months since we have had occasion to send him into this apartment of tears. We have no punishments, except such as appears to be, so far as we can determine, the immediate consequences that grow out of the offence. . . .

The father and William left us this morning. Mr. Montagu came to us unexpectedly. William has accompanied him to Bristol where they will spend about a fortnight. I am excessively pleased with Mr. M. He is one of the pleasantest men I ever saw, and so amiable and good that every one must love him. You perhaps have heard that our friend Mary Hutchinson is staying with me. She is one of the best girls in the world, and we are as happy as human beings can be, that is when

'William is at home; for you cannot imagine how dull we feel, and what a vacuum his loss has occasioned, but this is the first day. To-morrow we shall be better.... He is the life of the whole house. . . .

XLVII

William Wordsworth to William Mathews

RACEDOWN, NEAR CREWKERNE,
March 21st, [Postmark, 1796.]

Dear Mathews,

I could wish our correspondence were more frequent. I fully expected to hear from you by Azor Pinney, and was not a little surprized you omitted so good an opportunity of sending me the volume of fugitive poetry. Pray write to me at length, and give me an account of your proceedings in the Society, or any other information likely to interest me. Are your members much increased? and what is of more consequence have you improved I do not ask in the [art] of speaking, but in the more important one of thinking? I believe I put these questions to you once before, but they were never answered.

You were right about Southey; he is certainly a coxcomb, and has proved it completely by the preface to his *Joan of Arc*, an epic poem which he has just published. This preface is indeed a very conceited performance, and the poem, though in some passages of first rate excellence, is on the whole of very inferior execution. Our present life is utterly barren of such events as merit even the short-lived chronicle of an accidental letter. We plant cabbages; and if retirement, in its full perfection, be as powerful in working transformations as one of

Ovid's gods, you may perhaps suspect that into cabbages we shall be transformed. Indeed I learn that such has been the prophecy of one of our London friends. In spite of all this I was tolerably industrious in reading, if reading can ever deserve the name of industry, till our good friends the Pinneys came amongst us; and I have since returned to my books. As to writing, it is out of the question.

Not however entirely to forget the world, I season my recollection of some of its objects with a little ill-nature, I attempt to write satires; and in all satires, whatever the authors may say, there will be found a spice of malignity. Neither Juvenal nor Horace were without it, and what shall we say of Boileau, and Pope, or the more redoubted Peter?[1] These are great names, but to myself I shall apply the passage of Horace, changing the bee into a wasp to suit the subject.

> Ego apis Matinae
> More modoque, &c, &c.

I hope you have preserved the catalogue of my books left at Montagu's. You would oblige me much by calling there; and desiring James to procure a box sufficient to contain them. See that they are nailed up in it. Gilpin's tour into Scotland, and his northern tour, each 2 vols.,[2] ought to be amongst the number. Montagu

---

[1] Possibly John Wolcot (Peter Pindar), 1738–1819. Compare, on the subject of satire, Wordsworth's letter to Francis Wrangham, Nov. 7, 1806. — Ed.

[2] 1. *Observations relative chiefly to Picturesque Beauty, made in the year 1776, in Several Parts of Great Britain, particularly the Highlands of Scotland,* (1788, 2 vols.). 2. *Observations relative chiefly to Picturesque Beauty, made in the year 1772, on Several Parts of England, particularly the Mountains and Lakes of Cumberland and Westmoreland* (1787, 2 vols.). — Ed.

either did lend, or talked of lending, one of these to Miss Roby. Pray request that he would take care to have it returned immediately. I am the more solicitous on this account as the books, having been very expensive, are the *less likely* to be returned. Pray give my best compliment to Myers, and say I mean to write to him very soon. How are you now employed? and what do you do for money? If you could muster the cash to come down, we should be glad to see you during the course of this summer. If the outside of a coach should not disagree with you, you might come for a trifle, the fare being only 14 shillings. Pray write soon. Adieu. Your affectionate friend,

W. WORDSWORTH.

My sister would be very glad of your assistance in her Italian studies. She has already gone through half of Davila,[1] and yesterday we began Ariosto. I have received from Montagu, Godwyn's second edition. I expect to find the work much improved. I cannot say that I have been encouraged in this hope by the perusal of the second preface, which is all I have yet looked into. Such a piece of barbarous writing I have not often seen. It contains scarce one sentence decently written. I am surprized to find such gross faults in a writer, who has had so much practice in composition. Give me some news about the theatre. I have attempted to read Holcroft's *Man of Ten Thousand,*[2] but such stuff.

[1] Probably H. C. Davila's *Istoria delle Guerre Civile di Francia,* 1775. — Ed.

[2] Thomas Holcroft, a voluminous dramatic and miscellaneous writer, (1744–1809). *The Man of Ten Thousand, a Comedy* (1796). — Ed.

1797

XLVIII

Dorothy Wordsworth to Correspondent Unknown

RACEDOWN, [1797.]

. . . You had a great loss in not seeing Coleridge. He is a wonderful man. His conversation teems with soul, mind, and spirit. Then he is so benevolent, so good tempered and cheerful, and — like William — interests himself so much about every little trifle. At first I thought him very plain, that is for about three minutes. He is pale and thin, has a wide mouth, thick lips, and not very good teeth, longish loose-growing half-curling rough black hair. But if you hear him speak for five minutes you think no more of them. His eye is large and full, not dark but gray; such an eye as would receive from a heavy soul the dullest expression, but it speaks every emotion of his animated mind. It has more of the " poet's eye in a fine frenzy rolling " than I ever witnessed. He has fine dark eyebrows, and an overhanging forehead.

The first thing that was read after he came was William's new poem *The Ruined Cottage* with which he was much delighted; and after tea he repeated to us two acts and a half of his tragedy *Osorio*. The next morning William read his tragedy *The Borderers*. . . .

XLIX

Dorothy Wordsworth to Correspondent Unknown

[NETHER STOWEY, July 4th, 1797.]

. . . There is everything here ; sea, woods wild as
fancy ever painted, brooks clear and pebbly as in Cumberland, villages so romantic ; and William and I, in a
wander by ourselves, found out a sequestered waterfall in
a dell formed by steep hills covered with full-grown timber trees. The woods are as fine as those at Lowther,
and the country more romantic ; it has the character of the
less grand parts of the neighbourhood of the Lakes. . . .

L

Dorothy Wordsworth to Correspondent Unknown

ALFOXDEN, NEAR NETHER-STOWEY, SOMERSETSHIRE,
August 14, 1797.

Here we are in a large mansion, in a large park, with
seventy head of deer around us. But I must begin with
the day of leaving Racedown to pay Coleridge a visit.
You know how much we were delighted with the neighbourhood of Stowey. . . . The evening that I wrote to
you, William and I had rambled as far as this house, and
pryed into the recesses of our little brook, but without
any more fixed thoughts upon it than some dreams of
happiness in a little cottage, and passing wishes that
such a place might be found out. We spent a fortnight
at Coleridge's ; in the course of that time we heard that
this house was to let, applied for it, and took it. Our
principal inducement was Coleridge's society. It was a
month yesterday since we came to Alfoxden.

The house is a large mansion, with furniture enough for a dozen families like ours. There is a very excellent garden, well stocked with vegetables and fruit. The garden is at the end of the house, and our favourite parlour, as at Racedown, looks that way. In front is a little court, with grass plot, gravel walk, and shrubs; the moss roses were in full beauty a month ago. The front of the house is to the south, but it is screened from the sun by a high hill which rises immediately from it. This hill is beautiful, scattered irregularly and abundantly with trees, and topped with fern, which spreads a considerable way down it. The deer dwell here, and sheep, so that we have a living prospect. From the end of the house we have a view of the sea, over a woody meadow-country; and exactly opposite the window where I now sit is an immense wood, whose round top from this point has exactly the appearance of a mighty dome. In some parts of this wood there is an under grove of hollies which are now very beautiful. In a glen at the bottom of the wood is the waterfall of which I spoke, a quarter of a mile from the house. We are three miles from Stowey, and not two miles from the sea. Wherever we turn we have woods, smooth downs, and valleys with small brooks running down them through green meadows, hardly ever intersected with hedgerows, but scattered over with trees. The hills that cradle these valleys are either covered with fern and bilberries, or oak woods, which are cut for charcoal. . . . Walks extend for miles over the hill-tops, the great beauty of which is their wild simplicity: they are perfectly smooth, without rocks.

The Tor of Glastonbury is before our eyes during more than half of our walk to Stowey; and in the park wherever we go, keeping about fifteen yards above the house, it makes a part of our prospect. . . .

LI

Dorothy Wordsworth to Correspondent Unknown

November 20, 1797.

. . . William's play is finished, and sent to the managers of the Covent Garden theatre. We have not the faintest expectation that it will be accepted.

LII

William Wordsworth to Joseph Cottle[1]

LONDON, Wednesday, December 13 (1797).

Dear Cottle:

I received by the hands of Coleridge sometime since a volume of Icelandic poetry translated by your brother;[2] I begged Coleridge to return you my best thanks for it. The volume has afforded me considerable pleasure. It is generally executed in spirit, though there are many inaccuracies which ought to have been avoided. I have deferred writing to you till this time, hoping I might have to communicate some pleasant intelligence; but I am disappointed. Mr. Harris has pronounced it impossible that my play should succeed in the representation. My sister and I mean to quit London on Friday. We propose to take Bristol on our way. . We shall set out from the White-horse, Piccadilly, and be in Bristol on Friday night. . . .

[1] The publisher of *Lyrical Ballads.* — Ed.
[2] *Icelandic Poetry, or The Edda of Sæmund, translated into English verse*, by A. S. Cottle, 1797. —Ed.

LIII

Dorothy Wordsworth to Correspondent Unknown

BRISTOL, December 21, 1797.

. . . We have been in London : our business was the play ; and the play is rejected. It was sent to one of the principal actors at Covent Garden, who expressed great approbation, and advised William strongly to go to London to make certain alterations. Coleridge's play is also rejected. . . .

1798

LIV

William Wordsworth to James Tobin [1]

ALFOXDEN, 6th March, [1798.]

My dear Tobin,

I have long wished to thank you for your letter and Gustavus Vasa. They were both very acceptable to me in this solitude. The tragedy is a strange composition of genius and absurdity; as you have not read it I will take care of it for you. I am perfectly easy about the theatre, if I had no other method of employing myself Mr. Lewis's success would have thrown me into despair. The Castle Spectre is a Spectre indeed. Clothed with the flesh and blood of £400 received from the treasury of the theatre it may in the eyes of the author and his friend appear very lovely. There is little need to advise me against publishing; it is a thing which I dread as much as death itself. This may serve as an example of the figure by rhetoricians called hyperbole, but privacy and quiet are my delight. No doubt you have heard of the munificence of the Wedgwoods towards Coleridge. I hope the fruit will be good as the seed is noble. We leave Alfoxden at Midsummer. The house is let to Crewkshank of

---

[1] James Tobin, brother of the dramatist, and the "Dear brother Jim" of the suppressed line in *We are Seven*. See the Fenwick note to that poem. — Ed.

Stowey, so our departure is decided. What may be our destination I cannot say. If we can raise the money, we shall make a tour on foot; probably through Wales, and northwards. I am at present utterly unable to say where we shall be. We have no particular reason to be attached to the neighbourhood of Stowey, but the society of Coleridge, and the friendship of Poole. News we have none; our occupations continue the same, only I rise early in the mornings.

I have written 1300 lines of a poem in which I contrive to convey most of the knowledge of which I am possessed.[1] My object is to give pictures of Nature, Man, and Society. Indeed I know not any thing which will not come within the scope of my plan. If ever I attempt another drama, it shall be written either purposely for the closet, or purposely for the stage. There is no middle way. But the work of composition is carved out for me, for at least a year and a half to come. The essays[2] of which I have spoken to you must be written with eloquence, or not at all. My eloquence, speaking with modesty, will all be carried off, at least for some time, into my poem. If you could collect for me any books of travels you would render me an essential service, as without much of such reading my present labours cannot be brought to a conclusion. I have not yet seen the life of Mrs. Godwyn. I wish to see it, though with no tormenting curiosity. If you have three pounds, eighteen shillings to spare for a few months I will thank you to call at No. 6 little Ormond street, Queen square, and pay the bill for the newspapers. The bill is either a mistake, or a gross

[1] The projected *Recluse*, of which *The Excursion* and *The Prelude* are parts. — Ed.

[2] Projected essays on Poetry. — Ed.

imposition; but there is no remedy. Let me hear from you soon. If you can employ an amanuensis it would be better, as we find it difficult to read your letters.

Basil grows a stout fellow. He has not forgotten you. My sister declares to be kindly remembered to you.

Yours sincerely,
WILLIAM WORDSWORTH.

LV

William Wordsworth to Amos Cottle

Aug. 28, 1798.

. . . We arrived safely in town yesterday evening, after a very pleasant journey per foot, per waggon, per coach, per post-chaise; having expended for each passenger £1..18..6, and been admitted to the presence chamber at Blenheim, and seen the University of Oxford. . . . We forgot the letter of introduction to Longman. . . . God bless you, dear Cottle. Dorothy sends her best love. . .

LVI

William Wordsworth to Thomas Poole [1]

HAMBURG, October 3rd, [1798.]

My dear Poole,

It was my intention to have written to you from England, to bid you farewell. I was prevented by procrastination, and I now take up the pen to assure you that my sister and myself both retain the most lively recollection

[1] Thomas Poole of Nether Stowey, friend of Coleridge, Wordsworth, &c. See *Thomas Poole and his Friends*, by Mrs. Sandford. —Ed.

of the many kindnesses which we have received from you and your family. I believe my letter would be more acceptable to you if, instead of speaking on this subject, I should tell you what we have seen during our fortnight's residence at Hamburg. It is a *sad* place. In this epithet you have the soul and essence of all the information which I have been able to gather. We have, however, been treated with unbounded kindness by Mr. Klopstock, the brother of the poet; and I have no doubt this city contains a world of good and honest people, if one had but the skill to find them. I will relate to you an anecdote. The other day I[1] went into a baker's shop, put into his hand two pieces of money, for which I ought to have had five loaves, but I thought the pieces had only been worth two loaves each. I took up four loaves. The baker would not permit this, upon which I took from his hand one of the pieces, and pointed to two loaves, and then, re-offering to him the piece, I took up two others. He dashed the loaves from my hand into the basket in the most brutal manner. I begged him to return the other piece of money, which he refused to do, nor would he let me have any bread into the bargain. So I left the shop empty-handed, and he retained the money. Is there any baker in England who would have done this to a foreigner? I am afraid we must say, yes. Money, money is here the god of universal worship, and rapacity and extortion among the lower classes, and the classes immediately above them; and just sufficiently common to be a matter of glory and exultation.

The situation of the town is, upon the whole, pleasant; the ramparts present many agreeable views of the river

---

[1] It happened to his sister, not to himself. — Ed.

and the adjoining country.   The banks of the Elbe are
thickly sown with houses, built by the merchants for Saturday and Sunday retirement.   The English merchants
have set the example; the style is in imitation of the
English garden, imitated as Della Crusca might imitate
Virgil.   It is, however, something gained, the dawning
of a better day.

We set off this evening by the diligence for Brunswick.
We shall be two days and two nights constantly travelling
in a vehicle, compared with which Tanlin's long coach is
a very chariot of the gods — patience ! patience !   We
have one comfort travelling in this way, a very great one
for the poor, viz., that we cannot be cheated.   Coleridge
has most likely informed you that he and Chester have
settled at Ratzeburg.   Dorothy and I are going to specu-
late further up in the country.

I have seen Klopstock, the poet.   There is nothing
remarkable either in his conversation or appearance,
except his extreme gaiety, with legs swelled as thick as
your thigh.   He is in his seventy-fourth year.   He began
his *Messiah* at seventeen, — not the composition, for the
plan employed him three years.

I sent a copy of my tragedy by Wade.   Ward will
transcribe it as soon as he can, and you have the goodness to transmit the original to Wade.   It is in a sad
incorrect state.   Ward must use his best eyes and his
best sagacity in deciphering it.   Pray have the goodness
to remove those boxes of ours from that damp room at
Mr Coleridge's, and lodge them in some perfectly dry
place at Stowey.   I could wish also that they might be
well aired, I mean on the outside, as I am afraid the
things may have already sustained some injury.   Either
let them be put in the sunshine, or before a large fire.

My sister joins me in kindest remembrances to yourself, and your mother, not forgetting Ward. I hope Mrs Coleridge is well, and the children.—Yours most affectionately,

WM. WORDSWORTH.

I have one word to say about Alfoxden: pray, keep your eye upon it. If any series of accidents should bring it again into the market, we should be glad to have it, if we could manage it

LVII

Dorothy Wordsworth to Mrs. Marshall

[Oct. 3, 1798.]

. . . We quitted Hamburg on Wednesday evening, at five o'clock, reached Luneburg to breakfast on Thursday, and arrived at Brunswick between three and four o'clock on Friday evening. . . . There we dined. It is an old, silent, dull-looking place; the duke's palace a large white building, with no elegance in its external appearance. The next morning we set off at eight. You can have no idea of the badness of the roads. The diligence arrived at eight at night at the city of Goslar, on Saturday October 6, the distance being only twenty-five miles. . . .

LVIII

Dorothy Wordsworth to Mrs. Marshall

[GOSLAR. No date.]

. . . Coleridge is very happily situated at Ratzeburg for learning the language. *We* are not fortunately situated here, with respect to the attainment of our main object, a knowledge of the language.   We have, indeed, gone on improving in that respect, but not so expeditiously as we might have done, for there is no society at Goslar.   It is a lifeless town ; and it seems that here, in Germany, a man travelling alone may do very well, but, if his sister or wife goes with him, he must give entertainments.   So we content ourselves with talking to the people of the house, &c.,[1] and reading German.   William is very indus-trious.   His mind is always active ; indeed, too much so. He over-wearies himself, and suffers from pain and weak-ness in the side. . . .   We have plenty of dry walks ; but Goslar is very cold in winter. . . .

[1] Coleridge addressed them, "Chez Madame le Veuve Dippér-maer." — Ed.

1799

LIX

William Wordsworth to Joseph Cottle

SOCKBURN, 27th July, [Postmark, 1799.]

My dear Cottle,

I thank you for your draft, which I received on Friday evening. . . . I am not poor enough yet to make me think it right that I should take interest for a debt from a friend, paid eleven months after it is due. If I were in want, I should make no scruple in applying to you for twice that sum. I should be very glad to hear so good an account of the sale of the *Lyrical Ballads*, if I were not afraid that your wish to give pleasure, and your proneness to self-deception, had made you judge too favourably. I am told they have been reviewed in *The Monthly Review*, but I have not heard in what style. . . . God bless you, my dear Cottle. — Believe me, your very affectionate friend,

W. WORDSWORTH.

P.S.— My aversion from publication increases every day, so much so, that no motives whatever, nothing but pecuniary necessity, will, I think, ever prevail upon me to commit myself to the press again. . . .

LX

William Wordsworth to Joseph Cottle

SOCKBURN, 1799.

My dear Cottle,

. . . Southey's review I have seen. He knew that I published those poems for money and money alone. He knew that money was of importance to me. If he could not conscientiously have spoken differently of the volume, he ought to have declined the task of reviewing it.

The bulk of the poems he has described as destitute of merit. Am I recompensed for this by vague praises of my talents? I care little for the praise of any other professional critic, but as it may help me to pudding. . . . Believe me, dear Cottle, your affectionate friend,

W. WORDSWORTH.

1800

LXI

William Wordsworth to Humphry Davy[1]

GRASMERE, NEAR AMBLESIDE, 28th July, [1800.]

Dear Sir,

So I venture to address you, though I have not the happiness of being personally known to you. You would greatly oblige me by looking over the enclosed poems,[2] and correcting anything you find amiss in the punctuation, a business at which I am ashamed to say I am no adept. I was unwilling to print from the MS. which Coleridge left in your hands because, as I had not looked them over, I was afraid that some lines might be omitted or mistranscribed. I write to request that you would have the goodness to look over the proof-sheets of the second volume, before they are finally struck off. In future I mean to send the MS. to Biggs and Cottle, with a request that along with the proof-sheets they may be sent to you.

Coleridge left us last Wednesday. Mrs. C. and Hartley followed on Thursday. I hope they will both be pleased with their situation. From a note sent by Coleridge yesterday I learn that Mr. Biggs is prepared to print the second volume. In order that no time may be lost I have sent off this letter, which shall be followed by others every post

[1] The chemist, afterwards Sir Humphry Davy. — Ed.
[2] *Lyrical Ballads.* The second volume, published in 1800. — Ed.

day, viz. three times a week, till the whole is completed. You will be so good as to put the enclosed poems into Mr. Biggs's hands as soon as you have looked them over, in order that the printing may be commenced immediately. The preface for the first volume shall be sent in a few days.

Remember me most affectionately to Tobin. I need not say how happy I should be to see you both in my little cabin. I remain, with great respect, and kind feelings,

Yours sincerely,

W. WORDSWORTH.

LXII

Dorothy Wordsworth to Mrs. Marshall

GRASMERE, Sept. 10, 1800.

. . . She describes the vale as "one small green retired woody valley," and adds, "We are daily more and more delighted with Grasmere, and its neighborhood. Our walks are perpetually varied, and we are more fond of the mountains as our acquaintance with them increases. We have a boat upon the lake, and a small orchard, and a smaller garden; which, as it is the work of our own hands, we regard with pride and partiality. This garden we enclosed from the road, and pulled down a fence which formerly divided it from the orchard. The orchard is very small; but then it is a delightful one from its retirement and the excessive beauty of the prospect from it. Our cottage is quite large enough for us, though very small. We have made it neat and comfortable within doors, and it looks very nice on the outside, for though the roses and honeysuckles which we have planted against it are only of this year's growth, yet it is covered all over with green leaves and scarlet flowers; for we have trained scarlet beans upon threads, which are not only exceedingly beautiful, but very useful, as their produce is immense. The only objection we have to our house is that it is rather too near the road; and from its smallness, and the manner in which it is built, noises pass from one part of the house to the other; so that, if we had any visitors, a sick person could not be in quietness.

We have made a lodging room of the parlor below stairs, which has a stone floor. Therefore we have covered it all over with matting. The bed, though only a camp bed, is large enough for two people to sleep in. We sit in a room above stairs, and we have one lodging room with two single beds, a sort of lumber-room, and a small low unceiled room which I have papered with newspapers, and in which we have put a small bed without curtains. Our servant is an old woman, sixty years of age, whom we took partly out of charity and partly for convenience.

My brother John has been with us eight months, during which time we have had a good deal of company; for instance, Mary Hutchinson for five weeks, Coleridge a month, and Mr. and Mrs. Coleridge and their little boy nearly a month. . . . My brother Christopher is now in Norfolk. He is engaged to marry Miss Lloyd, sister of the author Charles Lloyd, and daughter of the Lloyds of Birmingham. He is so deeply engaged in college business that he could not come and see us this summer. . . . When John leaves he intends spending some time at Forncett. You may have heard that my uncle Crackanthorp left me £100.

William is going to publish a second edition of the
Lyrical Ballads, with a second volume. He intends to
give them the title of "Poems by W. Wordsworth," as
Mrs. Robinson has claimed the title, and is about to publish a volume of *Lyrical Tales*.[1] This is a great objection
to the former title, particularly as they are both printed at
the same press, and Longman is the publisher of both
works. The first volume sold much better than we
expected, and was liked by a much greater number of
people; not that we had ever much doubt of its finally
making its way, but we knew that poems, so different
from what have in general become popular immediately
after their publication, were not likely to be admired all
at once. The first volume I have no doubt has prepared
a number of purchasers for the second; and independent
of that, I think the second is much more likely to please
the generality of readers. William's health is by no
means strong. He has written a great deal since we first
went to Alfoxden, namely during the years preceding our
going into Germany, while we were there, and since our
arrival in England; and he writes with so much feeling
and agitation that it brings on a sense of pain.

... We have spent a week at Mr. Coleridge's since his
arrival at Keswick. His home is most delightfully situated, and combines all possible advantages both for his
wife and himself. *She* likes to be near a town, *he* in the
country. It is only half or a quarter of a mile from Keswick, and commands a view of the whole vale. Their
little boy Hartley, who is an original sprite, is to come
and stay with us. He is a sweet companion, always
alive, and of a delightful temper.

[1] A volume entitled *Lyrical Tales* written by Mrs. Mary Robinson
was published at London in 1800.—Ed.

William and John were in Yorkshire last summer at Goredale, Yordas, etc.[1] Thence they went to see our friends the Hutchinsons, and were absent a whole month. They talked of paying you a visit, but they found they had stayed so long at Scarborough that they did not like to leave me alone any longer. During their absence I felt myself very lonely. . . . We are very comfortably situated with respect to neighbors of the lower classes. They are excellent people, friendly in performing all offices of friendship and humanity, and attentive to us without servility. If we were sick, they would wait upon us night and day. We are also upon very intimate terms with one family in the middle rank of life, a clergyman with a very small income,[2] his wife, son, and daughter. The old man is upwards of eighty, yet he goes a-fishing to the tarns on the hill-tops with my brothers, and he is as active as any man of fifty. His wife is a delightful old woman, mild and gentle, yet cheerful in her manners, and much of the gentlewoman, so made by long exercise of the duties of a wife and mother, and the charities of a neighbor; for she has lived forty years in the vale, and seldom left her home. . . .

Our employments, though not very various, are irregular. We walk at all times of the day; we row upon the water; and, in the summer, sit a great part of our time under the apple trees of the orchard, or in a wood close by the lake side. William writes verses; John goes fishing. We read the books we have, and such as we can procure. I read German, partly as preparatory to translating; but I am

[1] They left Grasmere on May 14, and returned on June 7, 1800. —Ed.

[2] The Rev. Joseph Sympson, the "pastor" of *The Excursion.* —Ed.

unfit for the task alone, and William is better employed, so I do not know when it will turn to much account. If William's name rises among the booksellers, we shall have no occasion for it. We often have our friends calling in upon us. Anthony Harrison of Penrith, Mr. and Mrs. James Losh of West Gesmond near Newcastle, and Mr. and Mrs. Clarkson. Mr. Clarkson is the man who took so much pains about the slave trade. He has a farm at Ullswater, and has built a house. Mrs. C. is a pleasant woman. . . .

LXIII

William Wordsworth to Mr. Biggs, Printer[1]

Dear Sir,

It is my particular request that, if no part of the poem of *Christabel* is already printed off, the poems which I now send should be inserted before *Christabel*. This I wish to be done even if the press for *Christabel* be composed. I had no notion that the printing of *Christabel* would be begun till you received further intelligence from Mr. Coleridge, or I should have sent these poems before.[2] The Preface shall certainly be sent off in four days at furthest.

I am, dear Sir,
Your most obed^t Servt,

W. WORDSWORTH.

GRASMERE, 15th September [1800].

[1] Written in Coleridge's hand, signature and all. — Ed.
[2] This letter shows that it was originally intended that the *Christabel* of Coleridge should be included in the second edition of " Lyrical Ballads " (1800). It was not published, however, till 1816. — Ed.

LXIV

William Wordsworth to Messrs. Biggs and Cottle

[Postmark, KESWICK, Oct. 10 or 20, 1800.]

Sirs,

I sent off a short letter by the last post containing a paragraph concerning *Christabel*, which I wished to have inserted towards the conclusion of the Preface. I now write to say that this paragraph must not be inserted, or taken any notice of, and further, that I wish the first page of the Preface to be cancelled in order to be reprinted. If Mr Longman consents to alter the title page according as I stated, the first sentence of the Preface in the reprinted leaf must stand thus —

"The first volume of these poems, under the title of 'Lyrical Ballads' has already been presented &c."

The paragraph — I believe it is the second — beginning "For the sake of variety and from a consciousness of my own weakness, &c." down to the words " do almost entirely coincide" must be cancelled; and, when reprinted, must stand thus. " It is proper to inform the reader that the Poems entitled *The Ancient Mariner, The Foster Mother's Tale, The Nightingale, The Dungeon*, and *Love* are written by a Friend, who has also furnished me with a few of those poems in the second volume, which are classed under the title of 'Poems on the Naming of Places.' "

It is my wish and determination (whatever the expense may be, which I here take upon myself) that such pages of the poem of *Christabel* as have been printed, (if any such there be), be cancelled. I mean to have other poems substituted, a sheet of which will be sent by the next post, and you may now and thenceforth *depend* on being supplied without any intermissions.

> I am, dear Sir,
> Yours sincerely,
>
> W. WORDSWORTH.

LXV

William Wordsworth to Joseph Cottle

December, 1800.

My dear Cottle,

. . . Mrs. Coleridge and her youngest child are now with us. . . . Coleridge is at Keswick. . . . I wish much that I could have presented you with a copy of the *Lyrical Ballads*, but I foolishly did not stipulate with Longman for any copies for myself, so that I must depend upon his liberality, and must present the few copies which I shall have to a few persons who would be offended if they did not receive this mark of attention from me. . . . —I am, my dear Cottle, yours affectionately,

> W. WORDSWORTH.

LXVI

William Wordsworth to Messrs. Biggs and Cottle

[Postmark, Dec. 23, 1800.]

Dear Sirs,

Have you received a sheet containing three poems? namely, *The Pet-Lamb, Lines written in Germany*, and *The Childless Father?* Have you likewise received another containing *The Old Cumberland Beggar, Rural Architecture*, and part of a Poem entitled *A Poet's Epitaph.*

Likewise have you received a third letter containing the Remainder of *A Poet's Epitaph*, *A Character*, and two poems "On the Naming of Places"?

If you have not received these three letters pray be so good as to write immediately to let me know. This present sheet contains three other "Poems on the Naming of Places," which you will print as they are numbered. By the same post I send you two other sheets containing a poem entitled *Michael*. This poem contains 493 or 4 lines. If it be sufficient to fill the volume to 205 pages or upwards, printing it at 18 lines, or never more than 19, in a page — as was done in the first edition of the "Lyrical Ballads " — you will print this poem immediately after the "Poems on the Naming of Places," and consider it as (with the two or three notes adjoined) finishing the work. If it does not fill up so much space as to make the volume 205 pages, you must not immediately print the Poem of *Michael*, as I wish it to conclude the volume. If what I have sent does not make the volume amount to 205 pages, let me know immediately *how many pages* it amounts to, and I will send you something to insert between *Michael* and the "Poems on the Naming of Places."

By beginning the Preface the space of three or four lines lower down in the page there will be no occasion to reprint half the sheet. Omitting the note at the bottom the sentence will stand thus [1]

" For the sake of variety, and from a consciousness of my own weakness, I was induced to request the assistance of a Friend, who furnished me with the Poems of *The Ancient Mariner*, *The Foster Mother's Tale*, *The Nightingale*, *The Dungeon*, and the poem entitled *Love*. I should

[1] For obvious reasons this, which occurs in a different form in the preceding letter, must be repeated. — Ed.

not however have requested this assistance &c." The rest of the paragraph to stand as printed. If printing as I have said, the matter is not enough, or cannot be contrived to fill up the page, pray let me know.

I do not exactly like the title-page, tho' I do not know how to alter it to have a better effect. I must however particularly request that my name be printed in smaller character. If you can think of any other alterations that will improve the look of the title-page, pray make them. There is a sad mistake in the Preface, namely, " Lucretia " printed for " Lucretius." This ought in every copy to be corrected with a pen. If not, it must be mentioned in the *errata.* I mentioned to Mr. Longman my intention to prefix an Essay to the second volume, but this I must decline. N.B. It is my *particular desire* that no advertisements of books be printed at the end of the volume. I am sorry I have detained you so long [over] the printing of this work. I have been stopped by bad health.

I am, &c.,

W. WORDSWORTH.

LXVII

William Wordsworth to Messrs. Biggs and Cottle

[Postmark, KESWICK, Dec. 24, 1800.]

Mr. Biggs,
    Sir,
        I sent off the three last sheets of the L. B. in a great hurry yesterday; and I have to request that you will take your pen, and transcribe into the first sheet, which I sent yesterday, the three following verses, which I think I neglected to insert. They relate to the fourth " Poem on

the Naming of Places." If you look towards the end of
that poem you will find these words

> was chang'd
> To serious musing and to self-reproach.

Immediately after which ought to follow these three
verses.

> Nor did we fail to see within ourselves
> What need there is to be reserved in speech,
> And temper all our thoughts with charity.

These three lines are absolutely necessary to render
the poem intelligible. In the poem of *Michael*, about
the middle of the first part, you will find this line —

> The Clipping Tree a name which still it bears.

Take a pen, and alter the word "still" into the word
"yet" — Let the line be printed —

> The Clipping Tree, a name which yet it bears.

A few lines from the end of the first part of the same
poem you will find this line,

> But when the lad, now ten years old, could stand

Alter the manuscript with a pen, and let it be printed
thus

> But soon as Luke now ten years old could stand.

From a printed sheet I received yesterday from Mr.
Coleridge, I see that the sheet containing *The Pet Lamb*
&c., had been received, but I am afraid that the sheet

containing *The Old Cumberland Beggar*, &c. must either have miscarried, or reached you much later than it ought to have done; else I cannot conceive why in your last letter you should have said that four sheets were wanting to complete the work. If this sheet should have miscarried, do not begin to print the poem of *Michael* till you have written to tell me what poems have been received and printed. The sheet which contained *The Cumberland Beggar* contained also a part of *The Poet's Epitaph*, without which what followed in the next sheet would be nonsense. In the page of *errata*, let Lucretius be read for Lucretia, in the Preface. Second volume page 145 line first, Place a comma after the words " disconsolate creature," and omit the comma after "perhaps." Page 147 for "both grey, red, and green" substitute "grey, scarlet, and green."

.   .   .   .

1801

LXVIII

William Wordsworth to Charles James Fox

GRASMERE, WESTMORELAND, January 14th, 1801.

Sir,

It is not without much difficulty that I have summoned the courage to request your acceptance of these volumes.   Should I express my real feelings, I am sure that I should seem to make a parade of diffidence and humility.

Several of the poems contained in these volumes are written upon subjects which are the common property of all poets, and which, at some period of your life, must have been interesting to a man of your sensibility, and perhaps may still continue to be so.   It would be highly gratifying to me to suppose that even in a single instance the manner in which I have treated these general topics should afford you any pleasure ; but such a hope does not influence me upon the present occasion ; in truth I do not feel it.   Besides, I am convinced that there must be many things in this collection which may impress you with an unfavourable idea of my intellectual powers.   I do not say this with a wish to degrade myself, but I am sensible that this must be the case, from the different circles in which we have moved, and the different objects with which we have been conversant.

Being utterly unknown to you as I am, I am well aware that if I am justified in writing to you at all, it is necessary my letter should be short; but I have feelings within me, which I hope will so far show themselves, as to excuse the trespass which I am afraid I shall make.

In common with the whole of the English people, I have observed in your public character a constant predominance of sensibility of heart. Necessitated as you have been from your public situation to have much to do with men in bodies, and in classes, and accordingly to contemplate them in that relation, it has been your praise that you have not thereby been prevented from looking upon them as individuals, and that you have habitually left your heart open to be influenced by them in that capacity. This habit cannot but have made you dear to poets; and I am sure that if, since your first entrance into public life, there has been a single true poet living in England, he must have loved you.

But were I assured that I myself had a just claim to the title of a poet, all the dignity being attached to the word which belongs to it, I do not think that I should have ventured for that reason to offer these volumes to you; at present it is solely on account of two poems in the second volume, the one entitled *The Brothers*, and the other *Michael*, that I have been emboldened to take this liberty.

It appears to me that the most calamitous effect which has followed the measures which have lately been pursued in this country, is, a rapid decay of the domestic affections among the lower orders of society. This effect the present rulers of this country are not conscious of, or they disregard it. For many years past, the tendency of society, amongst almost all the nations of Europe, has been to produce it; but recently, by the spreading of

manufactures through every part of the country, by the
heavy taxes upon postage, by workhouses, houses of
industry, and the invention of soup-shops, &c., super-
added to the increasing disproportion between the price
of labour and that of the necessaries of life, the bonds of
domestic feeling among the poor, as far as the influence
of these things has extended, have been weakened, and
in innumerable instances entirely destroyed. The evil
would be the less to be regretted, if these institutions
were regarded only as palliatives to a disease; but the
vanity and pride of their promoters are so subtly inter-
woven with them, that they are deemed great discoveries
and blessings to humanity. In the meantime, parents
are separated from their children, and children from their
parents; the wife no longer prepares, with her own hands,
a meal for her husband, the produce of his labour; there
is little doing in his house in which his affections can be
interested, and but little left in it that he can love. I
have two neighbours, a man and his wife, both upwards
of eighty years of age. They live alone. The husband
has been confined to his bed many months, and has never
had, nor till within these few weeks has ever needed, any
body to attend to him but his wife. She has recently
been seized with a lameness which has often prevented
her from being able to carry him his food to his bed.
The neighbours fetch water for her from the well, and
do other kind offices for them both. But her infirmities
increase. She told my servant two days ago, that she
was afraid they must both be boarded out among some
other poor of the parish (they have long been supported
by the parish); but she said it was hard, having kept
house together so long, to come to this, and she was sure
that "it would burst her heart." I mention this fact to

show how deeply the spirit of independence is, even yet, rooted in some parts of the country. These people could not express themselves in this way without an almost sublime conviction of the blessings of independent domestic life. If it is true, as I believe, that this spirit is rapidly disappearing, no greater curse can befall a Land.

I earnestly entreat your pardon for having detained you so long. In the two poems, *The Brothers*, and *Michael*, I have attempted to draw a picture of the domestic affections, as I know they exist among a class of men who are now almost confined to the north of England. There are small independent *proprietors* of land, here called statesmen, men of respectable education, who daily labour on their own little properties. The domestic affections will always be strong amongst men who live in a country not crowded with population, if these men are placed above poverty. But if they are proprietors of small estates, which have descended to them from their ancestors, the power, which these affections will acquire amongst such men, is inconceivable by those who have only had an opportunity of observing hired labourers, farmers, and the manufacturing poor. Their little tract of land serves as a kind of permanent rallying point for their domestic feelings, as a tablet upon which they are written, which makes them objects of memory in a thousand instances, when they would otherwise be forgotten. It is a fountain fitted to the nature of social man, from which supplies of affection, as pure as his heart was intended for, are daily drawn. This class of men is rapidly disappearing. You, Sir, have a consciousness, upon which every good man will congratulate you, that the whole of your public conduct has, in one way or other, been directed to the preservation of this class of men, and those who hold similar situations. You have felt that the most sacred of all property is the property of the poor. The two poems, which I have mentioned, were written with a view to show that men who do not wear fine clothes can feel deeply. "Pectus enim est quod disertos facit, et vis mentis. Ideoque imperitis quoque, si modo sunt aliquo affectu concitati, verba non desunt."[1] The poems are faithful copies from Nature; and I hope whatever effect they may have upon you, you will at least be able to perceive that they may excite profitable sympathies in many kind and good hearts, and may in some small degree enlarge our feelings of reverence for our species, and our knowledge of human nature, by showing that our best qualities are possessed by men whom we are too apt to consider, not with reference to the points in which they resemble us, but to those in which they manifestly differ from us. I thought, at a time when these feelings are sapped in so many ways, that the two poems might co-operate, however feebly, with the illustrious efforts which you have made to stem this and other evils with which the country is labouring; and it is on this account alone that I have taken the liberty of thus addressing you.

Wishing earnestly that the time may come when the country may perceive what it has lost by neglecting your advice, and hoping that your latter days may be attended with health and comfort,

I remain,
With the highest respect and admiration,
Your most obedient and humble servant,

W. WORDSWORTH.

[1] See Quintilian *Inst. Orat.* X, vii, 15. — Ed.

LXIX

William Wordsworth to Francis Wrangham

[Jan. or Feb., 1801.]

My dear Wrangham,

The letter which you were so kind as to write to me some months ago arrived in due time. Notwithstanding my procrastinating spirit, I do honestly believe that I should have answered it immediately, had it not been, that at that time I was in bad health, and particularly engaged in preparing my second volume for the press; being also at that time three months behind hand in fulfilling my engagement with Longman. Soon afterwards I learned that Coleridge had received a letter from you to which, as in duty bound, he replied immediately. Now, I, being a wretched lazy fellow, as soon as I had heard this, said, as I imagine to myself, my duty to Wrangham is more than half discharged; therefore, *quoad* Wrangham, for three months to come I will live the life of a lazzarone, doing nothing; to which I cannot add thinking nothing, for I may honestly say that not a day has passed without thinking about him, and his kindness in remembering me, as he has done.

Your letter indeed, my dear friend, gave me very great pleasure. I need not say how much I was disappointed in not seeing you at your parsonage house. Though I was much pressed for time, I purposed to stop at least a couple of days with you. I called in company with a Mr. Hutchinson who lives at Gallowhill near Wykeham. He is one of Mr. Langley's farmers, and a particular friend of mine. At the time when we called at Hunmanby, my brother John and I were staying in Mr. Hutchinson's house, a visit which we prolonged for *three weeks*.[1] Mr. Hutchinson's house is kept by his sister, a woman who is a very particular friend both of my sister and myself. If ever you go that way it would be a great kindness done to me if you would call on them, and also at any future period render them any service in your power: I mean as to lending Miss Hutchinson books, or when you become acquainted with them, performing them any little service, *auprès de Monsieur ou Madame Langley*, with respect to their farm. Miss Hutchinson I can recommend to you as a most amiable and good creature, with whom you would converse with great pleasure. We live quite out of the way of new books. I have not seen a single one since I came here, now thirteen months ago. You will not therefore be surprized if your sermons, have [not] found their way to us. Had they done so, they must literally have come " Heaven-directed to the poor." Neither have we seen your poem. I congratulate you on your return to the muses. When you visit this country mind you bring your poems along with you, also your sermons, if possible. I read with great pleasure a very elegant and tender poem of yours in the second volume of the Anthology. It is a pity but that you could have avoided in the last stanzas of that poem a vulgar use of the word " charms ": in other respects the poem is very pleasing and as I rec-ollect altogether unobjectionable. As to your invitation into Yorkshire, I am afraid the day is distant. Coleridge, as a married man not over and above rich, is tethered. I also have my tether with which I have no inclination to quarrel. Besides, I am not strong enough to walk, and too poor to ride. Nevertheless I shall bear your invitation

[1] You will find a note upon these three weeks in postscript. W.W.

in mind, and keep the complying with it among the number of my pleasant wishes. We look forward to the thought of seeing you with great delight, you shall have a hearty welcome though very homely fare, no wine and even little beer, in our tiny cottage. Poor Coleridge has been very unwell, in a rheumatic fever, confined to his room, and often to his bed. He is however now, I hope, quite recovered. Let me hear from you soon. Your very affectionate friend,

                                        W. WORDSWORTH.

P.S. — Upon looking over my letter I find that it is probable you will think I portioned out my time very unjustly when I gave three weeks to my friends the Hutchinsons, and only allotted two days to you. The fact was that during the former part of my stay with the H—s, I knew that you were from home; it was during the last four or five days that I called on you, doubting even then, whether you would be returned.

My second volume of L. B. has been out a month; we have not yet seen it ourselves.

LXX

William Wordsworth to Thomas Poole

GRASMERE, KENDAL, WESTMORELAND,
                [Postmark, July, 1801.]

My dear Poole,

... At present I have taken up the pen solely on Coleridge's account, and must confine my letter to him and his affairs. I know how much you will be concerned to hear that his health cannot be said to be much better, indeed any better at all. He is apparently quite well one day, and the next the fit comes on him again with as much violence as ever. These repeated shocks cannot but greatly weaken his constitution; and he is himself afraid that, as the disease (which is manifestly gout) keeps much about his stomach, he may be carried off by it, with little or no warning. . . . We all here feel deeply persuaded that nothing can do him any effectual good, but a change of climate. And it is on this subject that I have now written to you.

The place which he thinks of going to is the Azores; both for the climate and the baths — which are known to be exceedingly salutary in cases of gout and rheumatism — and on account of the cheapness of living there, and the little expense in getting thither. But you know well how poor Coleridge is situated with respect to money affairs; indeed, it will be impossible for him to accomplish the journey without some assistance. . . . Further, it seems to me absolutely necessary that this should be procured in a manner the least burthensome to his feelings possible. If the thought of it should hang upon his mind when he is away, it will undo, or rather prevent, all the salutary effects of the climate. . . . I have thought it my duty to mention these circumstances to you, as being a person more interested than perhaps any other in what befalls our common friend. . . . As Coleridge at present does not intend to take his wife or children with him, I should hope that £50 might be enough; if she goes I am sure he will want £100, or near it. Now it is my opinion, and I dare say will be yours, that this money should be lent to him, in whatever way you think will ultimately hang the least upon his mind. He has mentioned to me a scheme of this sort, viz. : that he would write to Godwin, desiring him to call upon some bookseller, to request him to advance £100 upon some work to be written by Coleridge within a certain time, for the repayment of which £100 Coleridge would request you or some other of his friends to be security, if the work were not forthcoming at the time appointed. This plan, for my own part, though I did not like to say so abruptly to Coleridge, I greatly disapprove. As I am sure it would entangle him in an engagement, which it is ten to one he would be unable to fulfil; and, what is far worse, the engagement, while useless in itself, would prevent him from doing anything else. My dear Poole, you will do what you think proper on this statement of facts.

W. WORDSWORTH.

1802

LXXI

Dorothy Wordsworth to Mrs. Clarkson[1]

Tuesday Morning.

My dear Friend,

... I reached home before five o'clock on Sunday afternoon, without being in the least heated or fatigued. I daresay Mr. Clarkson was anxious about me, for he would see the clouds upon the tops of the mountains. There they were, but they never touched me, they only made my walk more interesting. They connected the whole vale of Brothers Water, with the sky enclosing it, so that there seemed no other place beyond ; and, indeed, it seemed as beautiful a place as there need be, in a beautiful world. I met William at the top of the hill above our own house. He was on the look-out for me. Mary was at home — Dear creature ! she was overjoyed to see me, after this short absence. She looked much better than she did, when I left her. ... Our garden is in great beauty. The brooms are covered with blossom, and we have a fine stock of flowers. I wish you could see it at this moment. Then I should wish the rain to stop, so that you might sit on the orchard-seat by the bower. ... Oh ! my dear friend, what a beautiful spot this is ! the

---

[1] The wife of the slave liberator, Thomas Clarkson, one of her chief friends. — Ed.

greenest in all the earth, the softest green covers the mountains even to the very top.   Silver How is before my eyes, and I forget that I have ever seen it so beautiful. Every bit of grass among the purple rocks (which are of all shades of purple) is green.   I am writing in my own room.   Every now and then I hear the chirping of a little family of swallows that have their abode against the glass of my windows.   The nest was built last year, and it has been taken possession of again about six weeks ago, needing no repairs whatever. William calls me again. God bless you, my very dear friend. . . .

1803

LXXII

William Wordsworth to Thomas De Quincey

GRASMERE, NEAR KENDAL, WESTMORELAND,
July 29th, 1803.

Dear Sir,

Your letter dated May 31, I did not receive till the day before yesterday, owing I presume to the remissness of Messr Longman and Rees, in forwarding it. I am much concerned at this; as though I am sure you would not suppose me capable of neglecting such a letter, yet still my silence must needs have caused you some uneasiness.

It is impossible not to be pleased when one is told that one has given so much pleasure; and it is to me a still higher gratification to find that my poems have impressed a stranger with such favorable ideas of my character as a man. Having said this, which is easily said, I find some difficulty in replying more particularly to your letter.

It is needless to say that it would be out of nature were I not to have kind feelings towards one who expresses sentiments of such profound esteem and admiration of my writings as you have done. You can have no doubt but that these sentiments, however conveyed to me, must have been acceptable; and I assure you that they are still more welcome coming from yourself. You will thus perceive that the main end which you proposed to yourself in writing to me is answered, viz., that I am already kindly disposed towards you. My friendship it is not in my power to give. This is a gift which no man can make; it is not in our own power. A sound and healthy friendship is the growth of time and circumstance. It will spring up and thrive like a wild-flower when these favour, and when they do not it is in vain to look for it.

I do not suppose that I am saying anything which you do not know as well as myself. I am simply reminding you of a commonplace truth which your high admiration of me may have robbed, perhaps, of that weight which it ought to have with you. . . .

And this leads me to what gave me great concern, I mean the very unreasonable value which you set upon my writings, compared with those of others. You are young and ingenuous, and I wrote with a hope of pleasing the young, the ingenuous and the unworldly, above all others; but sorry indeed should I be to stand in the way of the proper influence of other writers. You will know that I allude to the great names of past times, and above all to those of our own country.

I have taken the liberty of saying this much to hasten on the time when you will value my poems not the less, but those of others more. That time, I know, would come of itself, and may come sooner for what I have said, which, at all events, I am sure you cannot take ill. . . .

How many things there are in a man's character, of which his writings — however miscellaneous, or voluminous — will give no idea! How many thousand things which go to making up the value of a practically moral man, concerning not one of which any conclusion can be drawn from what he says of himself or of others in the world's ear! You probably would never guess from anything you know of me, that I am the most lazy and impatient letter-writer in the world. You will perhaps have observed that the first two or three lines of this sheet are in a tolerably fair, legible hand, and, now every letter, from A to Z, is a complete rout, one upon the heels of the other. Indeed so difficult do I find it to master this ill habit of idleness and impatience, that I have long since ceased to write any letters but upon business. In justice to myself and you, I have found myself obliged to mention this, lest you should think me unkind if you find me a slovenly and sluggish correspondent.

I am going with my friend Coleridge and my sister upon a tour into Scotland for six weeks or two months. This will prevent me hearing from you as soon as I could wish, as most likely we shall set off in a few days. If, however, you write immediately, I may have the pleasure of receiving your letter before our departure. If we are gone, I shall order it to be sent after me. I need not add that it will give me great pleasure to see you at Grasmere, if you should ever come this way.

I am, dear sir, with great sincerity and esteem,
Yours sincerely,
W. WORDSWORTH.

P.S. — I have just looked my letter over, and find that towards the conclusion I have been in a most unwarrantable hurry, especially in what I have said as to seeing you here. I seem to have expressed myself absolutely with coldness. This is not in my feelings, I assure you. I shall indeed be very happy to see you at Grasmere, if you ever find it convenient to visit this delightful country. You speak of yourself as being very young, and therefore may have many engagements of great importance with respect to your worldly concerns and future happiness in life. Do not neglect these on any account; but if consistent with these and your other duties you could find time to visit this country, which is no great distance from your present residence, I should, I repeat it, be very happy to see you. . . .

W. W.

LXXIII

Dorothy Wordsworth to Mrs. Clarkson

GRASMERE, Sunday, October 9th, [1803.]

My dear Friend,

. . . I was tired when I reached the inn at night, and glad to put my body in the state to receive all possible enjoyment of the few comforts a Scotch inn affords. I was glad to lay my legs up, and loll in indolence before the fire. . . . William had met him (Mr. Clarkson) at Ambleside on Monday, with the whole party. William had gone to volunteer his services [1] with the greatest part of the men of Grasmere. Alas! alas! Mary and I have no other hope than that they will not be called upon, out of these quiet far-off places, except in case of the French being successful after their landing, and in that case what matter? We may all go together. But we wanted him to wait till the body of the people should be called. For my part I thought much of the inconvenience and fatigue of going to be exercised twice or thrice a week. However, if he really enters into it heart and soul, and likes it, that will do him good; and surely there never was a

---

[1] Wordsworth — like his father — became a volunteer, in view of a possible French invasion. His father's sword is now at Dove Cottage, Grasmere. — Ed.

more determined hater of the French, nor one more willing to do his utmost to destroy them if they really do
come. . . .

LXXIV

William Wordsworth to Sir George Beaumont

GRASMERE, 14th October, 1803.

Dear Sir George,

If any person were to be informed of the particulars
of your kindness to me, — if it were described to him in
all its delicacy and nobleness, — and he should afterwards
be told that I suffered eight weeks to elapse without writing to you one word of thanks or acknowledgment, he
would deem it a thing absolutely *impossible*.

It is nevertheless true. This is, in fact, the first time
that I have taken up a pen, not for writing letters, but on
any account whatsoever, except once, since Mr. Coleridge
showed me the writings of the Applethwaite estate, and
told me the little history of what you had done for me,
the motives, etc. I need not say that it gave me the
most heartfelt pleasure, not for my own sake chiefly,
though in that point of view it might well be most highly
interesting to me, but as an act which, considered in all
its relations as to matter and manner, it would not be too
much to say, did honour to human nature. At least, I
felt it as such, and it overpowered me. . . .

I contented myself with breathing forth solitary gratu-
lations and thanksgivings, which I did in many a sweet
and many a wild place, during my late tour.[1] In this
shape, procrastination became irresistible to me; at last

[1] The tour with Coleridge and Dorothy Wordsworth in Scotland.
— Ed.

I said, I will write at home from my own fireside, when I
shall be at ease and in comfort. . . .

It is now high time to speak of the estate,[1] and what
is to be done with it.   It is a most delightful situation,
and few things would give me greater pleasure than to
realise the plan which you had in view for me, of building
a house there.   But I am afraid, I am sorry to say, that
the chances are very much against this, partly on account
of the state of my own affairs, and still more from the
improbability of Mr. Coleridge's continuing in the country.   The writings are at present in my possession, and
what I should wish is that I might be considered at
present as steward of the land, with liberty to lay out the
rent in planting, or any other improvement which might
be thought advisable, with a view to building upon it.
And if it should be out of my power to pitch my own tent
there, I would then request that you would give me leave
to restore the property to your own hands; in order that
you might have the opportunity of again presenting it to
some worthy person, who might be so fortunate as to be
able to make that pleasant use of it, which it was your
wish that I should have done.

Mr. Coleridge informed me that immediately after you
left Keswick he had, as I requested, returned you thanks
for those two elegant drawings, which you were so good
as to leave for me.   The present is valuable in itself, and
I consider it as a high honor conferred on me.   How
often did we wish for five minutes' command of your
pencil while we were in Scotland ! or rather that you had
been with us.   Sometimes I am sure you would have
been highly delighted.   In one thing Scotland is superior
to every country I have travelled in, I mean the graceful

---

[1] The Applethwaite property, near Keswick. — Ed.

beauty of the dresses and figures. There is a tone of imagination about them beyond anything I have seen elsewhere.

Mr. Coleridge, I understand, has written to you several times lately; so of course he will have told you when, and why, he left us. I am glad he did, as I am sure the solitary part of his tour did him much the most service. He is still unwell, though wonderfully strong. He is attempting to bring on a fit of the gout, which he is sure will relieve him greatly. I was at Keswick last Sunday, and saw both him and Mr. Southey, whom I liked very much. Coleridge looks better, I think, than when you saw him; and *is*, I also think, upon the whole much better. Lady Beaumont will be pleased to hear that our carriage, though it did not suit Mr. Coleridge (the noise of it being particularly unpleasant to him) answered wonderfully well for my sister and me, and that the whole tour far surpassed our most sanguine expectations.

They are sadly remiss at Keswick in putting themselves to trouble in defence of the country; they came forward very cheerfully some time ago, but were so thwarted by the orders and counter-orders of the Ministry and their servants that they have thrown up the whole in disgust. At Grasmere we have turned out almost to a man. We are to go to Ambleside on Sunday to be mustered, and put on, for the first time, our military apparel. I remain, dear Sir George, with the most affectionate and respectful regard for you and Lady Beaumont, yours sincerely,

W. WORDSWORTH.

My sister will transcribe three sonnets,[1] which I do not send you from any notion I have of their merit, but

[1] They were those entitled *Composed at —— Castle*, *To the Men of Kent*, and *Anticipation*. — Ed.

merely because they are the only verses I have written since I had the pleasure of seeing you and Lady Beaumont. At the sight of Kilchurn Castle, an ancient residence of the Breadalbane's, upon an island in Loch Awe, I felt a real poetical impulse : but I did not proceed. I began a poem (apostrophizing the castle) thus :

> Child of loud-throated war ! the mountain stream
> Roars in thy hearing : but thy hour of rest
> Is come, and thou art silent in thine age.

But I stopped.

LXXV

Dorothy Wordsworth to Mrs. Clarkson

Sunday, November 13th, [1803.]

My dear Friend,

... The vale and mountains of Grasmere have been in the fullest pride of their beauty this autumn. The fern has been more luxuriant than John Fisher (an old inhabitant of Grasmere) ever knew it, and we never saw it half so fine ; besides the colour of it has been more gorgeous than ever, owing I suppose to the gentleness of the autumn. Winter is now settled with us, yet the fern still retains some of its glorious orange hue. William and I had a fine walk this morning round the lake. It was a cold morning, but the mountains and lakes were in great beauty, all alive with sunshine and shadows. I can say but little in praise of our garden and orchard. They are not yet put into winter trim. ...

1804

LXXVI

William Wordsworth to Francis Wrangham

[Early in 1804.]

My dear Wrangham,

It is something less than ten minutes since I received your pacquet of songs, and kind admonishment accompanying them, for both of which receive my best thanks. I have indeed behaved very uncourteously to you, I will not say unkindly because that would be unjust, inasmuch as my own apparent neglect of you has called out more kind feelings towards you than I ever could have had, if I had done my duty. You do not know what a task it is to me to write a letter; I absolutely loathe the sight of a pen, when I have to use it. I have not written three letters, except upon indispensable business, during the last three years. I should not mention a circumstance so discreditable to me, were it not to justify myself from any apprehension on your part that I may have slighted you. It is not in my nature to neglect old friends. I live too much in the past for anything of that kind to attach to me. You wrote me a very friendly and pleasant letter long since, with a copy of verses which were very amusing; for both of these, if thanks late be better than thanks never at all, I now make you my acknowledgments. I have hurried through your songs which I think admirably adapted for the intended purpose. "A song or a story may drive away care," etc., pleased me best, but I shall be able to judge better upon a more leisurely perusal. You enquire how I am and what doing. As to the first, I am tolerably well; and for the second, I have great things in meditation, but as yet I have only been doing little ones. At present I am engaged in a poem on my own earlier life,[1] which will take five parts, or books, to complete; three of which are nearly finished. My other meditated works are a philosophical poem,[2] and a narrative one.[3] These two will employ me some, I ought to say several, years; and I do not mean to appear before the world again as an author, till one of them at least be finished.

As to my private affairs you would probably hear at Gallow.Hill, if you called there, that I have a son; and a noble one too he is, as ever was seen. He is a great comfort and pleasure to us in this lonely place. My sister continues to live with me. I read, walk, doze a little now and then in the afternoon; and live upon the whole what you may call a tolerably rational life, I mean as the world goes.

But should this letter grow in length, as it has grown in dullness, the Muses have mercy on you! but I will spare you! Farewell. Do not fail to present my kind remembrances to Mrs. Wrangham; and believe me, in spite of my remissness, and letter-phobia (forgive the uncouth wedlock of this compound), your very sincere and affectionate friend,

W. WORDSWORTH.

[1] *The Prelude.* — Ed.
[2] Doubtless *The Excursion.* — Ed.
[3] *The White Doe of Rylstone*, probably. — Ed.

P.S.—I shall send you on the other side **three sonnets**, the first and third of which I believe have been printed, though I myself have never seen them in print. I sent them to Sir George Beaumont, who informed me that he would forward them to some of the newspapers. The two or three last lines in the last I have altered from the copy sent to Sir George; if you think it worth while to circulate them with your own ballads and songs (or otherwise) you are perfectly at liberty so to do. They are however heavy-armed troops, and might perhaps stand in the way of the movements of your flying artillery. I conjecture that you have more songs to follow. Do not fail on any account to transmit them to me. Let me know also what you are doing, and how yourself and family are. I cannot promise to be a correspondent. I know my own infirmity too well. Therefore perhaps you may think this a request, little less than impudent, viz., that you should write to me upon such terms. Poor Coleridge who has been in very miserable health is now in London, whither he is gone with a view of trying to arrange matters for a voyage to Madeira for benefit of climate. Farewell, and all happiness attend you. My wife and sister send their best respects to you and Mrs. Wrangham.

W. W.

LXXVII

Dorothy Wordsworth to Mrs. Clarkson

February 13th, 1804.

My dear Friend,

. . . We have had a most mild Winter. The heart of it (December and January) has been a perfect South of England February-Spring, but these two days have been

intensely cold ; and indeed the mild weather was interrupted by chance days of mountain frosts and winds, that
made the snow-drops hang their heads.   The gardens are
gay with Spring flowers, and many primroses have been
found wild in the hedges.   The grass in many parts of
the vale is of a refreshing green.   We are all well.   William, which is the best news I can tell you, is cheerfully
engaged in composition, and goes on with great rapidity.
He is writing the poem on his own early life, which is to
be an appendix[1] to the *Recluse.* . . .   The weather, with
all its pleasant mildness, has been very wet in general.
He takes out the umbrella, and I daresay stands stock-still
under it, during many a rainy half-hour, in the middle of
road or field ! . . .

LXXVIII

Dorothy Wordsworth to Mrs. Clarkson

Sunday, February 26th, 1804.

My dear Friend,
    . . . William has been walking, and is now writing down
the verses which he has composed in his walk. . . .

[1] Preface rather. — Ed.

LXXIX

William Wordsworth to Thomas De Quincey [1]

GRASMERE, March 6th, 1804.

My dear Sir,

Your last amiable letter ought to have received a far earlier answer: I have been indeed highly culpable in my procrastination. It arrived just before we set off on our Scotch tour, and I am so sadly dilatory in matters of this kind, that unless I reply to a letter immediately, I am apt to defer it till the thought becomes painful, taking the shape of a duty rather than a pleasure; and then, Heaven knows when I may set myself to rights again, by doing what I ought to do. While I am on this subject, I must however say that I have a derangement which makes writing painful to me, and indeed almost prevents me from holding correspondence with anybody: and this (I mean to say the unpleasant feelings which I have connected with the act of holding a pen) has been the chief cause of my long silence.

Your last letter gave me great pleasure; it was indeed a very amiable one, and I was highly gratified in the thought of being so endeared to you by the mere effect of my writings. I am afraid you may have been hurt at not hearing from me, and may have construed my silence into neglect or inattention; I mean in the ordinary sense of the word. I assure you this has by no means been

---

[1] Addressed, Thomas De Quincey, Esq[r].
St. Johns' Priory,
Chester,
to be forwarded.
Re-addressed to Bath, and afterwards to Worcester College, Oxford. — Ed.

the case; I have thought of you very often and with great interest, and wished to hear from you again, which I hope I should have done, had you not perhaps been apprehensive that your letter might be an intrusion. Another letter might have roused me to discharge sooner the duty which I had shoved aside. . . .

We had a most delightful tour of six weeks in Scotland; our pleasure however was not a little dashed by the necessity under which Mr. Coleridge found himself of leaving us, at the end of something more than a fortnight, from ill health and a dread of the rains (his complaint being rheumatic), which then, after a long drought, appeared to be setting in. The weather however on the whole was excellent, and we were amply repaid for our pains.

As, most likely, you will make the tour of the Highlands some time or other, do not fail to let me know beforehand, and I will tell you what we thought most worth seeing, as far as we went. Our tour, though most delightful, was very imperfect, being nothing more than what is commonly called the short tour, with considerable deviations. We left Loch Ness, the Fall of Foyers, etc., unvisited.

By this time I conclude you have taken up your abode at Oxford. I hope this letter, though sent at random partly, will be forwarded, and that it will find you. I am anxious to hear how far you are satisfied with yourself at Oxford, and, above all, that you have not been seduced into unworthy pleasures or pursuits. The state of both the Universities is, I believe, much better than formerly in respect to the morals and manners of the students. I know that Cambridge is greatly improved since the time when I was there, which is about thirteen years ago. The manners of the young men were very frantic and dissolute at that time, and Oxford was no better, or worse. I need not say to you that there is no true dignity but in virtue and temperance, and, let me add, chastity; and that the best safeguard of all these is the cultivation of pure pleasures, namely, those of the intellect and affections. I have much anxiety on this head from a sincere concern in your welfare, and the melancholy retrospect which forces itself upon one, of the number of men of genius who have fallen beneath the evils that beset them. I do not mean to preach; I speak in simplicity and tender apprehension, as one lover of nature and of virtue speaking to another. Do not on any account fail to tell me whether you are satisfied with yourself since your migration to Oxford; if not, do your duty to yourself immediately. Love nature and books; seek these, and you will be happy; for virtuous friendship, and love, and knowledge of mankind must inevitably accompany these, all things thus ripening in their due season. I am now writing a poem on my own earlier life; I have just finished that part in which I speak of my residence at the University; it would give me great pleasure to read this work to you at this time, as I am sure, from the interest you have taken in the L. B., that it would please you, and might also be of service to you. This poem will not be published these many years, and never during my lifetime, till I have finished a larger and more important work to which it is tributary. Of this larger work I have written one book and several scattered fragments : it is a moral and philosophical poem ; the subject whatever I find most interesting in Nature, Man, and Society, and most adapted to poetic illustration. To this work I mean to devote the prime of my life, and the chief force of my mind. I have also arranged the plan of a narrative poem; and if I live to finish these three principal works I shall be content. That on my own life, the least important of the three, is better than half complete, viz., four books, amounting to about 2500 lines. They are all to be in blank verse. I have taken the liberty of saying this much of my own concerns to you, not doubting that it would interest you. You have as yet had little knowledge of me as a poet; but I hope, if we live, we shall be still more nearly united.

I cannot forbear mentioning to you the way in which a wretched creature of the name of Peter Bailey has lately treated the author of your favourite book, the "Lyrical Ballads." After pillaging them in a style of plagiarism, I believe unexampled in the history of modern literature, the wretch has had the baseness to write a long poem in ridicule of them, chiefly of *The Idiot Boy;* and, not content with this, in a note annexed to the same poem, has spoken of me, *by. name,* as the *simplest,* i.e. the most contemptible of all poets! The complicated baseness of this (for the plagiarisms are absolutely by wholesale) grieved me to the heart for the sake of poor human nature. That anybody could combine (as this man in some way or other must have done) an admiration and love of those poems, with moral feelings so detestable, hurt me beyond measure. If this unhappy creature's volume should ever fall in your way, you will find the plagiarisms chiefly in two poems, one entitled *Evening in the Vale of Festiniog,* which is a wretched parody throughout of *Tintern Abbey,* and the other *The Ivy Seat,* also *The Truest Fay,* and some others.

I must now conclude, not omitting however to say that Mr. Coleridge and my sister were much pleased with your kind remembrances of them, which my sister begs me to return. Mr. C—— is at present in London, sorry I am to say, on account of the very bad health under which he labours. Believe me to be, dear sir, your very affectionate friend,

W. WORDSWORTH.

P.S. — Do not fail to write me as soon as you can find time.

LXXX

William Wordsworth to Thomas De Quincey

GRASMERE, Monday, March 19th, [1804.]

Dear Sir,

. . . I cannot express to you how much pleasure it gave me to learn that my poems had been of such eminent service to you as you describe. May God grant that you may persevere in all good habits, desires, and resolutions.

Such facts as you have communicated to me are an abundant recompense for all the labour and pains which the profession of poetry requires, and without which nothing permanent or good can be produced. I am at present much engaged, and therefore I know you will excuse my adding more; I will only request that you will be so good as to write to me soon after you receive the letter above spoken of,[1] if you find a disposition so to do.

Believe me, with kind regard and esteem, your affectionate

W. WORDSWORTH.

[1] The preceding letter, addressed to De Quincey at Chester, after the De Quincey family had left the place. — Ed.

LXXXI

Dorothy Wordsworth to Mrs. Clarkson

Sunday Evening, March 24th, 1804.

My dear Friend,

. . . We have been engaged, Mary and I, in making a complete copy of William's poems for poor Coleridge, to be his companion in Italy; and it was really, towards the conclusion, a work of great anxiety, for we were afraid that they would not reach London or Portsmouth in time for him; and his desire to have them almost made him miserable, while there was any doubt about it. The last packet we sent off would arrive in London, as we now learn, three days before his departure; a great comfort to us. Thinking of his banishment, his loneliness, the long distance he will be from all the human beings that he loves, it is one of my greatest consolations that he has those poems with him. There are about eight thousand lines. A great addition to the poem on my brother's life has been made, since C. left us, fifteen hundred lines; and since we parted from you, a still greater. He has also written a few small poems. I hope, my dear friend, a happy time for you, and all of us, will come, when we shall read these poems to you. I am sure your heart will swell with exultation and joy. I ought to tell you that besides copying the verses for Coleridge, we have re-copied them entirely for ourselves as we went along; for the manuscripts which we took them from were in such a wretched condition, and so tedious to copy from — besides requiring William's almost constant superintendence — that we considered it as almost necessary to save them alive that we should re-copy them; for I think William would never have had the resolution to set us to work again. . . .

We have looked out for the Evening Star constantly since we knew what a dear companion she was of yours. She stares at us from the northern side of Silver How, and sets considerably below the highest point of the hill; but for two nights we have seen neither moon nor stars. It has been storm, rain, and snow. . . .

LXXXII

Dorothy Wordsworth to Mrs. Clarkson

PARK HOUSE, Wednesday, April 9th, 1804.

My dear Friend,

. . . I determined then to go to Eusemere as soon as possible, so yesterday afternoon Sara and I went. . . . We strolled about in the garden for about half an hour before Ellen arrived. The afternoon was warm, and we sat down upon the grass; the lake was beautiful and all about the house neat and flourishing — need I say how full our hearts were ? . . . When we entered the drawing room the view from the window struck us both in the same moment in the same way, as if it were an unearthly sight, a scene of *heavenly* splendour. . . .

LXXXIII

Dorothy Wordsworth to Mrs. Clarkson

[KESWICK, June 4, 1804.]

My dear Friend,

. . . I have always felt at Eusemere, when I have entered one of the rooms without thinking of what was to be seen — particularly when I had been there only a short time — that there was something unearthly in the prospect. So it seemed the last time. I was entirely occupied in the thought of you, and past times, when I went into the drawing room; and, indeed, I think that I never before saw any sight that was so purely, so *heavenly* beautiful. . . .

LXXXIV

Dorothy Wordsworth to Mrs. Clarkson

GRASMERE, 18th July, 1804.

My dear Friend,

. . . Your mother has been in her grave as I guess these fourteen days. . . . I trust you are now steadily calm, and I can think with pleasure of the quiet and silence in which she lies. My dear friend I need not speak *to you* of the many consolations that are to be found, while you lament this loss. . . . She has lived to see her children, men and women, grown; no longer *needing* her care, dutiful and good, a comfort to their father, and each other. . . .

LXXXV

William Wordsworth to Sir George Beaumont

GRASMERE, July 20, 1804.

Dear Sir George,

. . . If a man were what he ought to be, with such feelings and such motives as I have, it would be as easy for him to write to Sir George Beaumont as to take his food when he was hungry, or his repose when he was weary. But we suffer bad habits to grow upon us, and that has been the case with me, as you have had reason to find and forgive already. . . .

A few days ago I received from Mr. Southey your very acceptable present of Sir Joshua Reynold's Works, which, with the Life, I have nearly read through. Several of the Discourses I had read before, though never regularly together: they have very much added to the high opinion which I before entertained of Sir Joshua. Of a great part of them, never having had an opportunity of *studying* any pictures whatsoever, I can be but a very inadequate judge; but of such parts of the Discourses as relate to general Philosophy, I may be entitled to speak with more confidence; and it gives me pleasure to say to you, knowing your great regard for Sir Joshua, that they appear to me highly honourable to him.

The sound judgment universally displayed in these Discourses is truly admirable, — I mean the deep conviction of the necessity of unwearied labour and diligence, the reverence for the great men of his art, and the comprehensive and unexclusive character of his taste. Is it not a pity that a man with such a high sense of the *dignity* of his art, and with such industry, should not have given more of his time to the nobler departments of painting? I do not say this so much on account of what the world would have gained by the superior excellence and interest of his pictures, though doubtless that would have been very considerable, but for the sake of example. It is such an animating sight to see a man of genius, regardless of temporary gains, whether of money or praise, fixing his attention solely upon what is intrinsically interesting and permanent, and finding his happiness in the entire devotion of himself to such pursuits as shall most ennoble human nature. We have not yet seen enough of this in modern times; and never was there a period in society when such examples were likely to do more good than at present. The industry and love of truth which distinguish Sir Joshua's mind are most admirable; but he

appears to me to have lived too much for the age in
which he lived, and the people among whom he lived,
though this in an infinitely less degree than his friend
Burke, of whom Goldsmith said, with such truth, long
ago, that,

> Born for the universe, he narrowed his mind,
> And to party gave up what was meant for mankind.

I should not have said thus much of Reynolds, which
I have not said without pain, but because I have so great
a respect for his character, and because he lived at a
time when, being the first Englishman distinguished for
excellence in the higher department of painting, he had
the field fairly open for him to have given an example —
upon which all eyes must needs have been fixed — of a
man preferring the cultivation and exertion of his own
powers in the highest possible degree to any other
object of regard.

The weather has been most glorious, and the country,
of course, most delightful. Our own valley in particular
was last night, by the light of the full moon, and in the
perfect stillness of the lake, a scene of loveliness and
repose as affecting as was ever beheld by the eye of man.
We have had a day and a half of Mr. Davy's company
at Grasmere, and no more. . . . I went with him to Patterdale, on his road to Penrith, where he would take
coach. . . . He is a most interesting man, whose views are
fixed upon worthy objects.

That Loughrigg Tarn, beautiful pool of water as it is,
is a perpetual mortification to me when I think that you
and Lady Beaumont were so near having a summer-nest
there. This is often talked over among us; and we
always end the subject with a heigh-ho! of regret. . . .

I must add how much pleasure it gives me that Lady Beaumont is so kindly, so affectionately, disposed to my dear and good sister, and also to the other unknown parts of my family. Could we but have Coleridge back among us again! There is no happiness in this life but in intellect and virtue.

Farewell. Believe me, with the sincerest love and affection for you and Lady Beaumont, yours,

WM. WORDSWORTH.

LXXXVI

William Wordsworth to Sir George Beaumont

GRASMERE, August 30 (?), 1804.

Dear Sir George,

On Wednesday last Mrs. Coleridge received a letter from Coleridge. I happened to be at Keswick when it arrived; and she has sent it over to us to-day. I will transcribe the most material parts of it, first assuring you, to remove anxiety on your part, that the contents are, we think, upon the whole, promising. He begins thus (date, June 5, 1804, Tuesday noon; Dr. Stoddart's, Malta): "I landed, in more than usual health, in the harbour of Valetta, about four o'clock, Friday afternoon, April 18." ...

Mrs. Wordsworth and Lady B.'s little god-daughter[1] are both doing very well. Had the child been a boy, we should have persisted in our right to avail ourselves of Lady Beaumont's goodness in offering to stand sponsor for it. The name of *Dorothy*, obsolete as it is now grown, had been so long devoted in my own thoughts to the first

[1] Dora Wordsworth, born August 16, 1804. — Ed.

daughter that I might have, that I could not break this promise to myself — a promise in which my wife participated; though the name of *Mary*, to my ear the most musical and truly English in sound we have, would have been most welcome to me, including, as it would, Lady Beaumont and its mother.   This last sentence, though in a letter to you, Sir George, is intended for Lady Beaumont. . . .

When I ventured to express my regret at Sir Joshua Reynolds giving so much of his time to portrait painting and to his friends, I did not mean to recommend absolute solitude and seclusion from the world as an advantage to him or anybody else.   I think it a great evil; and indeed, in the case of a painter, frequent intercourse with the living world seems absolutely necessary to keep the mind in health and vigour.   I spoke, in some respects, in compliment to Sir Joshua Reynolds, feeling deeply, as I do, the power of his genius, and loving passionately the labours of genius in every way in which I am capable of comprehending them.   Mr. Malone, in the account prefixed to the *Discourses*, tells us that Sir Joshua generally passed the time from eleven till four every day in portrait painting.   This it was that grieved me, as a sacrifice of great things to little ones.   It will give me great pleasure to hear from you at your leisure.   I am anxious to know that you are satisfied with the site and intended plan of your house.   I suppose no man ever built a house without finding, when it was finished, that something in it might have been better done.   *Internal* architecture seems to have arrived at great excellence in England; but, I don't know how it is, I scarcely ever see the *outside* of a new house that pleases me. . . . Believe me, yours, with the greatest respect and regard,

W. WORDSWORTH.

My poetical labours have been entirely suspended during the last two months. I am most anxious to return to them.

LXXXVII

William Wordsworth to Sir George Beaumont

GRASMERE, September 8th.[1]

... You will be glad to hear that I have been busily employed lately. I wrote one book of *The Recluse*, nearly a thousand lines, then had a rest. Last week I began again, and have written three hundred more. I hope all tolerably well, and certainly with good views. ...

I have been at Whitby several times. Once in particular I remember seeing a most extraordinary effect from the pier, produced by the bold and ragged shore in a misty and showery day. The appearance was as of a set of huge faces in profile, one behind the other, with noses of prodigious prominence. The whole was very fantastic, and yet grand. ...

LXXXVIII

Dorothy Wordsworth to Mrs. Clarkson

GRASMERE, Monday, about the 13th or 14th October, [1804 probably.]

My dear Friend,

... Coleridge will be heart struck at the thought of no more returning to his old books in their old book-case looking to Skiddaw; his study, his study-fireside, Newlands, and Borrowdale, all taken from him; for there is no such situation, no such prospect anywhere as from his study window. ...

---

[1] No year is given, but it cannot be later than 1804. — Ed.

LXXXIX

William Wordsworth to Sir George Beaumont

GRASMERE, Dec. 25th, 1804.

My dear Sir George,

I was deeply sensible of your kindness in inviting me to Grosvenor Square, and then felt and still feel a strong inclination to avail myself of the opportunity of cultivating your friendship and that of Lady Beaumont, and of seeing a little of the world at the same time. But as the wish is strong, there are also strong obstacles against it: first, though I have lately been tolerably industrious, I am far behindhand with my appointed work; and next, my nervous system is so apt to be deranged by going from home that I am by no means sure that I should not be so much of a dependent invalid . . . as to make it absolutely improper for me to obtrude myself where neither my exertions of mind or body could enable me to be tolerable company. . . .

I think we are completely agreed upon the subject of Sir Joshua — that is, we both regret that he did not devote more of his time to the higher branches of the art; and further, I think you join with me in lamenting, to a certain degree at least, that he did not live more to himself. I have since read the rest of his *Discourses*, with which I have been greatly pleased, and wish most heartily that I could have an opportunity of seeing in your company your own collection of pictures and some others in town, Mr. Angerstein's for instance, to have pointed out to me some of those finer and peculiar beauties of painting; pictures which I am afraid I shall never have an occasion of becoming sufficiently familiar with to discover of myself. There is not a day in my life when I am at home in which that exquisite little drawing of yours of Apple-thwaite does not affect me with a sense of harmony and grace which I cannot describe. Mr. Edridge, an artist whom you know, saw this drawing along with a Mr. Duppa, another artist, who published *Hints from Raphael and Michael Angelo;* and they were both most enthusiastic in their praise of it, to my great delight. By the by, I thought Mr. Edridge a man of very mild and pleasing manners, and as far as I could judge, of delicate feelings, in the province of his art. Duppa is publishing a life of Michael Angelo, and I received from him a few days ago two proof-sheets of an appendix which contains the poems of Michael Angelo, which I shall read, and trans-late one or two of them, if I can do it with decent suc-cess. I have peeped into the sonnets, and they do not appear unworthy of their great author.

You will be pleased to hear that I have been advancing with my work. I have written upwards of two thousand verses during the last ten weeks. I do not know if you are exactly acquainted with the plan of my poetical labour. It is twofold — first, a poem, to be called *The Recluse;* in which it will be my object to express in verse my most interesting feelings concerning Man, Nature, and Society; and next, a poem (in which I am at present chiefly engaged) on my earlier life, or the growth of my own mind, taken up upon a large scale. This latter work I expect to have finished before the month of May; and then I purpose to fall with all my might on the former, which is the chief object upon which my thoughts have been fixed these many years. Of this poem, that of The Pedlar, which Coleridge read you, is part, and I may have written of it altogether about two thousand lines. It will consist, I hope, of about ten or twelve thousand.

May we not hope for the pleasure of seeing you and Lady Beaumont down here next summer? I flatter myself that Coleridge will then be returned, and though we would not on any account that he should fix himself in this rainy part of England, yet perhaps we may have the happiness of meeting all together for a few weeks. We have lately built in our little rocky orchard a circular hut, lined with moss, like a wren's nest, and coated on the outside with heath, that stands most charmingly, with several views from the different sides of it, of the Lake, the Valley and the Church — the latter sadly spoiled of late by being white-washed. The little retreat is most delightful, and I am sure you and Lady Beaumont would be highly pleased with it. Coleridge has never seen it. What a happiness would it be to us to see him there, and entertain you all next summer in our homely way under its shady thatch. I will copy a dwarf inscription which I wrote for it the other day, before the building was entirely finished, which indeed it is not yet.

> No whimsy of the purse is here,
> No pleasure-house forlorn;
> Use, comfort, do this roof endear;
> A tributary shed to cheer
> The little cottage that is near,
> To help it and adorn.

I hope the young Roscius,[1] if he go on as he has begun, will rescue the English theatre from the infamy that has fallen upon it, and restore the reign of good sense and nature. From what you have seen, Sir George, do you think he could manage a character of Shakespeare? Neither Selim nor Douglas requires much power; but

---

[1] William H. W. Betty. — Ed.

even to perform them as he does, talents and genius I should think must be necessary. I had very little hope, I confess, thinking it very natural that a theatre which had brought a dog upon the stage as a principal performer would catch at a wonder whatever shape it might put on.

We have had no tidings of Coleridge these several months. He spoke of papers which he had sent by private hands, none of which *we* have received. It must be most criminal neglect somewhere, if the fever be suffered to enter Malta. Farewell, and believe me, my dear Sir George, your affectionate and sincere friend,

W. WORDSWORTH.

1805

XC

Dorothy Wordsworth to Mrs. Clarkson

PARKHOUSE,[1] January 6, 1805.

. . . We have now little thought of leaving our cottage till Coleridge's return, which surely will not be long — we shall go wherever he goes — and why may not you be near us too? . . .

XCI

William Wordsworth to Walter Scott

GRASMERE, Jan. 16, 1805.

. . . If you come next summer Southey will almost certainly be at Keswick, and I hope Coleridge also; although it will be the duty of all his friends to do their utmost in forcing him from the country, to which he is so much attached; but the rainy climate disagrees with him miserably. When Coleridge has found out a residence better suited to his state of health, we shall remove and settle near him. I mention these things that you may be prevailed upon to come and see us while we are yet such near neighbours of yours, and inhabitants of a

---

[1] A house on the eastern side, and at the lower end of Ulles water, where the Wordsworths' friends the Luffs resided. — Ed.

country the more retired beauties of which we can lead you to better than anybody else. . . .

I am very glad to hear of your farm on Tweedside. You will be quite in the district of your own most interesting local feelings, — a charming country besides ; and I was not a little glad it brought you so much nearer to us, instead of removing you so much further away from us. I sincerely wish you fortune in your farming labours, good crops, thriving cattle, and little vexation.

On the other side you will find a few stanzas, which I hope (for the subject at least) will give you some pleasure.[1] I wrote them, not without a view of pleasing you, soon after our return from Scotland, though I have been too lazy to send them to you till now. They are in the same sort of metre as the *Leader Haughs*, and I have borrowed the name " Burn-mill meadow " from that poem, for which I wish you would substitute something that may really be found in the Vale of Yarrow. . . . Believe me, your sincere friend,

W. WORDSWORTH.

XCII

John Wordsworth to William Wordsworth[2]

Ship *Abergavenny* at Portsmouth,
Jan. 24, 1805.

My dear Wm.,

I ought to have written to you long ago, but I have a most utter dislike to writing if I can avoid it. And I can assure you, though no man of business myself,

[1] *Yarrow Unvisited.* — Ed.
[2] This was the last letter which John Wordsworth wrote to his brother. He perished by shipwreck on February 6, 1805. — Ed.

I have had quite enough to engage the attention of a man more fitted for it than myself. I have the pleasure to inform you that the *Abergavenny* is arrived safe at Portsmouth; and if the wind continues fair, which it is at present, shall expect to leave this place to-morrow. We had a very narrow escape in the Downs. The *Warren Hastings*, Indiaman, drifted foul of us, in a heavy gale of wind, but fortunately did us little damage. She has suffered so much that we are ordered to proceed to sea without her. The purser is dispatched, and I expect him at Portsmouth every hour. The convoy appointed is the Weymouth frigate of 44 guns. I have been so much engaged since I arrived in England that I regret very much it has been out of my power to pay you a visit in the North of England, and I can assure you that except to see the ship, I have not been three miles out of London since we arrived.

My investment is well laid in, and my voyage thought by most persons the first of the season; and if we are so fortunate as to get safe and soon to Bengal, — I mean before any other ship of the season, — I have no doubt but that I shall make a very good voyage of it, if not a *very great* one. At least this is the general opinion. I have got my investment upon the best of terms, having paid ready money for great part of it, which I was enabled to do by one gentleman lending me £5000. It amounts to about £20,000 in money.

The passengers are all down, and we are anxiously expecting to sail. We shall muster at my table 36 or 38 persons. This must alone have given me a great deal of trouble, to provide provisions, etc. for them. I was obliged to apply to the Court of Directors to have some of the passengers turned out of the ship, which was granted.

I thought at one time I should have had 45 persons at my table.

In ship's company we have 200, and soldiers and passengers 200 more, amounting all together to 400, so that I shall have sufficient employment on my hands to keep all these people in order.

I should have liked very much to have seen the poetry you have written (which I have not seen). In the "Lyrical Ballads" my favourites are *The Mad Mother*, part of *The Indian Woman*, and *Joanna*. I like *Michael*, and all the *Poems on the Naming of Places*, but *Joanna* best, and I also like —.[1] The poem on *The Wye* is a poem that I admire, but after having read it I do not like to turn to it again. Among those unpublished that I have seen my favourite is *The Leech Gatherer*, *The Sparrow's Nest*, *The Butterfly*, and *The Cuckoo*. There is a harshness in many of the rest which I do not like. I think the "Lyrical Ballads" taken all together far superior to the last poems.

Remember me most affectionately to Mary and Dorothy. Give my little namesake and his sister a kiss from me, and believe me to be,
                    Your affectionate brother,

                                JOHN WORDSWORTH.

XCIII

William Wordsworth to Sir George Beaumont

                              GRASMERE, Feb. 20th, 1805.
My dear Friend,

My father, who was an attorney of considerable eminence, died intestate, when we were children: and the

---

[1] The name is illegible from sealing wax on the MS. It may be *The Brothers*, or it may be *Beggars*. — Ed.

chief part of his personal property after his decease was expended in an unsuccessful attempt to compel the late Lord Lonsdale to pay a debt of about £5000 to my father's estate. Enough, however, was scraped together to educate us all in different ways. I, the second son, was sent to college with a view to the profession of the church or law; into one of which I should have been forced by necessity, had not a friend left me £900. This bequest was from a young man with whom, though I call him friend, I had had but little connection; and the act was done entirely from a confidence on his part that I had powers and attainments which might be of use to mankind. This I have mentioned, because it was his due, and I thought the fact would give you pleasure. Upon the interest of the £900, £400 being laid out in annuity, with £200 deducted from the principal, and £100 a legacy to my sister, and £100 more which the " Lyrical Ballads " have brought me, my sister and I contrived to live seven years, nearly eight. Lord Lonsdale then died, and the present Lord Lowther paid to my father's estate £8500. Of this sum I believe £1800 apiece will come to my sister and myself ; at least, would have come : but £3000 was lent out to our poor brother, I mean taken from the whole sum, which was about £1200 more than his share, which £1200 belonged to my sister and me. This £1200 we freely lent him : whether it was insured or no, I do not know ; but I dare say it will prove to be the case ; we did not however stipulate for its being insured. But you shall faithfully know all particulars as soon as I have learned them.

XCIV

Dorothy Wordsworth to Christopher Wordsworth

Feb. 22, 1805.

[After the death of her brother John.]

. . . A thousand times have I repeated to myself his last words, "The will of God be done"; and be it so. I trust I shall always be both better, and happier too, because he has lived; though I seem to myself that I could never more be *cheerful* as heretofore. Wherever we turn, wherever we look, we see something that he knew and loved. . . .

XCV

William Wordsworth to Richard Sharp

February, 1805.

My dear Sir,

. . . We have no tidings of poor Coleridge. For heaven's sake, should you hear of him, write to me; and also do let me know whether we shall see you, as you said, this next June. Woe to poor Grasmere for ever and ever! A wretched creature, wretched in name and nature, of the name of *Crump*, goaded on by his still more wretched wife, — (for by-the-bye, the man, though a Liverpool attorney, is, I am told, a very good sort of fellow, but the wife as ambitious as Semiramis), — this same wretch has at last begun to put his long impending threats in execution; and when you next enter the sweet paradise of Grasmere you will see staring you in the face, upon that beautiful ridge that elbows out into the vale, (behind the church, and towering far above its steeple), a temple of abomination, in which are to be enshrined Mr. and Mrs. Crump. Seriously, this is a great vexation to us, as this house will stare you in the face from every part of the vale, and entirely destroy its character of simplicity and seclusion.

I now see no newspapers — not even a weekly one — so that I am in utter ignorance of what is going on in the world. My poem advances, quick or slow as the fit comes ; but I wish sadly to have it finished, in order that, after a reasonable respite, I may fall to my principal work.

I purpose to make a tour somewhere next summer, if I can possibly muster the cash, but where I have not fixed. I incline much to Norway, but five or six weeks' sea voyage — as thither and back again it will be — frightens me ; else I could sail most conveniently from Stockton-upon-Tees, Mrs. Wordsworth having a brother who is a timber merchant, and has vessels regularly passing to and fro. Could you give me any information that would be of use in case of such a scheme taking effect? . . . Believe me, my dear friend, yours with great respect,

W. WORDSWORTH.

XCVI

William Wordsworth to Walter Scott

March 7th, 1805.

Dear Scott,

We have at last received your poem,[1] for which my sister returns you her sincere thanks. High as our expectations were, I have the pleasure to say that the

---

[1] *The Lay of the Last Minstrel.* — Ed.

poem has surpassed them much. We think you have completely attained your object. The book is throughout interesting and entertaining, and the picture of manners as lively as possible. . . .

XCVII

Dorothy Wordsworth to Mrs. Marshall

March 16th, 1805.

Our house is too small for us, and there is no other in the vale: so we must move at some time, and the sooner it is done the better. We shall most likely go southward; but we do not talk of change and we shall find it hard to resolve. . . . I can think of nothing. . . .

XCVIII

Dorothy Wordsworth to Mrs. Clarkson

GRASMERE, March 18th, [1805.]

. . . I trust that the example of our dear brother, who though taken from our earthly sight is forever with us — and will be so to our dying day — that his example will teach us to submit, in all calmness, to the divine will; and that the memory of his happy and innocent life, his joy in all good and lovely things, will help us again to take pleasure in the same objects as before, and with a more holy feeling, though it can never be so gladsome. . . .

XCIX

Dorothy Wordsworth to Mrs. Clarkson

[Postmark, KESWICK, April 19, 1805.]

My dear Friend,

. . . I have great pleasure in thinking that you may see
Miss Lamb.   Do not miss it, if you can possibly go without injury to yourself.   They are the best good creatures,
blessings be with them!   They have sympathized in our
sorrow as tenderly as if they had grown up in the same
town with us, and known our beloved John from his childhood.   Charles has written to us the most consolatory
letters, the result of diligent and painful enquiry of the
survivors of the wreck.   For this we must love him as
long as we have breath.   I think of him and his sister
every day of my life, and many times in the day, with
thankfulness and blessings.   Talk to dear Miss Lamb
about coming into this country, and let us hear what she
says of it.   I cannot express how much we all wish to
see her and her brother while we are at Grasmere.   We
look forward to Coleridge's return with fear and painful
hope, but indeed I dare not look to it.   I think as little
as I can of him.   Oh, my dear friend, my heart seems to
be shut against worldly hope!   Our poor John was the
life of the best of all our hopes.   I seek to be resigned
to the will of God, and find my comfort in his innocent
life and noble death.   These contemplations strengthen
my inner convictions of the glory of our nature, and that
he is now in blessedness, in peace. . . .

C

William Wordsworth to Sir George Beaumont

GRASMERE, May 1st, 1805.

My dear Sir George,

I have wished to write to you every day this long time, but I have also had another wish, which has interfered to prevent me; I mean the wish to resume my poetical labours. Time was stealing away fast from me, and nothing done, and my mind still seeming unfit to do anything. At first I had a strong impulse to write a poem that should record my brother's virtues, and be worthy of his memory. I began to give vent to my feelings, with this view; but I was overpowered by my subject, and could not proceed. I composed much, but it is all lost except a few lines, as it came from me in such a torrent that I was unable to remember it. I could not hold the pen myself, and the subject was such that I could not employ Mrs. Wordsworth or my sister as my amanuensis. This work must therefore rest a while till I am something calmer; I shall, however, never be at peace till, as far as in me lies, I have done justice to my departed brother's memory. His heroic death (the particulars of which I have now accurately collected from several of the survivors) exacts this from me, and still more his singularly interesting character, and virtuous and innocent life.

Unable to proceed with this work, I turned my thoughts again to the poem on my own life, and you will be glad to hear that I have added 300 lines to it in the course of last week. Two books more will conclude it. It will be not much less than 9000 lines,[1] — not hundred but thousand lines long, — an alarming length! and a thing unprecedented in literary history that a man should talk so much about himself. It is not self-conceit, as you will know well, that has induced me to do this, but real humility. I began the work because I was unprepared to treat any more arduous subject, and diffident of my own powers. Here, at least, I hoped that to a certain degree I should be sure of succeeding, as I had nothing to do but describe what I had felt and thought; therefore could not easily be bewildered. This might certainly have been done in narrower compass by a man of more address; but I have done my best.

If, when the work shall be finished, it appears to the judicious to have redundancies, they shall be lopped off, if possible; but this is very difficult to do, when a man has written with thought; and this defect, whenever I have suspected it, or found it to exist in any writings of mine, I have always found incurable. The fault lies too deep, and is in the first conception. If you see Coleridge before I do, do not speak of this to him, as I should like to have his judgment unpreoccupied by such an apprehension. I wish much to have your further opinion of the young Roscius,[2] above all of his Hamlet. It is certainly impossible that he should understand the character, that is, the composition of the character. But many of the sentiments which are put into Hamlet's mouth he may be supposed to be capable of feeling, and to a certain degree of entering into the spirit of some of the situations. I never saw *Hamlet* acted myself, nor do I know what kind of a play they make of it. I think I have heard that

---

[1] It reached to 7884 lines. — Ed.

[2] See p. 174. — Ed.

some parts which I consider among the finest are omitted; in particular, Hamlet's wild language after the ghost has disappeared.

The players have taken intolerable liberties with Shakespeare's plays, especially with *Richard the Third*, which, though a character admirably conceived and drawn, is in some scenes bad enough in Shakespeare himself; but the play, as it is now acted, has always appeared to me a disgrace to the English stage. *Hamlet*, I suppose, is treated by them with more reverence. They are both characters far, far above the abilities of any actor whom I have ever seen. Henderson was before my time, and, of course, Garrick.

We are looking anxiously for Coleridge; perhaps he may be with you now.

Is your building going on? I was mortified that the sweet little valley, of which you spoke some time ago, was no longer in the possession of your family; it is the place, I believe, where that illustrious and most extraordinary man, Beaumont the poet, and his brother, were born. One is astonished when one thinks of that man having been only eight-and-twenty years of age, for I believe he was no more when he died. Shakespeare, we are told, had scarcely written a single play at that age. I hope, for the sake of poets, you are proud of these men.

Lady Beaumont mentioned some time ago that you were painting a picture from *The Thorn:* is it finished? I should like to see it; the poem is a favourite with me, and I shall love it the better for the honour you have done it. We shall be most happy to have the other drawing which you promised us some time ago. The dimensions of the Applethwaite one are eight inches high, and a very little above ten broad; this, of course, exclusive of the margin. . . .   When we look back upon this spring it seems like a dreary dream to us.   But I trust in God that we shall yet " bear up and steer right onward."

Farewell.   I am, your affectionate friend,

W. WORDSWORTH.

. . . Have you seen Southey's *Madoc?*   We have it in the house, but have deferred reading it, having been too busy with the child.   I should like to know how it pleases you.

CI

William Wordsworth to Sir George Beaumont

GRASMERE, June 3d, 1805.

My dear Sir George,

I write to you from the moss-hut at the top of my orchard, the sun just sinking behind the hills in front of the entrance, and his light falling upon the green moss of the side opposite me.   A linnet is singing in the tree above, and the children of some of our neighbours, who have been to-day little John's visitors, are playing below, equally noisy and happy.   The green fields in the level area of the vale, and part of the lake, lie before me in quietness.

I have just been reading two newspapers, full of fractious brawls about Lord Melville and his delinquencies, ravage of the French in the West Indies, victories of the English in the East, fleets of ours roaming the sea in search of enemies whom they cannot find, etc. etc. etc.; and I have asked myself more than once lately if my affections can be in the right place, caring as I do so little about what the world seems to care so much for.

All this seems to me, "a tale told by an idiot, full of sound and fury, signifying nothing."

It is pleasant in such a mood to turn one's thoughts to a good man and a dear friend. I have, therefore, taken up the pen to write to you. And, first, let me thank you (which I ought to have done long ago, and should have done, but that I knew I had a license from you to procrastinate) for your most acceptable present of Coleridge's portrait, welcome in itself, and more so as coming from you. It is as good a resemblance as I expect to see of Coleridge, taking it altogether, for I consider Coleridge's as a face absolutely impracticable. Mrs. Wordsworth was overjoyed at the sight of the print; Dorothy and I much pleased. We think it excellent about the eyes and forehead, which are the finest parts of Coleridge's face, and the general contour of the face is well given; but, to my sister and me, it seems to fail sadly about the middle of the face, particularly at the bottom of the nose. Mrs. Wordsworth feels this also; and my sister so much that, except when she covers the whole of the middle of the face, it seems to her so entirely to alter the expression as rather to confound than revive in her mind the remembrance of the original.

We think, as far as mere likeness goes, Hazlitt's is better; but the expression in Hazlitt's is quite dolorous and funereal; that in this is much more pleasing, though certainly falling far below what one would wish to see infused into a picture of Coleridge. Mrs. Coleridge received a day or two ago a letter from a friend who had letters from Malta, not from Coleridge, but a Miss Stoddart, who is there with her brother. These letters are of the date of the fifth of March, and speak of him as looking well and being well, and talking of coming home, but doubtful whether by land or sea.

I have the pleasure to say that I finished my poem [1] about a fortnight ago. I had looked forward to the day as a most happy one; and I was indeed grateful to God for giving me life to complete the work, such as it is. But it was not a happy day for me; I was dejected on many accounts: when I looked back upon the performance it seemed to have a dead weight about it, — the reality so far short of the expectation. It was the first long labour that I had finished; and the doubt whether I should ever live to write *The Recluse*, and the sense which I had of this poem being so far below what I seemed capable of executing, depressed me much; above all, many heavy thoughts of my poor departed brother hung upon me, the joy which I should have had in showing him the manuscript, and a thousand other vain fancies and dreams. I have spoken of this because it was a state of feeling new to me, the occasion being new. This work may be considered as a sort of *portico* to *The Recluse*, part of the same building, which I hope to be able, ere long, to begin with in earnest; and if I am permitted to bring it to a conclusion, and to write, further, a narrative poem of the epic kind, I shall consider the task of my life as over. I ought to add that I have the satisfaction of finding the present poem not quite of so alarming a length as I apprehended.

I wish much to hear from you, if you have leisure; but as you are so indulgent to me, it would be the highest injustice were I otherwise to you.

[1] *The Prelude.* — Ed.

We have read *Madoc* and been highly pleased with it. It abounds in beautiful pictures and descriptions, happily introduced, and there is an animation diffused through the whole story; though it cannot, perhaps, be said that any of the characters interest you much, except, perhaps, young Llewellyn, whose situation is highly interesting, and he appears to me the best conceived and sustained character in the piece.   His speech to his uncle at their meeting in the island is particularly interesting.   The poem fails in the highest gifts of the poet's mind — imagination in the true sense of the word — and knowledge of human nature and the human heart.   There is nothing that shows the hand of the great master, but the beauties in description are innumerable ; for instance, that of the figure of the bard, towards the beginning of the convention of the bards, receiving the poetic inspiration ; that of the wife of Thalala, the savage, going out to meet her husband ; that of Madoc and the Aztecan king with a long name, preparing for battle ; everywhere, indeed, you have beautiful descriptions, and it is a work which does the author high credit, I think.   I should like to know your opinion of it.   Farewell !   Best remembrances and love to Lady Beaumont.   Believe me, my dear Sir George, your most sincere friend,

W. WORDSWORTH.

My sister thanks Lady Beaumont for her letter, and will write in a few days.   I find that Lady Beaumont has been pleased much by *Madoc*.

CII

Dorothy Wordsworth to Mrs. Clarkson

Saturday, June 8th [Postmark, KENDAL, 1805.]

My dear Friend,

. . . We had let everything remain neglected, and in ruin. We had not dared to look at the garden, and a little shed which we had begun at the top of the orchard remained unfinished. We durst not look in the face of anything we loved that was not forced upon us. For three months I was only once at the top of the orchard. We have summoned up our hearts, and done everything; and now we spend many sweet hours in this shed, where I write to you at half past six o'clock, Saturday evening. The sun yet a considerable height above the mountain tops shines in upon me. Oh! my friend, we remember our brother every moment of our lives, and begin even to feel in happiness how great a blessing the memory of him will ever be to us. It is too much sometimes, but God is merciful. We glory in the goodness of our dear brother, and so we comfort ourselves. We are all pretty well. . . .

CIII

William Wordsworth to Sir George Beaumont

GRASMERE, July 29th, 1805.

My dear Sir George,

We have all here been made happy in hearing that you are so much better. I write now chiefly on account of a mistake which you seem to be under concerning Coleridge. I guess from your letter that you suppose him to be appointed to the place of secretary to Sir A. Ball. This is by no means the case. He is merely an occasional substitute for Mr. Chapman — who is secretary — and no doubt must have resumed his office long before this, as he had been expected every day some time before the date of Coleridge's last letter. The paragraph in the paper (which we also saw) positively states that Coleridge is appointed secretary. This is an error, and has been merely put in upon common rumour.

When you were ill I had a thought which I will mention to you. It was this: I wished to know how you were at present situated as to house-room at Coleorton, that is, whether you could have found a corner for me to put my head in, in case I could have contrived to have commanded three weeks' time or so. I am at present, and shall be for some time, engaged with a sick friend, who has come all the way from Bristol on purpose to see us, and has taken lodgings in the village; but should you be unwell again, and my company be like to tend in the least to exhilarate you, I should like to know, that were it in my power to go and see you, I might have the liberty to do so.

Having such reason to expect Coleridge at present (were we at liberty in other respects), I cannot think of taking my family a tour, agreeable to your kind suggestion. Something has, however, already been added by your means to our comforts, in the way of books, and probably we shall be able to make an excursion ere the summer be over.

By the by, are you possessed of Houbraken and Vertue's *Heads of Illustrious Persons*, with anecdotes of their lives by Birch? I had an opportunity of purchasing a handsome copy (far below the price at which it now sells,

I believe, in London) at Penrith, a few weeks ago ; and
if you have not a copy, and think the work has any merit,
you would please me greatly by giving it a place in your
library.

I am glad you like the passage in *Madoc* about Llewellyn.   Southey's mind does not seem strong enough to
draw the picture of a hero.   The character of Madoc is
often very insipid and contemptible ; for instance, when
he is told that the Hoamen have surprised Caermadoc,
and of course (he has reason to believe) butchered or
carried away all the women and children, what does the
author make him do?   Think of Goervyl and Llayan
very tenderly forsooth; but not a word about his people !
In short, according to my notion, the character is throughout languidly conceived, and, as you observe, the contrast
between her and Llewellyn makes him look very mean.   I
made a mistake when I pointed out a beautiful passage
as being in the beginning of the meeting of the bards ; it
occurs before, and ends thus :

> His eyes were closed ;
> His head, as if in reverence to receive
> The inspiration, bent ; and as he raised
> His glowing countenance and brighter eye
> And swept with passionate hands the ringing harp.

The verses of your ancestor, Francis Beaumont the
younger, are very elegant and harmonious, and written
with true feeling.   Is this the only poem of his extant?
There are some pleasing verses (I think by Corbet, Bishop
of Norwich) on the death of Francis Beaumont the elder.
They end, I remember, thus, alluding to his short life :

> Beaumont is dead ! by whose sole death appears,
> Wit 's a disease consumes men in few years.

I have never seen the works of the brother of the dramatic poet ; but I know he wrote a poem upon the battle of Bosworth Field. Probably it will be in the volume which you have found, which it would give me great pleasure to see, as also Charnwood Rocks, which must have a striking effect in that country. I am highly flattered by Lady Beaumont's favourable opinion of me and my poems. ...

The letter which you will find accompanying this is from an acquaintance of ours to his wife. He lives at Patterdale, and she was over at Grasmere. We thought it would interest you. Farewell. I remain, in hopes of good news of your health, your affectionate and sincere friend,

W. WORDSWORTH.

CIV

William Wordsworth to Sir George Beaumont

GRASMERE, August 1st, [1805.]

My dear Friend,

It was very good in you to write to me, much more than I deserved, as I have shown by suffering your letter to remain so long unanswered. I deserve your friendship, I hope, but not your letters ; indeed, I am unworthy of anybody's, being a correspondent intolerably remiss. I am glad you liked the verses.[1] I could not but write them with feeling, having such a subject, and one that touched me so nearly. Your delicacy in not leading me to the picture[2] did not escape me. It is a melancholy

---

[1] The *Elegiac Stanzas suggested by a picture of Peele Castle in a Storm.* — Ed.

[2] Sir George's own picture which suggested the *Stanzas.* — Ed.

satisfaction to me to connect my dear brother with anybody whom I love much; and I knew that the verses would give you pleasure as a proof of my affection for you. The picture was to me a very moving one; it exists in my mind at this moment as if it were before my eyes. . . .

I do not know whether my sister has written since we had another account of Coleridge, — I am sorry I cannot say *from* him. He was at Leghorn, with a friend, on their way to England: so that we still continue to look for him daily. He had lost *all* his papers; *how* we are not told. This grieves and vexes me much; probably (but it is not on this account — his loss being I daresay irreparable — that I am either much vexed or grieved) a large collection of the poems is gone with the rest; among others five books of the poem upon my own life, but of all these I have copies. He, I am afraid, has none of his old writings.

Within this last month I have returned to *The Recluse*, and have written 700 additional lines. Should Coleridge return, so that I might have some conversation with him on the subject, I should go on swimmingly. We have been very little interrupted with tourist company this summer, and, of course, being for the most part well, have enjoyed ourselves much. I am now writing in the moss-hut, which is my study,[1] with a heavy thunder shower pouring down before me. It is a place of retirement for the eye (though the public road glimmers through the apple-trees a few yards below), and well suited to my occupations.

I cannot, however, refrain from smiling at the situation in which I sometimes find myself here; as, for instance, the other morning when I was calling some lofty notes out of my harp, chanting of shepherds, and solitude, etc.,

[1] In the orchard garden. — Ed.

I heard a voice (which I knew to be a male voice, whose also it was) crying out from the road below, in a tone exquisitely effeminate, "Sautez, sautez, apportez, apportez; vous ne le ferez pas, venez donc Pandore, venez, venez." Guess who this creature could be, speaking thus to his lap-dog in the midst of our venerable mountains? It is one of two nondescripts who have taken the cottage for the summer which we thought you might occupy, and who go about parading the valley in all kinds of fantastic dresses, green leather caps, turkey half-boots, jackets of fine linen, or long dressing-gowns, as suit them. Now you hear them in the roads ; now you find them lolling in this attire, book in hand, by a brook side. Then they pass your window in their curricle, — to-day the horses tandem-wise, and to-morrow abreast, or on horseback, as suits their fancies. One of them we suspect to be painted, and the other, though a pale-cheeked puppy, is surely not surpassed by his blooming brother. If you come you will see them, and I promise you they will be a treat to you.

We still think it possible that we may winter at Coleorton, but we shrink from the thought of going so far without seeing you, and if we procure a house in this neighbourhood we certainly shall. We are the more willing to be kept in a state of suspense as long as Coleridge is unarrived. I don't know that after expressing my thanks for your many kindnesses to me when under your roof, and at all times, and the happiness I derive from your friendship, I can fill this paper better than by adding a sonnet from Michael Angelo, translated some time since. Farewell. Yours most affectionately,

W. WORDSWORTH.

[Then followed the sonnet *To the Supreme Being*, beginning "The prayers I make."]

CV

William Wordsworth to Sir George Beaumont

GRASMERE, October 17th, 1805.

My dear Sir George,

I was very glad to learn that you had room for me at Coleorton, and far more that your health was so much mended. Lady Beaumont's last letter to my sister has made us wish that you were fairly through your present engagements with workmen and builders, and, as to improvements had smoothed over the first difficulties, and gotten things into a way of improving themselves. I do not suppose that any man ever built a house, without finding in the progress of it obstacles that were unforeseen, and something that might have been better planned; things teasing and vexatious when they come, however the mind may have been made up at the outset to a general expectation of the kind.

With respect to the grounds, you have there the advantage of being in good hands, namely, those of Nature; and, assuredly, whatever petty crosses from contrariety of opinion or any other cause you may now meet with, these will soon disappear, and leave nothing behind but satisfaction and harmony. Setting out from the distinction made by Coleridge which you mentioned, that your house will belong to the country, and not the country be an appendage to your house, you cannot be wrong. Indeed, in the present state of society, I see nothing interesting either to the imagination or the heart, and, of course, nothing which true taste can approve, in any interference with Nature, grounded upon any other principle.

In times when the feudal system was in its vigour, and the personal importance of every chieftain might be said to depend entirely upon the extent of his landed property and rights of seignory; when the king, in the habits of people's minds, was considered as the primary and true proprietor of the soil, which was granted out by him to different lords, and again by them to their several tenants under them, for the joint defence of all — there might have been something imposing to the imagination in the whole face of a district, testifying, obtrusively even, its dependence upon its chief. Such an image would have been in the spirit of the society, implying power, grandeur, military state, and security; and, less directly, in the person of the chief, high birth and knightly education and accomplishments; in short, the most of what was then deemed interesting or affecting. Yet, with the exception of large parks and forests, nothing of this kind was known at that time, and these were left in their wild state, so that such display of ownership, so far from taking from the beauty of Nature, was itself a chief cause of that beauty being left unspoiled and unimpaired. The *improvements*, when the place was sufficiently tranquil to admit of any, though absurd and monstrous in themselves, were confined (as our present laureate has observed, I remember, in one of his essays) to an acre or two about the house in the shape of garden with terraces, etc.; so that Nature had greatly the advantage in those days, when what has been called English gardening was unheard of. This is now beginning to be perceived, and we are setting out to travel backwards. Painters and poets have had the credit of being reckoned the fathers of English gardening; they will also have, hereafter, the better praise of being fathers of a better taste.

Error is in general nothing more than getting hold of good things, as everything has two handles, by the wrong one. It was a misconception of the meaning and principles of poets and painters which gave countenance to the modern system of gardening, which is now, I hope, on the decline ; in other words, we are submitting to the rule which you at present are guided by, that of having our houses belong to the country, which will of course lead us back to the simplicity of Nature. And leaving your own individual sentiments and present work out of the question, what good can come of any other guide, under any circumstances ? We have, indeed, distinctions of rank, hereditary legislators, and large landed proprietors; but from numberless causes the state of society is so much altered, that nothing of that lofty or imposing interest formerly attached to large property in land, can now exist ; none of the poetic pride, and pomp, and circumstance ; nor anything that can be considered as making amends for violation done to the holiness of Nature.

Let us take an extreme case, such as a residence of a Duke of Norfolk or Northumberland ; of course you would expect a mansion, in some degree answerable to their consequence, with all conveniences. The names of Howard and Percy will always stand high in the regards of Englishmen ; but it is degrading, not only to such families as these but to every really interesting one, to suppose that their importance will be most felt where most displayed, particularly in the way I am now alluding to. This is contracting a general feeling into a local one. Besides, were it not so as to what concerns the past, a man would be sadly astray who should go, for example, to modernise Alnwick and its dependencies,

with his head full of the ancient Percies.   He would find
nothing there which would remind him of them, except
by contrast ; and of that kind of admonition he would,
indeed, have enough.   But this by the by ; for it is against
the principle itself I am contending, and not the misapplication of it.

After what was said above I may ask if anything connected with the families of Howard and Percy, and their
rank and influence, and thus with the state of government and society, could, in the present age, be deemed a
recompense for their thrusting themselves in between us
and Nature.   Surely it is a substitution of little things
for great when we would put a whole country into a noble-
man's livery.   I know nothing which to me would be so
pleasing or affecting as to be able to say, when I am in the
midst of a large estate, This man is not the victim of his
condition ; he is not the spoiled child of worldly grandeur;
the thought of himself does not take the lead in his
enjoyments ; he is, where he ought to be, lowly-minded,
and has human feeling ; he has a true relish of simplicity,
and therefore stands the best chance of being happy ; at
least, without it there is no happiness, because there can
be no true sense of the bounty and beauty of the creation,
or insight into the constitution of the human mind.

Let a man of wealth and influence show, by the appearance of the country in his neighbourhood, that he treads
in the steps of the good sense of the age, and occasionally
goes foremost ; let him give countenance to improvements
in agriculture, steering clear of the pedantry of it, and
showing that its grossest utilities will connect themselves
harmoniously with the more intellectual arts, and even
thrive the best under such connection ; let him do his
utmost to be surrounded with tenants living comfortably,

which will always bring with it the best of all graces
which a country can have, — flourishing fields and happy-
looking houses; and, in that part of his estate devoted to
park and pleasure-ground, let him keep himself as much
out of sight as possible. Let Nature be all in all, taking
care that everything done by man shall be in the way of
being adopted by her. If people choose that a great
mansion should be the chief figure in a country, let this
kind of keeping prevail through the picture, and true
taste will find no fault.

I am writing now rather for writing's sake than anything else, for I have many remembrances beating about
in my head which you would little suspect. I have been
thinking of you, and Coleridge, and our Scotch tour,
and Lord Lowther's grounds, and Heaven knows what.
I have had before me the tremendously long ell-wide
gravel walks of the Duke of Athol, among the wild glens
of Blair, Bruar Water, and Dunkeld, brushed neatly,
without a blade of grass or weed upon them, or anything that bore traces of a human footstep; much indeed
of human hands, but wear or tear of foot was none.
Thence I passed to our neighbour, Lord Lowther. You
know that his predecessor, greatly, without doubt, to
the advantage of the place, left it to take care of itself.
The present Lord seems disposed to do something, but
not much.

He has a neighbour, a Quaker, an amiable, inoffensive
man,[1] and a little of a poet too, who has amused himself,
upon his own small estate upon the Emont, in twining
pathways along the banks of the river, making little cells
and bowers with inscriptions of his own writing, all very

[1] Thomas Wilkinson. — Ed.

pretty as not spreading far. This man is at present *arbiter elegantiarum*, or master of the grounds, at Lowther; and what he has done hitherto is very well, as it is little more than making accessible what could not before be got at.

You know something of Lowther. I believe a more delightful spot is not under the sun. Last summer I had a charming walk along the river, for which I was indebted to this man, whose intention is to carry the walk along the river-side till it joins the great road at Lowther Bridge, which you will recollect, just under Brougham, about a mile from Penrith. This to my great sorrow! for the manufactured walk, which was absolutely necessary in many places, will in one place pass through a few hundred yards of forest ground, and will there efface the most beautiful specimen of a forest pathway ever seen by human eyes, and which I have paced many an hour when I was a youth, with some of those I best love.[1] This path winds on under the trees with the wantonness of a river or a living creature; and even if I may say so, with the subtlety of a spirit, contracting or enlarging itself, visible or invisible as it likes. There is a continued opening between the trees, a narrow slip of green turf besprinkled with flowers, chiefly daisies; and here it is, if I may use the same kind of language, that this pretty path plays its pranks, wearing away the turf and flowers at its pleasure. When I took the walk I was speaking of, last summer, it was Sunday. I met several of the people of the country posting to and from church, in different parts; and in a retired spot by the river-side were two musicians (belonging probably to some corps of

[1] Before he went to Hawkshead, Wordsworth was for some time at a dame-school in Penrith, with his sister. — Ed.

volunteers) playing upon the hautboy and clarionet. You may guess I was not a little delighted ; and as you had been a visitor at Lowther, I could not help wishing you were with me..

And now I am brought to the sentiment which occasioned this detail, I may say brought back to my subject, which is this, — that all just and solid pleasure in natural objects rest upon two pillars, God and Man. Laying out grounds, as it is called, may be considered as a liberal art, in some sort like poetry and painting; and its object, like that of all the liberal arts, is, or ought to be, to move the affections under the control of good sense ; that is, of the best and wisest. Speaking with more precision, it is to assist Nature in moving the affections; and surely, as I have said, the affections of those who have the deepest perception of the beauty of Nature, who have the most valuable feelings, — that is, the most permanent, the most independent, the most ennobling, — connected with Nature and human Life. No liberal art aims merely at the gratification of an individual or a class, the painter or poet is degraded in proportion as he does so. The true servants of the Arts pay homage to the human kind as impersonated in unwarped and enlightened minds.

If this be so when we are merely putting together words or colours, how much more ought the feeling to prevail when we are in the midst of the realities of things ; of the beauty and harmony, of the joy and happiness, of living creatures ; of men and children, of birds and beasts, of hills and streams, and trees and flowers; with the changes of night and day, evening and morning, summer and winter ; and all their unwearied actions and energies, as benign in the spirit that animates them as they are beautiful and grand in that form and clothing which is given to them for the delight of our senses ! But I must stop, for you feel these things as deeply as I ; more deeply, if it were only for this, that you have lived longer. What then shall we say of many great mansions with their unqualified expulsion of human creatures from their neighbourhood, happy or not, houses which do what is fabled of the upas-tree ? — that they breathe out death and desolation ! I know you will feel with me here, both as a man and a lover and professor of the Arts.

I was glad to hear from Lady Beaumont that you did not think of removing your village. Of course much here will depend upon circumstances ; above all, with what kind of inhabitants, from the nature of the employments in that district, the village is likely to be stocked. But for my part, strip my neighbourhood of human beings, and I should think it one of the greatest privations I could undergo. You have all the poverty of solitude, nothing of its elevation. In a word, if I were disposed to write a sermon (and this is something like one) upon the subject of taste in natural beauty, I should take for my text the little pathway in Lowther woods ; and all that I had to say would begin and end in the human heart, as under the direction of the Divine Nature conferring value on the objects of the senses, and pointing out what is valuable in them.

I began this subject with Coleorton in my thoughts, and a confidence that whatever difficulties or crosses (as of many good things it is not easy to choose the best) you might meet with in the practical application of your principles of Taste, yet, being what they are, you will soon be pleased and satisfied. Only (if I may take the freedom to say so) do not give way too much to others ;

considering what your studies and pursuits have been, your own judgment must be the best : professional men may suggest hints, but I would keep the decision to myself.

Lady Beaumont utters something like an apprehension that the slowness of workmen, or other impediments, may prevent our families meeting at Coleorton next summer. We shall be sorry for this, the more so as the same cause will hinder your coming hither. At all events, we shall depend upon her frankness, which we take most kindly indeed — I mean, on the promise she has made, to let us know whether you are gotten so far through your work as to make it comfortable for us all to be together.

I cannot close this letter without a word about myself. I am sorry to say I am not yet settled to any serious employment. The expectation of Coleridge not a little unhinges me, and still more, the number of visitors we have had ; but winter is approaching, and I have good hopes. I mentioned Michael Angelo's poetry some time ago ; it is the most difficult to construe I ever met with, but just what you would expect from such a man, showing abundantly how conversant his soul was with great things. There is a mistake in the world concerning the Italian language ; the poetry of Dante and Michael Angelo proves that if there be little majesty and strength in Italian verse, the fault is in the authors, and not in the tongue. I can translate, and have translated, two books of Ariosto at the rate, nearly, of 100 lines a day ; but so much meaning has been put by Michael Angelo into so little room, and that meaning sometimes so excellent in itself, that I found the difficulty of translating him insurmountable. I attempted, at least, fifteen of the sonnets, but could not anywhere succeed. I have sent you the only one I was able to finish;[1] it is far from being the best or most characteristic, but the others were too much for me.

I began this letter about a week ago, having been interrupted. . . .

I am glad the Houbraken will be acceptable, and will send it any way you shall think proper, though perhaps, as it would only make a small parcel, there might be some risk in trusting it to the wagon or mail, unless it could be conveniently inquired after. No news of Coleridge. The length of this letter is quite formidable; forgive it. Farewell, and believe me, my dear Sir George, your truly affectionate friend,

W. WORDSWORTH.

CVI

William Wordsworth to Walter Scott

PATTERDALE, November 7, 1805.

My dear Scott,

. . . Your letter was very welcome. I am not apt to haunt myself with fears of accident from flood and field, etc. It was nevertheless pleasant to hear that you had got home well. . . . I often think with delight of the few days you were with us, and live in hope that we may enjoy something of the same kind at some future period. I should like exceedingly to meet you somewhere next summer, either here or in your own country, or both; and certainly (if an engagement, under which I am at present partly bound, does not take place) shall do so, provided you have as much leisure and inclination as I. I long

---

[1] The one beginning, " Yes ! Hope may with my strong desire keep pace." — Ed.

much to see more of Scotland, both north and south.   It is (not excepting the Alps) the most poetical country I ever travelled through.

Like you, I had been sadly disappointed with Todd's *Spenser;* not with the Life, which I think has a sufficient share of merit, though the matter is badly put together ; but three parts of four of the notes are absolute trash. That style of compiling notes ought to be put an end to. I was much pleased to hear of your engagement with Dryden ; not that he is, as a poet, any great favourite of mine.   I admire his talents and genius highly, but his is not a poetical genius.   The only qualities I can find in Dryden that are *essentially* poetical are a certain ardour and impetuosity of mind with an excellent ear.   It may seem strange that I do not add to this great command of language; *that* he certainly has, and of such language, too, as it is most desirable that a poet should possess, or rather, that he should not be without.   But it is not language that is, in the highest sense of the word, poetical, being neither of the imagination nor of the passions — I mean of the amiable, the ennobling, or intense passions. I do not mean to say that there is nothing of this in Dryden, but as little, I think, as is possible, considering how much he has written.   You will easily understand my meaning when I refer to his versification of *Palamon and Arcite*, as contrasted with the language of Chaucer. Dryden has neither a tender heart nor a lofty sense of moral dignity.   Whenever his language is poetically impassioned, it is mostly upon unpleasing subjects; such as the follies, vices, and crimes of classes of men or of individuals.   That his cannot be the language of imagination must have necessarily followed from this ; that there is not a single image from Nature in the whole body of his works ; and in his translation from Virgil, whenever Virgil can be fairly said to have his *eye* upon his object, Dryden always soils the passage.

But too much of this ; I am glad that you are to be his editor. His political and satirical pieces may be greatly benefited by illustration, and even absolutely require it. . . . I have read Dryden's works (all but his plays) with great attention, but my observations refer entirely to matters of taste. Things of this kind appear better anywhere than when tagged to a poet's works, where they are absolute impertinences. In the beginning of the *Absalom* you find an allusion to a freak or revel of the Duke of Monmouth of rather a serious kind. This I remember is mentioned in Andrew Marvel's poem, which I have not seen these many years, but that I think you might peep into with advantage for your work. One or two of the Prologues may be illustrated from Cibber's *Apology*. A correct text is the first object of an editor ; then such notes as explain difficult or unintelligible passages, or throw light upon them ; and lastly, which is of much less importance, notes pointing out passages or authors to whom the poet has been indebted, not in the paddling way of a phrase here and phrase there (which is detestable as a general practice), but where the poet has had essential obligations as to matter or manner.

Let me hear from you as soon as convenient. If I can be of any use, do not fail to apply to me. One thing I may take the liberty to suggest, which is, when you come to the *Fables*, might it not be advisable to print the whole of the *Tales* of Boccaccio in a smaller type in the original language ? If this should look too much like swelling a book, I should certainly make such extracts as would show where Dryden had most strikingly improved upon, or fallen below, his original. I think his translations from Boccaccio are the best, at least the most poetical, of his poems. It is many years since I saw Boccaccio, but I remember that Sigismunda is not married by him to Guiscard (the names are different in Boccaccio in both tales, I believe, certainly in Theodore, etc.). I think Dryden has much injured the story by the marriage, and degraded Sigismunda's character by it. He has also, to the best of my remembrance, degraded her still more by making her love absolute sensuality and appetite; Dryden had no other notion of the passion. With all these defects, and they are very gross ones, it is a noble poem. Guiscard's answer, when first reproached by Tancred, is noble in Boccaccio, — nothing but this : *Amor può molto più che ne voi ne io possiamo.* This, Dryden has spoiled. He first says very well, " The faults of love by love are justified," and then come four lines of miserable rant, quite *à la Maximin.* Farewell, and believe me ever,

Your affectionate friend,

WILLIAM WORDSWORTH.

CVII

Dorothy Wordsworth to Mrs. Clarkson

[Postmark, PENRITH] Saturday, December 11th, 1805.

My dear Friend,

. . . I have for many days been intending to send you a copy of a poem which William has written for the Journal,[1] suggested by that beautiful passage in Thomas Wilkinson's Tour about the solitary Highland lass singing at her harvest work, but I put off in the hope of hearing from you. . . .

[1] Her Journal of the Tour in Scotland, 1803. — Ed.

CVIII

Dorothy Wordsworth to Mrs. Clarkson

GRASMERE, Christmas Day, 1805.

My dear Friend,

. . . I do not think anything which may be numbered among the *accidents* of life is so delightful as meeting again the companions of one's youth after a long separation, when it does not end in disappointment, which, alas! too often happens. . . . This day I have completed my thirty-fourth year. Six Christmases have we spent at Grasmere, and though the freshness of life was passed away even when we came hither, I think these years have been the very happiest of my life, — at least, they seem as if they would bear looking back upon better than any other, — though my heart flutters and aches, striving to call to my mind more perfectly the remembrance of some of the more thoughtless pleasures of former years, and though till within this late time I never experienced a real affliction.

Poor John was in London last Christmas, all his heart set upon the accomplishment of that fatal voyage as the termination of his labours, and so it proved to him, a happy and glorious termination of them, — to us only sorrow and pain. Dear and blessed creature, he in those last moments of trial bequeathed us a large share of consolation and ennobling thought, and confident trust in the goodness of Divine Providence. . . . In numbering over the blessings of the last six years, first and foremost are present with me the pleasures and consolations of friendship. How many excellent and kind friends have been tried, and proved to me, within that time! When we came here, you were but a *name* to me! . . .

CIX

William Wordsworth to Sir George Beaumont

[1805.]

. . . We anxiously expected a letter yesterday from Lady Beaumont, hoping to hear that you continue to advance towards recovery; but no letter coming, we have many fears, and I can no longer defer writing, which, however, I would not do if I thought you would consider yourself as obliged to write again. For Heaven's sake, my dear friend, let us both be quite easy on this head. I assure you I do not measure the interest you take in me or mine either by the length or frequency of your letters; if I but hear from time to time how you are going on in health, or upon any occasion when my sympathies can give you comfort or pleasure, this is all I look for. Lady Beaumont is so good as to write often to my sister, so that through her we may learn these things; and, therefore, never think of writing to me. Should such an impulse of genial spirits as one sometimes feels at the thought of taking a walk, making a sketch, or playing a tune ever prompt you to take up the pen, let me hear from you, but not otherwise; never trouble your head about it a moment.

I am glad my verses gave you pleasure; I have been hunting over and over in my mind through all that I have written for something to send you, and cannot pitch upon anything. I have composed lately two small poems in memory of my brother, but they are too melancholy, else I would willingly copy them. My sister, however, shall transcribe something or other, though I have not a single line in my possession which quite satisfies me for such a purpose. . . .

[Then follows a quotation from *The Prelude*, Book VIII, — from line 1, " What sounds are these, Helvellyn, that are heard " to "their calm abode," line 69.]

The above is from the beginning of one of the books upon my own earlier life.   It has been extracted not so much from any notion of its merit, as from its standing more independent of the rest of the poem than perhaps any other part of it.   The few lines which you will find on the next page require a long preface, which my sister begs you will excuse.   It is from her Journal of our tour in Scotland.   We had visited the Trossachs and Loch Katrine, and were so much pleased as to return thither towards the end of our tour.   We had been entertained at a ferryman's house, a Highland hut on the banks of the lake, and were again making our way thither on foot, a journey of about six miles, along the bank of the lake.

My sister then proceeds thus : "The path, or road (for it was neither one nor the other, but something between both), was the pleasantest I have ever travelled in my life for the same length of way ; now with marks of sledges or wheels, or none at all, bare or green, as is might happen ; now a little descent, now a level, sometimes a shady lane, at others an open track through green fields ; then again it would lead us into thick coppice woods, which often entirely excluded the lake, and again admitted it by glimpses.   We have never had a more delightful walk than this evening ; Ben Lomond, and the three pointed-topped mountains of Loch Lomond, which we had seen from the Garrison, were very majestic under the clear sky ; the lake was perfectly still, the air sweet and mild. I felt how much more interesting it is to visit a place where we have been before, than it can possibly be the

first time, except under peculiar circumstances.   The sun
had been set some time, when, being within a quarter of
a mile of the ferryman's hut, and close to the shore of
the calm lake, we met two neatly-dressed women without
hats, who had probably been taking their Sunday evening's
walk.   One of them said to us in a friendly, soft tone of
voice, 'What, you are stepping westward?'   I cannot
describe how affecting this simple expression was in that
remote place, with the western sky in front *yet* glowing
with the departed sun.   William wrote the following
poem[1] long after, in remembrance of his feelings and
mine." . . .

[1] See the poem *Stepping Westward*, in "Memorials of a Tour in
Scotland," 1803. — Ed.

1806

CX

William Wordsworth to Sir George Beaumont

GRASMERE, February 11th, 1806.

My dear Sir George,

Upon opening this letter you must have seen that it is accompanied with a copy of verses.[1] I hope they will give you some pleasure, as it will be the best way in which they can repay me for a little vexation, of which they have been the cause. They were written several weeks ago, and I wished to send them to you, but could not muster up resolution, as I felt that they were so unworthy of the subject. Accordingly I kept them by me from week to week, with a hope, (which has proved vain,) that, in some happy moment, a new fit of inspiration would help me to mend them; and hence my silence, which, with your usual goodness, I know you will excuse.

You will find that the verses are allusive to Lord Nelson; and they will show that I must have sympathized with you in admiration of the man, and sorrow for our loss. Yet, considering the matter coolly, there was little to regret. The state of Lord Nelson's health, I suppose, was such that he could not have lived long; and the first

---

[1] *The Character of the Happy Warrior.* — Ed.

burst of exultation upon landing in his native country, and his reception here, would have been dearly bought, perhaps, by pain and bodily weakness, and distress among his friends, which he could neither remove nor alleviate.

Few men have ever died under circumstances so likely to make their death of benefit to their country : it is not easy to see what his life could have done comparable to it. The loss of such men as Lord Nelson is, indeed, great and real; but surely not for the reason which makes most people grieve — a supposition that no other such man is in the country. The old ballad has taught us how to feel on these occasions :

> I trust I have within my realm
> Five hundred good as he.

But this is the evil, that nowhere is merit so much under the power of what (to avoid a more serious expression) one may call that of fortune, as in military and naval service; and it is five hundred to one that such men will not have attained situations where they can show themselves, so that the country may know in whom to trust. Lord Nelson had attained that situation; and, therefore, I think (and not for the other reason), ought we chiefly to lament that he is taken from us.

Mr. Pitt is also gone! by tens of thousands looked upon in like manner as a great loss. For my own part, as probably you know, I have never been able to regard his political life with complacency. I believe him, however, to have been as disinterested a man and as true a lover of his country as it was possible for so ambitious a man to be. His first wish (though probably unknown to himself) was that his country should prosper under his administration; his next that it should prosper. Could the order of these wishes have been reversed, Mr. Pitt would have avoided many of the grievous mistakes into which, I think, he fell.

I know, my dear Sir George, you will give me credit for speaking without arrogance; and I am aware it is not unlikely you may differ greatly from me in these points. But I like, in some things, to differ with a friend, and that he should *know* I differ from him; it seems to make a more healthy friendship, to act as a relief to those notions and feelings which we have in common, and to give them a grace and spirit which they could not otherwise possess.

There were some parts in the long letter which I wrote about laying out grounds, in which the expression must have been left imperfect. I like splendid mansions in their proper places, and have no objection to large or even obtrusive houses in themselves. My dislike is to that system of gardening which, because a house happens to be large or splendid, and stands at the head of a large domain, establishes it therefore as a principle that the house ought to *dye* all the surrounding country with a strength of colouring, and to an extent proportionate to its own importance. This system, I think, is founded in false taste, false feeling, and its effects disgusting in the highest degree. The reason you mention as having induced you to build was worthy of you, and gave me the highest pleasure. But I hope God will grant you and Lady Beaumont life to enjoy yourselves the fruit of your exertions for many years.

We have lately had much anxiety about Coleridge. What can have become of him? It must be upwards of three months since he landed at Trieste. Has he returned to Malta, think you, or what can have befallen him? He has never since been heard of.

We are all well at present, and unite in affectionate wishes to you and Lady Beaumont.   Believe me, your sincere friend,

W. WORDSWORTH.

I have thoughts of sending the verses to a newspaper.

CXI

Dorothy Wordsworth to Mrs. Clarkson

GRASMERE, Sunday Evening, March 2nd, [1806.]

My dear Friend,

We have long been anxiously expecting to hear from you ; and I have daily intended writing, but I had not the resolution to set about it till this present day, when having good news for you of Coleridge, I am assured that my letter will give you pleasure.   Last night we received a note from Mrs. C., enclosing a letter to her from Miss Lamb, from which I will transcribe the whole that relates to Coleridge.   It is dated Feb. 25th.   " My brother has received a letter from Stoddart (Stoddart, you probably know, is at Malta) dated December 26th, in which he tells him that Coleridge was then at Naples. We have also heard from a Mr. Dawe that a friend of his had received a letter of the same date, which mentioned Coleridge having been lately travelling towards Rome with a party of gentlemen; but that he changed his mind, and returned back to Naples.   Stoddart says nothing more than that he was driven back to Naples in consequence of the French having taken possession of Trieste."   Thus, my dear friend, a heavy load is removed from our minds.   We were wearied out with conjectures, and expectation was worn out : for though every post-day we trembled when the news was coming up stairs, "no letters," yet we had scarcely anything like expectation left. Yet we had a comfort that if anything so bad as imprisonment among the French had happened we should have heard of it in some way or other. Such were our sober, steady day-thoughts, but when I was alone in bed at night I could not banish the most dreadful images, and Mary and Sara have suffered in the same way. All is over now, if it please God to preserve him from the perils of the sea, and in health of body. We conjectured that he would go from Naples to Sicily with the troops, and we trust that he is now there, or on his way home. There is now, I hope, no danger whatever from the French except by sea: but oh! what dreadful winds we have had lately! I never remember such a winter of storms. The last woful one for us was nothing to it. As I have said I had not resolution to write while we remained in such a miserable state of uncertainty, for I knew that I could impart no cheerfulness to you ; and I am afraid you have been in a state to need it, for it is your way not to write when you are not in your *better fashion.*

I think William seems to consider it as almost indifferent what Administration we have, that there is no true honour or ability amongst them. He wants to have all the people of England instructed in the use of arms. . . .

CXII

William Wordsworth to Lady Beaumont

GRASMERE, Tuesday, June 3.

My dear Lady Beaumont,

I arrived at happy Grasmere Sunday before last, i.e. ten days ago, so that you see I have taken time to breathe before I informed you how I sped; but I know I have an unlimited indulgence from you and Sir George in these respects. I found everybody well, little Dorothy the most altered, — I ought to say improved, — for she is grown the most delightful chatterer ever seen; all acquired in two months; nor is it the least of her recommendations that she is more delighted with me than with a new toy, and is never easy, if in my sight, when out of my arms.

Since I reached home I have passed the chief part of my time out of doors, much of it in a wood by the lake-side, a spot which you would love. The Muses, without any wooing on my part, came to me there one morning and murmured a few verses, in which I did not forget Grosvenor Square, as you will know if I ever take up the strain again, for it is not finished. We have had a great deal of talk about your summer visit, and we cannot satisfy ourselves entirely about the inn ; we have fears concerning the sitting-room, which, having no prospect, you would find dull. There is a small cottage close to the lake with two pleasant sitting-rooms that look upon it, under and between two very respectable pollard oaks, and these two rooms are charming in summer; but then the house is ill-provided with bedrooms; but my sister shall describe it for you, and you shall judge.

I have received a very obliging letter from Mr. Price,

who seems much pleased with what I said upon the Sublime. He speaks in warm terms of Sir George, and the many obligations he has to his friendship, and is kind enough to invite me to Foxley, holding out the inducement of the neighbouring scenery of the Wye.

I shall write to Sir George in a short time ; meanwhile you will remember me most affectionately to him. And believe me, my dear Lady Beaumont, most sensible of your goodness, most happy in possessing your friendship, and now faithfully yours,

WM. WORDSWORTH.

CXIII

Dorothy Wordsworth to Lady Beaumont

My dear Friend,

My brother has put his letter into my hands to direct and fold up, and I cannot let it go without a word. A thousand thousand thanks for all your goodness to him ! and you have sent him home to us with looks and health so much improved that we knew not how to express our happiness.

I shall write as soon as we have an answer respecting the possibility of your having the house which my brother speaks of, the cottage near the lake. I am afraid you would not be at ease in the small confined room at the inn. Adieu, my dear Lady Beaumont. Believe me ever faithfully and affectionately yours,

D. WORDSWORTH.

I am very sorry you have had so much trouble about the Journal. You are very good in taking charge of my brother's concerns. I am afraid he left you a great deal to do, for he is a very bad manager of his own affairs, being so much used to leave all little things to us.

CXIV

Dorothy Wordsworth to Lady Beaumont

GRASMERE, Tuesday Evening, June 17th.

My dear Friend,

You will rejoice with us in my sister's safety, and the birth of a son. There was something peculiarly affecting to us in the time and manner of this child's coming into the world. It was like the very same thing over again which happened three years ago; for on the 18th of June, on such another morning, after such a clear and starlight night, the birds singing in the orchard in full assembly as on this 15th, the young swallows chirping in the self-same nest at the chamber window, the rose-trees rich with roses in the garden, the sun shining on the mountains, the air still and balmy, — on such a morning was Johnny born, and all our first feelings were revived at the birth of his brother two hours later in the day, and three days earlier in the month; and I fancied that I felt a double rushing-in of love for it, when I saw the child, as if I had both what had been the first-born infant John's share of love to give it, and its own.

We said it was to be called William at first, but we have since had many discussions and doubts about the name; and Southey, who was here this morning, is decided against William; he would keep the father's name distinct, and not have two *William Wordsworths*. It never struck us in this way; but we have another objection which does not go beyond our own household and our own particular friends, i.e. that my brother is always called *William* amongst us, and it will create great confusion, and we cannot endure the notion of giving up the sound of a name, which, applied to him, is so dear to us. In the case of Dorothy there is often much confusion; but it is not so bad as it would be in this case, and besides, if it were only equally confusing, the inconvenience would be doubled.

Your kind letter to my brother arrived yesterday, with your sister's most interesting account of her sensations on ascending the Mont Denvers. I shuddered while I read; and though admiration of the fortitude with which she endured the agony of her fear was the uppermost sentiment, I could not but slightly blame her for putting herself into such a situation, being so well aware of her constitutional disposition to be so affected. For my own part, I do think that I should have died under it, and nothing could prevail upon me to undertake such an expedition. When I was in the whispering gallery at St. Paul's, I had the most dreadful sensation of giddiness and fear that I ever experienced. I could not move one foot beyond another, and I retired immediately, unable to look down; and I am sure when the sense of personal danger should be added to that other bodily fear, it would be too much for me; therefore I had reason to sympathize with your sister in the course of her narrative.

I hope you will find the inn tolerably comfortable, as I am informed that one of the upper rooms, which was formerly a bedroom, is converted into a sitting-room, which entirely does away our objections to the house for you; the upper rooms being airy and pleasant, and out of the way of noise. Among my lesser cares, and hopes, and wishes, connected with the event of your coming to Grasmere, the desire for fine weather is uppermost; but it will be the rainy season of this country, and we have had so much fine and dry weather that we must look forward to some deduction from our comfort on that score. We received your second letter with the tidings of the finding of the Journal, the day after we had received the first. You may be sure we were very glad that it was found. It is a delicious evening, and after my confinement to the house for these two days past I now doubly enjoy the quiet of the moss-hut, where I am writing. Adieu! Believe me, my dear Lady Beaumont, your affectionate friend,

D. WORDSWORTH.

I have expressed myself obscurely about our objections to calling the child by William's name.[1] I meant that we should not like to call him but as we have been used to do. I could not change William for brother, in speaking familiarly, and his wife could not endure to call him Mr. Wordsworth. Dorothy is in ecstasies whenever she sees her little brother, and she talks about him not only the day through but in her dreams at night, "Baby, baby!"

CXV

Dorothy Wordsworth to Lady Beaumont

GRASMERE, June 24th, 1806.

My dear Friend,

I begin my letter with an expectation of being summoned at every moment to deliver it up, along with others which I have been writing, to my brother and Miss Hutchinson, who are going to meet the post at Rydal; but I cannot omit informing you how we go on, as I know you will be anxious about us; besides, we have received the

[1] The child was christened Thomas. — Ed.

box, etc., and it is fit that I should release your mind of all further care respecting its contents, which came in perfect safety, and have given general satisfaction, and great joy to your god-daughter (for poor Johnny is not here to look at the beautiful library which you have sent him); but could you see Dorothy, how she spreads her hands and arms, and how she exclaims over each book, as she takes it from the case, and the whole together — such a number ! — (when by special favour she is permitted to view them), then you would indeed be repaid for the trouble and pains you have taken ! She lifts her arms, and shouts and dances, and calls out, "Johnny, book ! Dear god-mother sent Johnny book !" She looks upon them as sacred to Johnny, and does not attempt to abuse them. She is also very much delighted with her little almanac, but not in such an enthusiastic manner; for I never saw anything like her joy over the whole library of books. But enough of this. I spoil a pen with every letter I write. The binding of the manuscript destined for Coleridge is exactly to our minds, and Mr. Tuffin is not only forgiven, but we feel a little compunction for the reproaches which slipped from us when we supposed it to be lost.

I am called for. My brother and Miss Hutchinson are ready. Adieu ! Yours ever,

D. WORDSWORTH.

Tuesday Evening. They were too late for the post this morning, and brought back my letter, which I open, to copy a part of a letter relating to Coleridge, which we have just received from Dr. Stoddart of Malta. He begins :

"As it is probable that you have neither heard of nor from Coleridge for some time, I have determined to write to you in order to relieve in some measure your anxiety and that of his family. I have not, however, any very precise information to communicate. The sum of the whole is that he is probably safe at Rome, but may be obliged to reside there privately, and perhaps under a borrowed name, till he finds an opportunity of returning either to Malta or England. He left this place in September last, intending to go through the kingdom of Naples to Trieste, and so through Germany home.

"On the 26th of September he wrote me a short note from Syracuse, which is the only letter that has been received from him at Malta. He was then on his way to Messina, and meant to go from thence to Venice or Trieste, having at these three places a credit of £500 on respectable bankers, correspondents of Mr. Noble, a friend of mine here. From Naples at the approach of the French in January he withdrew with a Mr. B., son of the Member for H., to Rome; but a little after his departure, sent a box of papers and other things to Mr. G. Noble, who with his family escaped to Messina, and took the box with him soon after the French entered Naples in February. From this precaution I conclude that Coleridge wished to travel *incog.*, as he might with justice apprehend that the official character in which he acted here might expose him to suspicion; and, as the French so openly violate all the rights of neutrality, they might think fit to seize him even at Rome. However, I think he has sufficiently obviated all danger of that kind, and being with Mr. B., he will probably be in no want of money. I imagine his object will be to get to Trieste, which is now restored to the Emperor, and where his banker's credit will be of service to him."

This letter is certainly not calculated to set us entirely at ease, for if there be need of so much caution there

must be some danger, and we have reason yet to apprehend further delay; but we are furnished with a probable
reason for his silence, and we may be satisfied that he is
not in want of money, which is very comfortable. I am
afraid the other side of the sheet will be scarcely legible.
I wrote in great haste in the morning, and had hardly
room left for Stoddart's letter. Adieu, dear Lady B.

Yours ever,

D. W.

CXVI

Dorothy Wordsworth to Lady Beaumont

GRASMERE, July 9th, Monday, [1806.]

My dear Friend,

My brother received Sir George's letter on Friday
evening, and his intention of replying to it himself prevented me from writing to you, which I was going to do
when Sir George's letter arrived; but my brother having
been obliged to go with Miss Hutchinson for a few days
to Park House, *I* take the pen merely to tell you what
accommodations we are likely to have for you at the inn,
and to give you our opinions and feelings respecting our
journey into Leicestershire for the winter. I need not
say how deeply sensible we are of Sir George's kindness
and yours in this instance, and we have so many reasons
to be grateful to you that I am little inclined to dwell
upon this particular one.

In the first place, then, we seem to have no other spot
to turn to, for there is not a house in this neighbourhood;
and our continuing here during another winter would be
attended with so many serious inconveniences, especially
to my brother, who has no quiet corner in which to pursue

his studies, no room but that where we all sit (to say nothing of the unwholesomeness of these low small rooms for such a number of persons), that we feel that nothing short of absolute impossibility should prevent us from moving. Ever since my brother's return from London we have thought about our removal to Coleorton as the only scheme in our power; but I abstained from speaking of it to you, thinking that at our meeting all things might be better explained.

The solitude would be no evil to us with such a treasure of books, and even the dirty roads a trifling one, the house being so large that it would not be irksome or unhealthful to be confined there in rainy weather. But there is one circumstance which casts a damp upon our prospects, and is the only one that prevents us from looking forward to the journey with unmingled pleasure, — the being in your house and you not there; so near you, as it were, and not enjoying your society. On this account we could not but have many regrets; therefore, if any house should become vacant in this neighbourhood before the beginning of winter, of course it would be desirable to take it, and defer our journey till the end of next summer, when you will be there also, — for I hope there will be no further delay in the finishing of your building.

One week of the month of July is gone by, and you thought it possible you might be with us before the end of the month, so I hope it will not be long before you have arranged your plans. As to the house at Grasmere, I think there is no doubt but that you may be very comfortable there. I daresay that you might have lodgings at Keswick (if you have no objections to being in the town), where you might be well enough accommodated for a week or a fortnight; but I believe there are no entire houses to be let even in the town, and I know there are none in the neighbourhood; therefore our removing thither is out of the question, for my brother could not endure the thought of living in the town, and we have all great objections to it. Now, if you wish for lodgings in Keswick, you must let us know as soon as you have settled your plans, and we will write to Mr. Edmondson. I have just begun to read Mr. Knight's book,[1] which you were very kind in sending. *The Lay of the Last Minstrel* was also in the box, which we think must have come by mistake. We have two copies of our own sent to us by Mr. Scott. Adieu! Yours affectionately,

D. WORDSWORTH.

CXVII

Dorothy Wordsworth to Lady Beaumont

July 23d, GRASMERE, [1806.]

My dear Friend,

. . . A few minutes before your letter arrived William had set forward with his daughter on his back, and our little nursemaid and I were on foot following after, all on our road over the high mountain pass betwixt Grasmere and Patterdale, by which road we were going to Park House, to remove the child from the danger of whooping-cough, which is prevalent at Grasmere. The letter was sent after us and we halted by the wayside to read it. This was a sad damping at our setting out. We had, however, on the whole a prosperous journey. A young man assisted my brother in bearing the child over the mountains. We went down Ullswater in a boat, and arrived in

---

[1] Doubtless Richard Payne Knight's *Analytical Enquiry into the Principles of Taste.* — Ed.

the evening at Park House, about three miles further.
Our little darling had been the sweetest companion that
ever travellers had.   She noticed the crags, the streams,
everything we saw, and when we passed by any living
creatures, sheep or cows, she began to sing her baby
songs which she has learned from us, "Baa! baa! black
sheep" and "Curly cow bonny."   She was not frightened
in the boat, but for half an hour she screamed dreadfully,
wanting to be out and in the water.   This was all the
trouble we had with her in the whole journey, for she fell
asleep, and did not wake till we landed.

We found Johnny perfectly well, and overjoyed to see
us.   Poor fellow! he had met with an accident a few weeks
before, which one cannot but lament, as it entirely mars
the expression of his countenance.   He fell through a
hay-rack, and got a severe blow on his cheek, which,
though there is no scar, has left an indention or hole in
the cheek, which appears, to those who do not know him,
like a dimple; and, indeed, it is like a dimple; but it has
changed his rich, joyous smile into a silly simper.

I have had a letter from an old servant, whose distresses
my brother related to you, and to whom you so kindly
sent the sum of £5.   She overflows with gratitude; goes
on to tell me that by the means of your liberality, and
that of others who have been interested for her, she is in
no worse condition than she was before the fire happened.
Poor soul!   She says, "I can never be sufficiently thankful that our lives were spared.   We were all fast asleep in
bed, and, as God would have it, my little baby waked,
and wakened me, and the flames were rushing in at the
window."   She is an uncomplaining sufferer, for, since
she left our home, she has endured very much from
many causes, especially the cruelty of her husband, and

sickness and death of children, and her own weak health; yet, though she had no other means of support but the labour of her husband and her own for several years, she never uttered one expression which might induce me to think she needed any comfort which money could procure; quite the contrary, yet when we sent her any assistance it was plain how much she needed it by her account of the manner in which she disposed of that little money, chiefly in fuel! Then comes this sorrow, and now again they are going into the house, which has been rebuilt, and she will patiently again enter upon a way of life which I know is utterly discordant with all her feelings, except a spirit of submission to the will of her husband and the hope of providing a maintenance for her children. I had not intended to detain you so long with talking of this poor woman, but knowing that you would sympathize with me in the pleasure I feel in contemplating a conduct so delicate and disinterested with respect to money in a person placed in so low a rank in society, I went on, and was loath to stop. Believe me, dear Lady Beaumont, your affectionate friend,

D. WORDSWORTH.

I have said nothing about our residence for the winter. The truth is that the thought of being in your house and not seeing you always hangs heavy upon us, and if we can meet with a place here (but I am afraid we shall not) we shall take it, and next autumn, if your house be still at liberty, we can spend two or three months near you. I must again add, however, that we do not dread any of the inconveniences you mention.

We left both John and Dorothy at Park House. William's disposition to procrastinate has yet prevented him from writing to Sir George, who will, he knows, excuse him. He is going on with *The Recluse.*

CXVIII

William Wordsworth to Sir George Beaumont

August 5th, [1806.]

My dear Sir George,

I wrote to you a few days ago. I now write again under a considerable embarrassment of mind occasioned by the enclosed letter, which I wish you would be so good as to 'read after I have furnished you with the necessary preface.

In consequence of this house being too small for us, I have for some time wished to purchase, somewhere or other in this neighbourhood, a few acres of land, with a house attached to them, which might be made large enough by expending upon it £200 or £300. I have sought in vain for such a thing in this vale, and at last I fixed upon a beautiful spot in Patterdale, which I think is worth £700, and for which I offered £800, the utmost farthing I was resolved to give, thinking it nothing but reasonable, as the property was not offered to sale, that I should pay £100 more than it was worth.

Now, it happens that the property in question adjoins an estate of a clergyman of considerable fortune, who also applied for it, and in consequence, chiefly, I believe, of this double application, the proprietors fixed upon it the price of £1000. Of course I gave up all thoughts of the thing, merely writing to the person whom I employed to manage the affair for me, that if he could get the estate for £800 he was to do so. The people stood to their demand of £1000.

In this state of the business, Thomas Wilkinson, the Quaker, whom I mentioned to you in a letter some time ago, the writer of the enclosed, and my agent in the affair, mentioned the circumstance to Lord Lowther, as you will see in the letter, which I beg you would now read. The unhandsome conduct alluded to is that of the clergyman, to whom I wrote, stating my reasons for wishing to purchase this property, and begging him to give up his claim, as the property, I knew, was of no real consequence to him. My letter produced no effect but that of sending him to treat with the people in an ungentlemanly and underhand way.

I suppose you now to have read the enclosed, and your astonishment will be little less than mine. I could scarce believe my eyes when I came to the conclusion. This good Quaker, for an excellent simple-hearted man he is, no doubt is eagerly waiting for a letter of thanks and joyful congratulation from me; and alas! I know not which way to turn me in the affair. Undo the bargain I cannot; to pay the whole money out of my own pocket would be an inhuman return to Lord Lowther for his generous kindness. Strange it is that Wilkinson could not perceive that, if I was unwilling to pay an exorbitant price out of my own money, I should be still more unwilling to pay it out of another's, especially of a person who had shown to me so much kindness, treated me with such respectful delicacy, and given such striking proof of his desire to apply his property to beneficent purposes.

My dear Sir George, I do not ask your advice in the case, for I must be obliged to act before I receive it, and how to act I am sure I do not know. In the first place, if I could possibly avoid it I would not wound the feelings of Thomas Wilkinson, who has been animated by the best and purest motives through the whole course of his innocent and useful life.   He has been betrayed into this hasty step by imagining this purchase to be of far more consequence to me than it really is.   I was by no means *determined* to build upon it, but I wished to have such a place where I might do so if I liked; and, above all, I had no doubt that I could dispose of it at any time for as much as I meant to give for it.   Why, I am led to say to myself, have I troubled you with this letter? I can only say that I have satisfaction in opening out my mind to you, and perhaps you may suggest something that will assist me to see my way, as I think now of writing to T. Wilkinson merely to say that I have received his letter, and shall be over at his house in a few days. In this case I may have time to receive your answer, for which I shall be most thankful.   Pray address me at Mr. John Monkhouse's, Penrith, Cumberland.   Most affectionately yours,

WM. WORDSWORTH.

My sister will express my thanks to Lady Beaumont for her forethought about my accommodation at Coleorton. I ought not to have left this to a postscript.

CXIX

Postscript by Dorothy Wordsworth to Lady Beaumont

MOSS-HUT, Wednesday Morning.

Being compelled to give up all remaining hope of seeing you here this season, it is indeed time we should talk decidedly about our plans for the winter.   In three months more, unless the frosts and winds spare some chance corner of this quiet nook, all the trees which are now rustling in the breeze with their green boughs will be leafless and bare. The prospect of seeing you, though but for a day or two, at Coleorton makes us look to the journey with entire satisfaction; and the moment we received your first letter we determined to seek no further for a house in this neighbourhood, except in case of Coleridge's wintering at Keswick. Should he determine so to do, if within three or four miles of Keswick (which is very improbable) a suitable house should be vacant, my brother will take it for the sake of being near to Coleridge. When we meet you will know how deeply we feel your goodness, my dear Lady Beaumont, in attending with such minuteness to our wants and comforts. I would thank you now again and again; but something more than words is needed to express the habitual sentiments of gratitude and love with which we think of you.

As to the manner of our journey, we must not go in the car. Perhaps my sister might receive no injury, if she be tolerably strong, but we should be afraid for the little baby, and for Dorothy, she being liable to attacks of the croup whenever she is exposed to cold. We shall, therefore (that is, my brother and sister, the three children and I), travel in a postchaise, which we shall certainly "fill," as well as did Mrs. Gilpin when she repaired to Edmonton, "her sister and her sister's child, herself and children three"; and our servant and the girl who helps us to take care of the children must go in the coach to the town nearest to Coleorton. Since the birth of Thomas we have had this girl, whom we find very useful, and could not now (having three children so young to look after) do without, except at the expense of sacrificing all opportunities of leisure and quiet; at least leisure and quiet enjoyed in common by their mother and me, for one of us must be with them the day through. Having these two servants, therefore, we shall have no occasion for assistance from the farmer's servant except in case of accidents.

Mrs. Wordsworth is perfectly well, and thinks of going with William in a few days to Park House to see John and Dorothy, whom we are afraid we shall hardly be able to have at home again before we leave Grasmere, as whooping-cough is in every quarter of the vale, and there are yet a great number of children who have not had it. The house seems strangely dull without them. Every day we may look for news of Coleridge's arrival. I thank you for taking the trouble to transcribe those excellent lines from Sir John Beaumont's poems. They interested us very much, and we wish for the pleasure of reading his works when we are on the ground which he and his brother trod. Adieu! Your affectionate friend,

DOROTHY WORDSWORTH.

I am sure you will enter into our feelings about the purchase of the estate. It is a most mortifying affair, and perplexing too, though nothing can be done to prevent completing the purchase.

CXX

Dorothy Wordsworth to Lady Beaumont

GRASMERE, Aug. 15th, [1806.]

My dear Friend,

I have at last the happiness of telling you that Coleridge is actually in sight of his own dear country. He is now off Portsmouth, where he must remain to perform quarantine. A Mr. Russel, an artist, is with him, and by his means we have heard; for Coleridge has not written himself. I have no doubt (as Mrs. Coleridge thinks also) that he is afraid to inquire after us, lest he should hear of some new sorrow. We have only had one letter from him, written since our poor brother's death. Mr. Russel had written to his friends at Exeter, they to the Coleridges at Ottery, and the Coleridges to Mrs. Coleridge, so at least ten days of the time of his imprisonment must be gone by; but the letter does not mention when they arrived, nor the name of the ship. My brother and sister and little Thomas are at Park House.

My joy at Coleridge's return will be quite a burden to me till I know that they too have received the news. I never felt the want of them at home half so much as for these three last hours, since Mrs. Coleridge's note came. William intends calling upon Lord Lowther before his return. He hoped to find a letter from Sir George at Penrith, and intended writing to him. We were deeply affected by Sir George's last letter, which came the day before my brother and sister went to Park House. William said he should write again to him immediately. I write in great haste to save the post. God bless you, my dear friend! I hope we shall hear from you, when you next write, that Sir George has recovered his spirits after the severe and painful shock he has had; for death, when it comes to a young person, is a *shock* for the survivors, however truly we may feel that it was a merciful dispensation. Adieu, my good and dear friend, yours ever,

D. W.

When I next write I will transcribe the sonnet of Michael Angelo, of which my brother sent Sir George the translation.

CXXI

William Wordsworth to Lord Lonsdale (then Viscount Lowther)

Aug. 19th, 1806.

. . . I called to thank you for the high honour with which you have lately distinguished me.[1]

I cannot help adding that a place which its own beauty first recommended to me will be greatly endeared by being connected in my mind with so pleasing a remembrance of your particular kindness towards me, and of your general benevolence, . . .

CXXII

William Wordsworth to Sir George Beaumont

GRASMERE, Aug. 21st, 1806.

My dear Sir George,

First let me congratulate you on Coleridge's arrival, and upon what is a still nearer and deeper subject of congratulation, — his recovery from a most dangerous illness, which prevented his writing to us. Their passage had been long, irksome, and dreadful; he having been ill, I believe, the whole of the time, and much worse on their arrival, and while performing quarantine; so much so that his life was despaired of. He had dictated a letter to me under that feeling, to be sent to me in case he did

[1] Can the reference be to the purchase, or gift, of Place Fell? They had not met previously. — Ed.

not recover. Have we not reason to be thankful? As soon as he set his foot upon land he was greatly renovated, and last Monday, the day on which he wrote, was uncommonly well. He was at his friend Lamb's chambers in London. His letter is very short, and he does not say a word when we are to expect him down.

Many thanks for your prompt reply to my troublesome letter. I wrote in a great hurry, and must have expressed myself ill, or your view of the subject could not have differed so much from mine. My uneasiness did not arise so much from being thus betrayed into an obligation to Lord Lowther, as from the specific circumstances attending that obligation. It is my opinion that a man of letters (and indeed all public men of every pursuit) ought to be severely frugal. If I ought to be frugal of my own money, much more ought I to be so of another person's, particularly of a generous-minded person. Now the object here was not worth an additional £200 of my own money, and therefore much less of Lord Lowther's. Had indeed the object been very important, such as putting me in possession of a place where I had long lived, and with which I had connected many interesting feelings, I might not have thought that any sense of honour or independence, however nice, ought to call upon me to shrink from such an act of kindness and munificence. But this was not the case here; the spot had little to recommend it to me but its own beauty, and Providence has dealt so kindly with this country that this is little distinction.

Applethwaite, I hope, will remain in my family for many generations.[1] With my will it should never be

---

[1] It does still (1907). — Ed.

parted with, unless the character of the place be entirely changed, as I am sorry to say there is some reason to apprehend; a cotton-mill being, I am told, already planted, or to be planted, in the glen. I shall see the place to-morrow. The matter of your advice about building I have long laid to my heart; and it has (as is common in these cases) just answered the purpose of quickening the temptation to be dabbling. The *temptation* I like, and I should content myself with the pleasure it gives me, through my whole life (I have at least built five hundred houses, in five hundred different places, with garden, grounds, etc.), but I have no house to cover me, and know not where to get one. But seriously, I do not mean to entangle myself with rashness. What then shall I say? My object is not to build a new house, only to add two rooms to an old one, and this on the supposition that we do not go southward with Coleridge.

I called at Lowther, and did not find his lordship at home. Since my return hither I wrote him a letter, in which I confined myself to expressing my thanks for the great honour he had done me. I told Wilkinson frankly, yet in as gentle a manner as I could, that I should not have accepted Lord Lonsdale's offer if I had been consulted, and upon what principle I should have refused. This he took very well, and seemed quite happy that he had not consulted me. The spot I re-examined last Sunday, and a most beautiful one it is. How happy should I be to show it to you and Lady Beaumont! I don't know any place where more recommendation lies in so little room.

I have not yet thanked you for your former letter, which gave me very great pleasure. Lady Beaumont had mentioned your friend's death, but I did not know that he was one to whom you were so much attached. Do not be afraid of dividing any of your painful sensations with me. I know no passion where sympathy is of so much use as in grief. I like your idea of republishing your ancestor's poems, and promise myself great pleasure in reading them. If I could be of any service in editing the book, nothing would give me more satisfaction, either in the way of prefixing a life, carrying the work through the press, or anything else.

As soon as we have seen Coleridge we shall be able to say something positive about our journey to Coleorton; at present we indulge great hopes of seeing you.

The vale is relieved of our harlequins, to the great loss of my daughter, who had conceived a great attachment to them and their doggy.

Farewell. Affectionate remembrance to yourself and Lady Beaumont from us all. Ever yours,

W. WORDSWORTH.

Keep T. Wilkinson's letter till we meet.

CXXIII

William Wordsworth to Sir George Beaumont[1]

My dear Sir George,

When my last letter was gone I was much mortified. I seemed to myself a thankless spirit, having said so much of the different view we had taken of my perplexity, and little or nothing of your goodness in writing, giving yourself so much trouble about the business. But let us

[1] This letter is undated and was unfinished; but internal evidence shows that it was written the autumn of 1806. — Ed.

dismiss it.   Whether I have done right or no I know not,
but I acted to the best of my judgment.   I like your
ancestor's verses the more, the more I see of them ; they
are manly, dignified, and extremely harmonious.   I do
not remember in any author of that age such a series of
well-tuned couplets.

The picture of the Thorn has been ten days under our
roof.   It has pleased us greatly ; and the more it is looked
at, the more it pleases.   Yet we have two objections to
it : one, that the upright bough in the thorn is, we think,
too tall for a tree in so exposed a situation ; and the
other, — which I remember you mentioned as having been
made by somebody in town, — that the woman appears
too old.   I did not feel this much myself, but both my
wife and sister have felt it.   The picture is, I think, beautifully coloured ; and assuredly if it be the best praise of
a picture that it should be often looked at, that praise
yours has in abundant measure, and is likely to have.
Our servant (observe, she is a Quaker by birth and breed-
ing) thought that the colours were too grave.   Our old
Molly, of whom you have heard, did not venture to give
her opinion in our presence; but as we learned afterwards, she laid her head close to a neighbour's of ours,
whispering, "What do ye think of it?"   "To be sure, the
frame's varra bonny, but, for my part, I can mak nowt
on 't" (meaning "nothing of it"); to which her neighbour
replied that she thought it was very natural.   She was
well acquainted with the poem, and said that the thorn
in the picture was as like a thorn as it could stare ; but
that, upon a high place; the boughs never grew so high
as the middle bough.   This confirmed in me the belief
that our objection, which she had not heard, was well
founded.

What shall I say of Coleridge? or what can I say? My dear friend, this is certain, that he is destined to be unhappy. I would not distress you and Lady Beaumont with this, but it is not to be kept from you, and ought not, loving him and us as you do. I believe I have spoken to Lady Beaumont of his domestic situation, so that the little which I shall now say will not be altogether new, and therefore will, I hope, be less felt. In fact, he dare not go home, he recoils so much from the thought of domesticating with Mrs. Coleridge, with whom, though on many accounts he much respects her, he is so miserable that he dare not encounter it. What a deplorable thing! I have written to him to say that if he does not come down immediately I must insist upon seeing him somewhere. If he appoints London, I shall go. I believe if anything good is to be done for him, it must be done by me. I will say no more of this at present; only be assured, if we have not written to you, this is the cause. He has no plan for his own residence, and as yet has taken no notice of anything we have said of our movements depending upon him and his. . . .

CXXIV

Dorothy Wordsworth to Lady Beaumont

GRASMERE, 26th August.[1]

My dear Friend,

I have been prevented from answering your last letter by several accidental interruptions. Otherwise I should not have been so long in expressing our sense of the kindness of your proposal. Whatever may come of it, it

[1] No year is given, but it must have been 1806. — Ed.

is a pleasure to us to think and talk of the scheme; and
your delicate and most friendly care for our comfort and
happiness in this instance, as in so many others, has made
impressions upon us that cannot pass away, and will for
ever be a source of delight.   That you may have an accurate notion of our house my brother insists that I send
you a measurement of the sitting-room, and I intend to
give you a plan or drawing of the whole at the end of my
letter.   We do indeed seriously think of visiting you next
summer, and we have said so much about it in Johnny's
hearing that he already talks in his lisping way of " doing to see Lady Beaumont."   It is a long time beforehand, and far to look forward; but if all goes on well with
you and us, I do not see it may not happen, and at all
events it is pleasant to think of it.

The end of the month of June is the time we have fixed
upon for setting forward, the spring and early part of the
summer being the season of our quiet enjoyment of home,
and the end of summer and the autumn the season of
bustle; for we are directly in the highway of the tourists.
Of course, I mean that time *should it suit you;* and also,
it being uncertain whether we shall remain another year
in this country, we perhaps may be ourselves obliged to
defer the journey till the end of summer, as my brother
and I are determined that Mrs. Wordsworth shall see a
part of Scotland before we finally quit the north of
England.

As to the two houses the picture you have sketched of
the cottage is delightful, and made me long to sit with you
under the shade of its old elm tree; yet do not think
that if the other house can be prepared for us with less
trouble we should not therefore be more contented with
it, though we might love the cottage better; and let me

add too that we trust you will not put yourselves to any expense or trouble that may not turn to account hereafter. You know it is but waiting another year; that is, to be sure, a long time in life at our age, but we may meet in some other way. I shall say no more upon this subject, depending upon your perfect openness with us.

Mr. Davy is probably with you at this time. He will have told you that he spent two or three pleasant days with my brother and Walter Scott. William went to Keswick to meet Mr. Scott, and after having stayed a couple of days to our great surprise Mr. Davy also came home with him over Helvellyn. We all went upon Windermere the next day, and parted from Mr. Davy at Bowness; it being then his intention to see you at Coleorton in about a week. I had been very much pleased to see him thus unexpectedly, both on his own account and as a friend of yours, and I was really quite delighted when I heard that he intended to be with you so soon. My brother and sister join me in kindest remembrance. Believe me, your affectionate friend,

D. WORDSWORTH.

Now for my drawings. They will make you smile at my little skill.

 This is the front of the house.

The door is at one end, and there is at the other end an out-jutting, which I really have not the power to delineate. We enter at the kitchen door. On the same floor is a parlour which we have converted into a bedroom, and my brother and sister sleep there. Above stairs over the kitchen is the sitting-room — five yards by four, and two yards and a half in height—and over the other room is a lodging room, where our visitors lodge. *My* room is in the outjutting, of which I have spoken; and then in the same part is also the pantry, lumber room, etc. So you see that, small as our house is, we have one spare apartment; and three rooms are all that will be necessary for us in your cottage, except a place for the servant to sleep in. Dorothy will be weaned at that time, and she will sleep with me; and John will sleep with the servant. All the rooms of this house are low, and each room has only one window. I have written in great haste. Excuse blunders. You may lament with me that I have not been taught to exercise the pencil. It is indeed true that I scarcely ever take a walk without lamenting it.

CXXV

Dorothy Wordsworth to Lady Beaumont

[Sept., 1806.]

My dear Friend,

I have put off writing to you for many days, hoping always that the next post would bring us a letter from Coleridge himself, from which some comfort might be gathered and a more accurate estimate formed of the state of his mind. But no letter has arrived. I have, however, the satisfaction of telling you that he is to be at home on the 29th of this month. He has written to acquaint Mrs. Coleridge with this, and has told her that he has some notion of giving a course of lectures in London in the winter. This is all we know; I do not imagine he has mentioned the subject of the lectures to Mrs. Coleridge.

Whatever his plan may be, I confess I very much wish he may not put it in practice, and for many reasons: first, because I fear his health would suffer from late hours, and being led too much into company; and, in the second place, I would fain see him address the whole powers of his soul to some great work in prose or verse, of which the effect would be permanent, and not personal and transitory. I do not mean to say that much permanent good may not be produced by communicating knowledge by means of lectures, but a man is perpetually tempted to lower himself to his hearers, to bring them into sympathy with him, and no one would be more likely to yield to such temptation than Coleridge; therefore at every period of his life the objection would have applied to his devoting himself to this employment. But at this present time it seems almost necessary that he should have one grand object before him, which would turn his thoughts away in a steady course from his own unhappy lot, and so prevent petty irritations and distresses, and in the end produce a habit of reconcilement and submission.

My dear friend, you will judge how much we have suffered from anxiety and distress within the few last weeks. We have long known how unfit Coleridge and his wife were for each other; but we had hoped that his ill-health, and the present need his children have of his care and fatherly instructions, and the reflections of his own mind during this long absence would have so wrought upon him that he might have returned home with comfort, ready to partake of the blessings of friendship, which he surely has in an abundant degree, and to devote himself to his studies and his children. I now trust he has brought himself into this state of mind, but as we have had no letters from him since that miserable one which we received a short time before my brother mentioned the subject to Sir George, I do not know what his views are. Poor soul! he had a struggle of many years, striving to bring Mrs. Coleridge to a change of temper, and something like communion with him in his enjoyments. He is now, I trust, effectually convinced that he has no power of this sort, and he has had so long a time to know and feel this that I would gladly hope things will not be so bad as he imagines when he finds himself once again with his children under his own roof. If he *can* make use of the knowledge which he has of the utter impossibility of producing powers and qualities of mind which are not in her, or of much changing what is unsuitable to his disposition, I do not think he will be unhappy; I am sure I think he ought not to be *miserable*.

While he imagined he had anything to hope for, no wonder that his perpetual disappointments made him so! But suppose him once reconciled to that one great want, an utter want of sympathy, I believe he may live in peace and quiet. Mrs. Coleridge has many excellent properties, as you observe: she is unremitting in her attentions as a nurse to her children, and, indeed, I believe she would have made an excellent wife to many persons. Coleridge is as little fitted for her as she for him, and I am truly sorry for her. When we meet you at Coleorton I trust we shall have been with Coleridge long enough to know what comfort he is likely to have. In the meantime I will say no more on this distressing subject unless some change should happen much for the better or the worse. I hope everything from the effect of my brother's conversation upon Coleridge's mind; and bitterly do I regret that he did not at first go to London to meet him, as I think he might have roused him up, and preserved him from much of the misery that he has endured.

Now I must speak of the delight with which we look forward to seeing you. We think that nothing will prevent our accepting your kind offer; for it is plain that Coleridge does not wish us to go to Keswick, as he has not replied to that part of William's letter in which he spoke of our plans for the winter. We shall therefore prepare ourselves to be ready to set off at any time that you shall appoint, so as to be with you a few days before your departure from Coleorton. . . .

CXXVI

Dorothy Wordsworth to Mrs. Clarkson

COLEORTON, ASHBY DE LA ZOUCHE, LEICESTERSHIRE,
November 6th, 1806, begun the 5th.

My dear Friend,

I hope you have hit upon the true reason of my long silence, or you may have felt as if I am either negligent or positively unkind. In fact from Coleridge's arrival till the time when we saw him at Kendal we were so unhappy on his account, and so distracted with doubt and painful conjectures, that I could not bear to write. You could do us no good, and to set about explaining so perplexing a distress would have been a miserable task. William would have gone up to London before we received your letter, but he was afraid of missing him on the road; and when C. wrote in answer to William's proposal, he replied in three lines that he was coming, and wrote to Mrs. C. to the same effect, time after time. Meanwhile we knew not what to do. We were obliged to come to Coleorton

at the very time we did come, or we should not have
seen Sir George and Lady Beaumont; and we resolved
to come as the only means of seeing Coleridge, being
informed by Mrs. C., and others, that he had engaged
to begin a course of lectures in London in November.

During the last week of our stay at Grasmere we had
reason (from his having told Mrs. C. that he should be
·at Keswick by the end of the preceding week) to expect
him every day, and judge of our distress at being obliged
to set off without having seen him; but when we got to
Kendal we heard from Sara Hutchinson that she had
just received a letter from him from Penrith, written immediately on his arrival there, i.e. little more than half
an hour after her departure from P.[1] to meet us at K.[2]
He said he *could* not come to Kendal, just to see us,
and then to part. Notwithstanding this, however, we
resolved to see him, and wait one day at Kendal for that
purpose. Accordingly we sent off a special messenger to
Keswick to desire him to come over to us; but before
seven o'clock that evening he himself arrived at an inn,
and sent for William. We all went thither to him, and
never never did I feel such a shock, as at first sight of
him. We all felt exactly in the same way — as if he were
different from what we had expected to see; almost as
much as a person of whom we had thought much, and of
whom we had formed an image in our own minds, without having any personal knowledge of him.

Thursday Evening. Your letter to Mary reached us
this afternoon and bitterly am I distressed that I did
not write when we were at Kendal, or since our arrival
here. As to poor Coleridge I am afraid he has not

[1] Penrith. — Ed.   [2] Keswick. — Ed.

written to you, and you are still in the same miserable suspense. I cannot forgive myself, but I must not take up my paper with regrets and self-accusations, but go on with my tale. We, that is Mary and I, stayed with him from Sunday evening till Tuesday morning at nine o'clock; but Sara Hutchinson and William did not part from him till the morning following. Alas! what can I say? I know not what to hope for, or what to expect. My wishes are plain and fair, that he may have strength of mind to abide by his resolution of separating from Mrs. C., and hereafter may continue unshaken; but his misery has made him so weak, and he has been so dismally irresolute in all things since his return to England, that I have more of fear than hope. He is utterly changed; and yet sometimes, when he was animated in conversation concerning things removed from him, I saw something of his former self; but never when we were alone with him. He then scarcely ever spoke of anything that concerned him, or us, or our common friends, except we forced him to it; and immediately he changed the conversation to Malta, Sir Alexander Ball, the corruptions of government, anything but what we were yearning after. All we could gather from him was that he must part from her, or die and leave his children destitute, and that to part he was resolved.

We would have gone back to Grasmere, or taken a house near Hawkshead (Belmont), but this he was against, and indeed it would have been worse than useless, for he gave us a promise to come to us here in a month; and, if he do part, the further the better. So matters stood when we left him, and we are now in anxious expectation of a letter from him. He did not complain of his health, and his appetite appeared to be not bad; but that he is ill I am well assured, and that he must sink if he does not grow more happy. His fatness has quite changed him. It is more like the flesh of a person in a dropsy than one in health; his eyes are lost in it — but why talk of this? you must have seen and felt all. I often thought of Patty Smith's[1] remark. It showed true feeling of the divine expression of his countenance. Alas! I never saw it, as it used to be — a shadow, a gleam there was at times, but how faint and transitory! I think however that, if he have courage to go through the work before him, William's conversation and our kind offices may soothe him, and bring on tranquillity; and then, the only hope that remains will be in his applying himself to some grand object connected with permanent effects. . . .

CXXVII

William Wordsworth to Francis Wrangham

COLEORTON, NEAR ASHBY DE LA ZOUCHE,
        LEICESTERSHIRE, Novbr. 7th, 1806.

My dear Wrangham,

Your kind letter deserved an earlier, indeed an immediate, answer; but it happened that the very day I received it I caught a violent cold, by far the worst I ever had in my life, which hung upon me for five weeks. I do not mention this as entitling me to your absolute pardon, but it was in fact the reason why I put off writing, as I did every other business, expecting every day to become better. I am now with my family at Coleorton, near Ashby de la Zouche, Leicestershire; occupying a house of Sir George

---

[1] A daughter of W. Smith, the member of Parliament for Norwich. — Ed.

Beaumont's for the winter; our own cottage at Grasmere being far too small for our family to winter in, though we manage well enough in it during the summer.

Now for the subject of your last; I am afraid what I have to say will not be welcome to you. I have long since come to a fixed resolution to steer clear of personal satire; in fact I never will have anything to do with it as far as concerns the *private* vices of individuals on any account; with respect to public delinquents or offenders I will not say the same, though I should be slow to meddle even with these. This is a rule which I have laid down to myself, and shall rigidly adhere to;[1] though I do not in all cases blame those who think and act differently. It will, therefore, follow that I cannot lend any assistance to your proposed publication. The verses which you have of mine I should wish to be destroyed. I have no copy of them myself, at least none that I can find. I would most willingly give them up to you, — fame, profit, and everything, — if I thought either true fame or profit could arise out of them. I should even with great pleasure leave you to be the judge in the case, if it were unknown to everybody that I had ever had a concern in a thing of this kind; but I know several persons are acquainted with the fact, and it would be buzzed about; and my name would be mentioned in connection with the work, which I would on no account should be. Your imitations seem well done; but as I have not the intermediate passages, I could not possibly judge of the effect of the whole.

I have never seen those works of yours which you mention, being entirely out of the way of new books. I was

---

[1] Compare Wordsworth's letter to William Matthews, March 21st, 1796. — Ed.

indeed in London last spring, but was so much engaged that I did not read five minutes all the time I was there.

I think of publishing a volume of small pieces in verse this winter. How shall I get a copy conveyed to you?

I should be very happy to see you, Mrs. Wrangham, and your family; but you are sadly out of the way; and whatever wings poets may boast of, they are useless in cases of this kind. Here the richest man is the best flyer; and I am neither rich, nor ever likely to be.

My children are as follows: a son, three years old; a daughter, two; a son, under five months. . . . When I am upon this subject, may I ask a favour of you which I have long thought of. It is this: Have you any friends who draw, and may happen to be at Sir George Cayley's, or Mr. Langley's? and could you procure for me by their means two drawings of Brompton Church? It is the place where I was married. One I should like to have taken at a small distance, where the church has the most picturesque effect in connection with the land-scape; and the other the best looking picture of the build-ing itself. My wife, and Miss Hutchinson who is here, beg their best respects to you, and will thank you to take the trouble of remembering them to Sir George and Lady Cayley.

My wife and sister also beg to be remembered to Mrs. Wrangham. Do write soon, and believe me, dear Wrangham, ever affectionately yours,

WM. WORDSWORTH.

CXXVIII

William Wordsworth to Walter Scott

COLEORTON, November 10, 1806.

My dear Scott,

Here I am, with my whole family, a flight of 160 miles south, . . . for six months, about the end of which time we shall return to Grasmere.   I hope to have a sight of the last primroses.   You see therefore that I cannot profit by your friendly invitation to take up abode with you for any part of the ensuing winter.

. . . Your second copy of the *Minstrel* I gave away. It was a beautiful book, but when I wished for another copy it was for one of a pocket size.   Any poetry which I like, I wish for in that size, to which no doubt you will one day descend.

I am going to the press with a volume[1] which I publish with great reluctance; but the day when my long work[2] will be finished seems further and further off. . . . It would look like affectation if I were to say how indifferent I am to its present reception ; but I have a true pleasure in saying to you that I put some value upon it, and hope that it will one day or other be thought well of by the public.   By the by you will not be displeased to find that you and I have (as I understand) fallen upon the same subject, the melancholy catastrophe of the dog in the coves of Helvellyn.   What a happy day we had together there.   I often think of it with delight. . . .

---

[1] The *Poems* of 1807. — Ed.   [2] *The Recluse.* — Ed.

CXXIX

William Wordsworth to Sir George Beaumont

Nov. 10, 1806.

My dear Sir George,

I was moved even to weakness by your letter. It is indeed a great happiness to me to be beloved by you, and to think upon what foundation that love rests. We were as sorry to part with you as you could be to part with us; perhaps even more so, as I believe is almost always the case with those who are left behind. We did not see the rising sun, which you describe so feelingly; but the setting was as glorious to us as to you. We looked at it with great delight from your fireside; but were foolish enough — at least I was — to believe that we should have such every night; that it was a gift of our new situation, and so the colours and motions which touched you so much were thrown away upon me, — at least it seems so now. You know that at Grasmere the high mountains conceal from us in a great measure the splendour of a western sky at sunset. We have often regretted this, and we congratulated ourselves that evening on the opportunity which our present comparatively flat situation would give us of enjoying a sight from which we had long been excluded. We have had one or two fine evenings since, but nothing like that first, which was, I think, the most magnificent I ever beheld. The whole day had been uncommonly fine.

We have not yet rambled much about. Once I have been at the fir-wood with Miss Hutchinson, once at the pool with Mrs. Wordsworth, and once had a long walk with my sister about the house and in the kitchen garden.

Your new building and its immediate neighbourhood improve upon me much. I am particularly pleased with the spot — a discovery since your departure — which Lady Beaumont has chosen, I conjecture, for a winter garden. It will be a delightful place. By the by, there is a pleasing paper in the *Spectator* (in the 7th vol., No. 477) upon this subject. The whole is well worth reading, particularly that part which relates to the winter garden. He mentions hollies and horn-beam as plants which his place is full of. The horn-beam I do not know, but the holly I looked for in Lady Beaumont's ground, and could not find. For its own beauty, and for the sake of the hills and crags of the North, let it be scattered here in profusion. It is of slow growth, no doubt, but not so slow as generally supposed; and then it does grow, and somebody, we hope, will enjoy it. Among the barbarisers of our beautiful lake-region, of those who bring and those who take away, there are few whom I have execrated more than an extirpator of this beautiful shrub, or rather tree — the holly. This worthy, thank Heaven! is not a native, but he comes from far; and his business is to make bird-lime, and so down go these fair creatures of Nature wherever he can find them. (You know probably that bird-lime is made of the bark of the holly.)

I would also plant yew, which is of still slower growth. One thought struck me, too, relating to the grounds, which I will mention. I should not be for planting many forest-trees about the house, by the side of those which are already at their full growth. When I planted at all there, I should rather choose thickets of underwood, hazels, wild roses, honeysuckle, hollies, thorns, and trailing plants, such as traveller's joy, etc. My reason, in addition to the beauty of these, is that they would never be compared

with the grown-up trees, whereas young trees of the same
kind will, and must, appear insignificant. Observe my
remark only applies to placing these young trees *by the
side* of the others; where there is an open space of any
size it does not hold.

Miss Hutchinson and I were at church yesterday. We
were pleased with the singing; and I have often heard a
far worse parson — I mean as to reading. His sermon
was, to be sure, as village sermons often are, very injudi-
cious : a most knowing discourse about the Gnoştics, and
other hard names of those who were *h*adversaries to Chris-
tianity and *h*enemies of the Gospel. How strangely inju-
dicious this is ! — and yet nothing so frequent. I remember
hearing Coleridge say that he was once at Keswick Church,
and Mr. Denton (you know him) was very entertaining
in guarding his hearers against the inordinate vice of
ambition, what a shocking thing it was to be a courtier,
and sacrifice a man's hopes in heaven for worldly state
and power. I don't know that I ever heard in a country
pulpit a sermon that had any special bearing on the condition of the majority of the audience.

I was sorry to see at Coleorton few middle-aged men,
or even women ; the congregation consisted almost entirely
of old persons, particularly old men, and boys and girls.
The girls were not well dressed. Their clothes were
indeed clean, but not *tidy;* they were in this respect a
shocking contrast to our congregation at Grasmere. I
think I saw the old man (not he with the spectacles)
whose face, especially the eyes, Mr. Davie has drawn so
well. Lady Beaumont will remember that I objected to
the shoulders in the drawing as being those of a young
man. This is the case in nature, — in this instance
I mean; for I never saw before such shoulders and

unwithered arms with so aged a face as in the person I allude to.

I have talked much chit-chat. I have chosen to do this rather than give way to my feelings, which were powerfully called out by your affecting and beautiful letter. I will say this, and this only — that I esteem your friendship one of the best gifts of my life. I and my family owe much to you and Lady Beaumont. I need not say that I do not mean any additions to our comfort or happiness, which — with respect to external things — you have been enabled to make ; but I speak of soul indebted to soul. I entirely participate your feelings upon your birthday. It is a trick of kings and people in power to make birthdays matter of rejoicing. Children, too, with their holiday and plum-pudding, rejoice ; but to them, in their inner hearts, it is a day

> That tells of time misspent, of comfort lost,
>   Of fair occasions gone forever by.

I long to see Wilkie's picture. From Lady Beaumont's account it seems to have surpassed your utmost expectations. I am glad of this, both because the picture is yours, and as it is an additional promise of what he is to do hereafter. No doubt you will read him my Orpheus of Oxford Street,[1] which I think he will like. In a day or two I mean to send a sheet of my intended volume to the press; it would give me pleasure to desire the printer to send you the sheets as they are struck off if you could have them free of expense. There is no forming a true estimate of a volume of *small* poems by reading them all together; one stands in the way of the other. They must either be read a few at once, or the book must remain some time by one, before a judgment can be made

[1] His poem entitled *Power of Music.* — Ed.

of the quantity of thought and feeling and imagery it contains, and what (and what variety of) moods of mind it can either impart or is suited to.

My sister is writing to Lady Beaumont, and will tell her how comfortable we are here, and everything relating thereto. Alas! we have had no tidings of Coleridge — a certain proof that he continues to be very unhappy. Farewell, my dear friend. Most faithfully and affectionately yours,

WM. WORDSWORTH.

CXXX

Dorothy Wordsworth to Lady Beaumont

COLEORTON, Friday, 14th November, [1806.]

My dear Friend,

We like the place more and more every day, for every day we find fresh comfort in having a roomy house. The sitting-room, where by the fireside we have seen some glorious sunsets, we far more than like — we already *love* it. These sunsets are a gift of our new residence, for shut up as we are among the mountains in our small deep valley, we have but a glimpse of the glory of the evening through one gap called the Dunmail Gap, the inverted arch which you pass through in going to Keswick. On Wednesday evening my brother and I walked backwards and forwards under the trees near the hall just after the sun was gone down, and we felt as if we were admitted to a new delight. From the horizon's edge to a great height the sky was covered with rosy clouds, and I cannot conceive anything more beautiful and glorious and solemn than this light seen through the trees, and the majestic trees themselves; and afterwards, when we went lower down, and had the church spire and your new house backed by the west, they had a very fine effect. We continued to walk till the sky was gloomy all over, and two lights (we supposed from coal-pits) on the hill opposite to the hall, where the grove stands whither you want to decoy the rooks, were left to shine with full effect, and they looked very wild.

We have not been much further than your grounds (except to Ashby, whither we have gone several times on business). The roads, if you do not go very far from home, are by no means so bad as I expected; for instance, the Ashby road, till you come to the turnpike, is very well; afterwards, to be sure, it is shocking, and I have no doubt the Ashby people think we are marvellous creatures to have the courage to wade through it. In consequence of your hint my sister and I walked to the Hospital the next day, and the day after we sent John to school; and a proud scholar he is. He goes with his dinner in a bag slung over his shoulder, and a little bottle of milk in his greatcoat pocket, and never man was fuller of pride and self-importance. . . . Mr. Craig has planted honeysuckles beside the pillars at the door. I wish they may thrive, for in a few years the spot will be very beautiful if they do. It makes a charming walk, and I think the effect of the pillars when you are under the shed will be very elegant. We have requested Mr. Craig to plant some of the clematis or traveller's joy, a plant which is very beautiful, especially by moonlight in winter, grows rapidly, and makes a delicious bower. What above all things I delight in is the piece of ground you have chosen for your winter garden; the hillocks and slopes and the hollow shape of the whole will make it a perfect wilderness when the trees get up. The wall at the end which supports the bank is very handsome, — that is, it will be so when it is overgrown; but I hope you will not wall the garden all round. The natural shelving earthy fence which it has at present might be made perfectly beautiful, as I should think.

I recognized the old steps which are in Sir George's drawing, and oh ! how very pretty that wych-elm cottage might be made; but go it must, that I see, being so very near your house; yet I will and must mourn for it. My sister and I are very fond of the parsonage-house, and should like to live there, as we said to each other one morning when we were walking beside it — if we could but persuade William to take orders; and he being a very "delightful creature" you know, it would suit you, and we should all be suited. My brother works very hard at his poems, preparing them for the press. Miss Hutchinson is the transcriber. She also orders dinner and attends to the kitchen; so that the labour being so divided we have all plenty of leisure. . . .

I do not understand anything by that line of Michael Angelo's but this, that he — seeing in the expression and light of her eye so much of the divine nature, that is, receiving from thence such an assurance of the divine nature being in her — felt therefrom a more confirmed belief or sentiment or sensation of the divinity of his own, and was thereby purified. If I write more I shall have no room for the poem. God bless you, my good dear Lady Beaumont! Remember me kindly to Sir George.

[Then follows the poem *Star-Gazers*.]

We shall be anxious to know how you find Lady Beau-

¹ I have kept back from speaking of

? Dowager Lady Beaumont, who lived usually at

Coleridge, for what can I say? We have had no letter,
though we have written again. You shall hear of it when
he writes to us.

CXXXI

Dorothy Wordsworth to Lady Beaumont

16th November, 8 o'clock, Sunday Evening.[1]

My dear Friend,

I write to you from the nursery fireside, and a very
warm and comfortable spot it is; and seems more quiet
for the gentle regular breathing of the two little boys, who
are in bed at the other end of the room. I do not know
what to say to you about poor Coleridge. We have had
four letters from him, and in all he speaks with the same
steadiness of his resolution to separate from Mrs. Coleridge, and she has fully agreed to it, and consented that
he should take Hartley and Derwent, and superintend
their education, she being allowed to have them at the
holidays. I say she has agreed to the separation, but in
a letter which we have received to-night he tells us that
she breaks out into outrageous passions, and urges continually that one argument (in fact the only one which
has the least effect upon her mind), that this person, and
that person, and everybody will talk.

He would have been with us here before this time but
for the chance of giving H. and D. the whooping-cough,
and, on that account, he is miserably perplexed, for he
has no other place to carry them to where they would be
under the care of females on whom he could rely ; and if
he were to leave them with her, he must be obliged to

---

[1] The postmark is December 10, 1806. — Ed.

return to fetch them, for she would not give them up to any one but him; and if he leaves them, and has to return, the worst part of the business will be undone, and he cannot possibly regain his tranquillity. As he says himself: "If I go away without them I am a bird who has struggled himself from off a bird-lime twig, and then finds a string round his leg pulling him back." My brother has written to advise him to bring the boys to us. . . .

He has also given several other reasons which I need not detail. There is one sentence in one of Coleridge's letters which has distressed us very much, and indeed all is distressing; but it is of no use to enter into particulars. He says, after speaking of the weakness of his mind during the struggle: "I cannot, therefore, deny that I both have suffered, and am suffering hourly, to the great injury of my health, which at times alarms me as *dropsical.*" This confirms what we had observed in his appearance; but I trust these bad symptoms will wear away when he is restored to quiet, and settled in some employment. It is his intention to instruct the boys himself one part of the day, and the other part to send them to school to learn writing and arithmetic, and to have the advantage of being with children of their own age. I hope my brother's letter will make him determine to come with them here, and that I shall have to tell you that they are here before the end of this week.

My brother has been frequently with Mr. Gray since he received your letter, and has spoken to him about planting thickets in the grove. He has also frequently paced over and studied the winter garden, and laid some plans; but I will not anticipate what he has to say, for he intends writing to you himself when he has fully settled in his own mind what seems to him the best. We

have had workmen near the house planting the other part
of the enclosed ground. All they have done is already
an improvement. The place looks the better even for
the dead fence, it gives it a snug appearance; and in a
very few years there will be a nice sheltered walk. Mr.
Gray is making the new path. He consulted my brother
respecting the direction it should take.

You were very kind in transcribing the passage from
Pascal. I entirely go along with you in your sentiments
of pleasure and admiration. It is a beautiful passage
indeed — very beautiful; but there is always a something
wanting to the fulness of my satisfaction in the expression of all elevated sentiments in the French language;
and I cannot but think, simple as the conception is, and
suitable as is the expression, that if Pascal had been an
Englishman having the same exalted spirit of piety and
the same genius and had written in English, there would
have been more of dignity in the language of the sentences you have quoted, and they would have been more
impressive. There is a richness and strength in the language of our own great writers that I could never perceive
in the French; but I have not read much in French,
except poetry and common light reading such as everybody
reads, so I have little right to suppose myself a judge.

William has written two other poems, which you will
see when they are printed. He composes frequently in
the grove, and Mr. Gray is going to put him up a bench
under the hollies. We have not yet received a sheet
from the printer. We have had no evening walks lately,
the weather has been so stormy. On Saturday fortnight
we had a terrible wind, which blew down a wind-mill on
the moor. William and I went to Grace Dieu last week.
We were enchanted with the little valley, and its rocks,

and the rocks of Charnwood upon the hill, on which we rested for a long time. Adieu, my dear friend. Accept the best wishes and most affectionate remembrance of all our family. Yours ever,

DOROTHY WORDSWORTH.

CXXXII

Dorothy Wordsworth to Mrs. Clarkson

Monday, Nov. 24th, [1806.]

My dear Friend,

I have at last the comfort of writing to you with a settled hope that poor Coleridge may be restored to himself and his friends. Lost he has been, oppressed even to the death of all his noble faculties (at least for any profitable work either in himself or for the good of others): but, Heaven be praised, his weakness is conquered (I trust it is), and all will be well. Last night William and I walked to the post office (two miles off), tempted through miry roads by the *possibility*, not the *hope*, of a letter; but a letter we found, and I will give you his own words. I dare not believe that he has written to you, or that he will be able to write to anybody, or fulfil any of the duties of friendship, till he has left Keswick. He says, "We have *determined* to part absolutely and finally; Hartley and Derwent to be with me, but to visit their mother as they would do if at a public school." The sentence preceding that I have quoted I will copy, and you may judge from it of the state of his mind, and what he has had to go through — he who is so weak in encountering moral suffering. "I am very glad, deeply conscious as I am of my own weakness, that I had seen you before I came to

Keswick; indeed the excess of my anguish occasioned by the information given me at Penrith was a sort of oracle to me of the necessity of seeing you. Every attack that could be made on human weakness has been made; but, fortunately for so weak a moral being as I am, there was an indelicacy and artifice in them which tho' they did not perceptibly lessen my anguish, yet made my shame continually on the watch, made me see always, and without the possibility of a doubt, that mere selfish desire to have a *rank* in life, and not to be believed to be that which she really was, without the slightest wish that what was should be otherwise, was at the bottom of all. Her temper, and selfishness, her manifest dislike of me (as far as her nature is capable of a *positive* feeling) and her self-encouraged admiration of Southey, as a vindictive feeling in which she delights herself as satirizing me &c &c." He concludes, "I think it probable I shall leave this place for your mansion of sojourn before an answer can reach me." I am sure, my dear friend, you will be comforted when you have read so far. Depend upon it when we know any thing further you shall hear. In the meantime we hope that after he has conquered in the struggle, he will regain his cheerfulness with us, and be able to set himself to some work. . . . William and I have some very pleasant evening walks under the tall trees near the Hall (Sir G.'s house that he is building). We have scarcely missed one evening since the new moon. . . .

CXXXIII

Dorothy Wordsworth to Lady Beaumont

Friday Evening.

My dear Friend,

We are in expectation every moment of poor Coleridge and his son Hartley. They were to leave Kendal on Wednesday, and if they had come as quickly as my brother and Miss Hutchinson, they would have been here last night. Coleridge says that Mrs. Coleridge intends removing southward in the spring, and is to meet him in London with Derwent, who till that time is to stay with her. . . .

He writes calmly and in better spirits. Mrs. Coleridge had been outrageous; but for the last two or three days she had become more quiet, and appeared to be tolerably reconciled to his arrangements. I had a letter from her last week — a strange letter! She wrote just as if all things were going on as usual, and we knew nothing of the intentions of Coleridge. She gives but a very gloomy account of Coleridge's health, but this in her old way, without the least feeling or sense of his sufferings. I do think, indeed, that the state of his health will absolutely prevent him from lecturing. It is a sad pity that he did not formally decline accepting the proposal, as I believe his heart was never in it, and nothing but the dreamy and miserable state of his mind (which prevented him from *doing* anything) kept him from saying that he would *not* lecture.

I trust, gloomy as his own apprehensions are (for he talks of a dropsy in the chest), that when he is more tranquil a tolerable state of health will return. As to drinking brandy, I hope he has already given over that practice; but *here*, I think, he will be tolerably safe, for we shall not have any to set before him, and we should be very loath to comply with his request if he were to ask for it. There may be some danger in the strong beer, which he used formerly to like, but I think, if he is not inclined to manage himself, *we* can manage him, and he will take no harm, while he has not the temptations which variety of company leads him into of taking stimulants to keep him in spirits while he is talking.

My brother, who is writing a long letter to you himself, which you will probably receive the post after this, has had his thoughts full of the winter garden, as you will see. His poetical labours have been at a stand for more than a week. We have had boisterous and very rainy weather, which has kept us chiefly in the house; but yesterday the air was very mild, and to-day the sun shone from nine o'clock in the morning till he set in glory in the west. Then we had the moon, and William and I walked for more than an hour and a half in the grove. The Hall looks exceedingly well by moonlight from the walk near the fish-pond (which, by the bye, adds greatly to the effect of it). The turrets looked very beautiful to-night; great part of the front was in shade, and all the end of the house enlightened.

There is one improvement to this house which seems to be wanted — a spout along the edge of the penthouse, or shed; the rain-drops will otherwise entirely destroy the border of tuft and other flowers; besides, in very rainy weather the walk is often even plashy; and also — another reason for placing a spout — soft water (which might be caught by setting a tub under the spout) is very much needed for household purposes, the pump water being, though excellent, very hard. I have often intended to mention to you, but have forgotten it when I wrote, that in reading my journal of our tour in Scotland, you must bear in mind that it is only *recollections* of the tour, therefore do not wonder if you or Sir George should detect some inaccuracies, often misspelt and even miscalled, for I never looked into a book, and only bore in mind my own remembrance of the sounds as they were pronounced to us. Add to this, that the last part was written nearly two years after we made the journey, and I took no notes. My sister and Miss Hutchinson beg to be affectionately remembered to you. Believe me ever, my dear Lady Beaumont, your grateful and sincere friend,

DOROTHY WORDSWORTH.

Saturday morning. — No Coleridge last night, and it is now twelve o'clock, and he is not arrived; therefore we cannot expect him till the arrival of another coach, and if that be late, he will probably stay all night at Loughborough.

CXXXIV

Dorothy Wordsworth to Lady Beaumont

December 23, 1806.

Coleridge and his son Hartley arrived on Sunday afternoon. My dear Lady Beaumont, the pleasure of welcoming him to your house mingled with our joy, and I think I never was more happy in my life than when we had had him an hour by the fireside: for his looks were much more like his own old self, and though we only talked of common things, and of our friends, we perceived that he was contented in his mind, and had settled things at home to his satisfaction. He has been tolerably well and cheerful ever since, and has begun with his books. Hartley, poor boy! is very happy, and looks uncommonly well. . . . I long to know your opinion and Sir George's of my brother's plan of the winter garden. Coleridge (as we females are also) is much delighted with it, only he *doubts* about the fountain, and he thinks it is possible that an intermingling of birch trees somewhere, on account of the richness of the colour of the naked twigs in winter, might be an advantage; I may add also from myself, that we have often stood for half an hour together at Grasmere, on a still morning, to look at the rain-drops or hoar-frost glittering in sunshine upon the birch twigs; the purple colour and the sparkling drops produce a most enchanting effect. . . . God bless you, my kind good friend. We shall drink a health to you on Christmas Day. You may remember that it is my birthday; but in my inner heart it is never a day of jollity. Believe me, ever yours,

D. WORDSWORTH.

CXXXV

William Wordsworth to Lady Beaumont

[December, 1806.]

My dear Lady Beaumont,

There's penmanship for you! I shall not be able to keep it up to the end in this style, notwithstanding I have the advantage of writing with one of your steel pens with which Miss Hutchinson has just furnished me. I have a long work to go through, but first let me tell you that I was highly gratified by your letter, and I consider the request that I would undertake the laying out your winter garden as a great honour. You kindly desire me not to write, but I cannot enter upon my office till I have had your opinion on my intended plan, and solicited the improvement which your taste and intention, and those of Sir George, may suggest.

Before I explain my ideas I must entreat your patience. I promise you I will be as brief as may be; but, meaning to be minute, I fear I shall be tiresome.

First, then, to begin with the boundary line. Suppose ourselves standing upon the terrace above the new-built wall; that, of course, would be open, and we should look down from it upon the garden; and, winding round upon the left bank, I would plant upon the top of it, in the field, a line of evergreen shrubs intermingled with cypress, to take place of the present *hedges;* and, behind these, a row of firs, such as were likely to grow to the most majestic height. This kind of fence, leaving visible such parts of the cottages as would have the best effect (I mean the beautiful one with ivy, and the other, which is of a very picturesque form, but very shabby surface), I would continue all round the garden, so as to give it the greatest appearance of depth, shelter, and seclusion possible.

This is essential to the *feeling* of the place, with which, indeed, I ought to have begun : and that is of a spot which the winter cannot touch, which should present no image of chilliness, decay, or desolation, when the face of Nature everywhere else is cold, decayed, and desolate. On this account, keeping strictly to the example of the winter garden in the *Spectator*, I should certainly exclude all deciduous trees, whatever variety and brilliancy of colour their foliage might give at certain seasons intermingled with the evergreens, because I think a sufficiency of the same effect may be produced by other means, which would jar less with what should never be out of mind, the sentiment of the place. We will, then, suppose the garden to be shut up within this double and tall fence of evergreen shrubs and trees. Do you remember the lines with which Thomson concludes his *Ode on Solitude?*[1]

> Oh ! let me pierce thy secret cell,
> And in thy deep recesses dwell ;
> Perhaps from Norwood's oak-clad hill,
> When meditation has her fill,
> I just may cast my careless eyes
> Where London's spiry turrets rise,
> Think of its crimes, its cares, its pain,
> Then shield me in the woods again.

In conformity to the spirit of these beautiful lines, I would make one opening, but scarcely more, in this boundary fence, which should present the best view of the most interesting *distant* object.

Having now done with the double evergreen fence, we will begin again with the wall ; and, first, let me say that this wall with its recesses, buttresses, and towers, I very much admire. It should be covered here and there with ivy and pyracanthus (which probably you know), or any other winter plants that bear scarlet berries, or are rich and luxuriant in their leaves and manner of growing.

From the wall, going round by the left, the first thing we meet is a mound of rubbish which should be planted. Then, before we reach the ivied cottage, we come to a perpendicular bank or scar ; this should be planted along the top, in addition to the double evergreen fence mentioned before, with ivy, periwinkle, and other beautiful or brilliant evergreen trailing plants, which should hang

---

[1] Thomson called it a *Hymn on Solitude*. A draft of it was given in a letter to Mallet in July, 1725, and it was first printed in 1729. — Ed.

down and leave the earth visible in different places. From the *sides* of the bank also might start juniper and yew, and it might be sprinkled over with primroses. Coming to the second cottage, this — if not entirely taken away — should be repaired, so as to have nothing of a patchy and worn-out appearance, as it has at present, and planted with ivy; this, and the shrubs and trees, hereafter to conceal so much of the naked wall, as almost to leave it doubtful whether it be a cottage or not.

I do not think that these two cottages would in an unwelcome manner break in upon the feeling of seclusion, if no window looking directly upon the garden be allowed. This second cottage is certainly not *necessary*, and if it were not here nobody would wish for it ; but its irregular and picturesque form, its tall chimney in particular, plead strongly with me for its being retained. I scarcely ever saw a building of its size which would show off ivy to greater advantage. If retained, — which with a view to *what it is to become* I should certainly advise, — it ought to be repaired, and made as little unsightly in its surface as possible, till the trailing plants shall have overspread it. At first I was for taking this cottage away, as it is in such ruinous plight, but now I cannot reconcile myself to the thought; I have such a beautiful image in my mind of what it would be as a supporter to a grove of ivy, anywhere beautiful but particularly so in a winter garden; therefore let it stand.

Following the fence round, we come to the remains of the little quarry (for such I suppose the excavation to be, nearly under the wych-elm cottage) ; I would scratch the bank here, so as to lay bare more of the sand rock, and that in as bold a way as could be done. This rock, or *scar*, like the one before mentioned, I would adorn with trailing plants, and juniper, box, and yew-tree, where a very scanty growth would soon show itself. The next part of the fence we come to in its present state is an unsightly corner, where is an old ugly wall (made still uglier with nettles and rubbish) which has been built to prevent the bank from falling in. Here I would plant, to cover this wall, a hedge of hollies, or some other evergreen, which should not be suffered to grow wildly, but be cropped, making a wall of verdure to ascend up to the roots of the fir-trees that are to be planted upon the top of the bank.

This form of boundary would revive the artificial character of the place in a pleasing way, preparing for a return to the new stone wall; the parts of the whole boundary thus, as you will perceive, either melting into each other quietly, or forming spirited contrasts. I must however not forget that there is here a space of boundary between this unsightly corner (where I would have the holly hedge) and the new stone wall; and this space would be diversified, first by the steps which now descend into the garden, and next, and most beautifully, by a conception which I have of bringing the water — which I am told may be done without much expense — and letting it trickle down the bank about the roots of the wych elm, so as to make if not a waterfall (there might not be enough for that) at least a dripping of water, round which might gather and flourish some of those vivid masses of water plants, a refreshing and beautiful sight in the dead time of the year; and which, when cased in ice, form one of the most enchanting appearances that are peculiar to winter.

In order to be clear I wish to be methodical, at the risk, as I forewarned you, of being tedious. We will therefore begin with the wall once more. This, as the

most artificial, ought to be the most splendid and ornamental part of the garden ; and here I would have,
betwixt the path and the wall, a border edged with boxwood, to receive the earliest and latest flowers. Within
and close to the edging of boxwood, I would first plant a
row of snowdrops, and behind that a row of crocus ; these
would succeed each other. Close under the wall I would
have a row, or fringe, of white lilies, and in front of
this another of daffodils ; these also would succeed
each other, the daffodils coming first ; the middle part
of the border, which must be of good width, to be richly
tufted, or bedded over with hepatica, jonquils, hyacinths,
polyanthuses, auriculas, mezereon, and other spring flowers, and shrubs that blossom early ; and, for the autumn,
Michaelmas-daisy, winter-cherry, china-asters, Michaelmas and Christmas rose, and many other shrubs and
flowers. I mentioned before what I would wish to have
done with the wall itself. The path of which I have been
speaking should wind round the garden mostly near the
boundary line, which would in general be seen or felt as
has been described ; but not always, for in some places,
particularly near the high road, it would be kept out of
sight, so that the imagination might have room to play.
It might perhaps with propriety lead along a second border under the clipped holly hedge ; everywhere else it
should only be accompanied by wild-flowers.

We have done with the circumference ; now for the
interior, which I would diversify in the following manner.
And to begin, as before, with the wall : this fronts nearly
south, and a considerable space before it ought to be
open to the sun, forming a glade, enclosed on the north
side by the wall ; on the east by a ridge of rubbish, to be
planted with shrubs, trees, and flowers ; on the west by

another little long hillock, or ridge of the same kind; and on the south by a line of evergreen shrubs, to run from the southern extremities of the ridges, and to be broken by one or two trees of the cypress kind, which would spire up without excluding the sun from the glade. This I should call the first compartment of the garden, to be characterised by ornament of architecture as in the wall, by showiness and splendour of colours in the flowers (which should be chiefly garden flowers), and in the choice of the shrubs.

In this glade, — if the plan of bringing the water should not be found impracticable, or too expensive, — I would have a stone fountain of simple structure to throw out its stream or even *thread* of water; the stone-work would accord with the wall, and the sparkling water would be in harmony with the bright hues of the flowers and blossoms, and would form a lively contrast to the sober colours of the evergreens, while the murmur in a district where the sound of water (if we except the little trickling that is to be under the wych elm) is nowhere else heard, could not but be soothing and delightful. Shall I venture to say here, by the bye, that I am old-fashioned enough to like in certain places even *jettes d'eau;* I do not mean merely in towns, and among buildings, where I think they always are pleasing, but also among rural scenes where water is scarce. They certainly make a great show out of a little substance, and the diamond drops of light which they scatter round them, and the halos and rainbows which the misty vapour shows in sunshine, and the dewy freshness which it seems to spread through the air, are all great recommendations of them to me; so much so, that, for myself, I should not be ashamed of seeing one here, if a fountain, which is a

thing of more simplicity and dignity, would not answer
every important purpose, and be quite unobjectionable.
If we had a living stream bustling through rocks, as at
Grace Dieu, and could decoy it among our evergreens, I
should not think either of fountain or *jettes d'eau;* but,
alas ! Coleorton is in no favour with the Naiads.

The next compartment (if you look at the accompanying plan you will clearly understand me) is to be a glade
unelaborate and simple, surrounded with evergreens, and
a few scattered in the middle.   N.B. — The former glade
to be entirely open with the fountain ; and of this second
glade so much of the ancient cottage as could be shown
with effect would be the presiding image.   No border or
garden flowers here, but wild-flowers to be scattered
everywhere.   Then (still look at the plan) we come to a
dark thicket or grove, the path winding through it, under
the other cottage ; then the path crosses the outlet where
the door leads into the high road, which door ought to be
entirely concealed, and led up to, under a thick arch of
evergreen.

Proceeding with the paths, we cross the end of a long
alley, of which I shall speak afterwards.   We then are
brought to a small glade or open space, belted round with
evergreens, quite unvaried and secluded.   In this little
glade should be a basin of water inhabited by two gold
or silver fish, if they will live in this climate all the year
in the open air; if not, any others of the most radiant
colours that are more hardy: these little creatures to be
the " genii " of the pool and of the place.   This spot
should be as monotonous in the colour of the trees as
possible.   The enclosure of evergreen, the sky above,
the green grass floor, and the two mute inhabitants, the
only images it should present, unless here and there a

solitary wild-flower. From this glade the path leads on through a few yards of dark thicket, and we come to the little quarry, and this (adopting an idea of yours, which I had from Mr. Craig, and which pleases me much) I should fill with a pool of water that would reflect beautifully the rocks with their hanging plants, the evergreens upon the top, and, shooting deeper than all, the naked spire of the church. The path would wind along on one side of the pool under the ridge of rubbish, the slope of which should be bare and grassy (if it will not in its present state grow smooth grass it should be seeded for that purpose). It should be planted only on the top, and with trees that would grow to the greatest height, in order to give the recess as much depth as possible.

You would appear to be shut up within this bottom, till, turning with the path round a rocky projection of the mound of rubbish, you are fronted by a flight of steps, not before visible, which will be made to bring you out of the quarry close under the clipt holly hedge spoken of before. Here you open into a large glade, one side formed by the trees on the mound of rubbish, the other by the holly hedge, and still further by those other steps near the wych-elm cottage, which now lead down into the garden; these steps, not visible till you come at them, and still further on by the principal object in the glade, the waterfall, for so I will call it, from the root of the wych elm.

Having passed through this glade, you go on a few steps through a thicket, and before you come to the new-built wall you cross the other end of the alley spoken of before, — this alley to run down from the boundary path the whole length of the garden in this part, as you will see in the plan. The alley to be quite straight, the ground perfectly level, shaded with evergreens; laurels I think the best, as they grow tall and so much faster than any other evergreen I know; the floor not gravelled, but green, which, when the trees overshadow the walk, would become mossy, so that the whole would be still, unvaried, and cloistral, soothing and not stirring the mind, or tempting it out of itself. The upper end of this alley should appear to be closed in by trees, the lower to be terminated by a rising bank of green turf which would catch the light, and present a cheerful image of sunshine; as it would always appear to do, whether the sun shone or not, to a person walking in the alley when the vista shall have become a complete shade.

Out of this alley, towards the middle of it, on the left side, should be a small blind path leading to a bower, such as you will find described in the beginning of Chaucer's poem of *The Flower and the Leaf*, and also in the beginning of the *Assembly of Ladies*. This little parlour of verdure should be paved with different-coloured pebbles, chiefly white, which are to be found in great plenty sprinkling the sandy roads of this country; these wrought into a careless mosaic would contrast livelily, if the white were predominant, with the evergreen walls and ceiling of this apartment. All around should be a mossed seat, and a small stone table in the midst. I am at a loss what trees to choose for this bower. Hollies (which would be clipped in the inside, so that the prickles would be no annoyance) I should like best, but they grow so slowly.

I have now mentioned everything of consequence. You will see by the plan that there were several spaces to be covered with evergreens, where there might or might not be bypaths, as you should like — one by way of specimen

I have chalked out (see the plan) along the foot of one of the ridges of rubbish. These intermediate plantations, when they get up, will entirely break any unpleasing formality, which the alley and bower, or any other parts of the garden, might otherwise give to it, when looked at from above. If you add to these features or passages a seat in some sunny spot, or perhaps a small shed or alcove, you have introduced as much variety within the compass of an acre as my fancy is capable of suggesting.

I had some thoughts that it might be possible to scoop out of the sandy rock a small cell or cavern on the stony side of the quarry, but the rock there is not continuous or firm enough. That part of the rock on which the decayed cottage stands, as it is much firmer, might perhaps admit of something of this kind with good effect. Thus laid out, the winter garden would want no variety of colouring beyond what the flowers and blossoms of many of the shrubs, such as mezereon and laurustinas, and the scarlet berries of the evergreen trees, and the various shades of green in their foliage would give. The place is to be consecrated to Winter, and I have only spoken of it in that point of view, confining myself to the time when the deciduous trees are not in leaf. But it would also be a delightful retreat from the summer sun. We think, in this climate only, of evergreens as a shelter from the cold, but they are chiefly natives of hot climates, and abound most there. The woods of Africa are full of them.

A word before I conclude: I have only given the garden two settled inhabitants, the pair of fishes in the pool; but, in the early spring, bees — much more attended to in the stillness of that season — would murmur round the flowers and blossoms, and all the winter long it would be enlivened by birds, which would resort thither for covert. We never pass in our evening walk the cluster of holly bushes, under one of which Mr. Craig has placed my seat, but we unsettle a number of small birds which have taken shelter there for the night. The whole bush seems in a flutter with them, while they are getting out of it. Mentioning holly, I must defend Mr. Craig for having fallen in with my proposal of placing me a seat there. Since Burns's time the holly has been a poetical tree as well as the laurel. His muse in the poem of *The Vision* takes leave of him in this manner —

> " And wear thou this " — she solemn said,
> And bound the holly round my head:
> The polished leaves, and berries red,
>   Did rustling play;
> And, like a passing thought, she fled
>   In light away.

With respect to trees, shrubs, and flowers, Mr. Craig has a considerable collection. You might add to these by your suggestions, and it might be worth your while for this purpose to take the trouble of visiting some large nursery garden in the neighbourhood of London, and to consult some of your friends.

I am sensible that I have written a very pretty romance in this letter, and when I look at the ground in its present state, and think of what it must continue to be for some years, I am afraid that you will call me an enthusiast and a visionary. I am willing to submit to this, as I am seriously convinced that if proper pains were taken to select healthy and vigorous plants, and to forward their growth, less than six years would transform it into something that might be looked at with pleasure;

fifty would make it a paradise. O that I could convert my little Dorothy into a fairy to realise the whole in half a day!

As to the thickets under the forest trees in the walks about the Hall, I have pressed Mr. Craig, and his wishes are good; but lately he has seemed fully occupied: and, to speak the truth, as he has very carefully given up the winter garden to my control, I do not like to intermeddle much with the other. It looks like taking the whole of the intellectual part from him, which would dispirit him, and be both unjust and impolitic, as he has a good taste, and seems a truly respectable man. He has already, in a general way, had my opinion, which I will continue at all favourable opportunities to remind him of. He has constructed the new walk with judgment, and a sweet spot it is. There are a few hollies here which have an excellent effect; I wish almost the whole hedge to be made of them, as they would be comfortable in winter, excluding the field, which is cold, and of no beauty ; and in summer, by being intermingled with wild roses, and hung with honeysuckles, they would be rich and delightful.

I never saw so beautiful a shrub as one tall holly which we had near a house we occupied in Somersetshire; it was attired with woodbine, and upon the very top of the topmost bough that "looked out at the sky" was one large honeysuckle flower, like a star, crowning the whole. Few of the more minute rural appearances please me more than these, of one shrub or flower lending its ornaments to another. There is a pretty instance of this kind now to be seen near Mr. Craig's new walk; a bramble which has furnished a wild rose with its green leaves, while the rose in turn with its red hips has to the utmost of its power embellished the bramble. Mr. Graham in his

Birds of Scotland has an exquisite passage upon this subject, with which I will conclude —

> The hawthorn there,
> With moss and lichens grey, dies of old age.
> Up to the upmost branches climbs the rose
> And mingles with the fading blooms of May,
> While round the brier the honeysuckle wreaths
> Entwine, and with their sweet perfume embalm
> The dying rose.

My dear Lady Beaumont, I have now written you the longest letter I ever wrote in my life; Heaven forbid that I should often draw so largely upon the patience of my friends.   Farewell,

W. W.

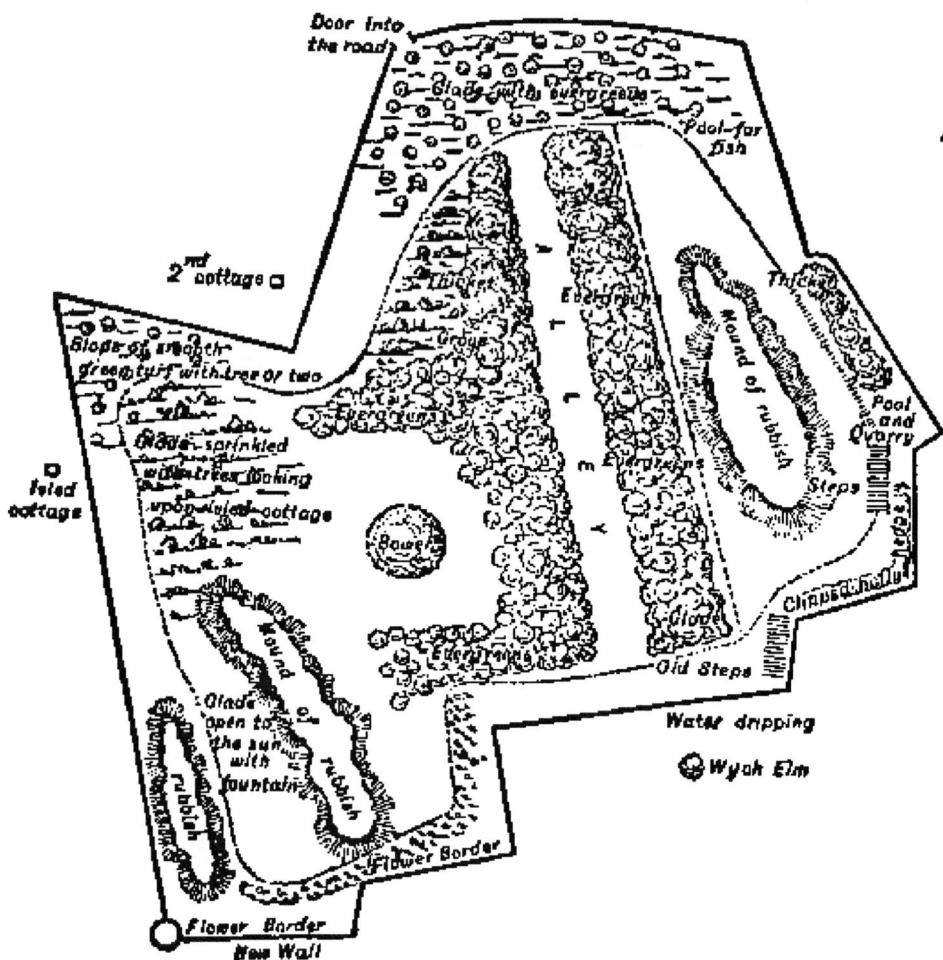

Door into
the road
Glade with evergreens
Pool for fish
2nd cottage
Thicket
Evergreen
Thicket
Mound of rubbish
Pool and Quarry
Slope of smooth green turf with tree or two
Group
Steps
Glade sprinkled with trees looking upon 2nd cottage
Evergreen
Evergreens
1st cottage
Bough
Clipped holly hedge
Glade
Evergreens
Mound of rubbish
Old Steps
Water dripping
Glade open to the sun with fountain
rubbish
Wych Elm
Flower Border
Flower Border
New Wall

PLAN OF THE WINTER GARDEN

285

1807

CXXXVI

William Wordsworth to Walter Scott

COLEORTON, January 20, 1807.

. . . Could you furnish me, by application to any of your Gaelic friends, a phrase in that language which would take its place in the following verse of eight syllables, and have the following meaning?

> Lega, lega, thus did he cry,
> Lega, lega, most eagerly
> Thus did he cry, and thus did pray;
> And what he meant was, " Keep away,
> And leave me to myself."

The above is part of a little poem which I have written on a Highland story told me by an eye-witness.[1] . . .

CXXXVII

Mary Wordsworth to Mrs. Clarkson

COLEORTON, January 20th, [1807.]

My dear Friend,

. . . We hear nothing of a house in the North of England. I do not see that any is likely to be vacant except Mr. Jackson's,[2] in case the Southeys do not give up their

---

[1] See *The Blind Highland Boy.* — Ed.
[2] Greta Hall, Keswick. — Ed.

intention of leaving it, and that Mrs. Coleridge removes southward. For my part I shall be reconciled to it by *necessity;* but pleasant as the situation of that house is, I never liked it, and I have always thought that I had rather live in any other part of the Lake country than so near to Keswick as that house. At any rate we shall go into the North next summer. . . . Dorothy is grown hardy, and a delightful lively creature she is, and far less trouble than John was at her age. As to your old friend honest John (who by the bye remembers you very well, and how he used to go and see you) I must say that at times he is very wilful and unmanageable, which makes him dangerous from his exceeding strength. Whenever he is disposed to quarrel with his sister (which is not seldom) he uses blows, and not contented with his own heavy hand, when he is very angry he takes up whatever is nearest to him, stool, chair, table, stick, or even poker. Yet he has a sweet temper, and certainly the most delightful smile I ever saw. Dorothy looks exceedingly lively, and has great variety in her countenance; but the expression of John's is far richer. You remember his dear uncle John's smile. Johnny's reminds me of it, that is in the quantity of effect which it produces; but it is very different. Little Thomas, God bless him! is neither boastful nor boasted of, but he wins his way silently into all hearts. He has a quiet, sensible, grave smile, yet full of light, which fixes in his pretty blue eyes; and while he smiles he points his tongue, and puts it out upon his under lip. We call it a serpent tongue, it moves about, and changes so prettily. John's used to occupy the whole den of his mouth, and his father called it the Dragon of Wantley. . . .

CXXXVIII

Dorothy Wordsworth to Lady Beaumont, sent from Coleorton

Saturday Morning, [Postmark, Jan. 27, 1807.]

My dear Friend,

We should have been very unjust to you if we had not felt ourselves as free as before. We were only induced to mention the circumstance that, in case any complaints should be made to you, you might be prepared to meet these with a perfect knowledge of the state of the case as far as we were concerned. And I must take this opportunity of repeating again that we are as perfectly at home as ever we were in our lives, and have never once suffered from that sense of difference or any of those little wants which you speak of.

We use all that you have left for us with freedom exactly as if it were our own : only, believe me, with more pleasure for your sakes. It is a most delightful morning. My brother and sister are gone to the winter garden. He visits the workmen generally twice in the day, and one of us accompanies him. When it is pleasant we afterwards walk in the grove, hundreds and hundreds of times have we paced from one end of that walk to the other. When the air is calm we take the whole of the walk, but in windy weather we stop before we come to the pond. The seat under the hollies is a great comfort to us.

My brother makes no complaints of Mr. Craig; he is very willing to give his opinion respecting the manner in which my brother's ideas are to be executed. I believe he may be inwardly rather petted; for he gives no *opinion* whatever; and we had long ago found out that his character was exactly what you describe — very obstinate, and somewhat self-conceited; withal industrious, ingenious, and faithful. You have misunderstood me respecting the floor of the alley. It is simply meant to be *green-grown*, which it will in a short time be with short moss after there is any shade. The moss will not be soft; it will be merely a gravel walk mossed over. My brother wishes the alley not merely to be screened at the sides but over-arched. Alas! it will need a long time for this, however tall and strong the evergreens may be when they are planted. Coleridge is pretty well at present, though ailing at some time in every day. He does not take such strong stimulants as he did, but I fear he will never be able to leave them off entirely. He drinks ale at night and mid-morning and dinner-time; and, according to your desire, we have got some from Loughborough. Hartley is thoroughly happy. He spends a great deal of time in Mr. Ward's room; sometimes drinks tea and dines with him, for Mr. Ward takes to him exceedingly. Little Dorothy also continues to be in high favour with him.

Adieu, my good friend. Believe me, ever affectionately yours,

D. WORDSWORTH.

CXXXIX

A Postscript to the Same Letter

Excuse haste. Mr. Bailey is very attentive and kind to us. I have opened my letter to ask you if you have Cowper's translation of Homer. We do not want it unless you have it, or have a desire to purchase it. Coleridge says that the *last* edition of Bruce's *Travels*[1] is a

[1] *Travels between the Years 1768 and 1773, through Part of Africa, Syria, Egypt, and Arabia into Abyssinia, to discover the Source of the Nile* (1805). — Ed.

book that you ought by all means to have. He does not know the name of the editor, but it is published by Longman. If you purchase it we should be very glad to have the reading of it. William and I were in the inside of the new house yesterday. The upper rooms are very much nearer being finished than when we saw them last. William has thought about the laying out of the piece of ground before the house, but he has not yet made up his mind.

CXL

William Wordsworth to Lady Beaumont

[Postmark, Feb. 3, 1807.]

My dear Lady Beaumont,

Lord Redesdale's letter contains several things that will be of use to us; I must however make two or three remarks upon it. Our garden is to be a winter garden, a place of comfort and pleasure from the fall of the leaf to its return, nearly half of the year. Great part of this time you now perhaps pass in London, but if you live that probably will not always be so. Infirmities come on with age, that render tranquillity every year more welcome and more necessary. Lord Redesdale seems to have overlooked this, as far as the greatest part of his letter applies to a summer garden. His plan of avoiding expense in digging, weeding, and mowing — particularly the last — may be carried too far; a wilderness of shrubs is a delightful thing as part of a garden, but only as a part. You must have open space of lawn, or you lose all the beauty of outline in the different tufts or islands of shrubs, and even in many instances in their individual forms. This lawn cannot be had without mowing.

Digging and weeding ought to be avoided as much as possible; and his method is a good one.

With his Lordship, I should wish my strength to lie in perennial plants and flowers; but a small quantity of annuals, such as flower very late, may with little trouble and great advantage be interspersed among the others. His objection to an over-arched walk of evergreens, except for summer, at first appears well founded; but there is an oversight in it. In summer you may have a shade of *deciduous* trees or plants; but what are you to do in April or March, and sometimes even in February, when the heat and glare of the sun are often oppressive, notwithstanding the general cloudiness of our climate? For my own part, I can say with truth that in the month of April I have passed many an hour under the shade of a green holly, glad to find it in my walk, and unwilling to quit it because I had not courage to face the sun. Our winter garden is four parts out of five planned for the sun. If the alley or bower, the only parts exclusively designed for shade, should appear too damp or gloomy, you pass them by; but I am sure this will not always be the case; and even in those times when it is so, will not a peep into that gloom make you enjoy the sunshine the more? But the alley I designed for March and April, when there is often a heat in the sun, and a conflict of sun and wind, which is both unpleasant and dangerous, and from which neither walls nor bare leafless trees can protect you. . . . His Lordship's practical rules about making walks, propagating plants, etc., seem all to be excellent; and I much like his plan of a covered walk of vines, but not for our own winter garden.

I shall read the whole to Mr. Craig. He and I propose to go to a nursery garden about fourteen miles off to procure such plants as we are most likely to want. I would not have them bought of any great size; it is a needless expense, and surely it will be some pleasure to see them grow up as from infancy. I never saw any American plants growing with their bog-earth about them, and know not whether it has an unsightly appearance. If not, it certainly would be advisable to have some of the most brilliant in the first compartment of the garden, rather than under the wall. This is to be the most splendid and adorned. I have removed the rubbish from under the wall; part of it is thrown upon the ridge running from the wall on the right, and part against the straight hedge between the two ivied cottages. I am afraid we must give up the fountain, as Mr. Craig tells me the quantity of water will be too small to produce any effect even in winter. This consideration does not sway with me much; but Captain B—— told me there would be little or *none* sometimes in summer, and upon reflection I think this would be so melancholy, and would make such open declaration of the poverty of the land, that it is better to abandon the idea. We may easily have enough for as many pools or basins as we like.

Before I conclude I will add two or three words in further explanation of my general plan. The first compartment, as I have said, is to be as splendid as possible; to be divided by a fence of shrubbery twelve feet in width, interspersed with cypress. My present thought is to have that side of this fence which looks towards the first compartment to consist probably altogether of laurustinus rather than of a variety of plants; plants in rows or masses in this way always are more rich and impressive. The next compartment, of which the ivied cottage is to be the master object, I meant, in contrast to the

preceding one, to present the most delightful assemblage
of English winter shrubs and flowers, mingled with some
foreign shrubs, as are so common in English cottage
gardens as to be almost naturalised. Then comes the
second cottage, which I cannot find in my heart to pull
down; and I am sure it may be repaired in a manner
that will give no offence. I do not mean the encircling
path to pass *through* the glade with the gold and silver
fish, but only on one side of it, so that it may be entered
or not at pleasure. The quarry will be a delightful spot;
but this, with the English spire that will so feelingly
adorn it, I would have in all its ornaments entirely English. From it we should pass to the clipped holly or boxwood hedge and its accompanying glade, and this should
be mixed, and elaborate in its ornaments : something mid-
way betwixt the compartment under the wall and the rest
of the garden.

Farewell. Most affectionately yours, and Sir George's,

WM. WORDSWORTH.

CXLI

Dorothy Wordsworth to Lady Beaumont

COLEORTON, Sunday Evening.
[Postmark, Feb. 17, 1807.]

My dear Friend,

What reason have we not to bless the Poets, our friends
and companions in solitude or sorrow, who elevate our
thoughts beyond our weak poor selves, and him chiefly
who was your sister's consolation, that holy bard, and
greatest of men! I often think of the happy evening
when, by your fireside, my brother read to us the first

book of the *Paradise Lost*, and not without many hopes
that we may again have the same pleasure together.   We
received the books a week ago, all but Park's *Travels*,[1]
which, the bookseller informs us, are out of print, adding
that a new edition would be out in a fortnight.   We have
all already to thank you for a great deal of delight which
we have received from them.

In the first place, my brother and sister have read the
Life of Colonel Hutchinson,[2] which is a most valuable and
interesting book.   My brother speaks of it with unqualified approbation, and he intends to read it over again.
I wait for the time when the reading this work is to fall
to my share, with great patience.   I shall next begin with
Barrow's *Travels*,[3] and I have not quite finished the Anecdotes of Frederick,[4] which I find exceedingly amusing,
and instructive also, as giving a lively portrait of the
hard-heartedness, and selfishness, and servility of the
courtiers of a tyrant, and of the unsatisfactoriness of
such a life.

For more than a week we have had the most delightful weather.   If William had but waited a few days, it
would have been no anticipation when he said to you the
" songs of spring were in the grove," for all this week the
birds have chanted from morn till evening, — larks,
blackbirds, thrushes, and far more than I can name ; and
the busy rooks have joined their happy voices.

[1] *Travels in the Interior Districts of Africa, in 1795, 1796, and
1797*, by Mungo Park (1799). — Ed.

[2] *Memoirs of the Life of Colonel Hutchinson* (1746). — Ed.

[3] *Travels in South Africa*, by Sir John Barrow (1800–1804). — Ed.

[4] Probably *Original Anecdotes of Frederick the Second, King of
Prussia, and of his Family, his Court, his Ministers, his Academies,
and his Literary Friends*, by Dicadowne Thiebault.   Translated from
the French, 2 vols.   London (1805). — Ed.

As soon as dinner was over to-day, Coleridge, Miss
Hutchinson, my brother, and I set forward upon a ram-
ble through Spring Wood; then we came to a cottage at
the edge of another wood, which, I believe, does not
belong to Sir George (I have forgotten the name of
the wood), but I dare say you will recollect the spot.
The cottage stands so sweetly in a sloping green field,
which is enclosed and sheltered by the woods in a semi-
circle. We went still further, and saw many traces of
the coming spring, two or three primroses amongst the
honeysuckles, but what was most pleasant of all to us,
the paths were in most places perfectly dry, and we hope
that we shall henceforth be able frequently to wander in
the woods.

I must not forget to tell you that we have discovered
a favourite cottage of yours within this fortnight, and
visited it several times — the little dwelling under two
holly-trees, about a hundred yards from the wayside,
going to Mr. Bailey's. The situation of the cottage is
beautiful; the peep of the lake (lake I will call it here,
for it looks exactly like one) is very sweet, and the village, when you turn your eyes to the other side, has a
very cheerful appearance. It gave us great satisfaction,
when we were sitting with the old man and his wife by
their fireside, to hear them let out the history of their
love for the holly-trees. He told us how long ago he had
planted them (" when he was a *young youth* going to service "), and that they were now a shelter for his house,
and nothing could prevail upon him to part with them.
You can hardly conceive with what pride he directed our
attention to the richness of the berries, and at the same
time lamented that some idle boys had robbed one tree
of its prettiest branches, which arched over, and almost

touched the cottage window; he would not have had it cut away for half a guinea.

We longed not for *those* trees, but for half a score as beautiful in the winter garden. Such a sight neither you nor we can hope to see there; but a very few years will, I doubt not, make it a delicious winter retreat. When the shrubs and trees once get forward they will begin to look pretty, and the situation and the form of the ground is such that it is already sheltered and warm without the help of trees. The men work industriously, I am sure, for we never find them idle; but little seems yet to be done, the labour having been all employed in clearing away, removing rubbish, and digging soil out for the border. My brother thinks that, by all means, the terrace should be terminated by another tower. He is here very happy in his employment, and I assure you that you need not give yourself a moment's care about interrupting him in his poetical labours; for those will and must go on when he begins, and any interruption, such as attending to the progress of the workmen, and planning the garden, is of the greatest use to him.

After a certain time the progress is by no means proportioned to the labour in composition, and if he is called from it by other thoughts, he returns to it with ten times the pleasure, and his work goes on proportionally more rapidly. He and Mr. Craig intend to visit the nursery at Nottingham next week, or the week following. It was a most kind and friendly deed when Sir George wrote to Coleridge. He had begun to write several days before he received Sir George's letter; but I do not know how long it might have been before he would have been able to finish the letter. At some future time my brother hopes to have it in his power to profit from Sir George's kindness; he is very proud of such mutual records of their friendship; and I need not say what a grace and a value one of Sir George's beautiful sketches would add to any volume of poems; nor (what would be of more importance in Sir George's feelings) the great delight that we all in common by our own fireside should receive from it. Adieu, my dear Lady Beaumont. Believe me, with sincerest gratitude, your affectionate friend,

D. WORDSWORTH.

CXLII

Dorothy Wordsworth to Mrs. Clarkson

COLEORTON, February, Monday Morning,
I believe the 17th, [1807.]

My dear Friend,

You can scarcely conceive how much pleasure your
last letter gave us; but I wish you would not go to
Church so often (I am not going to disturb your religious
sentiments, or to argue against going to Church in general; for we are become regular churchgoers, that is, we
take it by turns, two at a time, and always two every
Sunday when the weather will permit): but I do think
that you have no business at Church in winter, and that
you are more likely to catch cold there than anywhere
else.   I speak seriously that I did not read without alarm
that you had been at church four successive Sundays,
though no doubt the pleasure of knowing that you had
done so without injury was inexpressibly great.   I have
taken up the pen after half an hour's absence.   Coleridge
called me up stairs to read a letter from Mrs. C. who,
poor woman! is almost frantic, being now convinced that
C. is determined not to live with her again, which she
never fully believed before; though she herself, as far as
words could go, had fully assented to it.   I have been
agitated by the letter, and the thoughts which it led to.
Coleridge has determined to make his home with us; but
where?   There is no house vacant in the North, and we
cannot spend another winter in the cottage, nor even a
summer with Coleridge and his two boys, therefore how
can we go again into the North this summer?   Besides
there would be something very unpleasant (not to say

indelicate, for that in a case of *necessity* might be got over) in going so near to Mrs. Coleridge immediately after their separation; for, after she has been with C. at Ottery, she intends to return to Greta Hall, and remain there as long as the Southeys do.

At present, after the short consideration we have given the matter, it seems as if we ought to seek out a ready-furnished house in this neighbourhood, or further south. Coleridge had an idea that S.[1] intended leaving Keswick in the autumn, in which case, he wished to have the house; and we consented to take it — though *very very* reluctantly — Mary and I having many objections to Keswick, and a hundred more to taking Mrs. C.'s place in that house. But in consideration of Coleridge's inclinations, the convenience of having his books already there, and for the sake of Mrs. Wilson and Hartley, we had consented; but, as Mrs. C.'s letter informs C. that Southey has no thought of leaving Keswick, it is out of the question, and we are all right glad in our hearts to be released. Perhaps we might have a house near you. . . . As to poor Mrs. Coleridge, I cannot but pity her, because she *does* suffer, though I feel and know that wounded pride, and the world's remarks, are all that give her pain. . . .

William is engaged in superintending the making of a winter garden for Lady B. Her idea she took from one of Addison's papers in the *Spectator*, but the plan, and I may say the *invention*, is entirely William's. A beautiful picture, or romance, it is; and, when time has helped the work, it will be a substantial and true paradise. . . . Coleridge often talks of you, and wishes to write; but

---

[1] Southey. — Ed.

he never writes any letters except from necessity, and I believe will not be able to do so, till he has seen Mrs. Coleridge again, and parted from her for ever; by "for ever" I mean made it public, and taken up his home elsewhere. It is his wish that she should be in such a state of mind as to be able to visit her in a friendly way. . . .

CXLIII

William Wordsworth to Walter Scott

2nd March, 1807.

. . . I am very glad to hear that Flodden Field is to be celebrated by you.[1] . . .

CXLIV

William Wordsworth to Thomas De Quincey

36 Thornhaugh Street, LONDON, Sat. 5 o'clock.
[Postmark, April 25, 1807.]

Dear Sir,

I have but this moment received your letter which has travelled half the world over after me. I have only time to say that Mr. Coleridge though at present in Town will not be here many days — but if you come hither in the course of ten days or a fortnight you will find me here, and I shall be most happy to see you. I have not time for more.

Yours sincerely,

W. WORDSWORTH.

[1] Referring to *Marmion.* — Ed.

CXLV

William Wordsworth to Thomas De Quincey

36 Thornhaugh St., 28th April.[1]

My dear Sir,

The time of my leaving Town does not depend upon myself, but a gentleman who accompanies me into Leicestershire where I have been resident for the last 6 or 7 months. The time of his departure is uncertain but he hopes to be ready to attend me on Tuesday next. I write now to say that if you are not in Town before Sunday I shall in all probability have left this house; however if you do not find me here, I shall be at the Rev. Christopher Wordsworth's, Essex Place, Lambeth. You will most likely meet with Mr. Coleridge, as he has been detained in Town longer than he expected. I am very happy at the prospect of seeing you, for believe me I have been much interested in you. I am, dear Sir, in great haste, your sincere friend,

W. WORDSWORTH.

CXLVI

William Wordsworth to Lady Beaumont

COLEORTON, May 21, 1807.

My dear Lady Beaumont,

Though I am to see you so soon, I cannot but write a word or two, to thank you for the interest you take in my poems, as evinced by your solicitude about their immediate reception. I write partly to thank you for this and to express the pleasure it has given me, and partly to remove

---

[1] [Postmark obscure, but it must be 1807.]

any uneasiness from your mind which the disappointments you sometimes meet with in this labour of love may occasion. I see that you have many battles to fight for me, — more than, in the ardour and confidence of your pure and elevated mind, you had ever thought of being summoned to; but be assured that this opposition is nothing more than what I distinctly foresaw that you and my other friends would have to encounter. I say this, not to give myself credit for an eye of prophecy, but to allay any vexatious thoughts on my account which this opposition may have produced in you.

It is impossible that any expectations can be lower than mine concerning the immediate effect of this little work upon what is called the public. I do not here take into consideration the envy and malevolence, and all the bad passions which always stand in the way of a work of any merit from a living poet; but merely think of the pure absolute honest ignorance, in which all worldlings of every rank and situation must be enveloped, with respect to the thoughts, feelings, and images, on which the life of my poems depends. The things which I have taken, whether from within or without, what have they to do with routs, dinners, morning calls, hurry from door to door, from street to street, on foot or in carriage; with Mr. Pitt or Mr. Fox, Mr. Paul or Sir Francis Burdett, the Westminster election or the borough of Honiton? In a word, — for I cannot stop to make my way through the hurry of images that present themselves to me, — what have they to do with endless talking about things nobody cares anything for except as far as their own vanity is concerned, and this with persons they care nothing for but as their vanity or *selfishness* is concerned? what have they to do (to say all at once) with a life without love? In such a life there can be no thought; for we have no thought (save thoughts of pain) but as far as we have love and admiration.

It is an awful truth, that there neither is, nor can be, any genuine enjoyment of poetry among nineteen out of twenty of those persons who live, or wish to live, in the broad light of the world; among those who either are, or are striving to make themselves, people of consideration in society. This is a truth, and an awful one, because to be incapable of a feeling of poetry, in my sense of the word, is to be without love of human nature and reverence for God.

Upon this I shall insist elsewhere; at present let me confine myself to my object, which is to make you, my dear friend, as easy-hearted as myself with respect to these poems. Trouble not yourself upon their present reception; of what moment is that compared with what I trust is their destiny? to console the afflicted; to add sunshine to daylight, by making the happy happier; to teach the young and the gracious of every age to see, to think, and feel; and, therefore, to become more actively and securely virtuous; this is their office, which I trust they will faithfully perform, long after we (that is, all that is mortal of us) are mouldered in our graves. I am well aware how far it would seem to many I overrate my own exertions, when I speak in this way, in direct connection with the volume I have just made public.

I am not, however, afraid of such censure, insignificant as probably the majority of those poems would appear to very respectable persons. I do not mean London wits and witlings, for these have too many foul passions about them to be respectable, even if they had more intellect than the benign laws of Providence will allow to such a heartless existence as theirs is ; but grave, kindly-natured, worthy persons, who would be pleased if they could. I hope that these volumes are not without some recommendations, even for readers of this class : but their imagination has slept ; and the voice which is the voice of my poetry, without imagination, cannot be heard.

Leaving these, I was going to say a word to such readers as Mr. ———. Such ! — how would he be offended if he knew I considered him only as a representative of a class, and not an unique ! " Pity," says Mr. ———, " that so many trifling things should be admitted to obstruct the view of those that have merit." Now, let this candid judge take, by way of example, the sonnets, which, probably, with the exception of two or three other poems, for which I will not contend, appear to him the most trifling, as they are the shortest. I would say to him, omitting things of higher consideration, there is one thing which must strike you at once, if you will only read these poems, viz. that those *To Liberty*, at least, have a connection with, or a bearing upon, each other ; and, therefore, if individually they want weight, perhaps, as a body, they may not be so deficient. At least, this ought to induce you to suspend your judgment, and qualify it so far as to allow that the writer aims at least at comprehensiveness.

But, dropping this, I would boldly say at once, that these sonnets, while they each fix the attention upon some important sentiment, separately considered, do, at the same time, collectively make a poem on the subject of civil liberty and national independence, which, either for simplicity of style or grandeur of moral sentiment, is, alas ! likely to have few parallels in the poetry of the present day. Again, turn to the " Moods of my own Mind." There is scarcely a poem here of above thirty

lines, and very trifling these poems will appear to many ;
but, omitting to speak of them individually, do they not,
taken collectively, fix the attention upon a subject eminently poetical, viz., the interest which objects in Nature
derive from the predominance of certain affections, more
or less permanent, more or less capable of salutary
renewal in the mind of the being contemplating these
objects? This is poetic, and essentially poetic. And
why? Because it is creative.

But I am wasting words, for it is nothing more than
you know ; and if said to those for whom it is intended,
it would not be understood.

I see by your last letter that Mrs. Fermor has entered
into the spirit of these "Moods of my own Mind." Your
transcript from her letter gave me the greatest pleasure;
but I must say that even she has something yet to receive
from me. I say this with confidence, from her thinking
that I have fallen below myself in the sonnet beginning —

With ships the sea was sprinkled far and nigh.

As to the other which she objects to, I will only observe
that there is a misprint in the last line but two —

And *though* this wilderness

for

And *through* this wilderness —

that makes it unintelligible. This latter sonnet, for many
reasons (though I do not abandon it), I will not now
speak of ; but upon the other, I could say something
important in conversation, and will attempt now to illustrate it by a comment, which, I feel, will be inadequate to

convey my meaning. There is scarcely one of my poems which does not aim to direct the attention to some moral sentiment, or to some general principle, or law of thought, or of our intellectual constitution. For instance, in the present case, who is there that has not felt that the mind can have no rest among a multitude of objects, of which it either cannot make one whole, or from which it cannot single out one individual, whereupon may be concentrated the attention, divided among or distracted by a multitude? After a certain time, we must either select one image or object, which must put out of view the rest wholly, or must subordinate them to itself while it stands forth as a head:

> Now glowed the firmament
> With living sapphires! Hesperus, that *led*
> The starry host, rode brightest ; till the moon,
> Rising in clouded majesty, at length,   '
> Apparent *Queen*, unveiled *her peerless* light,
> And o'er the dark her silver mantle threw.

Having laid this down as a general principle, take the case before us. I am represented in the sonnet as casting my eyes over the sea, sprinkled with a multitude of ships, like the heavens with stars. My mind may be supposed to float up and down among them, in a kind of dreamy indifference with respect either to this or that one, only in a pleasurable state of feeling with respect to the whole prospect. " Joyously it showed." This continued till that feeling may be supposed to have passed away, and a kind of comparative listlessness or apathy to have succeeded, as at this line,

> Some veering up and down, one knew not why.

All at once, while I am in this state, comes forth an object, an individual ; and my mind, sleepy and unfixed, is awakened and fastened in a moment.

> Hesperus, that *led*
> The starry host,

is a poetical object, because the glory of his own nature gives him the pre-eminence the moment he appears. He calls forth the poetic faculty, receiving its exertions as a tribute. But this ship in the sonnet may, in a manner still more appropriate, be said to come upon a mission of the poetic spirit, because, in its own appearance and attributes, it is barely sufficiently distinguished to rouse the creative faculty of the human mind to exertions at all times welcome, but doubly so when they come upon us when in a state of remissness. The mind being once fixed and roused, all the rest comes from itself; it is merely a lordly ship, nothing more:

> This ship was nought to me, nor I to her,
> Yet I pursued her with a lover's look.

My mind wantons with grateful joy in the exercise of its own powers, and, loving its own creation,

> This ship to all the rest I did prefer,

making her a sovereign or a regent, and thus giving body and life to all the rest ; mingling up this idea with fondness and praise —

> where she comes the winds must stir ;

and concluding the whole with

> On went she, and due north her journey took;

thus taking up again the reader with whom I began, letting him know how long I must have watched this favourite vessel, and inviting him to rest his mind as mine is resting.

Having said so much upon mere fourteen lines, which Mrs. Fermor did not approve, I cannot but add a word or two upon my satisfaction in finding that my mind has so much in common with hers, and that we participate so many of each other's pleasures. I collect this from her having singled out the two little poems, *The Daffodils*,[1] and *The Rock crowned with Snowdrops*.[2] I am sure that whoever is much pleased with either of these quiet and tender delineations must be fitted to walk through the recesses of my poetry with delight, and will there recognise, at every turn, something or other in which, and over which, it has that property and right which knowledge and love confer. The line,

> Come, blessed barrier, etc.,

in the sonnet upon *Sleep*, which Mrs. F. points out, had before been mentioned to me by Coleridge, and, indeed, by almost everybody who had heard it, as eminently beautiful. My letter (as this second sheet, which I am obliged to take, admonishes me) is growing to an enormous length ; and yet, saving that I have expressed my calm confidence that these poems will live, I have said nothing which has a particular application to the object of it, which was to remove all disquiet from your mind on account of the condemnation they may at present incur from that portion of my contemporaries who are called the public.

[1] See *I wandered lonely as a cloud*, composed in 1804. — Ed.
[2] See *Who fancied what a pretty sight*, composed in 1803. — Ed.

I am sure, my dear Lady Beaumont, if you attach any importance to it, it can only be from an apprehension that it may affect me, upon which I have already set you at ease ; or from a fear that this present blame is ominous of their future or final destiny. If this be the case, your tenderness for me betrays you. Be assured that the decision of these persons has nothing to do with the question ; they are altogether incompetent judges. These people, in the senseless hurry of their idle lives, do not *read* books, they merely snatch a glance at them, that they may talk about them. And even if this were not so, never forget what, I believe, was observed to you by Coleridge, that every great and original writer, in proportion as he is great or original, must himself create the taste by which he is to be relished; he must teach the art by which he is to be seen ; this, in a certain degree, even to all persons, however wise and pure may be their lives, and however unvitiated their taste. But for those who dip into books in order to give an opinion of them, or talk about them to take up an opinion — for this multitude of unhappy, and misguided, and misguiding beings, an entire regeneration must be produced ; and if this be possible, it must be a work *of time*.

To conclude, my ears are stone-dead to this idle buzz, and my flesh as insensible as iron to these petty stings ; and, after what I have said, I am sure yours will be the same. I doubt not that you will share with me an invincible confidence that my writings (and among them these little poems) will co-operate with the benign tendencies in human nature and society, wherever found ; and that they will, in their degree, be efficacious in making men wiser, better, and happier. Farewell. I will not apologise for this letter, though its length demands an apology.

Believe me, eagerly wishing for the happy day when I shall see you and Sir George here, most affectionately yours,

W. WORDSWORTH.

Do not hurry your coming hither on our account : my sister regrets that she did not press this upon you, as you say in your letter, " we cannot *possibly* come before the first week in June "; from which we infer that your kindness will induce you to make sacrifices for our sakes. Whatever pleasure we may have in thinking of Grasmere, we have no impatience to be gone, and think with full as much regret at leaving Coleorton. I had, for myself, indeed, a wish to be at Grasmere with as much of the summer before me as might be ; but to this I attach no importance whatever, as far as the gratification of that wish interferes with any inclination or duty of yours. I could not be satisfied without seeing you here, and shall have great pleasure in waiting.

CXLVII

William Wordsworth to Francis Wrangham

GRASMERE, July 12, [1807.]

My dear Wrangham,

I received your letter (directed to Coleorton) at Halifax in your own county, yet seventy or eighty miles from your place of abode. I am in your debt for two letters, one received many months ago : to that I made reply from London (which I visited this spring) in a sheet which was to be filled up by Montagu : but as you do not mention this letter, I take for granted that Montagu, with his usual fidelity in the art of forgetting, neglected not only to add his own part but to forward mine.

Your epigrams were amusing enough; the last, I think, was the best. I heard a good deal of the Yorkshire election where I was, but my friends were among the blues; of course I did not hear much good of Lord Milton, except in the streets: and there indeed I heard enough.

I am glad you had received so much pleasure from those of my poems which you had read. I am so much of your opinion with respect to Lord Nelson that I shall omit the note in future. Is your objection to the word " immediately " or to its connection with the others? The word itself seems to have sufficient poetical authority, even the highest.

Immediately a place
Before his eyes appeared, sad, noisome, dark.

I am well aware that the *nimia simplicitas* of my diction will frequently be complained of. I am prepared for that, being confident that the more an intimacy with our best writers is cultivated, the less dislike of this kind shall I have to encounter.

Do not you write in the *Critical Review*[1] occasionally? I know you are intimate with the publisher, Mawman. I put this question to you because there is a most malignant spirit (his fleshly name is Legrice)[2] whose gall and venom are discharged upon the public through that review. This wretch, for such I cannot but call him, has taken Coleridge, his quondam school-fellow at Christs hospital and contemporary at Cambridge, into his most deadly hatred, and persecutes him upon all occasions, in which hatred all Coleridge's friends have a share, and I among

[1] *The Critical Review* was started in 1756 and continued till 1817. — Ed.

[2] Possibly Charles Valentine Le Grice. — Ed.

the rest.   I have therefore to request that you would take
so much trouble as to keep the review of my poems in
the *Critical* out of this creature's hands, either by reviewing them yourself (which I should like best) or in any
other way.   I have requested this of you, not that I think
the criticisms of this man would have the slightest influence on the final destiny of these poems, — or that they
would give me a moment's concern on any other account
than this, that some of my relations and friends who
have not strength of mind to judge for themselves might
be wounded — but chiefly because the immediate sale of
books is more under the influence of reviews than is generally supposed, and the sale of this work is of some consequence to me.   If you stir in this affair there is no
time to be lost.

Are we not likely to see you here?   Your place is too
much out of the way for my purse.   Affectionately yours,

WM. WORDSWORTH.

Pray let a copy of your sermon be sent by Mawman
to Longman's, to be forwarded by him in the first parcel
of books he sends to Southey.

CXLVIII

Dorothy Wordsworth to Mrs. Clarkson

Sunday, July 19.[1]

My dear Friend,

. . . Bolton Abbey.   I hope you have been there.
The abbey stands in the most beautiful valley that ever

---

[1] No year is mentioned, but it must have been 1807. — Ed.

was seen; the ruin is greatly inferior to Kirkstall; but the situation infinitely more beautiful — a retired woody winding valley, with steep banks and rocky scars, no manufactories, no horrible forges, and yet the forge near Kirkstall has often a very grand effect.   We spent a very pleasant day in the neighbourhood of Bolton with our friends, and parted from them at six miles distant from Burnsall, the place where we were to lodge.   We had a *delightful* walk to Burnsall, and there we were received at the little Inn with that true welcoming which you only meet with in lonely places; and we had an hour's very interesting conversation with the landlord, a most intelligent man.   Burnsall is a pretty little village, by the side of the Wharfe — now not a very large stream — the fields green, but wanting wood, and fenced with stone walls.

From Burnsall we walked with a guide over bare hills to Gordale, and there we rested under the huge rock for several hours, and drank of its cold waters, and ate our dinner.   We then climbed up the side of the waterfall and made our way over the crags to Malham Cove, then drank tea at the Inn, and returned again in the evening to Gordale. . . .   On our arrival here[1] our spirits sank, and our first walk in the evening was very melancholy. Many persons are dead.   Old Mr. Sympson, his son the parson,[2] young George Dawson.[3] . . . All the trees at Bainriggs are cut down; and even worse, the giant sycamore near the parsonage house, and all the finest fir trees that overtopped the steeple tower.   At home we found all well. . . .

[1] At Grasmere. — Ed.

[2] There is a mistake here.   Joseph Sympson, the clergyman, died on June 27, 1807, aged 92 years. — Ed.

[3] See *The Excursion*, Book VII, ll. 695-714. — Ed.

CXLIX

Dorothy Wordsworth to Mrs. Marshall

GRASMERE, September 19, [1807.]

[Referring to the Scottish tour of the Marshalls.]

... I think there is no sensation more elevating to the
heart and the imagination than what we take in on viewing distant mountains and plains, hills and valleys, towns
and seas, from some superior eminence. I do not wonder
that you were disappointed in Glencroe, passing through
it on a sunny morning, with expectations of something
tremendous or terrible. It may be *sublime* under certain
accidents of weather, but can never be " tremendous " or
" terrible "; and I think the glen itself is unjustly treated,
when such epithets are used in describing it. It is a wild
and solitary spot, where you feel that you are in *Scotland*.
Black cattle were the only living things, except birds
and sheep, that we saw in travelling through it. The
town of Inverary is a miserable place, when you are
in it; but I think the effect of the first view of it — in
connection with the broad expanse of water, fishing-boats,
hills, and distant mountains, and afterwards with the castle
and bridges — is very impressive and beautiful. The sun
was shining on the water when we first came in view of
this prospect, and it made an impression on my mind of
festive gaiety which I shall never forget. Loch Tay,
though very pretty to live beside, is — except at Killin
and Taymouth — an insipid place to visit. It is inferior
in beauty to all our Lakes, and not equal in grandeur to
the most insignificant of them. ... I cannot agree with
you in admiring the abbey at Melrose more than the

chapel at Roslin.   As far as it goes that chapel appeared to me to be perfection, most beautiful in form, and of entire simplicity.   Melrose has no doubt been a much grander place, but *as a whole* it now produces little effect. The minute sculpture there is excessively beautiful, but oh ! how much more delight have I in the remembrance of Bolton in its retired valley, and the venerable Kirkstall ! ... William and Mary spent twelve days at Ullswater of late, and returned with Sir George and Lady Beaumont, who stayed a week at Grasmere ; and two days after their departure, W. and M. set forward again upon a tour to Wastdale, Ennerdale, Whitehaven, Cockermouth, etc. . . .   They returned yesterday night, were at Cockermouth, our native place, saw the terrace that you have heard me speak of many a time, with the privet hedge still full of roses as it used to be thirty years ago.   Yes! I remember it for more than thirty years.   If it were not for dates, and other artificial aids to memory, I should forget that I am not as young as when you were married, for I feel no bodily difference. . . .

CL

Dorothy Wordsworth to Mrs. Marshall

GRASMERE, October 18, 1807.

. . . I cannot express how much pleasure my brother has already received from Dr. Whitaker's books, though they have only been two days in his possession.   Almost the whole time he has been greedily devouring the *History of Craven*[1]; and (what is of more importance) he has found all the information which he wanted for the

[1] *The History and Antiquities of the Deanery of Craven*, by Thomas Dunham Whitaker (1805). — Ed.

possession of his plan. I have great pleasure in thinking that you may receive gratification from the poem
which William is writing. I will not tell you the subject of it, that you may not anticipate anything. In the
meantime (but that is a foolish plan, for it may be many
months before the poem he is now writing is finished,
and many more before it is *published*), I have prevailed
upon him to let me transcribe a short one, which he
wrote about a month ago, on the story of young Romelli
and the Strid; which, as it may remind you of the day
we passed together at Bolton, I hope you will read with
pleasure. [She quotes,

> What is good for a bootless bene? etc.,

and adds a request to Mrs. M. to read this poem to Dr.
Whitaker when she sees him.] My brother has made
great use of Mr. Marshall's observations on planting,[1]
with which he has been greatly pleased, as they coincide
with his own previous ideas of what should be. He recom-
mends every one to plant larches on their *high* rocky
grounds, and oak, ash, etc., etc., on their richer and low
grounds. . . . Lady Beaumont is very busy planting and
laying out the grounds at Coleorton. . . .

CLI

Dorothy Wordsworth to Lady Beaumont

1807.

. . . I cannot but admire the fortitude, and wonder at
the success, with which he [her brother] has laboured,

---

[1] Doubtless William Marshall's *Practical Treatise on Planting
and Ornamental Gardening*, 1796. — Ed.

in that one room, common to all the family, to all visitors, and where the children frequently play beside him. . . .

CLII

William Wordsworth to Francis Wrangham

GRASMERE, Nov. 4th, [1807.]

My dear Wrangham,

I have just received from Montagu two letters of yours to him, by which I learn that your application to have the review of my poems taken out of Le Grice's hands was successful; for the trouble you have taken in this business I thank you, but alas! either for me, or for the *Critical Review*, or for both! it has been out of the frying-pan into the fire

> —*primo avulso non deficit alter*
> *Aureus, et simili frondescit virga metallo,*[1]

for I am told that there has appeared in the said journal an article purporting to be a review of those poems which is a miserable heap of spiteful nonsense, even worse than anything that has appeared hitherto, in these disgraceful days. I have not seen it, for I am only a chance-reader of reviews, but from what I have heard of the contents of this precious piece, I feel not so much inclined to accuse the author of malice as of sheer honest insensibility and stupidity. With what propriety did I select my motto for the "Lyrical Ballads," which might have been continued with equal or greater propriety on the present occasion.

> *Quam nihil ad genium, Papiniane, tuum!*[2]

[1] Virgil, *Æneid*, vi. 143–144. — Ed.
[2] This motto is not discoverable in classical literature. — Ed.

But peace to this gentleman, and all his brethren: as Southey neatly says "they cannot *blast* our *laurels*, but they may *mildew* our *corn*"; and it is only on account of this latter power, which to a certain degree they unfortunately possess, that I troubled you, or deemed them worth a moment's thought.   To turn to a more agreeable subject.   I am indeed much pleased that Mrs. Wrangham and yourself have been gratified by these breathings of simple Nature, the more so, because I conclude, from the character of the poems which you have particularized, that the volumes cannot but improve upon you.   I see that you have entered into the spirit of them.   You mention the Daffodils ; you know Butler, Montagu's friend, not Tom Butler, but the conveyancer.   When I was in Town in Spring he happened to see the volumes lying on Montagu's mantel-piece and to glance his eye upon this very poem of the Daffodils ; " aye," says he, "a fine morsel this for the reviewers."   When this was told me, for I was not present, I observed that there were two lines in that little poem which if thoroughly felt, would annihilate nine tenths of the reviews of the Kingdom, as they would find no readers ; the lines I alluded to, were those

> They flash upon that inward eye,
> Which is the bliss of solitude.

I should not have been sorry to have had an opportunity of saying this to Butler himself.   Before I finish the subject of these poems let me request you to take a pen and correct in your copy the following gross blunders of the press, as some of them materially affect the sense.

1st volume, page 37 rightful Heir
"   "   "   113 and *through* this wilderness.
"   "   "   121 while I was framing beds *for*.

2d volume, page 84 small wooden isle.
"   "   "   91 wheels hither *her* store.
"   "   "   127 His Thrift thy use*less*ness.

"Guilt-burther'd" you have already noted; I will also
thank you if any of your friends happen to possess the
book, and their copy should fall in your way, to take the
trouble of correcting the grossest of the above blunders.
"In Gaelic or the English tongue" the language in your
substitution is certainly more correct, and is the *proper*
language, but somehow it sounds ill. *In I*nglish. Your
other corrections I shall adopt and thank you for them;
and should be glad of more. Bring*i* tales is a gross error
of the press.

Pray let me now ask how you are employed. I had
heard a rumour of the offence you had given to Dr. Symmonds by the review, but I never either saw it or the
book itself. In fact I might as well live at St. Kilda for
any commerce I have with passing literature, especially
bulky works; for I have no neighbour that buys them,
and we have no Book-club. Have you any good old libra-
ries near you? or how are you accommodated with books,
new or old? You speak kindly in your letter of the pleasure you would have in seeing Montagu, and me, in your
neighbourhood; I should like it much, but can[not]
encourage the hope, for a reason which I believe I have
heretofore specified. Yorkshire is a favorite region with
me, both your side of the country, and the vallies on the
western side, among the ribs of the British Apennine.
I know it all well, almost every corner in it; and should
like better to wander through it on that very account. If
Montagu comes down to you next summer, I shall expect
you to find your way to Grasmere : remember this. I am
pleased to find you do not forget the drawing or drawings.

Mrs. W. desires me to say that when you see Mrs. Langley she will thank you to mention her name as a person who remembers her kindness with pleasure. With best regards to yourself and Mrs. Wrangham, I remain, affectionately yours,

WM. WORDSWORTH.

CLIII

William Wordsworth to Thomas Wilkinson

COLEORTON, ASHBY DE LA ZOUCHE,
LEICESTERSHIRE, November.

My dear Friend,

I was prevented by a most severe cold from seeing you as I intended, and meeting the person at Patterdale about the horses. I was indeed much indisposed for six or seven weeks. You will excuse me with your usual goodness for not having written sooner ; but what shall I say in apology for your Journal; which is now locked up with my manuscripts at Grasmere. As I could not go over to your part of the country myself, my intention was to have taken it with me to Kendal and then have delivered it to George Braithwaite or some friend of yours to be carefully transmitted to you ; unluckily, most unluckily, in the hurry of departure I forgot it, together with two of my own manuscripts which were along with it and I am afraid you will be standing in great need of it. If you do, it may be procured, for I can write to Grasmere to that effect ; it is there in perfect safety along with papers of my own. If you wish it I shall write to have it taken out and carried over to you by some trusty person, or if you or any of your friends should be passing that way I could send such orders to Grasmere that it may be in readiness for you or them whenever it should be convenient to call for it. If you do not want it, it is in a place where it can take no injury, and I may have the pleasure of delivering it to you myself in the spring.

I am now at Coleorton in Leicestershire with all my family, our house at Grasmere being too small for us to winter in ; we shall return in spring : the house we occupy is one of Sir George Beaumont's and very roomy and convenient. We like our situation very well, and are all well in health.

On the other page you will find a copy of verses addressed to an implement of yours ;[1] they are supposed to have been composed that afternoon when you and I were labouring together in your pleasure-ground, an afternoon I often think of with pleasure; as indeed I do of your beautiful retirement there.

I have in the press a poetical publication that will extend to a couple of small volumes,[2] 150 pages or so a-piece ; and I mean to publish the above verses in it, to which I do not suppose you will have any objections. If you should, I cannot permit them to have any force, therefore not a word upon the subject! I shall send you the books as soon as they are out; tell me how. My wife, sister, and Miss Hutchinson who is with us, join with me in most kind remembrances to yourself and both your sisters. Write soon.

Farewell, most affectionately yours,

WM. WORDSWORTH.

[1] *To the Spade of a Friend.* — Ed.
[2] The *Poems* of 1807. — Ed.

[This letter appears to have been written in 1806 and should more properly follow Letter CXXXI at p. 267. — Ed.]

CLIV

Dorothy Wordsworth to Mrs. Clarkson

[Postmark, KENDAL], December 2nd, [1807.]

My dear Friend,

. . . Since I wrote to you we have had two letters from dear Coleridge. They were short; but it was a great satisfaction after his dreary silence, which we know him too well not to attribute to unhappiness and irresolution of mind; which he himself was suffering from most, and would *most feelingly* condemn. I believe I had finished my letter to you when the Coleridges came, and that what I wrote about them was scribbled hastily across the paper. To give you a general idea of the state of things I must tell you that Mrs. Coleridge was in great spirits, and talked of Coleridge's coming down with her as what had been chiefly prevented by her having Mr. De Quincey as a companion, and that she and the children did not go to London with him on account of the expense, etc. But observe this was all said in Mr. De Quincey's presence. When we were alone together she entreated us to say nothing to Mr. De Q. that should make him suspect anything amiss between her [and C.,] spoke of the disgrace of a separation, that she had never mentioned it, nor would mention it, to any living soul, and a great deal more. To this M. and I answered that their present or rather past way of going on was disgraceful, but that if each declared openly that they were separated we could see no disgrace whatever that was likely to follow, that there would be a buzz, and all would be over; whereas now every body was ready to sneer. "Well," she replied, "he may stay away if he likes. I care nothing about it, if he will not talk of it "; and then she began again about disgrace, and the children. As to the children we replied that the evil was mighty indeed; but, however they went on, she saw plainly that *they* were not likely to be much with both parents at once.

The fact then is this, that Coleridge, not knowing how to manage with the boys, or where to place them, consented that they should come with her ; and he has parted from her, just as he did before, with positive assurances that he will never live with her ; but without having had the resolution to persist in declaring it among his and her friends ; so people will go on saying that he forsakes his wife and children, etc., etc., and he will always have something to make him uneasy and disturbed, something hanging over his head to be done, till all the world knows how they are situated. Of course the part that we, and all the friends of both parties, should take is this ; to keep silence, and if the subject is ever discussed in our presence, to say we know nothing about it.

Mrs. Coleridge seems disposed to be more friendly with us than ever, and if she had not so little feeling I should pity her very much for having been so often put into disagreeable situations, by his delays of coming to her at the time promised, and the like. For instance, I believe she was kept several weeks at Bristol in hourly expectation of him. These things are very wrong, and it is a sad pity that he should have done anything at such a time, which his best friends cannot help condemning. If after he came home he had acted with dignity and firmness, how easy would all have been, compared with what it is I Sara,[1] in a letter which I have just received from

---

[1] Sarah Hutchinson, Mrs. Wordsworth's sister. — Ed.

her, says that she thinks you must have misunderstood what I said in my last, as you "lament his irresolution respecting his wife." I hope I have now explained myself so that you cannot misunderstand me. I wrote in such a hurry that I hardly know what I said, but I did not then think differently from what I do now of his general resolution not to live with her; and now as then I equally lament the weakness which has prevented him from putting it out of her power to torment him any more.

Coleridge's last letter was written the day after his arrival in London. His lectures are to begin on Monday. He says nothing of his private feelings, but that his thoughts have been with us continually, and that he has been very unhappy. He adds that his lectures are likely to be very profitable, and that, if he is in a state to be other than a discomfort to us, he will certainly be at Grasmere in the course of the first fortnight in March. I am afraid his health will suffer from the bustle and fatigue he will have to go through in London, and I shall be very anxious to hear regularly from him. He had been detained more than a fortnight at Bristol by illness. . . . The best news contained in his letter was that he had been going on with *Christabel*, and had written almost as much as we have already seen, and *re*-written his tragedy.[1] If he has no more to do with Mrs. C. in the way of discussions, arrangements, or disputes, and comes hither in a mood to continue to compose verses, I shall have yet hopes that he may fulfil the promise of his great endowments, and be a happy man. . . . William has written above 500 lines of a new poem, a tale,[2] very beautiful. He has not yet quite done half of it. . . .

[1] *Osorio*, which was re-written under the title *Remorse.* — Ed.
[2] Evidently *The White Doe of Rylstone.* — Ed.

CLV

Dorothy Wordsworth to Lady Beaumont

GRASMERE, December 6th.
[Postmark, Dec. 14, 1807.]

My dear Friend,

I hope you are arrived in safety at Dunmow, and have found Lady Beaumont[1] not in worse health and spirits than when you left her, though it can scarcely be expected but that after every summer's absence you must perceive some shade of difference in her, some little decay of strength. This excessive cold weather must be very trying to old persons, though they never should stir out of doors. How does she bear it? You do not mention Sir George's health, so I hope he is well. Coleridge's lectures, as he told us (for we have had another letter from him), were to begin last Monday, and I had hopes that you would be present at the first; but I gather from your letter that you were to leave town before that time, which I am very sorry for. Mr. De Quincey, the gentleman whom I mentioned to you, who had come with Mrs. Coleridge from Bristol to see my brother, has promised to take down the heads of the whole course of lectures (and he is very capable of doing it accurately), of which he will send a copy to us. He is a remarkable and very interesting young man; very diminutive in person, which, to strangers, makes him appear insignificant; and so modest, and so very shy, that even now I wonder how he had ever the courage to address himself to my brother by letter. I think of this young man with extraordinary

[1] The Dowager Lady Beaumont, who lived at Dunmow in Essex. — Ed.

pleasure, as he is a remarkable instance of the power of my brother's poems over a lovely and contemplative mind, unwarped by any established laws of taste (as far as it is in my power to judge from his letters, and the little I have seen of him) — a pure and innocent mind!

It will be a week to-morrow since William left me, which was as soon as the roads would permit. I have not yet heard of his arrival at Stockton; but I will give you the account of his journey to Penrith in his own brief words, which perhaps may amuse you. He left home between ten and eleven o'clock on Tuesday morning, and he says, " I arrived here (at Penrith) between five and six. It was a pleasant morning; Skiddaw from the top of the Raise (Dunmail Raise) one huge mass of snow, spotless and smooth even to sublimity." (By the bye, I must tell you that we, in the vale of Grasmere, have no opportunity of observing this appearance, all our mountains being rocky, and therefore spotted with black.) He goes on: " The road was tolerably good all down St. John's.[1]   Within half a mile of Threlkeld I overtook a man of the country on horseback on a pad, told him whither I was going, and that I wished to hire a horse. He said he himself was busy, but if I could get a lad at Threlkeld to bring back the horse, he had no objection to let me have his a little way.   Procured a lad at Threlkeld, had a quart of ale with the man, and set off with the lad on the horse behind me.   Rode on to Hutton Moor, had four miles' riding on the whole, and then parted with the lad; gave the man for his horse a shilling, the boy six-pence.   At Penruddock saw a man before me in a gig, and, with smart running, overtook him.   He asked me

1 St. John's vale. — Ed.

to get in and ride, but had not rode above 100 yards before we met a man, who told us that the gig could not get along. The gentleman turned back to Penruddock, and I walked on. It rained very hard. Lost one of my gloves on the road, turned back, and, poring in the dark, found it. Got here very little tired. The journey has been a very interesting one: the long avenues of snow, which have been cut through some places half a mile long, and often between two and three yards deep, had a very solemn and lovely appearance. I passed several parties of men cutting; in one place at least twenty-five. Saw a shepherd in the wildest part of Hutton Moor collecting his sheep, on horseback, not on the road, but on the wildest part of the moor. The wind was at my back all the way, and helped me on; and I am surprised to find myself so little fatigued, for the road was often very slippery and trying."

I hope you will not be tired with this extract, which, though it seemed to me short before I began, has, I find, filled half my paper. At least you will be pleased to find that my dear brother was in such good health and spirits. Since his departure we have had a fine thaw, but the frost has begun again keener than ever; everything freezes in the house, which was not the case before, and there is again a thin covering of snow upon the fields. The mountains, of course, have never been clear, and long will it be before the huge snow-drifts are melted away. If we had had any reason to expect such weather as this, my sister had not gone to Stockton this year, but when she left home, the weather was very pleasant, and such a storm at this season of the year is not remembered by any person living in this country; and it is, indeed, forty years since there has been such a fall of snow at any season.   Forty years ago the roads were blocked up for three weeks, and it is still remembered by numbers, and goes by the name of the "great snow."

My sister was prevailed upon to leave home by the earnest entreaties of her friends, especially of her sister Joanna, who was going thither, and they travelled from Penrith together; but (as I have said) nothing could have prevailed upon us to trust her, if we could have foreseen what has happened.   I hope, however, she has not suffered in any respect from the storm, except that her return will have been delayed by it, for William must stay a fortnight with her amongst her friends.   She writes in good spirits, and her sister tells us her looks are much improved.   I have to thank you for a hamper of game, which arrived on Friday.   When I saw the hamper, I began directly to grieve that William and Mary were not at home to share it with me; but I soon recollected that I might make a present of a part to a neighbour who had been very civil to us, and to whom we had had no opportunity of making any return.   Accordingly I did so, and the gift was much prized.   There was a mistake both in the address and the manner of sending it.   It had been sent by *Leicester*, and was directed to Keswick, instead of Kendal; also it is proper to say, when the package requires expedition, *To be forwarded by the Ambleside Post.*   Luckily, the weather being so severe, the game was quite sweet, but it had been ten days on the road.

I am sorry to trouble you with this explanation of mistakes; but I think it proper, as the like might occur again, and by mentioning it to Captain Bailey, when you have occasion to write to him, it might be prevented.   I had heard from Coleridge of Davy's illness, and his great discoveries.   I am very anxious to hear that he is restored to health. Poor Wilkie! I am very sorry, too, to hear of his illness. I fear that by too much application, though in very different ways, they may have both irreparably injured their constitutions. Pray make my most respectful and affectionate remembrances to Sir George. Adieu, my dear friend. Ever yours,

D. W.

CLVI

William Wordsworth to Sir George Beaumont

[1807.[1]]

My dear Sir George,

I am quite delighted to hear of your picture for Peter Bell; I was much pleased with the sketch, and I have no doubt that the picture will surpass it as far as a picture ought to do. I long much to see it. I should approve of any engraver approved by you. But remember that no poem of mine will ever be popular; and I am afraid that the sale of Peter would not carry the expense of the engraving, and that the poem, in the estimation of the public, would be a weight upon the print. I say not this in modest disparagement of the poem, but in sorrow for the sickly taste of the public in verse. The *people* would love the poem of Peter Bell, but the *public* (a very different being) will never love it.

[1] No date is given to this letter; but from its reference to a subject for a picture to be found in a poem just written, from the fact that *The White Doe of Rylstone* contained such a subject, and that Sir George Beaumont did illustrate that poem, the date may be approximately fixed as about Christmas, 1807. Wordsworth left Grasmere for Stockton-on-Tees on December 1, 1807. At Stockton he composed the first half of *The White Doe*; and returned to Grasmere on the Wednesday before Christmas, 1807. — Ed.

Thanks for dear Lady Beaumont's transcript from your friend's letter; it is written with candour, but I must say a word or two not in praise of it. "Instances of what I mean," says your friend, "are to be found in a poem on a Daisy" (by the bye, it is on *the* Daisy, a mighty difference!) "and on the *Daffodils reflected in the Water!*" Is this accurately transcribed by Lady Beaumont? If it be, what shall we think of criticism or judgment founded upon, and exemplified by, a poem which must have been so inattentively perused? My language is precise; and, therefore, it would be false modesty to charge myself with blame.

> Beneath the trees, ·
> Ten thousand dancing in the *breeze*.
> The *waves beside* them danced, but they
> Outdid the *sparkling waves* in glee.

Can expression be more distinct? And let me ask your friend how it is possible for flowers to be *reflected* in water where there are *waves?* They may, indeed, in *still* water; but the very object of my poem is the trouble or agitation, both of the flowers and the water. I must needs respect the understanding of every one honoured by your friendship; but sincerity compels me to say that my poems must be more nearly looked at before they can give rise to any remarks of much value, even from the strongest minds. With respect to this individual poem, Lady Beaumont will recollect how Mrs. Fermor expressed herself upon it. A letter also was sent to me, addressed to a friend of mine, and by him communicated to me, in which this identical poem was singled out for fervent approbation.

What then shall we say? Why, let the poet first consult his own heart, as I have done, and leave the rest to posterity, — to, I hope, an improving posterity. The fact is, the English *public* are at this moment in the same state of mind with respect to my poems, if small things may be compared with great, as the French are in respect to Shakespeare, and not the French alone, but almost the whole Continent. In short, in your friend's letter, I am condemned for the very thing for which I ought to have been praised, viz., that I have not written down to the level of superficial observers and unthinking minds. Every great poet is a teacher : I wish either to be considered as a teacher, or as nothing.

To turn to a more pleasing subject. Have you painted anything else beside this picture from *Peter Bell*? Your two oil-paintings (and, indeed, everything I have of yours) have been much admired by the artists who have seen them. And, for our own parts, we like them better every day; this, in particular, is the case with the small picture from the neighbourhood of Coleorton, which, indeed, pleased me much at the first sight, but less impressed the rest of our household, who now see as many beauties in it as I do myself. Havell, the water-colour painter, was much pleased with these things ; he is painting at Ambleside, and has done a view of Rydal Water, looking down upon it from Rydal Park, of which I should like to know your opinion; it will be exhibited in the Spring, in the Water-Colour Exhibition.

I have purchased a black-lead pencil sketch of Mr. Green, of Ambleside, which, I think, has great merit, the materials being uncommonly picturesque and well put together : I should dearly like to have the same subject (it is the cottage at Glencoign, by Ullswater) treated by you. In the poem I have just written, you will find one situation which, if the work should ever become familiarly known, would furnish as fine a subject for a picture as anything I remember in poetry, ancient or modern. I need not mention what it is, as when you read the poem you cannot miss it. We have at last had, by the same post, two letters from Coleridge, long and melancholy; and also, from Keswick, an account so depressing as to the state of his health, that I should have set off immediately to London, to see him, if I had not myself been confined by indisposition.

I hope that Davy is by this time perfectly restored to health. Believe me, my dear Sir George, most sincerely yours,

W. WORDSWORTH.

CLVII

Dorothy Wordsworth to Lady Beaumont

My dear Friend,

Many thanks for your kind letter. We received it on a morning as delightful to the feelings as any I can remember. My brother and I walked to Ambleside to meet the post; the birds were singing joyfully, and the sun shone so warm, and the air was so mild that with closed eyes we might have believed it was the month of May; but the ground was almost covered with snow, and to-day we have had cold dismal rain, and we may expect more snow. It has been a long and most severe winter, particularly unfortunate for us, as it has added to the inconveniences of our two small houses, and has also often compelled my brother to the sitting-room, when in a milder season he would have composed his verses in the open air; indeed, I cannot but admire the fortitude, and wonder at the success, with which he has laboured, in that one room, common to all the family, to all visitors, and where the children frequently play beside him. I spoke rashly when I said that I hoped you might receive the printed poem at Dunmow. Much time will be lost in sending it backwards and forwards, and Southey did not go to Leeds till last Tuesday.

It gave us great delight to hear that Sir George has painted the picture from *Peter Bell.* I should think, independent of its own connection with the poem, that the *painting* must gain very much by the change of time, from moonlight to early morning; and, as separating that scene entirely from the action contained in the poem, it is very judicious. There would have been some confusion if the *moon*light had been preserved. I hope the day will come when we shall see the picture itself, whether ever the poem be graced with an engraving from it or not. We have been informed that Davy is perfectly recovered. I hope that this good news is true.

Poor Coleridge! I have deferred speaking of him to the last, for I have nothing good to say. We have been exceedingly distressed by the two letters we have had from him, and still more by an account that came from Keswick; insomuch that my brother was only prevented by his own illness from setting off to London. He wrote to Coleridge requesting an immediate answer, and also wrote to Miss Lamb to desire her to go to him, and see exactly how he is, and inform us; and upon the nature of her answer and Coleridge's, it will depend whether my brother goes to London or not. His object will be to attend upon Coleridge as long as he (Coleridge) is obliged to stay in London, or to see that he is likely to be attended to, and to prevail upon him, as soon as he is at liberty, to come into the North. He had said to Southey that he "*could* not live many months." Now I do not think he spoke thus, rashly or lightly, still less to give pain; and I believe that, if he were wholly left to himself, it might, in a few months even, be impossible to save him; but I have no doubt that his low spirits have made him look at his condition of body as so hopeless, and that if he could be cheered, as formerly, by the society of his friends, and would take common care of himself, he might yet be well, and live long, to the benefit of mankind. We anxiously expect his letter, and still more anxiously Miss Lamb's, as her account will be more to be depended upon, because dear Coleridge will be unwilling to draw my brother away from his home. Adieu, my dear Lady Beaumont. Forgive this scrawl; I write with a bad pen, and in *haste*, for it is late, and my letter goes in the morning. Believe me ever your affectionate friend,

DOROTHY WORDSWORTH.

CLVIII

Dorothy Wordsworth to Mrs. Clarkson

Monday, 28th December, [1807.]

My dear Friend,

... When we engaged this house [1] it was under the idea that Coleridge, with his two boys, would come and live with us, a plan to which we consented, in the hope of being of service to Coleridge, though we were well aware of the odium which we should draw upon ourselves by having the children under our roof. We do not, however, now think that Coleridge will have the resolution to put

[1] Allan Bank. It was let to Wordsworth six months before the building was finished. The Wordsworths entered it in the summer of 1808. — Ed.

this plan in practice; nor do we now even think it would be prudent for us to consent to it, C. having been so very unsteady in all things since his return to England. Had he acted with firmness we should willingly have encountered blame as the only means of preserving C. in quiet, and promoting his schemes for the education of his sons; but we had long experience at Coleorton that it was not in our power to make him happy; and his irresolute conduct since has almost confirmed our fears that it will never be otherwise; therefore we should be more disposed to hesitation, and fear of having our domestic quiet disturbed, if he should now wish to come to us with the children. I do not say that we *should not consent;* but it would be with little hope; and we shall never *advise* the measure.

We have not, however, the least expectation that we shall see Coleridge for more than two or three months at a time, in which case he might be well accommodated with you in the house; but you will see that we cannot come to any determination till after March, when he talks of being with us; and also we should wish you not to mention the affair to any body, as, if C. were to hear of it — either from ourselves, or by any other means — it might serve as a handle for despair, and an excuse for considering himself as utterly homeless; and we would fain give him all possible assistance, if any thing can be done. I need not say what pleasure we should have in being so near to you, and the house is so large that we need not be any annoyance to each other; for we need never meet but when it is more agreeable to us than not, and Mr. Clarkson and William may each pursue their separate studies as much apart as if they were not in the same house. This for William is of the utmost importance; for all his

work is disarranged and his mind made uneasy, whenever
he is obliged from the smallness of our house, to be in
company with any but our own family except in hours of
relaxation. The matter then may stand thus. If Coleridge
makes our house only an *occasional* residence, there is no
objection whatever on our side. . . .

We were very comfortable during the frost, and the
scene out of doors was exquisitely beautiful — the lake
firm transparent ice ; the trees, for days together covered
with sparkling white, as thick as the foliage itself. I
never saw anything like it before. I never saw the hoar-
frost so thick, and so lasting. . . . But the review itself is
so senseless, so contradictory, and plainly so spiteful,
that it can do no harm with any wise or feeling mind ;
and for me, I have not laughed so heartily this long time
(except now and then at dear little Sissy) as I did at the
reading of it. You will not accuse me of being selfish or
vain, when I say that I should feel disposed to like your
cousin Henry Robinson for his love of William's poems ;
if I had not before been prepossessed in his favour from
your having spent many happy hours of your youth in
his society. I am not more confident of any truth than
of this that there must be something good in the heart
that is much attached to my brother's poems, and I trust
too that they make better the heart that loves them. . . .

1808

CLIX

Dorothy Wordsworth to Lady Beaumont

GRASMERE, December[1] 3d, 1808.

My dear Friend,

Three or four times have I been about to write to you, and far oftener have wished to do it since I received your interesting letter from Dunmow, and to-day arrives your note enclosed in the parcel with Walton's *Complete Angler*. I should have felt the bitterness of self-reproach for my long silence, if I had been betrayed into it by a procrastinating disposition, or by negligence; but I wished to write to you in quiet and leisure, and some ordinary every-day occurrence always prevented me. My dear Lady Beaumont, I cannot say how much I am gratified by Sir George's kind remembrance of me, nor how highly I shall value his gift, for *his* sake, as well as that of the pure innocent spirit that breathed out the tender sentiments contained in that book, so many years ago. I have read a few pages here and there, and have seen enough to be convinced that it has not been overpraised. I was greatly delighted with one passage, where Walton speaks familiarly of Sir Henry Wotton, Milton's friend, and his frequent companion in his favourite pleasure, and he repeats some of the expressions of Sir Henry, which are very beautiful.

[1] Evidently a mistake for January.— Ed.

My brother has seized upon the book for his own reading this night, as he fancies that the imagery and sentiments accord with his own train of thought at present, in connection with his poem, which he is just upon the point of finishing. I think it will be finished in the course of three or four days. He has written above 1200 lines ; it is in irregular eight-syllable verse, and will be called *a tale*.[1] I certainly misled you when I said that it would be a sort of romance, for it has nothing of that character; yet it is very different from any other poem that my brother has written. I hope that you will be pleased with it ; indeed, I am sure you will, and I can hardly conceive how any feeling heart can be otherwise. My brother has fixed upon the day of his finishing this poem as the day of his writing to Sir George. He would have written a week ago, but, as he said, having waited so long, he would now wait till the work was done, when he should have the pleasure of telling Sir George what he knew he would be glad to hear. My sister, with my brother, arrived at home on the Wednesday before Christmas Day, she having been absent six weeks, and he three weeks. They had not an unpleasant journey, though the weather was excessively severe; the trees, hedges, and every blade of grass or withered stalk having been covered as thick with hoar-frost, all day through, for many days together (in spite of sunshine and blue sky), as ever I have seen them covered with snow after a heavy snow-shower; and the appearance was exquisitely beautiful. I could not but think that during the whole eight years of our residence, we had never before seen these mountain vales in the full possession of their *peculiar* grandeur and power over the imagination. The lakes were firm ice, as clear as crystal.

[1] *The White Doe of Rylstone.* — Ed.

But I have strayed from the point where I set out. The inconvenience of our small house (for we have been driven out of the kitchen on the opposite side of the road by the late rainy weather) often reminds us of the comforts we enjoyed last year at Coleorton; but we are so very glad that we are not in the *new* house, that we are disposed to make the best of everything, and to fancy ourselves very comfortable; though I must confess we are never thoroughly so till after seven o'clock in the evening, when the children are put to bed, and the business of the house is over; for the kitchen not being ceiled, we can almost hear every word that is spoken when we are in the sitting-room, and every foot that stirs. Spite of this, my brother has worked most industriously, and, I think, successfully; but of that you will one day judge. When I recollect the happy evening we spent together at the reading of *Peter Bell*, I long for the time when this last poem shall be read to you and Sir George.

We have anxiously expected a letter from Coleridge, with some account of his valuable friend Davy; but we have had no letter from him since I wrote to you. Mr. Stuart, the Editor of the *Courier*, whom my brother saw at Stockton, had however reported that he was pronounced to be out of danger, and this morning we have had a confirmation of the happy tidings (through Southey) from Sir George. I am very much afraid that we may hear of a relapse, and at best, one scarcely ventures to hope that, after such a shock, his constitution will be unimpaired; yet how Coleridge does rise up, as it were, almost from the dead! It is next to marvellous to hear of his good looks after the two severe fits of illness that he has lately had. I do hope that the work in which he is engaged will be of service to him, especially as his exertions for the cause of human nature (such I may call them) will be animated by his strong sentiments of friendship and veneration for my brother.

As to the *Edinburgh Review*, to which I suppose you allude, it is so very silly, and, as you express it, *ignorant*, that I think it must do good with the judicious, though I fear its influence upon the many who buy books will for a time affect the sale of the poems. It is a harsh transition to turn from these busy malevolent creatures, to that pious, gentle soul, the mother of your friend, who was soothed in pain and sickness and old age by the tender effusions of my brother's heart. I had always a firm conviction that such would be his power over the innocent and pure ; yet every single proof of this must needs be most pleasing to me. What a beautiful picture of filial piety does that short extract from Lady Susan Bathurst's letter present ! and how sweetly did her mother's breath pass away!

I received your letter when I was alone, and I will not attempt to tell you how much it employed my thoughts, or how grateful I was to you for it. I read the passage to my brother on the evening of his return home, and I hardly need to add that he was much affected by it. Such facts as these we may lay to the heart, and surely they may soothe us in worldly sorrow ! We were exceedingly glad to receive such an account of your dear mother. I recollect you gave me a very interesting description of her manner of spending Christmas Day twelve months ago, and on the same day this year I thought of her and you, with many wishes for your happiness and tranquillity in the coming year, and for her, that whenever her end comes it may be bright and cheerful as her life has been, and without severe bodily suffering. Again I must repeat how much I value Sir George's gift. Pray desire him to accept my best thanks. Adieu, my dear friend. May God bless you. Your affectionate and grateful

DOROTHY WORDSWORTH.

Though the Journal would have arrived safely, it was better not to run the risk of sending it, as our own copy is very incomplete, and it is possible that Coleridge may lose his; and also if it is likely to afford any pleasure to Mrs. Fermor, I should have been sorry that it had come. I wish I had not mentioned the mis-sending of the game, as I caused you the trouble of writing about it ; and we have since received a hamper (just.at the beginning of Christmas festivities), which was properly directed, and came in a very short time.

There is one part of your last letter which I have not noticed. Do not think from this that it made no impression upon me ; but I have left no room for such a subject: I mean the over-indulgence of children. No person can be more seriously convinced of the bad effects of over-indulgence than I am, and though I am far from thinking that I entirely avoid the fault, yet I hope I do not very grievously err. More of this hereafter. I should be very glad of an opportunity of reading Mrs. Carter's Life. Perhaps it may be sent to Southey to review, and we may see it through him.

CLX

Dorothy Wordsworth to Mrs. Marshall

23rd February, 1808.

We have had such alarming accounts of the state of our poor friend Coleridge's health, that my brother has determined to go up to London to see him, and if he be strong enough, to endeavour to persuade him to return to this country. He had engaged to deliver a course of lectures at the Royal Institution, and having got through two (as we have heard from others, to the great delight of the listeners) he has been obliged to give up the attempt. He himself told us that he got through the last with the utmost fear and difficulty. My brother leaves home to-morrow. . . . Our spirits are greatly depressed by this sad news. Coleridge himself thinks that he cannot live many months; but we hope that he looks on the worst side of his condition, and that my brother's presence may be of service to him.

CLXI

Dorothy Wordsworth to Mrs. Marshall

[Feb. 24, 1808.]

. . . William left us yesterday. Mary accompanied him to Kendal. I went as far as Low Wood. The day was delightful, warm and sunny; the lake glittered, the birds sang in full concert, and we could not but be cheered at parting. It seemed as if the heavens looked favourably upon our hopes, but alas! Coleridge is very ill; yet we gather consolation from past experience. He has often appeared to be dying, and has all at once recovered health and spirits. No doubt, however, his constitution must be weakened more and more by every attack. . . .

CLXII

Dorothy Wordsworth to Mrs. Clarkson

Monday, 28th March, [1808.]

My dear Friend,

We have had no letter from William since he was with you. He wrote on the very day he was to see you; and from Coleridge we have heard of his having been with you; and from Lady Beaumont that he was at Dunmow, and well, last Tuesday. I wonder whether he read his poem[1] to you. I hope he did; for I am sure you would be delighted. Nay that is too cold a word, enraptured with it, and may perhaps have had some influence in persuading him to publish it, which he very much dislikes now that it comes to the point, though he left us fully determined. I can never expect that poem, or any which he may write, to be immediately popular, like *The Lay of the Last Minstrel;* but I think the story will help out those parts which are above the common level of taste and knowledge, and that it will have a better sale than his former works, and perhaps help them off. . . . We have had frequent letters from Coleridge, and his health seems to be much amended. He has been too much employed in thinking of his friends to have time to brood over his own misfortunes, and *that* I am sure is much better for him; though I believe he has a thousand times over more care and sorrow for his friends than for himself. He has been exceedingly anxious about dear Sara H. I trust much more so than there was occasion; for she is at present very well, and though I have not skill to measure the danger, I hope (for Hope is in my nature) seeing

---

[1] *The White Doe of Rylstone.* — Ed.

her well, though not looking very well in the face, not worse than when she came to Grasmere.

Most likely you have read in the papers of the dismal event which happened in our neighbourhood on Saturday sen-night, but I am sure you will wish to know further particulars. Our thoughts have been almost wholly employed about the poor sufferers or their family ever since. George and Sarah Green, two inhabitants of this vale, went to a sale in Langdale in the afternoon; and set off homewards in the evening, intending to cross the fells and descend just above their own cottage, a lonely dwelling in Easedale. They had left a daughter at home eleven years old, with the care of five brothers and sisters younger than herself, the youngest an infant at the breast. These dear helpless creatures sate up till eleven o'clock expecting their parents, and then went to bed thinking that they had stayed all night in Langdale because of the weather. All next day they continued to expect them, and on Monday morning one of the boys went to a house on the opposite side of the dale to borrow a cloak. On being asked for what purpose? he replied that his sister was going to Langdale to *lait their folk* [1] who had never come home. The man of the house started up, and said that they were lost; and immediately spread the alarm. As long as daylight lasted on that day, and on Monday and till Tuesday afternoon, all the men of Grasmere, and many from Langdale, were out upon the fells. On Tuesday afternoon the bodies were found miserably mangled, having been cut by the crags. They were lying not above a quarter of a mile above a house in Langdale where their shrieks had been distinctly heard by two different

[1] To search for their people. — Ed.

persons who supposed that the shrieks came from some drunken people who had been at the sale. The bodies were brought home in a cart, and buried in one grave last Thursday. The poor children all the time they had been left by themselves suspected no evil; and as soon as it was known by others that their father and mother were missing, the truth came upon them like a thunder-stroke. The neighbouring women came to look after them, and found them in a pitiable state, all crying together. In a little time, however, they were pacified, and food was brought into the house, for they had scarcely anything left.

Their parents were the poorest people in the vale, though they had a small estate of their own and a single cow. This morsel of land, now deeply mortgaged, had been in the possession of the family for several generations; they were loath to sell it, and consequently they had never had any assistance from the parish. He had been twice married. By his former wife he had left one son and three daughters, and by her who perished with him four sons and four daughters. They must have very soon parted with their land if they had lived, for their means were reduced by little and little, till scarcely anything but the land was left. The cow was grown old, and they had not money to buy another. They had sold their horse, and were in the habit of carrying bridles, or anything that they could spare, to barter for potatoes or bread. Luxuries they had none. They never made tea, and when the neighbours went to the children on Monday they found nothing in the house but two boilings of potatoes, a very little meal, and a few [pieces] of lean dried mutton. The cow at this time does not give a quart of milk in a day. You will wonder how they lived at all,

and indeed I can hardly tell you. They used to sell a
few peats in the summer, which they dug out of their own
heart's heart — their land — and perhaps the old man (he
was sixty-five years of age) might earn a little money by
doing odd jobs for his neighbours; but it was never
known till now (by us at least) how much distressed they
must have been. See them when you would, they were
always cheerful; and when they went from home they
were decently dressed. The children too, though very
ragged, were clean; and are as pure and innocent, and
in every respect as promising children as I ever saw.
Since this melancholy event our thoughts have been
chiefly employed in laying schemes to prevent the children from falling into the hands of persons who may use
them unkindly, and for giving them decent education.
One of the eight is in place, and can provide for herself.
The next is with us. She has attended the children since
we came from Coleorton; but we had intended parting
with her at Whitsuntide if her parents had lived, and
have hired an elder servant in her place, thinking it bad
for the children's tempers to be under one so young. We
shall however now keep her, not as a servant, but send
her to Grasmere school, and teach her to sew; and do
our best to fit her for a good place. She is as innocent,
and as guileless, as a baby; but her faculties are rather
slow. After her there are six left, and it is probable they
will be boarded out by the parish. We hope that a sufficient
sum will be raised for the purposes I have mentioned.
Everybody who has the power seems disposed to assist
them. The Bishop of Llandaff will subscribe ten guineas,
and we have received five guineas from a Mr. Wilson[1];

[1] John Wilson, "Christopher North." — Ed.

a very amiable young man, a friend and *adorer* of William and his verses, who is building a house at Windermere. This sum we shall keep back till we see what is done by the parish and others, and we hope to get more from our friends. Perhaps your uncle Hardcastle may do something.[1] . . .

CLXIII

William Wordsworth to Sir George Beaumont

GRASMERE, April 8th, [Postmark, 1808.]

My dear Sir George,

I arrived here the day before yesterday, having given up my plan of going by Oxford, in consequence of the bad accounts received of the state of Miss Hutchinson's health. I found Mrs. Wordsworth and my sister well.

I left London on Sunday morning, the day, or day before, you would reach it. This was sufficiently morti-fying, but could not be prevented. I had a pleasant ride to town from Dunmow, the morning being, though cold, unusually beautiful. I heard Coleridge lecture twice, and he seemed to give great satisfaction; but he was not in spirits, and suffered much during the course of the week, both in body and mind. I did not write to you, or Lady Beaumont, at Dunmow, because my departure from town was deferred from day to day; and I wished to be able to speak with certainty of my intended motions. When you write to your mother, Lady Beaumont, pray do not fail to present to her my respectful remembrances and best thanks for her hospitable attention to me. I am very happy that I have seen her.

[1] See Wordsworth's poem, *George and Sarah Green*, and De Quincey's *Recollections of the Lakes.* — Ed.

Coleridge and I availed ourselves of your letters to Lawrence, and saw Mr. Angerstein's pictures. The day was very unfavourable, not a gleam of sun, and the clouds were quite in disgrace. The great picture of Michael Angelo and Sebastian pleased me more than ever. The new Rembrandt has, I think, much, very much, in it to admire, but still more to *wonder at*, rather than admire. I have seen many pictures of Rembrandt which I should prefer to it. The light in the *depth* of the Temple is far the finest part of it; indeed, it is the only part of the picture which gives me very *high* pleasure ; but that does highly please me. No doubt by this time you have seen Coleridge, and probably heard him lecture. I long to hear from you, and about him, what you think of the state of his health and spirits, etc. etc. Pray tell Lady Beaumont that I left my poem in Coleridge's possession ; so that, if she wishes to read it again, she may easily procure it of him.

We live in hope that our new house[1] will be ready for us in May. As you will guess, we are sadly cooped up here, particularly at this time. But O how happy are we altogether again ! If but poor Coleridge were in the right way, we should be content; in the fulness of contentment, as I trust that, with care, we shall bring Miss Hutchinson about again. When you have seen Havill's drawing of Rydale, pray tell me what you think of it. I have not much confidence in my judgment of pictures, except when it coincides with yours.

My heart has been so occupied since my return with my own family that I have scarcely greeted, or noticed, the beautiful vale in which we live, and our sheltering

[1] Allan Bank. — Ed.

mountains; but this is a pleasure to come. You will deem it strange, but really some of the imagery of London has, since my return hither, been more present to my mind than that of this noble vale. I left Coleridge at seven o'clock on Sunday morning, and walked towards the city in a very thoughtful and melancholy state of mind. I had passed through Temple Bar and by St. Dunstan's, noticing nothing, and entirely occupied with my own thoughts, when, looking up, I saw before me the avenue of Fleet Street, silent, empty, and pure white, with a sprinkling of new-fallen snow, not a cart or carriage to obstruct the view, no noise, only a few soundless and dusky foot-passengers here and there. You remember the elegant line of the curve of Ludgate Hill in which this avenue would terminate, and beyond, towering above it, was the huge and majestic form of St. Paul's, solemnised by a thin veil of falling snow. I cannot say how much I was affected at this unthought-of sight in such a place, and what a blessing I felt there is in habits of exalted imagination. My sorrow was controlled, and my uneasiness of mind — not quieted and relieved altogether — seemed at once to receive the gift of an anchor of security.

Little remarkable occurred during my journey. We had a guard to the coach, whose first journey it was; he had been a grocer, and taken to this new way of life — and for what reason, think you? — he did not like the confinement of his old business. At Lancaster I happened to mention Grasmere in hearing of one of the passengers, who asked me immediately if one Wordsworth did not live there. I answered "Yes." "He has written," said he, "some very beautiful poems; the critics do indeed cry out against them, and condemn them as

over-simple, but for my part I read them with great pleasure; they are natural and true." This man was also a
grocer. My sheet is exhausted. Affectionate remembrances to Lady Beaumont, and to Mrs. Fermor if with
you. And believe me, my dear Sir George, your sincere
friend,

W. WORDSWORTH.

CLXIV

William Wordsworth to Richard Sharp

GRASMERE, April 13, 1808.

My dear Sir,
Well-knowing your general humanity, and the particular
interest you take in this part of the country, I have been
unable to resist an impulse to send you the enclosed
paper, giving a brief account of a most melancholy event
[the death of the Greens] which took place lately in our
vale, and soliciting the assistance of such persons as
may be willing to do an act of kindness upon such an
occasion. Let me beg of you, for the sake of the children of whom you will read in this paper, and of the
pleasant remembrances which you will have in common
with me of Easedale, — that part of Grasmere vale of
which the unfortunate persons you will read of were
inhabitants, — that you would procure among your friends,
Mr. Boddington for example, and Mr. Philips, (I mention
these more particularly), and any others of your friends
unknown to me, a contribution however small for the
purposes specified in the paper. I beg you to do this
as a matter to which I, who am acquainted with all the
particulars of this pathetic case, and the merits of the
parties, attach no common interest. One of the orphans,

a little girl, is now in my service, and I shall myself take
care of her.

I am sorry that I did not see you again. . . . I found
Coleridge so unwell, and out of tune, that I had not
encouragement even to mention to him the breakfasting
with you we talked of. . . . I am, my dear Sharp, affectionately yours,
                                        W. WORDSWORTH.

There are many moving circumstances attending this
case, of which my sister will write a minute narrative;
and which, if we live to meet in this country again, I will
read to you, as they tend to throw much light upon the
state of moral feeling in the inhabitants of these vales.

CLXV

Dorothy Wordsworth to Mrs. Clarkson

[Postmark, KENDAL. No date. 1808?]
My dear Friend,
    . . . I cannot express what pain I feel in refusing to
grant any request of yours, and above all one in which
dear Mr. Clarkson joins so earnestly; but, indeed, I cannot have that narrative[1] published.

My reasons are entirely disconnected with myself,
much as I should detest the idea of setting myself up as
an author. I should not object on that score if it had
been an invention of my own. It might have been published without a name, and nobody would have thought
of me. But on account of the family of the Greens I
cannot consent. Their story was only represented to the

[1] The story of the Greens lost in the snowstorm in Langdale.
— Ed.

world in that narrative, which was drawn up for the collecting of a subscription, so far as it might tend to produce the aid desired; but, by publishing this narrative of mine, I should bring the children forward to notice as individuals, and we know not what injurious effect this might have upon them. Besides, it appears to me that the work is too recent to be published, in delicacy to others as well as to the children.

I should be the more hurt at being obliged to return such an answer to your request, if I could believe that the story would be of that service to the work which Mr. Clarkson imagines. I cannot believe that it would do much for it. Thirty or forty years hence, — when the characters of the children are formed, and they can be no longer objects of curiosity, — if it should be thought that any service would be done, it is my present wish that it should then be published, whether I am alive or dead. . . .

CLXVI

William Wordsworth to Francis Wrangham

GRASMERE, April 17th, [1808.]

My dear Wrangham,

Your last letter arrived just in time, viz., while I was busy in stirring among my more rich and powerful friends, among whom you yourself are to be ranked, to promote the interest of a cluster of little orphans, who have been left such in a most afflicting manner. . . .

I presumed far upon your indulgence when I left your last letter but one so long unanswered. The kindness which it displayed did not merit such a return, but I know not how it is, I can repay the love of my friends more punctually by any coin than that of letters. You offered to build me a cottage, and spoke of your sublime ocean scenery. I could not be easy under the thought of any body having the trouble of building a house for me, and since the loss of my dear brother, we have all had such painful and melancholy thoughts connected with the ocean, that nothing but a paramount necessity would make us live near it. Our common friend Montagu is doing and looking very well; he is advancing in his profession, and has in Mrs. Skipper an excellent friend for himself, and tutoress, and even mother for his children. Your Assize Sermon [1] I hope to receive through Longman's hands. About last Christmas I wrote a poem of the narrative kind of some length,[2] which, if I publish it, I shall send you. Excuse my writing more at length at present; for I am quite exhausted, having had to write and transcribe so much about this melancholy affair; and having had a course of dreadful suffering in our family last week, nothing less than an apprehension that our eldest boy — a child for his beauty, strength, and sweet disposition the admiration of every one — was labouring under that dreadful malady, water in the head. God be praised it has not proved so, and he is mending apace. But his bodily sufferings have been great, and ours (of mind) far more dreadful. I am, very affectionately yours,

W. WORDSWORTH.

My sole errand to London was to see Coleridge who had been dangerously ill, and is still very poorly. I have

[1] *Human Laws best supported by the Gospel; an Assize Sermon.* York, 1808. — Ed.

[2] *The White Doe of Rylstone.* — Ed.

read your quondam friend's, Dr. Symmonds, life of Milton.[1] On some future occasion I will tell you what I think of it. Your own prose translations from Milton are excellent, but you have not done justice (who indeed could?) to that fine stanza

> Gemelle cultu simplici gaudens liber, etc.[2]

It is untranslatable.

CLXVII

Dorothy Wordsworth to Lady Beaumont

GRASMERE, April 20th, 1808.

My dear Friend,

We received your letter this morning, enclosing the half of a five-pound note. I am happy to inform you that the orphans[3] have been fixed under the care of very respectable people. The baby is with its sister, she who filled the mother's place in the house during their two days of fearless solitude.[4] It has clung to her ever since, and she has been its sole nurse. I went with two ladies of the Committee (in my sister's place, who was then confined to poor John's bedside) to conduct the family to their separate homes. The two girls were together, as I have said, two boys at another house, and the third boy by himself at the house of an elderly man, who had a particular friendship for their father. The kind reception

---

[1] *The Life of John Milton*, by Charles Symmonds, D.D. (1806). — Ed.

[2] See the ode, *Ad Joannem Rousium Oxoniensis Academiæ Bibliothecarium.* Strophe 1, in " Sylvarum Liber." — Ed.

[3] The Greens of Easedale. — Ed.

[4] See pp. 344–346. — Ed.

that the children met with was very affecting. .... I am going to transcribe a poem composed by my brother a few days after his return. It was begun in the church-yard, when he was looking at the grave of the husband and wife, and is, in fact, supposed to be entirely composed there.

Who weeps for strangers? etc.

... The poem[1] is to be published. Longman has consented, in spite of the odium under which my brother labours as a poet, to give him one hundred guineas per thousand copies, according to the demand. ...

[Of Coleridge.] He is a wonderful creature, pouring out such treasures of thought and knowledge almost, we may say, without premeditation, and in language so eloquent. ...

CLXVIII

William Wordsworth to Richard Sharp[2]

GRASMERE, Monday, April 25, 1808.

My dear Sir,

Accept my warmest thanks for your generous donation to our poor orphans; be so good also as warmly to thank Mr. Boddington and Mr. Philips for their kindness. I have the satisfaction to say that a copy of the paper I sent you has been circulated in this neighbourhood with very good success; the neighbouring gentry having taken up the business with zeal. The Bishop of Llandaff and

[1] *The White Doe of Rylstone.* — Ed.
[2] Richard Sharp (1759-1835) of Mark Lane, M.P., friend of most of the literary men of his day, from Johnston and Burke to Wordsworth and Coleridge, a great traveller, essayist, minor poet, and very brilliant talker; hence the *sobriquet* " Conversation Sharp." — Ed.

Lord Muncaster have each subscribed ten guineas. Sir Daniel and Lady Fleming and Lady Diana each five, and other persons in the neighbourhood five, Lady Beaumont five, and Mr. Wilson, a friend of ours who is building a house near Ortest Head, has also subscribed five, and we have sums coming in from other quarters; so that the children will be well housed, well fed, well clad, taught to read and write, and the girls to sew; and we hope there will be a little overplus to set them forward in life. They are already all placed in respectable houses in Grasmere; and Mrs. Wordsworth, who is one of the managing committee, being upon the spot, will be able to see that justice is in all respects done to them.

If you and I ever meet in this country again, I should have great pleasure in showing you, I hope, the fresh cheeks of some of these orphans, and visiting with you the lonely and now deserted house which was occupied by them and their unfortunate parents. The house, in its appearance and situation, strikingly accords with the melancholy catastrophe; a brawling brook close by, with huge stones and scattered rocks on every side. The house itself is of grey mountain stone, as if it had grown out of the mountain, an indigenous dwelling for indigenous inhabitants.

As to the money, I shall immediately place your name on the list of subscribers. . . .

May I beg of you to transfer the statement to Mr. Rogers. . . .

I am, my dear Sharp, most truly yours,

W. Wordsworth.

I have only heard once from Coleridge, a week ago. He seemed then something better, but much occupied.

On second thoughts I find this to be an error. We had a short letter on Wednesday last, in which he said he was doing well.

CLXIX

Dorothy Wordsworth to Mrs. Marshall

[GRASMERE] May 11, 1808.

... My brother was very much pleased with your frankness in telling us that you did not perfectly like his poem.[1] He wishes to know whether the tale itself did not interest you, or whether you did not enter into the conception of Emily's character, or take delight in that visionary communion which is supposed to have existed between her and the doe. Do not fear to give him pain. He is far too much accustomed to be abused to receive pain from it, at least so far as he himself is concerned. My reason for asking you these questions is that some of our friends, who are equal admirers of *The White Doe* and of my brother's published poems, think that this poem will sell on account of the story; that is, that the story will bear up those parts which are above the level of the public taste: whereas the two last volumes are — except by a few solitary individuals who are passionately devoted to my brother's works — abused wholesale. Now, as his sole object for publishing this poem at present would be for the sake of the money, he would not publish it if he did not think from the judgments of his friends that it would be likely to have a sale. He has no pleasure in publishing. He even detests it ; and were it not that he is poor, he would leave all his works to be published after his death. William himself is sure that *The*

---

[1] *The White Doe of Rylstone.* — Ed.

White Doe will not sell, or be admired, except by a very few at first; therefore, though he once was inclined to publish it, he is very averse to it now, and only yields to Mary's entreaties and mine. We are determined, however, if we are deceived this time, to let him have his own way in future. . . .

CLXX

William Wordsworth to Walter Scott

GRASMERE, May 14, 1808.

My dear Scott,

. . . Thank you for the interesting particulars about the Nortons.[1] I shall like much to see them for their own sakes; but so far from being serviceable to my poem,[2] they would stand in the way of it, as I have followed (as I was in duty bound to do) the traditionary and common historic account. Therefore I shall say, in this case, a plague upon your industrious antiquarians, that have put my fine story to confusion.[3] . . .

CLXXI

William Wordsworth to Thomas De Quincey

GRASMERE, [1808.]

My dear Friend

As I neither see you nor hear tidings of you, I begin to fear you are suffering in health.

[1] Wordsworth had asked Scott to give him any particulars about "the Rising in the North," and the fate of the Norton family, with which he was acquainted. — Ed.

[2] *The White Doe of Rylstone.* — Ed.

[3] This letter and the letter of August 4, which follows, are in the Abbotsford Collection of MSS. — Ed.

I arrived at home ten days ago, and now write this to let you know that we have been disappointed in not seeing you, and further that it is not likely that I shall quit this place again for some time, where be assured I shall be happy to see you whenever it shall suit you. At all events let me hear from you, as I am afraid that you are unwell. Believe me most sincerely yours,

W. WORDSWORTH.

I wrote to you from London about a month or five weeks ago.

CLXXII

William Wordsworth to Francis Wrangham [1]

GRASMERE, June 5th, 1808.

My dear Wrangham,

I have this moment received your letter. Montagu is a most provoking fellow; very kind, very humane, very generous, very ready to serve, with a thousand other good qualities; but in the practical business of life the arrantest mar-plan that ever lived. When I first wrote to you, I wrote also to him, sending the statement which I sent to you, and begging his exertions *among his friends*. By and by comes back my statement having undergone a *rifaciamento* from his hands, and *printed;* with an accompanying letter saying that if some of the principal people in this neighbourhood who had already subscribed would

---

[1] This was published in the *Memoirs of William Wordsworth* (1851), Vol. II, pp. 171–179; also in the *Prose Works of William Wordsworth*, Vol. I, pp. 334–339. It is now transcribed more fully from the original MS. — Ed.

put their names to this paper testifying that this was a proper case for charitable interference ; or that the *persons mentioned were proper objects of charity*, that he would have the printed paper inserted in the public Newspapers, etc. etc. Upon which my sister wrote to him that in consequence of what had been already subscribed, and what we had reason to expect from those friends who were privately stirring in the business, — among whom we chiefly alluded to you, in our own minds, as one on whom we had most dependance, — that there would be no necessity for *public advertisements;* but that if, amongst his private friends, he could raise any thing for us, we should be *very glad* to receive it. And, upon this, does he write to you in this (what shall I call it, for I am really vexed) blundering manner!! I will not call upon you to undertake the awkward task of rebuilding that part of the edifice which Montagu has destroyed, but let what remains be preserved, and if a little could be added, there would be no harm. I must request you to transmit the money to me with the names of the persons to whom we are obliged, in order that they may be inserted in the book which is lodged with the treasurer.

With regard to the latter, and more important part of your letter, I am under many difficulties. I am writing from a window which gives me a view of a little boat gliding quietly about upon the surface of our basin of a lake. I should like to be in it, but what could I do with such a vessel in the heart of the Atlantic Ocean? As this boat would be to that navigation, so is a letter to the subject upon which you would set me afloat. Let me however say that I have read your sermon[1]

---

[1] Entitled, *The Gospel best promulgated by National Schools.* It was published at York. — Ed.

(which I lately received from Longman) with much
pleasure. I only gave it a cursory perusal, for since it
arrived our family has been in great confusion, we having
removed to another house, in which we are not yet half
settled. The appendix I had received before in a frank,
and of that I feel myself more entitled to speak, because
I had read it more at leisure.

I am entirely of accord with you, in chiefly recommending religious books for the poor, but of many of
those which you recommend I can neither speak in
praise nor blame, as I have never read them. Yet, as
far as my own observation goes, which has been mostly
employed upon agricultural persons in thinly-peopled
districts, I cannot find that there is much disposition to
read among the labouring classes, or much occasion for
it. Among manufacturers and persons engaged in seden-
tary employments it is, I know, very different. The
labouring man in agriculture generally carries on his work
either in solitude, or with his own family, — persons whose
minds he is thoroughly acquainted with — and with whom
he is under no temptation to enter into discussion, or to
compare opinions. He goes home from the field, or the
barn, and within and about his own house he finds a hundred little jobs which furnish him with a change of employment, which is grateful and profitable; then comes supper,
and to bed.

This for week-days : for Sabbaths he goes to church,
with us mostly twice a day ; on coming home some one
turns to the Bible, finds the text and probably reads the
chapter whence it is taken, or perhaps some other ; and
in the afternoon the master or mistress frequently reads
the Bible, if lone; and on this day the mistress of the
house *almost always* teaches the children to read, or as

they express it, hears them a lesson; or, if not thus employed, they visit their neighbours or receive them in their own houses as they drop in, and keep up by the hour a slow and familiar chat. This kind of life of which I have seen much, and which I know will be looked upon with little complacency by many religious persons, from its bearing no impression of their particular modes of faith and from its want of fervent piety and habitual godliness, is peaceable; and as innocent as (the frame of society and the practices of government being what they are) we have a right to expect; besides, it is much more intellectual than a careless observer would suppose.

One of our neighbours, who lives as I have described, was yesterday walking with me; and as we were pacing on, talking about indifferent matters, by the side of a brook, he suddenly said to me, with great spirit and a lively smile, " I like to walk where I can hear the sound of a beck " (the word, as you know in our dialect, for a brook). I cannot but think that this man, without being conscious of it, has had many devout feelings connected with the appearances which have presented themselves to him in his employment as a shepherd, and the pleasure of his heart at that moment was an acceptable offering to the Divine Being. But, to return to the subject of books, I find, among the people I am speaking of, halfpenny ballads, and penny and two-penny histories, in great abundance; these are often bought as charitable tributes to the poor persons who hawk them about (and it is the best way of procuring them). They are frequently stitched together in tolerably thick volumes, and such I have read; some of the contents, though not often religious, very good; others objectionable, either for the superstition in them (such as prophecies, fortune-telling, etc.) or more frequently for indelicacy. I have so much felt the influence of these straggling papers, that I have many a time wished that I had talents to produce songs, poems, and little histories, that might circulate among other good things in this way, supplanting partly the bad ; flowers and useful herbs to take the place of weeds. Indeed some of the poems which I have published were composed, not without a hope that at some time or other they might answer this purpose.

The kind of library which you recommend would not, I think, from the reasons given above, be of much direct use in any of the agricultural or pastoral districts of Cumberland or Westmorland with which I am acquainted, though almost every person can read : I mean of *general* use as to morals or behaviour. It might however with individuals do much in awakening enterprize, calling forth ingenuity, and fostering genius. I have known several persons who would eagerly have sought, not after these books merely, but any books, and would have been most happy in having such a collection to repair to. The knowledge thus acquired would also have spread, by being dealt about in conversation among their neighbours, at the door, or by the fire-side — so that it is not easy to foresee how far the good might extend; and harm I can see none, which would not be greatly overbalanced by the advantage.

The situation of manufacturers is deplorably different. The monotony of their employments renders some sort of stimulus, intellectual or bodily, absolutely necessary for them. Their work is carried on in clusters, men from different parts of the world, and perpetually changing; so that every individual is constantly in the way of being brought into contact with new notions and feelings, and of being unsettled in his own accordingly. A select library therefore, in such situations, may be of the same use as a public dial, keeping everybody's clock in some kind of order.

Besides, contrasting the manufacturer with the agriculturalist, it may be observed that he has much more leisure ; and in his over-hours (not having other pleasant employment to turn to) he is more likely to find reading a relief. What then are the books which should be put in his way? Without being myself a clergyman, I have no hesitation in saying, chiefly religious ones ; though I should not go so far as you seemed inclined to do, excluding others because they are not according to the letter, or in the spirit of your profession. I, with you, feel little disposed to admire several of those mentioned by Gilbert Burns ; much less others which you name, as having been recommended. In G. Burns' collection there may be too little religion ; and I should fear that you, like all other clergymen, may confine yourself too exclusively to that concern which you justly deem the most important, but which by being exclusively considered can never be thoroughly understood. I will allow with you that religion is the eye of the soul, but if we would have successful soul-oculists, not merely that organ, but the general anatomy and constitution of the intellectual frame must be studied. Farther, the powers of that eye are affected by the general state of the system. My meaning is, that piety and religion will be best understood by him who takes the most comprehensive view of the human mind, and that for the most part, they will strengthen with the general strength of the mind, and that this is best promoted by a due mixture of direct and indirect nourishment and discipline. For example, *Paradise Lost* and *Robinson*

Crusoe might be as serviceable as Law's *Serious Call*,[1] or Melmoth's *Great Importance of a Religious Life*[2]; at least, if the books be all good, they would mutually assist each other.

In what I have said, though following my own thoughts merely as called forth by your Appendix, is *implied* an answer to your request that I would give you "half an idea upon education as a national object." I have only kept upon the surface of the question; but you must have deduced, that I deem any plan of National Education in a country like ours most difficult to apply to practice. In Switzerland, or Sweden, or Norway, or France, or Spain — or anywhere but Great Britain — it would be comparatively easy. Heaven and Hell are scarcely more different from each other than Sheffield and Manchester, etc. differ from the plains and vallies of Surrey, Essex, Cumberland, or Westmorland. We have mighty cities, and towns of all sizes, with villages and cottages scattered everywhere. We are mariners, miners, manufacturers in tens of thousands: traders, husbandmen, everything. What form of discipline, what books or doctrines, I will not say would equally suit all these? but which, if happily fitted for one, would not perhaps be an absolute nuisance in another?

You will also have deduced that nothing romantic can be said with truth of the influence of education upon the district in which I live. We have, thank Heaven, free schools, or schools with some endowment, almost everywhere, and almost every one can read; not because we have free or endowed schools, but because our land

---

[1] *A Serious Call to a Devout and Holy Life* (1728). — Ed.

[2] William Melmoth, barrister and religious writer (1666–1743). The above work was published anonymously in 1711. — Ed.

is, far more than elsewhere, tilled by men who are the owners of it. As the population is not over-crowded, and the vices which are quickened and cherished in a crowded population do not therefore prevail, parents have more ability and inclination to send their children to school; much more than in the manufacturing districts ; and also, though in a less degree, more than in agricultural ones, where the tillers are not proprietors.

If in Scotland the children are sent to school, where the parents have not the advantage I have been speaking of, it is chiefly because their labour can be turned to no account at home. Send among them manufacturers, or farmers on a large scale ; and you may indeed substitute Sunday-schools, or other modes of instructing them, but the ordinary parish schools will be neglected. The influence of our schools in this neighbourhood can never be understood if this — their connection with the state of landed property — be overlooked. In fact that influence is not striking. The people are not habitually religious, in the common sense of the word, much less godly. The effect of their schooling is chiefly seen in the activity with which the young persons emigrate, and the success attending it ; and at home, by a general orderliness and gravity, with habits of independence and self-respect; nothing obsequious or fawning is ever to be seen amongst them.

It may be added that this ability (from the two causes, Land and Schools) of giving their children instruction contributes to spread a respect for scholarship through the country. If in any family one of the children should be quicker at his book, or fonder of it than others, he is often marked out in consequence for the profession of a clergyman. This (before these mercantile or manufacturing employments held out such flattering hopes) very generally happened; so that the schools of the North were the great nurseries of curates, several of whom got forward in their profession; some with, and others without, the help of a university education; and, in all instances, such connection of families (all the members of which lived in the humblest and plainest manner, working with their own hands as labourers) with a learned and dignified profession assisted — and still does, though in a less degree — not a little to elevate their feelings, and conferred importance on them in their own eyes.

But I must stop. My dear Wrangham, begin your education at the top of society; let the head go in the right course, and the tail will follow. But what can you expect of National Education conducted by a government which for twenty years resisted the abolition of the Slave Trade, and annually debauches the morals of the people by every possible device? holding out the temptation with one hand, and scourging with the other. The distilleries and lotteries are standing records that the government cares nothing for the morals of the people, and that all they want is their money. But wisdom and justice are the only true sources of the revenue of a people. Preach this, and may you not preach in vain! Wishing you success in every good work, I remain your affectionate friend,

WM. WORDSWORTH.

Thanks for your enquiries about our little boy. He is well, though not yet quite strong.

CLXXIII

Dorothy Wordsworth to Mrs. Clarkson

EUSEMERE, Wednesday, August 3rd, [1808.]

A breezy day, Hallin[1] before me clear with the lower mountains, Helvellyn shrouded in clouds. I write in the dining-room, i.e. your new room, not that room where you first received me. God bless you, my beloved friend. I have been led to this long preface by thoughts of you. I seem to see with your eyes. I have been here since Monday night, and Sara[2] is with me. . . .

I think I mentioned to you once a young man of the name of John Wilson, who is building a house near Windermere. He is a man of fortune, of good understanding, most affectionate heart, and very pleasing manners. The origin of our first acquaintance was his enthusiastic admiration of my brother's poems, and he is now scarcely less enthusiastic in his admiration of my brother. It seems as if he, and his whole family, thought they could hardly do enough to express their liking to us all, — no doubt in consequence of their reverence for him. His mother and sister are now at his cottage, which is close to his unfinished new house,[3] and is the most enchanting spot in the world, under the shade of a large sycamore tree, looking down upon the lake and all its lovely islands, and upwards to Langdale Pikes and sublime company of mountains. Well, at this place, about a month ago, we all spent a very pleasant day. Last Friday morning Mary Monkhouse and I rose at six o'clock, and breakfasted at

---

[1] Hallin Fell, on the east side of Ullswater. — Ed.
[2] Sarah Hutchinson, her sister-in-law. — Ed.
[3] Elleray. — Ed.

Ambleside with Mrs. Green. Mr. Wilson's boat met us
at the head of the water, and we stayed at his house till
Sunday, when Miss Wilson brought us home in her
mother's carriage. . . .

What do you think of a picnic upon Grasmere Island?
Nineteen of us were to have dined there, and were all
caught in a thunder shower, and all wet to the skin on
our way to the lake side. The Wilsons were of the party.
Mr. Wilson said to me, " I would not for the world that
that shower had not come. For the world I would not
have had nineteen persons racketing, and walking about
the whole day upon that island, disturbing those poor
sheep." By the bye what is the origin of the word picnic?
Our Windermere gentlemen have a picnic almost every
day. . . .

CLXXIV

William Wordsworth to Walter Scott

GRASMERE, August 4, 1808.[1]

. . . Thank you for *Marmion*, which I have read with
lively pleasure. I think your end has been attained.
That it is not in every respect the end which I should
wish you to purpose to yourself, you will be well aware,
from what you know of my notions of composition,
both as to matter and manner. . . . In the circle of my
acquaintance, it seems as well liked as the *Lay*, though
I have heard that in the world it is not so. Had the
poem been much better than the *Lay* it could scarcely
have satisfied the public, which, at best, has too much
of the monster, the moral monster, in its composition.

[1] This letter is quoted, imperfectly, in Lockhart's *Memoirs of the
Life of Sir Walter Scott*, Vol. II, p. 142. — Ed.

In the notes you have quoted two lines of mine from memory, and your memory, admirable as it is, has here failed you. The passage stands with you

The swans on *sweet* St. Mary's lake.

The proper reading is

The *swan* on *still* St. Mary's lake.

I mention this in order that the correction may be made in a future edition.

I had a peep at your edition of Dryden. I had not time to read the notes, which would have interested me much, namely the historical and illustrative ones; but some of the critical introductions I read, and am not surprised at the opinions they contain, but rather surprised at them coming from you, who in your infancy and childhood must have had so many of the strains of Nature-Poetry resounding in your ears. One passage in one of your notes I was grieved to see; not the language of praise applied to things which, according to my feelings, do not deserve it, but hard censure unjustly passed upon a great man, I mean Heywood, the dramatist. Only read (not to speak of any of his other things) his *Woman killed with Kindness*. There is an exquisite strain of pathos in many parts of that play, which Dryden not only was utterly incapable of producing, but of feeling when produced. The praise which has been given to Otway, Heywood is far better entitled to. He does not indeed write like a poet, but his scenes are, many of them, as *pathetic* as any that have been produced since the days of Euripides. . . . My dear Scott, most truly yours,

W. WORDSWORTH.

CLXXV

Dorothy Wordsworth to Lady Beaumont

Tuesday, 16th August, [1808.]

My dear Friend,

I will relate the history of my adventures in a few words from the time of my parting from you at Ashby to go to bed; for I had so hurried myself away at the last from Coleorton that I hardly felt as if I had bid you farewell till I had closed my letter, when I was much more at ease, though sad at heart. I lay down; although I did not sleep, I rose refreshed at twelve o'clock, when the coach arrived. Willy promised that he would call to inquire after me the next day, when the landlady assured me she would give him my letter to you. I hope that she did not at the same time tell him that I went on the outside of the coach; for I am sure you and Sir George would be uneasy about me, and dear Mrs. Fermor, if she had been with you, would have been completely miserable. I was, indeed (more for the sake of my friends than myself), greatly mortified to find that there was no room for me in the inside. Go I must; therefore there was no alternative but taking a chaise, or placing myself on the outside. I did not hesitate a moment, for I could not find in my heart to pay a guinea and a half (nay, it would have been five-and-thirty shillings) for travelling twenty miles, as the night was dry and pleasant; indeed, the air appeared to be very mild at Ashby, but I found it cold enough upon Charnwood Forest. There, by the light of the moon, and of our carriage lamps, I now and then discovered some scattered rocks; and they and everything reminded me of Coleorton, and many a time

I turned my head round to look back towards that quarter where I supposed Coleorton lay.

This is a pleasure I could not have had in the inside of the coach; and indeed I am sure, cold as I was, that I had a much more agreeable journey than I should have had if I had been shut up there; for the sky was very beautiful all night through, and when the dawn appeared there was a mild glory and cheerfulness in the east that was quite enchanting to me, being a sight I have so seldom seen. I warmed myself by the kitchen fire at Leicester, and went to bed at four o'clock. I did not fall asleep till very near six, and at six I was called upon to rise. I took my breakfast with a gentleman who was going on to Stamford on the outside; and, as he was very civil, and offered to take me under his protection, and as the morning was uncommonly promising, I resolved to go on the outside; for really I dreaded the heat within. Besides, as the coach was not likely to be full, I could change my place at any time. You must not therefore be angry with me, or charge me with imprudence. I determined, believe me, to take good care of myself. I had the best place on the coach, and all the passengers were civil and well-behaved — I am sure much better company than those within, for I could judge of both at breakfast-time.

Near Oakham I saw some fine woods on a hill to the left, and a large house. This they told me was Burley, and I was greatly disappointed (I supposed it to be Rugby House which Sir George had wished me to see), and hardly able to believe my own eyes, for, though a fine house, I could discover nothing but a great heavy mass, and no towers. I was not undeceived till I came to Stamford, when I passed by the gateway of the real

Burleigh House, and saw the irregular turrets and chimneys at a distance. By the bye the coach stopped at Stamford while the passengers dined, and I shared my sandwiches with a young woman who was my companion on the outside. I have several times, in the course of my travels, passed through Stamford, and used to think it a very ugly place; but, to my great surprise, whichever way I looked on Friday afternoon, I saw something to admire — an old house, a group of houses, the irregular line of a street, a church, or a spire; and it was a great satisfaction to me to be in this manner delighted with what I had passed over in my youth with indifference, perhaps even disgust.

At Huntingdon I had the offer of tea, but though it would have been very refreshing, I thought it was too expensive a luxury, being only one stage from the end of my journey; therefore I walked about in the town, which was all in a bustle with gay ladies here and there and everywhere, and I saw the sheriff in his state carriage. The evening was cold, therefore I got into the coach; and, though I was glad to be there at that time, I could not but rejoice in my past enjoyments on the outside in breathing the fresh air, and seeing all the cheerful sights of the country around me. We had six passengers — one young lady with a bunch of honeysuckles, which added a scented poison to the hot air, and when I got out of the coach at Cambridge I was quite sick and giddy. We reached Cambridge at half-past nine. In our way to the inn we stopped at the gate of St. John's College, to set down one of our passengers. The stopping of the carriage roused me from a sleepy musing, and I was awe-stricken with the solemnity of the old gateway, and the light from a great distance within, streaming along the pavement. When they told me that it was the entrance to St. John's College, I was still more affected by the gloomy yet beautiful sight before me; for I thought of my dearest brother, in his youthful days, passing through that gateway to his home; and I could have believed that I saw him there even then, as I had seen him in the first year of his residence.

I met with Mr. Clarkson at the inn, and was, you may believe, rejoiced to hear his voice at the coach door. We supped together, and immediately after supper I went to bed, and slept well; and at eight o'clock the next morning went to Trinity Chapel. There I stood for many minutes in silence before the statue of Newton, while the organ sounded. I never saw a statue that gave me one hundredth part so much pleasure — but pleasure, that is not the word: it is a sublime sensation, in harmony with sentiments of devotion to the Divine Being, and reverence for the holy places where He is worshipped. We walked in the groves all the morning, and visited the Colleges. I sought out a favourite ash-tree, which my brother speaks of in his poem on his own life — a tree covered with ivy. We dined with a fellow of Peter-house in his rooms; and after dinner I went to King's College Chapel. There, and everywhere else at Cambridge, I was even much more impressed with the effect of the buildings than I had been formerly; and I do believe that this power of receiving an enlarged enjoyment from the sight of buildings is one of the privileges of our latter years.

I have this moment received a letter from William. He reached Hindwell at ten o'clock on Friday morning and found all well, and was well himself, and Miss H. thought he looked remarkably so. He says that she is grown quite fat. I have had two letters from Grasmere — all well. I reached . . . at nine o'clock on Sunday night. I had not time to write yesterday, for I indulged myself with sleeping till twelve o'clock. Mrs. Clarkson was overjoyed to see me, and is in much better health. She says she never saw me look so well. I tell her she must give you, and Coleorton, the credit of this. Pray give my affectionate and grateful remembrances to Sir George. Do mention his health from time to time when you write. Tell me how Miss Wills is, and give my kind love to both your sisters, and do write soon, and tell me about everything that is done and that happens among you, and write as long letters as you can ; but this is very unreasonable. Let me hear from you, at all events; long or short. Adieu, my dear friend. Believe me, ever with affectionate gratitude, yours faithfully,

D. WORDSWORTH

CLXXVI

William Wordsworth to Samuel Rogers

GRASMERE, Sept. 29, 1808.

My dear Sir,

I am greatly obliged to you for your kind exertions in favour of our Grasmere orphans, and for your own contribution.

The bill you sent me — £31:8 — I have already paid into the hands of the secretary.

I was glad to hear that our friend Sharp was so much benefited in health by his late visit to our beautiful country. We passed one pleasant day together, but we were unlucky, upon the whole, in not seeing much of each other, as a more than usual part of his time was spent about Keswick and Ullswater. I am happy to find that we

coincide in opinion about Crabbe's verses; for poetry in
no sense can they be called. Sharp is also of the same
opinion. I remember that I mentioned in my last that
there was nothing in the last publication so good as the
description of the parish workhouse, apothecary, etc.
This is true, and it is no less true that the passage which
I commended is of no great merit, because the description, at the best of no high order, is — in the instance of
the apothecary — inconsistent, that is, false. It no doubt
sometimes happens, but as far as my experience goes
very rarely, that country practitioners neglect and brutally
treat their patients ; but what kind of men are they who
do so ? —not apothecaries like Crabbe's professional, prag-
matical coxcombs, "all pride, generally neat, business,
bustle, and conceit," — no, but drunken reprobates, fre-
quenters of boxing-matches, cock-fightings, and horse-races.
These are the men who are hard-hearted with their patients.
Any man who attaches so much importance to his profession as to have strongly caught in his dress and manner the
outward formalities of it, may easily indeed be much occupied with himself, but he will not behave towards his "victims," as Mr. Crabbe calls them, in the manner he has
chosen to describe. After all, if the picture were true to
nature, what claim would it have to be called poetry? At
the best, it is the meanest kind of satire, except the merely
personal. The sum of all is, that nineteen out of twenty
of Crabbe's pictures are mere matters of fact; with which
the Muses have just about as much to do as they have
with a collection of medical reports, or of law cases.

How comes it that you never favour these mountains
with a visit? You ask how I have been employed. You
do me too much honour, and I wish I could reply to the
question with any satisfaction. Since I saw you I have

written about 500 lines of my long poem, which is all I have done. What are you doing? My wife and sister desire to be remembered by you, and believe me, my dear sir,

With great truth, yours,

WM. WORDSWORTH.

CLXXVII

William Wordsworth to Francis Wrangham

GRASMERE, October 2nd, 1808.

My dear Wrangham,

Some time ago I received a letter from you enclosing a note for £6, which I immediately paid into the hands of the treasurer. You will be glad to hear that our subscription has sped well, amounting now to no less a sum than £500 which will be amply sufficient for all purposes. Rogers the poet to whom I had applied was so kind as to procure for us among his friends £32:8 including his own contribution.

Coleridge is now here, in tolerable health, and better spirits than I have known him to possess for some time. . . .

In what are you employed? I mean by way of amusement and relaxation from your professional duties. Is there any topographical history of your neighbourhood? Would it not be worth your while to give some of your leisure hours to a work of this kind. I remember reading White's *Natural History and Antiquities of Selborne* with great pleasure, when a boy at school; and I have lately read Dr. Whitaker's history of Craven and Whalley,[1] both

---

[1] *History of the Antiquities of the Deanery of Craven* (1805). *History of the Original Parish of Whalley*, and *Honour of Clitheroe* (1801). — Ed.

with profit and pleasure.   Make these partly your models, and add thereto from the originality of your own mind. . . . Pray think of this.   I am induced to mention it from a belief that you are admirably qualified for such a work; that it would pleasantly employ your leisure hours; and from a regret in seeing works of this kind, which might be made so very interesting, utterly marred by falling into the hands of wretched bunglers; e.g. the *History of Cleveland*, which I have just read, by a clergyman of Yarm of the name of Graves,[1] the most heavy performance I ever encountered; and what an interesting district ! Pray let me hear from you soon,

Affectionately and sincerely yours,

W. WORDSWORTH.

CLXXVIII

William Wordsworth to Richard Sharp

GRASMERE, September 27.
[Postmark, October 8, 1808.]

My dear Sharp,

I am much obliged to you for taking the trouble to send me Mackintosh's[2] opinion of my poems. If you think it worth while, tell him I was happy to have given a man like him so much pleasure, especially at such a distance from his own country, and in these distressful times. The sonnet beginning "Two voices are there," you will remember is the one which I mentioned to you as being the best I had written. . . .

---

[1] *History and Antiquities of Cleveland, in the North Riding of Yorkshire*, etc., 1808. — Ed.

[2] Doubtless Sir James Mackintosh. — Ed.

Two subjects are likely to be discussed in Parliament in which I feel interested. The one, Lotteries, in which I know you will bear a part, and which is surely of infinite importance, and the other, Copyright of Authors. I am told that it is proposed to extend the right from fourteen years, as it now stands, after the decease of authors, till twenty-eight. This I think far too short a period; at least I am sure that it requires much more than that length of time to establish the reputation of original productions, both in philosophy and poetry, and to bring them consequently into such circulation that the authors, in the persons of their heirs or posterity, can in any degree be benefited — I mean in a pecuniary point of view — for the trouble they must have taken to produce the works. The law, as it now stands, merely consults the interest of the useful drudges in Literature, or of flimsy and shallow writers, whose works are upon a level with the taste and knowledge of the age; while men of real power, who go before their age, are deprived of all hope of their families being benefited by their exertions. Take, for instance, in Philosophy, Hartley's book upon Man.[1] How many years did it sleep in almost entire oblivion? What sale had Collins' poems during his lifetime, or during the fourteen years after his death? and how great has been the sale since? The product of it, if secured to his family, would have been an independence to them.

Take a still stronger instance, but this you may say proves too much, I mean Milton's minor poems. It is nearly two hundred years since they were published, yet they were utterly neglected till within these last thirty

[1] *Observations on Man; his Frame, his Duty, and his Expectations.* — Ed.

years; notwithstanding they had, since the beginning of the past century, the reputation of *Paradise Lost* to draw attention towards them. Suppose that Burns or Cowper had each left at their deaths a child a few months old — a daughter for example — is it reasonable that those children, at the age of twenty-eight, should cease to derive benefit from their father's works, when every bookseller in the country is profiting by them? I merely remind you of these things, which cannot but have passed through your active mind. If you can be of any service to Literature in this case, I know you will not let slip the opportunity. ... I remain, dear Sharp, yours very sincerely,

W. WORDSWORTH.

We are all here cut to the heart by the conduct of Sir Hew and his brother knight in Portugal.[1] For myself, I have not suffered so much upon any public occasion these many years.

CLXXIX

Dorothy Wordsworth to Mrs. Clarkson

GRASMERE, November 4th, [1808.]

Mrs. C. about a month ago wrote that she was at Bristol in hourly expectation of C. who was to attend her and the children to Liverpool and Birmingham, where he had visits to pay; and that he was to leave her at L. and go to London, to deliver two courses of lectures.

[1] Sir Hew Dalrymple (1750–1830), the general who signed the Convention of Cintra, against which Wordsworth wrote his elaborate pamphlet. The "brother knight" was Sir Henry Burrand. — Ed.

. . . Coleridge has never written to us, and we have given over writing to him, for what is the use of it? We believe he has not opened one of our letters. Poor soul! he is sadly to be pitied; I fear all resolution and strength of mind have utterly deserted him. . . . Half an hour after I had closed this letter I heard a tumult in the house and Mary shouting. I was alarmed, and guess my surprise and joy at seeing Hartley skipping about the room. His mother and Derwent and Sara were at the door in a chaise, and a Mr. De Quincey, a young Oxonian, who long ago addressed a letter to William, expressive of his gratitude and veneration, and since that time has corresponded occasionally. He found out Coleridge, and is come for a week purposely to see William. Mrs. Coleridge is just as usual only more friendly than ever with us, looks well, and is in great spirits. They brought a short letter from Coleridge, which speaks of a long one sent the day before (ten days ago) which we have never received. I believe that no plans are settled between them, but all is just the same as when they parted at Keswick; yet that he will never live with her, and she deprecates its being spoken of, as the greatest disgrace and evil in the world. Therefore (especially as neither he nor she talk publicly of separation) the less that is said of the matter the better. She talks of Coleridge, and everything else just as usual. Coleridge's health and looks are much improved. They left him at Bristol, intending to set off to London immediately. He talks of coming into the North in March.

Poor dear Coleridge! I am almost afraid to wish him here, fearing that we may be of no service to him. Hartley looks uncommonly well, and Derwent is very much improved in activity and manliness. Sara is like a spirit, fair and beautiful, but far, far too delicate. She looks as if a single blast of wind would blow her into her grave. She is very little taller than Dorothy, and not so heavy. John is within an inch of Derwent's height. God bless you. Do write. The Coleridges stayed with us all night, and left us after dinner to-day. By lodging two at Peggy Ashburner's we contrived to harbour the whole party, not excepting Mr. De Quincey.

CLXXX

William Wordsworth to Robert Grahame[1]

GRASMERE, Nov. 26, [1808.]

My dear Sir,

My friend Mr. Coleridge, whose genius talents and comprehensive knowledge are well known to you, is about to enter upon the publication of a weekly Essay, the object of which is explained clearly and at length in a prospectus of it which by this time I hope you have received, as orders have been sent to the printer to forward to you a certain number ; trusting that from the nature of the prospectus, and what you know of the author, you would be inclined to distribute them among such persons in your neighbourhood, or elsewhere, as you deem likely to take interest in such a book and to become subscribers to it. The mode of the circulation and delivery of *The Friend* to the separate subscribers will be either by the post, or by coach ; but by which of these we cannot determine till the number of the subscribers, and

---

[1] Robert Grahame was a writer (or solicitor) in Glasgow. See the list of subscribers to *The Friend* in the appendix to *Letters from the Lake Poets to Daniel Stewart*, p. 461. — Ed.

the nature of their residence have been ascertained. If there should be a considerable proportion dwelling in the lesser towns and villages and single houses, that is, if the number of the places should compensate for the fewness of the subscribers living in each, the papers will then be stamped and sent by the post: in which case the Essay must be printed on one sheet, though by printing 40 lines on each page instead of 35, the number originally proposed, and by adopting a larger sized paper, the same quantity of matter will be given and even the market value remain the same. But if the scattered subscribers should be so few that the diminution of the cost of each paper by the additional number printed should bear no proportion to the increase of the cost by the stamp — in short, if almost the whole of the subscribers should be furnished by the great towns and cities — a packet will then be sent off by each Saturday's mail to some friend or bookseller in each place, to be delivered at the subscribers' houses, if desired, as soon as possible after the arrival of the mail. In order to determine the mode of circulation we are therefore anxious to know what number of subscribers we are likely to have in the large towns; and I beg you to be so kind as to take the trouble of transmitting to us the number and names of those who you may have an opportunity of hearing intend to be subscribers. Knowing how much you are engaged in business I should not have troubled you upon this occasion had we been acquainted with any gentleman in Glasgow who could have served as well, and whose time was less occupied.

A packet of prospectuses has also been ordered to be sent to your brother in Edinborough, to whom I beg you would be so kind as to transmit this letter; for I have several to write, with not much time. Pray give my compliments in which I am joined by my wife and sister to Mrs. Grahame and Miss Grahame.

I am, dear sir, very sincerely yours,

W. WORDSWORTH.

CLXXXI

William Wordsworth to Francis Wrangham[1]

GRASMERE, Dec. 3d, [1808.]

My dear Wrangham,

On the other side you have the prospectus of a weekly Essay, intended to be published by our friend Coleridge. He has given orders that a certain number of them should be sent to you from London, which I hope by this time you have received, and do not doubt that you will be happy to circulate them among those of your friends who are likely to take interest in such a work. Coleridge, who is desirous to have contributions from all his enlightened friends, requests me to say that — champion of religion as you are — he will make you re-polish your classical sword.

Your sermon did not reach me till the night before last.[2] I believe we have all read it, and are much pleased with it. Upon the whole I like it better than the last; it must have been heard with great interest. I differ however from you in a few particulars; first, the Spaniards " devoting themselves for an imprisoned Bourbon or the

[1] Written on a copy of *Prospectus of The Friend, a weekly Essay by S. T. Coleridge.* — Ed.

[2] Probably his published sermon entitled *Earnest Contention for True Faith.* York, 1808. — Ed.

crumbling relics of the inquisition." This is very fair for pointing a sentence, but it is not the truth. They have told us over and over again that they are fighting against a foreign tyrant who has dealt with them most perfidiously, and inhumanly, who must hate them for their worth, and on account of the injuries they have received from him, and whom they must hate accordingly; against a ruler over whom they could have no control, and *for* one whom they have told us they will establish as the sovereign of a *free* people, and who therefore must himself be a limited monarch. You will permit me to make to you this representation, for its own truth's sake, and because it gives me an opportunity of letting out a secret; viz. that I myself am very deep in this subject, and about to publish upon it; first, I believe in a newspaper for the sake of immediate and wide circulation; and next, the same matter in a separate pamphlet. Under the title of *The Convention of Cintra brought to the Test of Principles; and the People of Great Britain vindicated from the Charge of having prejudged it.* You will wonder to hear me talk of principles when I have told you that I also do not go along with you in your sentiments respecting the Catholic question. I confess I am not prepared to see the Catholic religion as the Established Church of Ireland; and how that can be consistently refused to them, if other things are granted on the plea of their being the majority, I do not see. Certainly this demand would follow, and how would it be answered?

There is yet another circumstance in which I differ from you. If Dr. Bell's plan of education be of that importance which it appears to be of, it cannot be a matter of indifference whether he, or Lancaster, have a rightful

claim to the invention. For Heaven's sake let all bene-
factors of their species have the honour due to them.
Virgil gives a high place in Elysium to the *improvers* of
life, and it is neither the least philosophical or least
poetical passage of the *Æneid*.[1] These points of difference being stated, I may say that in other things I greatly
approve both of the matter and manner of your sermon.

Do not fail to return my best thanks to the lady, to
whom I am obliged for the elegant and accurate drawing of Brompton Church. I should have written to thank
her, and you, for it immediately; but I foresaw that I
should have occasion to write to you on this or other
business.

All here desire their best remembrances, and believe
me, in great haste, for I have several other letters to
write, on the same subject,

Affectionately yours,

W. WORDSWORTH.

CLXXXII

Dorothy Wordsworth to Mrs. Marshall

4th December, 1808.

. . . We have grievous troubles to struggle with. A
smoky house, wet cellars, and workmen by the half dozen
making attempts (hitherto unsuccessful) to remedy these
evils. We are making one effort more; and, if that end
as heretofore, we shall be reduced to the miserable necessity of quitting Grasmere; for this house is at present

---

[1] Quique sui memores alios facere merendo. — *Æneid*, VI, 664.

literally not habitable,[1] and there is no other in the vale. You can have no idea of the inconvenience we have suffered. There was one stormy day in which we could have no fire but in my brother's study, and that chimney smoked so much that we were obliged to go to bed. We cooked in the study. . . . Partly on account of smoke and windy weather, and partly because of the workmen, we have been for more than a week together at different times without a kitchen fire. The servants, you may be sure, have been miserable ; and we have had far too much labour and far too little quiet. . . . At the time of the great storm, Mrs. Coleridge and her little girl were here, and Mr. Coleridge is with us constantly ; so you will make out that we were a pretty large family to provide for in such a manner. Mr. Coleridge and his wife are separated ; and I hope they will both be the happier for it. They are upon friendly terms, and occasionally see each other. In fact Mrs. Coleridge was more than a week at Grasmere under the same roof with him. Coleridge intends to spend the winter with us. On this side of the paper you will find the prospectus of a work which he is going to undertake ; and I have little doubt but that it will be well executed if his health does not fail him ; but on that score (though he is well at present) I have many fears.

My brother is deeply engaged writing a pamphlet upon the Convention of Cintra, an event which has interested him more than words can express. His first and his last thoughts are of Spain and Portugal. . . .

[1] Allan Bank. — Ed.

CLXXXIII

Dorothy Wordsworth to Mrs. Clarkson

December 8, Thursday Evening,
[Postmark, KESWICK, 1808?]

My dear Friend,

. . . I will not attempt to detail the height and depth
and number of our sorrows in connection with the smoky
chimneys. They are so very bad that if they cannot be
mended we must leave the house, beautiful as everything
will soon be out of doors, dear as is the vale where we have
lived so long. The labour of the house is literally doubled.
Dishes are washed, and no sooner set into the pantry
than they are covered with smoke. Chairs, carpets, the
painted ledges of the rooms, all are ready for the reception of soot and smoke, requiring endless cleaning, and
are never clean. . . . In fact we have seldom an hour's
leisure (either Mary or I) till after 7 o'clock (when the
children go to bed), for all the time that we have for sitting still in the course of the day we are obliged to employ
in scouring (and many of our evenings also). We are
regularly thirteen in the family, and on Saturdays and
Sundays 15 (for when Saturday morning is not very
stormy Hartley and Derwent come). I include the servants in the number, but as you may judge, in the most
convenient house there would be work enough for two
maids and a little girl. In ours there is far too much.
We keep a cow—the stable is two short field lengths
from the house, and the cook has both to fodder and
clean after the cow. We have also two pigs, bake all our
bread at home, and though we do not wash all our clothes,
yet we wash a part every week, and mangle or iron the

whole. . . . At Martinmas we were nearly at work without any servants at all. . . . Dear Coleridge is well and in good spirits, writing letters to all his friends and acquaintances, dispatching prospectuses, and fully prepared to begin his work. Nobody, surely, but himself would have ventured to send forth this prospectus with not one essay written, no beginning made! but yet I believe it was the only way for him. I believe he could not have made the beginning unspurred by a necessity which is now created by the promises therein made. I cannot, however, be without hauntings of fear, seeing him so often obliged to lie in bed more than half of the day — often so very poorly as to be utterly unable to do anything whatever. To-day, though he came down to dinner at three perfectly well, he did not rise till near two o'clock. I am afraid this account of him may give you some alarm. I assure you, however, that there is no need to be alarmed; his health is much, very much better, and his looks are almost what you would wish them to be ; and however ill he may have been in the mornings he seldom fails to be chearful and comfortable at night. Sara and he are sitting together in his parlour, William and Mary (alas! all involved in smoke) in William's study, where she is writing for him (he dictating). He is engaged in a work which occupies all his thoughts. It will be a pamphlet of considerable · length, entitled *The Convention of Cintra brought to the Test of Principles and the People of England justified from the Charge of Prejudging*, or something to that effect. I believe it will first appear in the *Courier* in different sections. Mr. De Quincey, whom you would love dearly, as I am sure I do, is beside me, quietly turning over the leaves of a Greek book — and God be praised we are breathing a clear air, for the night is calm, and this room (the dining-room) only smokes very much in a high wind. Mr. De Q. will stay with us, we hope, at least till the Spring. We feel often as if he were one of the family — he is loving, gentle, and happy — a very good scholar, and an acute logician — so much for his mind and manners. His person is unfortunately diminutive, but there is a sweetness in his looks, especially about the eyes, which soon overcomes the oddness of your first feeling at the sight of so very little a man. John sleeps with him and is passionately fond of him. Oh ! my dear friend ! Johnny *is* a sweet creature; so noble, bold, gentle, and beautiful — yes ! he is a beautiful boy. D. is very pretty, very kittenish, very quick, very clever, but not given to *thought.* Coleridge often repeats to her (altering a line of William's poem of *Ruth*) "the wild cat of the wilderness was not so fair as she."[1] To this she replies with a squall, inviting him to some fresh skirmish. C. says that John has all the virtues of a tame dog, she the qualities of the cat. God bless them ! They are both sweet in their way; but it must be allowed that John is the finer creature. . . .

CLXXXIV

[William Wordsworth to Thomas De Quincey]

My dear Friend,

I guess you would be truly glad when you received the last sheet, as were we when it was sent off yesterday. I do not mean to pester you with more alterations; but two

[1] The lines are:

The panther in the wilderness
Was not so fair as he.

— Ed.

suggested themselves to me this morning which must be adopted. A passage stands thus, "that the hearts of the many do languish and are not ready to answer to the sudden and continued requisitions of things." Let it stand thus, "do languish and therefore are not ready to answer to the requisitions of things," (and be followed thus). "Now the evidence of experience rightly understood not only gives no support to this belief, but proves that the truth is in direct opposition to it. The history of all ages — tumults after tumults, wars foreign or civil, etc."

Again in another place print "circles narrower and narrower, closer and closer *as they lie* more near to the centre of self" for *even to*, as it now stands.

As to the mode of publishing, advertising, etc. do not wait to consult me in anything. Mr. Stuart and you will do everything together. Ask him also whether he approves of printing the Armistice and Convention in the Notes. I think it would be better, if it were no great addition to the expense. Please to send fourteen copies hither.

Affectionately yours,

W. WORDSWORTH.

P.S. — Make any verbal alterations according to your better judgment. W. W.

[To the above letter the following postscript was added by Dorothy Wordsworth; no address or date, except "Monday morning," being given.[1]]

It is a heavenly morning. We are all a family party, Thomas, Catharine, and Johnny, whom we shall call on at

[1] [The text of all the letters from William and Dorothy Wordsworth to De Quincey is transcribed from the original MSS., now in the possession of his granddaughter, Miss Baird Smith.] — ED.

school going to the Town End, where your snow-drops are in full blossom to welcome us. William and I proceed to the post at Rydale, where we hope to find a letter from you. I am afraid you would hardly be able to make out what I wrote last night about the Manchester goods. Adieu.

Yours ever,

D. WORDSWORTH.

[It is possible that this letter was not written till February, 1809. Mr. Gordon Wordsworth writes : " It is not likely that the last sheets of the pamphlet could have been sent off before then and the reference (in Dorothy's postscript) to the snow-drops seems to confirm this." — Ed.]

1809

CLXXXV

William Wordsworth to Daniel Stuart [1]

February 9, 1809.

. . . Never did any public event cause in my mind so much sorrow as the Convention of Cintra, both on account of the Spaniards and Portuguese, and on our own. Every good and intelligent man of my friends or acquaintance has been in his turn agitated and afflicted by it.

. . . .

What you say upon Wellesley as to the French being *entitled* to such terms is exactly in its spirit what I had marked down upon the subject. . . . Buonaparte may rather be said to *inflict upon* than *to propose* terms *to* his adversaries.

Of Moore I know nothing further than that his forward movement is unaccountable, that his retreat appears to have been very disorderly, and that Dalrymple has told us he approved of the Convention. If this be true, he was either a fool, or a rascal, or both. Moore in his person was, I believe, a thoroughly brave man. If the Ministry do not mean to give up the Spaniards, which I suspect with you, they ought to be execrated to the latest posterity. . . . I have many apologies to make in having

---

[1] The editor of the *Morning Post* and of the *Courier*. — Ed.

been so dilatory in sending off copy. . . . But I cannot bear much confinement, and have many interruptions, and take little pleasure in composing, and penmanship is to me unendurable. . . .

CLXXXVI

Dorothy Wordsworth to Thomas De Quincey

Tuesday, [March 10, 1809.]

My dear Friend,

Yesterday morning my brother and I walked to Rydale; and he, intending to proceed to Brathay, sat upon a stump at the foot of the hill, while I went up to Ann Nicholson's, and there I found your letter. I did not break the seal, for it was already broken (you having sealed it so badly, I suppose); but I opened the letter in Ann's house, just to see if all were well with you, and I then hastened with my prize to William, and sat down beside him to *read* the letter; and truly a feast it was for us. You were very good in being so particular in your account of your journey, and that feeling of your goodness made the entertaining description of your fellow-travellers far more delightful. We rejoiced for the young American that he had met with so knowing an expounder of the state of nations, and agreed that in all England he probably could not have met with one so well qualified to instruct him, certainly not one so kindly willing. Two things we grieved for; your miserable cold ride on the outside of the coach, and that you should not have felt yourself at liberty to stay at Oxford for rest, and for arranging any business that you might have there. After this hurrying it would be very mortifying to you to have to wait day after day for our letters, even a whole week, for our earliest despatches could not reach you till last Saturday. I have explained the cause of this delay. My brother was indeed very poorly, his head having been continually tormented, and especially upon his pillow at night with those dreadful headaches, which you know he, in his gloomy way, calls apoplectic. He is now very well, and after he once got forward with his work, he went on rapidly with perpetual animation. Do tell us how you like the conclusion. Mary and I thought the whole was written with great dignity; but we, as well as my brother, could not help regretting that he had not more time to reconsider it. You know he never likes to trust anything away fresh from the brain. He is now engaged in making an addition to one paragraph, which is to be transcribed on the other side of this sheet. I hope he will have done in time to save this day's post (Tuesday); otherwise I fear the types will be arranged by the printer, and you and he will have a great deal of trouble.

It was a week yesterday since Coleridge went to Brathay, and we have not seen him since, for in consequence of a letter from his printer, and the regulator of the Stamps at Appleby not being able to settle that business without instructions from the Stamp Office in London, he thought it necessary to go to Penrith and Appleby, and accordingly he had set forward yesterday morning from Lloyd's about two hours before William's arrival there, on foot, intending to sleep at Patterdale last night, and go to Penrith to-day. On Saturday I had a note from him, in which he told me that, being deep in the *Tatler*, *Guardian*, *Spectator*, etc., he had stayed day after day at Lloyd's, and that he had finished his first essay all but one passage about Dr. Johnson. This was good news; but Mr. and Mrs. Lloyd told my brother that he had been very poorly during most of the week, and had never risen till near dinner-time. They said, too, that he looked wretchedly yesterday morning. I cannot but fear that the journey and one thing or other (to use one of his own favourite phrases) will knock him up, and that all will at last end in nothing. I wish he had not gone to Penrith, for we think that by letter he could have managed the matter just as well. And at this critical moment it will be for ever to be regretted if any accident of fatigue, bad accommodation, etc., etc., should disarrange his body or mind. If he had been able to stay quietly here, the trial would have been a fair one, and should he have failed, in future one could never, in case of any other scheme, be vexed with hopes or fears. Observe; he went from Lloyd's determined that the work should begin on the 1st of April, and that he would stay at Penrith till the first essay should be printed, and that essay being so nearly finished, this must be a very easy matter — but then there is the affair of the stamps, and what plague besides I know not, and he is so easily overturned — made ill by the most trifling vexations or fatigue.

I have just been writing to your landlord to hasten him with his work at the cottage. We have taken it for six years, for if you should have no use for it, it would be very easy to let it, being furnished. When your friend Johnny came from school last night, his mother said to him, "Here is a letter from ——." "From," he replied, "Mr. De Quincey?" And with his own ingenuous blush and smile he came forward to the fireside at a quicker pace, and asked me to read the letter; which I did, with a few omissions and levelling the language to his capacity, and you would have thought yourself well repaid for the trouble of writing it if you could only have seen how feelingly he was interested. When all was over he said, "But when will he come? Maybe he 'll tell us in his next letter." We hope that before you return he will be much improved in his reading, for he seems now to desire to learn, and takes a great deal of notice, not only of his own lessons, but of the lessons of the bigger boys. I cannot say that he seems much to love learning for its own sake. It is the hope of being a printer that moves him, and he knows that he must first be a scholar. I think no event has happened in the house of greater consequence since you left us than that a little mouse makes its appearance sometimes under the dining-room grate, and disappears we know not how, for we can find no hole for its escape! This John desired I would communicate to you. *He* thinks it is a fairy in the shape of a mouse, "For may I tell you what?" (at that time *I* had not seen the mouse, and he was relating the story to me); "it comes under the grate, and it does not come over the fender, and there is no hole under the grate for it to go through." You are therefore called upon to reflect on this prodigy, and favour us with your conjectures. This moment Johnny comes from school: "So Mr. De Quincey's letter came, that you said would be here to-day?" and then, "Have you told him about the mouse?" and he begged me to read to him what I had said. My brother tells me I must stop, or I shall not leave room for him.

Believe me, ever your affectionate friend,

D. WORDSWORTH.

My brother has just come upstairs to tell me that he cannot have transcribed in time for the Keswick post the addition which he has been making; therefore I send this to beg that you will *stop the Press* at the words "career in the fulness of —." The addition will be about a folio sheet. He sent off yesterday a letter with two or three corrections, addressed to you at Marybone. The next letter, which will be by to-morrow's post (from Ambleside), we shall direct as this. Adieu. God bless you! I hope your troubles and perplexities in this affair will end with this.

CLXXXVII

William Wordsworth to Thomas De Quincey

GRASMERE, Wed. Evening, 29th March, [1809.]

My dear Friend, . . .

I, William Wordsworth, employ Miss Hutchinson as my amanuensis, to spare you the trouble of puzzling out my bad penmanship, a labour which after all might be fruitless.

I received your letter, addressed to my sister, yesterday. I am truly sorry for the trouble you are put to, and beg that you would not be so anxious, particularly as to a misspelt word or so. I repeat to prevent mistake, that the long addition "in Ferrol in Corunna" is to follow after the paragraph about the conduct of the supreme Junta, ending with a sentence about "the old monarchy of Spain administered"; and that the words "In Madrid, etc." are to be preceded by a couple of sentences which I have already sent, and which will be found in the last of the four letters sent off together. I repeat this, fearful that my bad penmanship may have rendered the direction unintelligible. By a letter from Stuart to Coleridge

I learn that, in his opinion, the Armistice and Convention might as well be printed. I confess I am of the same mind, but do as you think best. Upon maturer thoughts, I withdraw the exhortation contained in my last, that you would expose the contradictions in the French bulletins, concerning the defence of Saragossa.

We stand upon too high ground there not to suffer by such a step. A few words said upon the base and cowardly charges of the French against the Saragossians, and particularly against their leader, might be well; but nothing more. It would also furnish a fair opportunity. of showing the different appearance which the French liars and defamers make when confronted by the heroic achievements of the people of Saragossa, and when backed by the cowardice and stupidity which our Generals showed in the Convention of Cintra. But do this, or let it alone, just as you like. Insert also that part of my note, or not, as you deem advisable, or feel an inclination; only let what is said about General Ferguson be inserted, both in justice to him, to me, and to the subject. About all this I am comparatively indifferent; but there is one point which I have much at heart. I will explain. Mr. Crump, my landlord, called here this morning; he did not stay much above two hours, and as soon as he had heard the dismal tale of the chimneys and the cellars, he began to crow; and over what, think you? The inert, the lazy, the helpless, the worthless Spaniards, clapping his wings at the same time in honour of Bonaparte. This was the truth, though he perhaps was not aware how his wings were employed. Mr. Crump introduced the subject, and his words were, "Well, Mr. W., is there no good to come of this? What do you say to rooting out the Friars, abolishing the Inquisition, sweeping away the feudal tenures?" in short, although I do not mean to defend Bonaparte, "Oh no, on no account; yet certainly he would be a great benefactor to the Spaniards: they are such vile slaves." In short, I found this good and excellent man (I do believe as kind hearted an attorney as breathes) completely saturated with Roscoism. I squeezed a little of it out of him, as much as the time would allow, but the sponge will be filled again the first dining party he is present at upon his return. In Mrs. Clarke's phrase, there are black sheep at Liverpool. This I had first heard from you; and it was confirmed by Mr. Wilson.[1] You may be sure I was not a little pleased with the remembrance of what I had added to the pamphlet upon this subject, and upon that of national independence in general. But to come to the point.

He quoted, as proofs of the miserable state of public spirit upon the Peninsula, the Letters of Sir J. Moore recently published by Government; and I found that these had made a great impression, to the prejudice of the Spaniards, both upon his mind and upon the minds of those with whom he associates. Now, what I wish is, that you would give a review of these Letters, not speaking with any asperity of Sir J. M., though the Letters would thoroughly justify it; but this the People of England would not bear, he being a Commander-in-Chief, shot and, of course in their tender estimations, *cannonized*. I have only seen such of those Letters as appeared in the *Courier* of Friday last (March 24). They are in number four, and at the end it is said they are to be continued. From these my opinion of Sir J. M. is completely made up, that he was a sober, steady-minded man, but without any

---

[1] John Wilson, "Christopher North." — Ed.

comprehensiveness or originality of mind, and totally unfit for so arduous a situation. I know that you have accurately in memory all the events of the campaign, and would find no difficulty in making such comments upon these Letters as would tend very much to obviate the unfavourable impression which, if left to themselves, I am sure they will make. I will just set down at random two or three thoughts such as struck me as a skeleton for the materials of such a note. First to remind the reader of the situation in which Sir J. Moore stood, and of the purpose for which these Letters were written — namely, under a conviction that his army could accomplish nothing; and to save himself and it from reproach in that quarter by which he had been sent, viz. the Ministry.

Now it was clear that the best way to succeed in this was not to charge those who had sent him with blame, but to fling the whole upon the Spaniards. Accordingly he enters into a dolorous account of the dispersion and defeat of Blake's army, flying in every direction, the Estremadura Army routed, and Castanos totally defeated. But nowhere do we hear a word of the gallant and desperate resistance which Blake made for so many days, of the courage and even temerity of the Estremadurans; and the fate of Castanos is totally misrepresented, inasmuch as his centre only was defeated, his two wings being untouched, part of which retired south and part threw themselves into Saragossa, where they made, as we know, a most valiant resistance. In fact, Sir John Moore nowhere speaks like a soldier, for he seems to be surprised that these raw levies could not stand their ground, upon all occasions, against the practised troops of Bonaparte, and seems surprised at the composition of the Spanish armies. The regular troops of Spain had, for the most part, been kidnapped by Bonaparte, and he ought to have known beforehand that the armies could be no other than what he found them, except as to numbers.

But we are interested in the question, not as a military one, but as the facts affect the dispositions of the Spanish People. Now, there can be no doubt, from the condition in which Sir J. M. found the armies and the spirit of the people in many parts of Spain, that the Supreme Junta had strangely neglected its duty. And it scarcely seems possible that any of its members can be men of talent; but this subject — I mean their talent — must in the note be touched gently. Sir J. M. seems to have thought literally with the lawyers, " De non apparentibus et non existentibus essilem est ratio ; " that is, because the people were not huzzaing and shouting like a mob at an election or a rout of drunkards reeling from a fair, that therefore they had no sense of their injuries. I know not that such was his sentiment, but assuredly many people in England will draw conclusions to the same purpose from his statement. All this apparent listlessness and languor is to be attributed solely to the Government not having taken proper means to circulate instructing and animating writings among the people; and to organise them in such a manner that an electric shock might pass from mind to mind, from one town to another, from one village to another, through all the land. He states that small parties of the French scoured the country of Leon without meeting any resistance from the inhabitants. This fact I cannot believe upon the evidence of any General, because my knowledge of human nature teaches me beforehand that it is impossible. That the resistance might fall far below what a superficial thinker would expect I can easily believe ; things of this sort, where regular arrangements have not been made to preclude such inactivity, and to give men a hope of embodying their passions in action by furnishing them with the means of so doing, depend upon accident. A single enterprising man, of a character like one of the old Buccaneers, would have drawn after him hundreds of the peasants of Leon for any service, however desperate.

But to keep to my text, I mean the unfairness of any conclusions drawn from Sir J. M.'s account to the prejudice of the elements or materials out of which Spanish regeneration was to arise. Take one instance, namely, that of Salamanca. It certainly was not his business, writing with such views as he had, when he represents the indifference and tranquillity which were then prevalent, to state to the Ministry that the flower of the students of Salamanca had formed themselves into a battalion, which had fought as volunteers in Blake's army, and with such conduct and valour, that their General had held them up to the especial admiration and gratitude of their countrymen. And who knows how many of the most active spirits among the townsmen of the same place had perished in that army? It was not his business to state this, but it becomes those who are in such a hurry to entertain unfavourable opinions of the Spanish nation to recollect it. In fact, with respect to the Spaniards, two conclusions may be fairly drawn from Moore's Letters, neither of which any sensible man ever doubted of before; first, that the Supreme Junta has been miserably remiss; and secondly, that the Spanish levies — *armies*, as they were foolishly called — could not stand against the French, except where situation greatly favoured them. A third conclusion may be drawn from the charge which, though he has pushed so hard upon the

Spaniard, Sir J. M. makes, in his own despite, upon the Ministry, viz. that he was sent with a pitiful force, and that force was never an efficient army. My wish, then, is fourfold; that you should clearly state what there is in these Letters that fairly tells against the Spanish people; what fairly against the armies, as made up of the people; what against the Spanish Government; and finally should accumulate upon that the achievements of the south and south-east of Spain. As to the note, let it be candid and quite respectful to Sir J. M. and his army, I mean candid even to *tenderness*. The British People are wretchedly cowardly in these feelings, and upon some future occasion it may be proper to tell them so. I do think, however, in justice to the subject, that some surprise at Sir J. M.'s apparent disappointment at the defeat of the Spanish armies should be expressed. The concluding paragraph need not be altered on account of Palafox's reported death. In the page which you will have been obliged to cancel with the footnote, you may, if you think proper, add a footnote of two words to "Saragossa," viz. "written in January."

P.S. — If you shrink from the responsibility of any of the opinions which you might like to express in this note, say that it is written by a friend of the author upon his suggestion, after having seen four of these Letters, he himself having not been able to complete the note owing to his distance from the press, without great delay, if he had waited till the whole of the Letters had reached him.

CLXXXVIII

William Wordsworth to Thomas De Quincey

Postmark, [March 30th, 1809.]

My dear Friend,

I have such a world of matter to write to you about minute particulars that I know not where to begin. But first let me say a word upon something important, viz. the disappointment which you must have had in not receiving the copy sooner, and the trouble and I fear vexation that has accompanied this business. On these accounts you have both my sincere sorrow and my zealous thanks. I have been long in sending the rest because I thought by straining a point I might be able to say in the present publication all that was necessary. Accordingly I wrote a great deal, but I have been obliged to give up the plan, and send what you will find, suppressing as much as I have sent. In fact I was exhausted in bodily strength. As the Duke of York's business is over, there is now a fair opening for a little of the public attention. Besides, I was very uneasy at the thought of detaining you in London.

Now for particulars. All your alterations are amendments. The hiatus about knowledge you supplied as I wrote it ; and how *re*fined slipped into the manuscript for *de*fined I cannot conceive. The footnote about Saragossa I am sorry you had the trouble of writing, as all the evil (if any) may be obviated by a word or two in the advertisement ; begging the reader to bear in mind that the work was begun in November or December and carried on since that period, the publication having been delayed partly by accidents, and still more from a wish to wait

for further evidence of facts; and that it seemed better
to leave passages of this kind as they were written than
to alter them.   Besides, you will see by what is now sent
that, so far from thinking that Saragossa has broken her
bond, in my estimation she has discharged it to the letter.
The last siege appears to have been even still more glorious than the former.   It will therefore be necessary to
cancel the page with the footnote, on account of what you
will find I have said in the text.   If you deem it advisable to add any remarks in the Appendix upon the iniq-
uitous, the infernal bulletin of the French, pray take the
trouble of doing so.   For my part, their own account
proves incontestably that the Spaniards have done as
much as ever was performed by human beings in like
circumstance.   Curse on our Ministers for not having
raised that siege, which would have been so easy!

I am afraid you will have had endless trouble about
the alterations, small and great.   You do not say what
you did about the petition part, and Charles the Second,
as talked about at Ambleside.   " Arm of the Almighty," I
wished rather to stand, " and gave to them the deep faith
which they have expressed that their power was favoured
and assisted by the Almighty"; perhaps you have substituted something better.   The great body of additions made, since the conclusion was sent, will begin
in this manner, after some expression like this which
I cannot recollect, " administered as the old Monarchy
of Spain."

But I began with hope, and hope goes along with me.
" In Madrid, in Ferrol," etc.   I cannot find the passage
in my MS.   Therefore if anything be wanting to smooth
the junction, you will be so kind as to add it.   I mean
to say that the heart of the people is sound; the first

direction given for the insertions is therefore set aside; it would indeed there have been quite out of its place, so near the conclusion. Any expressions which lead the reader to expect the conclusion too soon, such as "parting look," etc., etc., you will of course omit. As to concluding with a quotation, I don't know how to get over that; it could not conclude with the paragraph before, the simile not being sufficiently upon a level with ordinary imagination. Does what you will now find added require an alteration in the first words of the last paragraph? I ask this question because I cannot find the MS. If it does, be so good as to make it. I have alluded to the blasphemous address to Bonaparte made by some Italian deputies, which you remember we read at Grasmere some time ago, and his answer. I should like to have referred to the very words in the Appendix, but it is in vain to seek for the paper. If, without much trouble, you could find it in the file of *Couriers* at the office, I should exceedingly like such parts as you might approve of, both of address and answer, to be inserted in the Appendix. It is of considerable consequence; for, if I am not mistaken, there was there also the avowal which he has so repeatedly made to the Spaniards, that power is, in his estimation, the measure of right; in other words, that he will rule over them, whether they will or no. Many thanks for your trouble about the note on the Board of Inquiry. If any quotations which I have made from the proceedings of that Board should be grossly inaccurate, I don't mean as to words but in spirit, pray correct that by a note in the Appendix, as far as is possible.

The paragraph in the Advertisement must stand thus, to be inserted before the last sentence, not without a hope that you may be able to amend it.

"I must entreat the reader to bear in mind that I began to write upon this subject in November last, and have continued without bringing my work earlier to a conclusion, partly from accident, and partly from a wish to possess additional documents and facts. Passing occurrences have made a change in the situation of certain objects spoken of, but I have not thought it necessary to accommodate what I had previously written to these changes: the whole stands without alteration, except where additions have been made, or errors corrected."

I am obliged to put things down just as they come into my memory; but, as I know your habits of order, I can trust to you for correcting this. There is one passage which would stand better thus (the sentence would be clearer, and its connection with the preceding clearer), "The tendency of such education to warp, and therefore weaken the intellect," omitting what is said about "shutting out from common sympathies and genuine knowledge." I have said "deposited in the Escurial." Was that the place?

I have said "Swede or Norwegian," thinking that Norway has not forfeited its national independence, having, as I believe (and I have Hartley's authority to corroborate my opinion), fallen to the Crown of Denmark by marriage. But strange! we have here no book of Geography or History to give us information. If I should prove mistaken, let the word "Norwegian" be omitted.

I return to your proposed note upon the French bulletin on Saragossa. It would certainly be rendering good service if you could concisely expose the contradictions of this heinous document, and point the indignation of the public against its cowardly and execrable calumnies. I have a further reason for this, because I have done injustice to General Ferguson, by not mentioning in the body of the work his marked disapprobation of the Convention of Cintra, and therefore a note must be added upon this subject. A fair occasion was given awhile ago, by a passage in the *Moniteur;* and the note, after you had exposed the wickedness of the French Bulletin, might conclude in a manner like this. . . . I have stopped and hunted in vain all over the house for the *Courier* that contains the passage I wish to advert to. It may be easily found by consulting the file at the office. It is some observations in the *Moniteur*, which appeared within the course of a month past, upon the votes of thanks in the House of Commons concerning the campaign in Portugal. I wished to extract about six or seven lines, where the paper says, among other well-founded insults, " You were unable to drive the French out of Portugal."

"Official Papers of Governments containing such assertions in the face of such facts can only be injurious to their authors; but it is lamentably different when in an official journal of the French Government we meet with the following passage, supported by the documents of the Armistice and Convention of Cintra. In such combination there is sterling truth enough to give currency to a thousand lies;" then quote the passage from the *Moniteur*, interposing any other words which you may think proper, such as I cannot accommodate to the passage, not having it before me, and perhaps no words may be necessary.

> . . . pudet haec opprobria nobis
> Et dici potuisse, et non potuisse refelli.

> How can they be refuted ? and what avail
> Our virtues with such evidence against us ?

> . . . And all the while he read he did extend
> His sword high over him, if aught he did offend.

A picture like this must have presented itself to the imagination of men in all Europe, wherever those instruments travelled, and the people of Great Britain feel with heart-burning indignation in what hand the sword would appear to be.   To the victory of Vimeira these lines have been with propriety applied.

> Media fert tristis succos, tardumque saporem
> Felicis mali; quo non praesentius ullum,
> Pocula si quando saevae infecere novercae,
> Miscueruntque herbas et non innoxia verba,
> Auxilium venit, ac membris agit atra venena.
> Ipsa ingens arbos, faciemque simillima lauro;
> Et, si non alium late jactaret odorem,
> Laurus erat.[1]

I must be allowed upon this occasion to express my satisfaction that one of the Generals who was in Portugal stands clear of the shame of having countenanced the Convention of Cintra.   The gallant and patriotic General Ferguson has declared in the House of Commons his decided disapprobation of that measure.

N.B. — If Austria should not appear to join in the war, the two last paragraphs will require a slight alteration, an "*if*" or something that you can easily give.

The title-page need not state "first part."   I do not wish to engage myself so far, having now said so much. For the distribution of the work, I much approve of your sending it with a Latin note to the Spanish and Portuguese Ambassadors, but I cannot reconcile myself to the idea of your sending it with your own name to Sir

[1] Virgil, *Georgics*, II. 125-11. — Ed.

A. W. Let it not be done on any account. He may learn that you are an intimate friend of mine, and may suspect it to be an act of personal malice on my part. Consult with Mr. Stuart about sending any number to such public characters as you and he may think proper. Send one in my name to General Ferguson, one to Mr. Curwen, and one to Richard Sharpe, Esq., M.P., Mark Lane. Mr. Curwen's address in London I do not know. I dare say that I have forgotten many particulars, but this letter is a miserable jumble, and my head a perfect chaos. This will account for the heaviness of the note which I wish you would contrive to inspirit. With many thanks, and a very strong wish to see you again in Grasmere,

Very afftly yours,

WM. WORDSWORTH.

The poem you need not call for; it is come. Miss Monkhouse leaves Town on Friday week. If the pamphlet be out before that time, pray let a copy be sent to her (21 Budge row) for her brother in Wales. I should like a copy to be sent from me to the author of the *Narrative of the Siege of Saragossa*,[1] unless you should happen to know that he is not worthy of such a mark of notice. But as he must have connections in Spain, it might perhaps be a means of causing some part of the work to be translated into that language, which would give me great pleasure. Carleton's *Memoirs*[2] we have

---

[1] The book to which Wordsworth here refers is the *Narrative of the Siege of Zaragossa* by Richard Charles Vaughan, which had just been published (1809). — Ed.

[2] *Memoirs, including Anecdotes of the War in Spain*, etc., by Captain George Carleton (1808). — Ed.

procured, so you need not purchase them for us; but if the book falls in your way at a reasonable rate, buy it for yourself, for it is a most interesting work. . . .

Dorothy Wordsworth adds the following: —

My dear Friend,

Hartley and Derwent wait, therefore I have only a moment. Thomas has had measles, and is quite recovered; happier, lovelier, and handsomer than he has been for many weeks before; but poor Catherine is grievously reduced. . . . God bless you, my dear Friend.

Your ever-affectionate

DOROTHY WORDSWORTH.

Coleridge is not returned. We have heard nothing of him or *The Friend*, except that it is not to appear till the 14th of April. He is at Keswick. Miss H. is pretty well.

CLXXXIX

William Wordsworth to Thomas De Quincey

[Postmark, March 31, 1809.]

My dear Friend,

I have been not a little jeered this morning, when it was seen that I meant to trouble you with another letter; but I am haunted with notions, which I cannot get over in cases of this sort, that I leave my meaning undeveloped. Accordingly I must be permitted to submit to your judgment the following two sentences to be added after the words " But without national independence this is impossible."

"The difference between inbred oppression and that which is from without is *essential*, inasmuch as the former does not exclude from the mind of a people the feeling of being self-governed; does not imply (as the latter does when patiently submitted to) an abandonment of the first duty imposed by the faculty of reason. In reality, where this feeling has no place a people are not a Society but a herd; man being indeed distinguished among them from the brute but only to his disgrace. I am aware etc." Please also to put for "a change in the minds of the native French soldiery," "a *moral* change"; and for "this influence of moral causes," put "this *paramount* efficacy of moral causes," or any better words that may suggest themselves to you. Influence is too weak a word. It is in the sentence about the British troops. In the same paragraph read, "who by *submitting* to inglorious treaties, or by other misconduct."

In your note to Spanish and Portuguese Ambassadors, pray state that one of my principal objects was to refute the calumnies which selfish men had circulated in this country against those two nations.

I am happy to say that Thomas is quite well, and growing very handsome.

Do mend that stupid part of the note, which I sent you; in fact my brains were utterly dried up when I wrote it. The passage in the *Moniteur*, alluded to, is in some one of the *Couriers*, written a month past or less; and stands, if I am not mistaken, in the first page, something better than one third down the last column of it.

Of course we have not received the announced parcel.

Very affectionately your friend,

W. WORDSWORTH.

Tuesday Noon.

I am delighted to see reason for believing that Galicia is up again, and that the people have done summary justice to the traitorous governor of Cadiz. A little more of this, and the cause will go swing ; these traitors must be purged off. I should not be sorry to see one third at least of the supreme junta carried off in the same manner, or at least in some other equally effectual, in order that zealous and honest men might take their place.

CXC

William Wordsworth to Daniel Stuart

March 31, 1809.

Yesterday I sent off the last sheets of the pamphlet. ... As I found the public mind so completely engrossed with the Duke of York, I thought it better to avail myself of that opportunity to add general matter to the pamphlet concerning the hopes of the Spaniards, and the principles of the contest, so that, from the proportion of space which it occupied in the work, the Convention of Cintra might fairly appear — what in truth it is in my mind — an action dwelt upon only for the sake of illustrating principles, with a view to promote liberty and good policy, in the manner in which an anatomist illustrates the laws of organic life from a human subject placed before him and his audience.

I confess I have no hopes of the thing making any impression. The style of thinking and feeling is so little in the spirit of the age. This country is, in fact, fallen as low in point of moral Philosophy (and of course political) as it is possible for any country to fall. We should have far better *books* circulated among us, if we were as thoroughly enslaved as the Romans under their Emperors. Witness the state of literature in Germany till within these two or three years, when it has been overrun by the French. The voice of reason and nature was uttered and listened to under the Prussian despotism, and in the courts of the Princelings. But Books will do nothing of themselves, nor Institutions without books. Two things are absolutely wanted in this country: a thorough reform in Parliament, and a new course of education, which must be preceded by some genuine philosophical writings from some quarter or other, to teach the principles upon which that education should be grounded. We have in our language better Books than exist in any other, and in our land better Institutions; but the one nobody reads, and the others are fallen into disorder and decay. . . .

CXCI

Dorothy Wordsworth to Mrs. Clarkson, Bury St. Edmunds

ALLAN BANK, Sunday, April 5th, [1809.]

My dear Friend,

Sara and I have a delicious view from our several room windows — both look to the East — the mighty mountains of Fairfield and Seat Sandal, now green to their very summits. Oh that you could see that mass of clouds now resting over the pass, which we used to traverse in our visits to you, that pass where William and I were near being lost forever. Oh that you could see the bonny cottages, and their tufts of trees, and the sweet green fields ! It is a soothing scene, and I trust you will one day behold it, and sit with me in this my little castle, where I now

write. We already feel the comfort of having each a room
of our own, and begin to love them. But the dear cottage![1] I will not talk of it to-day, the loveliness of the
outside, the laburnums being in the freshness of their
beauty, made me quite sad, and all within how desolate! . . .

CXCII

Dorothy Wordsworth to Thomas De Quincey

Wednesday, 5th April, [1809.]

My dear Friend,

Since I wrote to you we have received three letters
from you, i.e., one dated 28th March, one enclosed with
the pamphlets, and one yesterday dated April 1st. I
merely write to set your mind at ease respecting the time
when you will receive a full answer from my brother to
your last letter, and to inform you that we received the
pamphlets duly on Saturday night, and next morning
there was perfect joy in the house over your sweet letter
to Johnny. But here I must tell you that in reading the
letter to him we omit that part after the description of the
carriage where you say you will buy one for him and
Sissy. My dear friend, I believe that you are serious,
because you have said so to Johnny; but I earnestly hope
that you will be prevailed upon not to buy it. We should
grieve most seriously that so much money should be expended for a carriage for them, when they are completely
happy and satisfied with their own, which answers every
important purpose of the other. What matter if it is a
little "harder" to pull? (Johnny often says it is very hard
uphill.) It is the better exercise for them! I have not

[1] Dove Cottage. — Ed.

time to say one half of what I wish, or to notice the particulars of your different letters. We are very much grieved that you have had so much perplexity and vexation about the note on Saragossa, and we (that is, we women) are exceedingly sorry that the sheet has been cancelled; for though we do not think that the note was *necessary* in that place, it does not seem to us that it could have done any harm, except what is always done by *any* note which stops the course of your reading at an animated or eloquent passage. I know not what my brother said to you; but sure I am that he did not in words utter any sentiment, any conjecture respecting your conceptions or intentions, which could have given you the slightest pain; therefore I conclude that he has expressed himself negligently in his hurry, and that you have misunderstood his meaning. I do not know what plan my brother fixed upon for explaining that passage; but certainly it is necessary that it should be known how long the pamphlet has been in being finished, for the sake of *perspicuity*, if there were no other reason. It is very strange about that imperfect sentence. We have hunted out the MS. from which your copy was taken, and it is exactly as you say, leaving off at the word "force." It is astonishing that this could have escaped any of us, much more my brother, who read it so often over. I have copied all the important parts of your letters relative to the pamphlet, and send them by this post to Kendal, and of course he will answer them, and you will receive his letter on Monday, for he will certainly come home by Kendal. We learn from Mrs. C. that Coleridge and Southey met William at Appleby on Saturday. C. is returned to Keswick, and goes with Southey to-morrow to Workington Hall. I know nothing more either of him, or his *Friend*.

Mrs. Kelsall[1] has written her "long story" to me, and I hope I have so explained matters to her, that neither she nor I need give you any more trouble about that business. I am quite vexed with her for plaguing you, and at a time too when *we* are giving you such never-ending plague of another kind. Oh, how I shall rejoice for your sake, and for the sake of your poor head and eyes, when the pamphlet is fairly published! Till then I cannot be easy, for I shall never feel sure that William will not have some changes to make. But for Mrs. K. I believe she suspects that we had some design to manufacture for ourselves quilts, curtains, or other things out of the spoils of your house. At least, she did not give us credit for knowing anything about *economy.* I trust she will not trouble you any more. We are in great spirits about the news from Spain. All are well. Catherine is as lively as a bird, and looks better and better every day. If you thought Totty handsome before, you would say he is beautiful now. Mrs. C. tells us that William was at Penrith, and they all saw Dorothy. She cried to go with her father to Appleby. I long to see her again, and to hear her dear lively voice in the house. John's pictures are put up in his own bedroom, and he is very proud of them. We gave Thomas the Parson and the two Ladies, and it has taken its place in the nursery below your works, the Giant's Castle and the Magician's Temple; Magician or Genius, I believe it is. The pamphlets came on Saturday night. Decius[2] looks so very

---

[1] The Mrs. Kelsall referred to here, at p. 433 and elsewhere, was the wife of a Mr. Kelsall at Manchester, in whose business a part of De Quincey's patrimony was invested, when he lived in Manchester. De Quincey was on very cordial terms with them both, and wrote that to their house only could he "come and go at all hours," but he added that they "had not one idea in common." — Ed.

[2] Probably *Letters of Decius*, in answer to a criticism *Upon the*

dry that I have not heart to attack him. I have read Cevallos[1]; also I have read Miss Smith's Translation of Klopstock's and Mrs. K.'s letters.[2] I wish she had never translated them; for they disturb that beautiful image which you conceive of Mrs. K.'s character from the few letters to Richardson; being full of indefinite breathings of godliness, exclamations without end, and "God" in every fourth line of a page.

Klopstock's letters to her are of the same kind, but being a man's letters, and the letters of a man who has had such a high reputation, one cannot read them with the same indulgence. I never in my life read a book in which there was so little sense or thought, — there is none, except in some of Mrs. K.'s letters, which have far more good in them than her husband's.

Hartley and Derwent are impatient to be gone with this letter. I write as fast as pen can go, but you are a "good scholar," and I hope can make it out. God bless you! We all beg our kindest love.

Your ever-affectionate
D. W.

We have engaged an excellent servant for you, to come at Martinmas, Mr. Lloyd's cook, formerly our servant; but we must hire another to serve you till that time.

Political Account of Trinidad, and upon the Defence of the Crimes of Governor Picton, in the Anti-Jacobin Review, under the Title of the "Pictonian Persecution." London, 1806. — Ed.

[1] Cevallos (Pedro), *An Exposure of the Arts and Machinations which led to the Usurpation of the Crown of Spain . . . translated from the Spanish,* by J. J. Stockdale. London, 1808. — Ed.

[2] Elizabeth Smith, 1776–1805, oriental scholar, went to Coniston in 1803, and died there. Her translation of the Memoir of Frederick and Margaret Klopstock was published in 1808. — Ed.

CXCIII

Dorothy Wordsworth to Thomas De Quincey

Sunday Afternoon, April, 1809.

My dear Friend,

Having an opportunity of sending a letter to Ambleside by Hartley and Derwent, I think it best to write a few lines for your satisfaction, though whether the pamphlet be published or not, there is no *necessity* for writing, as I do not think it likely that you would have " Author of the L. B.," printed in the title-page, which must by no means be done. My brother approves of your manner of disposing of General Ferguson. Let the " Corunna " be omitted. I fear your labours will not be over to-morrow; but soon you must have rest, and we shall all be thankful. You have indeed been a treasure to us while you have been in London, having spared my brother so much anxiety and care. We are very grateful for your kindness. We received your paper; not the *Times*, but the *Globe*. We very much enjoyed the hissings of the people in the presence of their slavish Chief Magistrate and his crew; but it is a pity they cannot conduct themselves with more temperance, in their common hall meetings. If the opposite party had been suffered to speak, the cause of the people would have gained rather than lost.

John is very proud of the pictures you have already sent. They are arranged with great taste in his bedroom. William and Mary were at Lloyd's on Friday, and stayed for the post; but we were not *much* disappointed at not hearing from you, supposing that you had not leisure, and that we should have a letter through Miss Crosthwaite yesterday evening. Accordingly my brother went down to the carrier's at nine o'clock, and brought home your letter. Thank you again and again for writing such "nice letters." You can hardly guess what pleasure we have in receiving them. Coleridge is still at Keswick. He goes to Workington Hall on Monday, was to have gone on Friday (with Southey); but, as usual, he caused the delay. You will have seen him advertised. Poor soul! he writes in bad spirits, and I have no hope. Adieu, my dear friend. Believe me ever affectionately yours,

D. WORDSWORTH.

Hartley and Derwent are impatient to be gone. It grieves me to send off a letter so little worth the postage. Friday was the sweetest day we have had all this year. John was much delighted with your account of the art of printing. You do not mention your brother.

CXCIV

[*William Wordsworth to Thomas De Quincey*]

GRASMERE, Friday,
[Postmark, April 10, 1809.]

My dear Friend,

I returned home last Wednesday after a very agreeable excursion of five days, and had the satisfaction of finding everybody well, though Catherine still looks very puny. I saw little Dorothy at Penrith for about an hour; she is very well, and was as glad to see me as sorry to part from me.

It gives me great concern to find that after all your fatigue, confinement, and vexation, you should have suffered such mortification as you express from such a quarter. As I have always found that explanations by letter in cases of this kind only aggravate the evil, by furnishing new matter for misconception on both sides, I shall not say much upon this subject, after having expressed the deep sorrow which I feel upon the occasion. Concerning your feelings I may be mistaken ; concerning my own I cannot ; I shall therefore confine myself to this subject, well aware however that — though I can be under no mistake myself here — it is not improbable that I may so imperfectly express myself as to occasion mistake on your part.

My reasons for suppressing the note were fourfold. First, that any note, especially in an animated part of a composition, checks the current of thought or feeling, and therefore is in its nature objectionable ; second, all that was *necessary* in this case might be provided for as well in the general advertisement ; third, and far above all, because it seemed to me that a note to the effect of yours would completely anticipate and therefore render intolerably heavy what had been said by me in the additions to the text where Saragossa is again mentioned, and it seemed desirable to say what I had said in the text ; at all events it was easier to strike out a note than a passage from the text which might render necessary other omissions ; and fourth, I thought that it was injurious to the cause and to the people of Saragossa to admit for a moment that any one could imagine that this prophecy had not been fulfilled. These were the considerations which inclined me to request that the leaf should be cancelled. Nor, though at the time I most exceedingly regretted the trouble you had been at, did I doubt that, after you had seen the additions I had sent, you would feel as strongly as myself the necessity that either the note should be suppressed, or those additions; and that, as the latter was not likely to be done without consulting me, the former would of course be deemed necessary as the lesser of two evils.

I never supposed that you drew conclusions unfavourable to Saragossa from the French bulletins. On the contrary, I was sure that your opinions and my own would be coincident. But I must quit the subject. My penmanship is very bad, and my head aches miserably. I am also in other respects not well.

I have seen a hint in one of the papers about some letters of David Baird to the same tune as Moore's. The letters themselves I have not seen; and am very sorry that, not having the whole of this correspondence, I cannot write the note on Moore's representation myself, to rid you of a responsibility which must be unpleasing to you. You will therefore act exactly as you think proper; either make a comment on these papers, or not. They are certainly a libel on the Spanish nation, and ought by some body or other to be exposed as such. Foolish fellow! with a Frenchified mind! to quote that miserable Frenchman's account of the state of public spirit in Spain with approbation. "Toujours la même incredulité sur nos avantages!" What symptom could be more favourable! does not it necessarily imply that the Spaniards had such confidence in their strength, and the justice of their cause, that their serenity could not be disturbed!

I am well satisfied with the manner in which you have filled up the imperfect sentence. How it happened to be left so I know not.

Pray let a copy be sent to Sir George Beaumont, Grosvenor Square!

The copy for Curwen may be sent down hither, as I learn he is at Workington Hall.

A body of the English were turned and broken, and therefore technically vanquished at the battle in Egypt, which decided the fate of the campaign ; that in which Abercrombie was killed. And General Reynier,[1] in his account, makes it matter of reproach to them that they did not surrender. This being the case, as I believe any other troops would have done, my argument is not affected by any subsequent formation of themselves, which these men might make, as it was to their individual courage that they were indebted for the power of making this formation, if it was made. As to the affair of Corunna the whole battle, from Hope's own account, appears to have been out of the rules of the Art of War from beginning to end, and is I believe the strongest case in point that could be given ; but on this I do not insist. Therefore, the word " Corunna " may be omitted.

I cannot pen better, and therefore must conclude,

Very affectionately yours,

W. WORDSWORTH.

CXCV

William Wordsworth to Daniel Stuart

April 26, 1809.

Do let me entreat of you to omit no opportunity, in the *Courier* or elsewhere, to exhort this country to be true to the Spaniards in their struggles, as they have been,

---

[1] Jean Louis Ebenezer Reynier (1771–1814), French general, lost the battle of Maida, 1806; author of *Campaign between the French Army of the East and the British and Turkish Forces in Egypt.* London, 1802. — Ed.

and will be found, true to themselves. Bonaparte cannot
have lost less than one hundred and forty, or one hundred and fifty, thousand men already in Spain. A man
must know little of human nature who despairs of the
cause because the country is overrun, or because the
Spaniards cannot beat the French yet in pitched battles.
... I wish to converse with you upon the military defence
of our own country, and to lay before you my reasons for
believing that nothing has yet been done towards it (I
mean in the arrangements concerning the Volunteers,
local Militia, etc.), which is not far worse than useless.
We are, in fact, in everything but our fleet, leaning upon
broken reeds, and these are perhaps (as has been apprehended by some wise men) sleeping upon gunpowder....

How strange that I should have so expressed myself as
to lead you to believe that I meant to lay it down as a
general proposition, that freedom of discussion could exist
under arbitrary governments, or under any modification
of them, for any good purpose. In the comparison which
I made between our own and other countries, I did not
mean to say any more than this, which might both be concluded *a priori*, and has been proved by fact, viz. that
under arbitrary Governments, which have been *long established in tranquillity*, and *are confident of their own security*,
works of bold disquisition, — both in religion, morals,
and politics — have been permitted to see the light; and,
what is of more consequence, have been generally read,
though not to any good purpose. And the reason is plain.
Under such governments, *in such circumstances*, opinions
excite no alarm either to the governors, or among any part
of the governed; there being no probable connection
between opinion and action. Whereas, in a country like
ours, where we have a considerable portion of practical

liberty, not only is the government afraid of opinions differing from those on which its own strength is founded; but another intolerance, still more to be deprecated, takes place in the minds of large bodies of the community, who set their faces against everything which is not in matter and manner perfectly orthodox, from the apprehension that, if such notions gain ground, a course of *action* will follow, and their privileges, or at least their tranquillity, be sacrificed. Hence for the most part such books only are written as flatter existing prejudice and ignorance; or, if others be produced, they are cried out against at first, and finally neglected. You will remember that I positively said in my letter that books avail nothing without *institutions*, that is, of course, institutions of civil liberty. I am sure that on these points not the smallest difference would exist between us, if we had an opportunity of sifting each other's thoughts thoroughly. . . . .

CXCVI

William Wordsworth to Francis Wrangham

[April, 1809.]

My dear Wrangham,

You will think, I am afraid, that I have used you ill in not replying sooner to your last letter; particularly as you were desirous to be informed in what newspaper my pamphlet was being printed. I should not have failed to give you immediately any information upon this subject which could be of use; but in fact, though I began to publish in a newspaper, viz. the *Courier*, an accidental loss of two or three sheets of the manuscript prevented me from going on in that mode of publication, after two sections had appeared. The pamphlet will be out in less than a fortnight, entitled at full length, *Concerning the Relations of Great Britain, Spain, and Portugal, to each other, and to the common Enemy, at this crisis, and specifically as affected by the Convention of Cintra; the whole brought to the test of those Principles by which alone the Independence and Freedom of Nations can be Preserved or Recovered.* This is less a Title than a Table of Contents!

I give it you at full length in order that you may set your fancy to work (if you have no better employment for it) upon what the pamphlet may contain! I sent off the last sheets only a day or two since, else I should have written to you sooner; it having been my intention to pay my debt to you the moment I had discharged this debt to my Country, and to the virtuous of all countries. What I have written has been done according to the best light of my conscience. It is indeed very imperfect, and will, I fear, be little read; but, if it is read, it cannot, I hope, fail of doing some good, though I am aware it will create me a world of enemies, and call forth the old yell of Jacobinism. I have not sent it to any personal friends as such, Therefore I have made no exception in your case. I have ordered it to be sent to two — the Spanish and Portuguese Ambassadors — and to three or four other public men, and Members of Parliament, but to none of my friends and relations. It is printed with my name, and I believe will be published by Longman.

Verses have been out of my head for some time; but in some inspiring moment, should such be vouchsafed, I may not be unmindful of the request which you do me the honour to make. You must permit me to return the same request on my part to you. There may not be much invention in this; the sincerity of it may make amends.

I am very happy that you have not been inattentive to my suggestion on the subject of topography. When I ventured to recommend this pursuit to you, I did not for a moment suppose that it was to interfere with your appropriate duties as a parish priest — far otherwise — but I know you are of an active mind; and I am sure that a portion of your time might be thus employed without any deduction from that which was due to your professional engagements. It would be a recreation to you, and also it appears to me that records of this kind ought to be executed by some one, both for the instruction of those now living, and for the sake of posterity; and if so, the duty devolves more naturally upon clergymen than upon other persons, as their opportunities and qualifications are likely to be better than those of other men. If you have not seen White's and Whitaker's books,[1] do procure a sight of them.

I was aware that you would think me fair game upon the Catholic question, but really I should be greatly obliged to any man who would help me over the difficulty I stated. If the Catholics upon the plea of their being the majority merely (which implies an admission on our part that their profession of faith is in itself as good as ours, as consistent with Civil Liberty) are to have these requests accorded, how can they be consistently refused the further prayer of being, upon the same plea, constituted the Established Church? I confess I am not prepared for this. With the Methodists on one side, and the Catholics on the other, what is to become of the poor Church and people of England, to both of which

---

[1] White's *Natural History and Antiquities of Selborne* (1789). Whitaker's *History and Antiquities of the Deanery of Craven, in the County of York* (1805). — Ed.

I am most tenderly attached ; and, to the former, not the less on account of the pretty little spire of Brompton Parish Church, under which you and I were made happy men, by the gift from Providence of excellent wives.

To Mrs. Wrangham present my cordial regards, and believe me, dear Wrangham,

Your very sincere and affectionate friend,

W. WORDSWORTH.

CXCVII

Dorothy Wordsworth to Thomas De Quincey

GRASMERE, Monday, May 1, 1809.

My dear Friend,

I have just dismissed Johnny with his shame-faced smile, telling him that I wanted to be alone to write to Mr. De Quincey. I asked him what I should say for him, and he could think of nothing but that I should tell you to come back again, and even of that he was ashamed, and seemed to struggle with other thoughts which he could not utter, while he blushed all over his face. He is a happy creature, more joyous than ever, and yet more thoughtful. I am sure you will say he is much improved, and will perceive his mind opening before you when you renew your long conversations with him. Reading is now no longer a painful exertion to him, though certainly he does not make out his words without great difficulty ; but he likes the exercise, not much yet for the sake of the matter contained in his book, but *as* an exercise, and I do not doubt that in a little time he will be able to read without spelling, though he is slow in learning.

I was called downstairs, and found Miss Hutchinson reading Coleridge's *Christabel* to Johnny. She was tired, so I read the greatest part of it. He was excessively interested, especially with the first part, but he asked "why she could not say her prayers in her own room," and it was his opinion that she ought to have gone "directly to her father's room to tell him that she had met with the Lady under the old oak tree and all about it."

My dear friend, I felt a pang when you complained of not having heard from us for so long a time, though I had written a hurried letter on Friday, the day when we received yours. It appeared to me as if I had been ungrateful and unfeeling in not writing; at least that there might be something like social intercourse between us while your mind was vexed and harassed by the labour which for our sakes you have taken upon you, though I could not have hoped to be very entertaining; for what have I to tell you but of the goings-on of our quiet household? We are indeed now a quiet family, wanting Sissy and, above all, Coleridge; who, though not noisy himself, makes a bustle in the house. Besides, we have been but little plagued with smoke lately, which makes us seem to have nothing to do but to sew, read, write, walk about and play with the children for our pleasure. I often wish that you were here now, that you might know that we are not always oppressed with business and labour.

We are to have workmen again at the chimnies, and they will revive past miseries; but we hope that they may do something to prevent our suffering next winter as we suffered the last; for we are assured by many persons that register stoves will entirely cure the evil in the parlours, and we would gladly submit to the inconvenience of having the kitchen chimney pulled down (which we think will be the only effectual remedy); but, alas! in two years more we fear we shall have to remove from this house, for Mr. Crump has taken a cottage at Ambleside for the next summer, a proof that he wishes at least to spend the summer months among the Lakes; and what is to be gained by letting his own house and renting another? It will be very grievous to be disturbed again, if we should get the chimnies cured, after having had one whole year's trouble and discomfort; and you will be left in the lurch, for if we quit this house there is no prospect but of our quitting Grasmere, for there is not another shelter for us here. But this is anticipating evils, and foolishly too, when we have had so many actual evils of the same kind to endure. We are greatly concerned at the delay of the pamphlet, but much more at your being detained in London so long and your having so much trouble. I will quit this subject with a hope that before the end of this week we may receive the parcel. By the bye, I hope you will have had leisure to think about Johnny's pictures, for he expects them with impatience, and is very proud of those which he already possesses.

My brother has begun to correct and add to the poem of the *White Doe*, and has been tolerably successful. He intends to finish it before he begins with any other work, and has made up his mind, if he can satisfy himself in the alterations he makes, to publish it next winter, and to follow the publication by that of *Peter Bell* and the *Waggoner*. He has also made a resolution to write upon public affairs in the *Courier*, or some other newspaper, for the sake of getting money; not wholly, however, on that account, for unless he were animated by the importance of his subject and the hope of being of use, he could do nothing in that way. Coleridge, however, writes to desire that he will not withdraw himself from poetry, for he is assured that there will be no need of it, as he (Coleridge) can get money enough. I have indeed better hopes of him at present than I have had for this long time, laying together his own account of himself and the account which Mrs. C. gives us of him. He intends to go to Penrith on Wednesday to superintend the press, therefore you may expect a visit from *The Friend* on Monday morning (I believe that is the day on which it will arrive in London). As to my brother's writing for a newspaper, I do not much like the thought of it; but unless the pamphlet (the most improbable thing in the world) should make his poems sought after, I know not how we can go on without his employing some portion of his time in that way. The misfortune is that he cannot lay down one work, and begin with another. It was never intended that he should make a trade out of his faculties. His thoughts have been much employed lately in the arrangement of his published poems, as he intends to blend the four volumes together whenever they are reprinted — or should I say *if* ever? for we hear no more from Longman, and I believe that the two last volumes scarcely sell at all.

This reminds me of the last *Edinburgh Review* which I saw at Mr. Wilson's. There never was such a compound of despicable falsehood, malevolence, and folly as the concluding part of the review of Burns's *Poems* (which was, in fact, all I thought it worth while to read, being the only part in which my brother's works are alluded to). It would be treating Mr. Jeffrey with too much respect to notice any of his *criticisms ;* but when he makes my brother censure himself, by quoting words as from his poems which are not there, I do think it is proper that he should be contradicted and put to shame. I mentioned this to my brother, and he agrees with me; not that he would do it himself, but he thinks it would be well for you, or some other friend of his, to do it for him, but in what way? I think a letter might be addressed to him in the Edinburgh papers and in one or two of the London papers. A private letter to himself would be of no use, and of course he would not *publish* any condemnation of himself in his own Review, if you were to call upon him to do so. I wish you would think about it. Mr. Wilson came to us on Saturday morning, and stayed till Sunday afternoon. William read the *White Doe* and Coleridge's *Christabel* to him, with both of which he was much delighted. He has promised to come again on Wednesday, and stay all night; and my brother, in return, has promised to read *Peter Bell* to him. They talked about going through Wales and thence into Ireland, and I do not think that the scheme will drop; therefore you must hold yourself in readiness to meet them in Wales, if you should not be here at the time. Miss Hutchinson has some thoughts of going into Wales in June; in which case William would accompany her, and Mr. Wilson would either go along with them or follow them; but if Miss H. does not go into Wales so soon, they most likely will defer the journey till the autumn, when you will, I hope, certainly be here.

Do excuse this scrawl. I left the parlour for the pleasure of being alone; and having no fire upstairs, I sat down in a sunny spot in a room without a table, and am writing with the writing desk upon my knee, — a lazy trick, I will allow, but it will be to you a sufficient excuse for my bad penmanship. Mrs. Kelsall has sent a very pretty carpet for your new house, but we are not at all

satisfied with the colour and pattern of the calico for
bed-curtains, etc., and are, upon the whole, sorry that we
did not make choice ourselves at Kendal. I am called
away. I go unwillingly, for I wanted to fill my paper.
God bless you! Believe me ever, my dear friend, your
affectionate

DOROTHY WORDSWORTH.

I dare say my sister will write to you soon, for the
pleasure of writing, not to spare me trouble, for I assure
you it never can be a trouble to me to write to you.
Again God bless you!

CXCVIII

William Wordsworth to Thomas De Quincey

Monday, May 5th, [1809.][1]

My dear Sir,

I take the first opportunity to inform you that I have
received your letter, which has been forwarded to me
from Grasmere. Be assured that I have read it with the
deepest interest, and with sorrow that you should have
suffered so much. I will not speak of this now; only let
me say that I never felt for a moment the least diminution of kindness towards you. When you spoke of your
health being re-established, I felt a great weight taken
from my mind. Be careful of yourself; but, to the point.
Could you defer your journey a fortnight, or three weeks?
I shall be detained here more than ten days, and also a
little time upon the road; but I cannot bear the thought
that you should be in the North, and I not see you. If it
be not in your power to defer your journey, do not fail on

[1] Mr. Gordon Wordsworth believes this letter may have been
written as early as 1806. — Ed.

any account to call at my Cottage. Wheresoever you may be, write to me ; and, if your letter could reach Grosvenor Square[1] within ten days of the date of this, write to me here. If not, at Grasmere.

Believe me, your sincere and affectionate friend,

W. WORDSWORTH.

CXCIX

Dorothy Wordsworth to Thomas De Quincey

GRASMERE, Saturday, 6th May, 1809.

My dear Friend,

I cannot let Mr. Jameson go without a greeting from us to you, though my brother and Miss Hutchinson wrote yesterday. I long for the carrier's return to-night, for assuredly we shall, at least, have a *letter* from you. Would that the pamphlets might come too ! William still continues to haunt himself with fancies about Newgate and Dorchester or some other gaol, but as his mind clings to the gloomy, Newgate is his favourite theme. We, however, have no fears, for even if the words be actionable (which I cannot but think they are not), in these times they would not dare to inflict such a punishment. Above all, the infamy alluded to, proceeding from the Convention of Cintra, would only be increased thereby. Though the expense of cancelling the leaf and the consequent delay would be serious evils, what I should most grieve for would be your trouble and vexation. I do not recollect that we want anything in London. Making presents is a very pleasant way of disposing of money; but, alas ! that is a commodity in which we do not much abound, and

[1] Sir George Beaumont's London residence. — Ed.

whatever wishes we might have of that sort we are forced
to suppress. Another week is gone by, and *The Friend*
does not appear. Coleridge at first talked of printing
upon unstamped paper, in case the stamped should not
arrive in time; but in the last letter we had from him he
says that is impossible. I suppose he has had some
fresh information on the subject since he talked of the
unstamped paper. The paper was sent off from London
some weeks ago, and has not yet arrived, and this is certainly an undeniable cause of delay; but I much fear that
there is little done on Coleridge's part, and that he himself is not sorry that there should be an excuse in which
he has no concern. He has written to London to desire
that a sufficient quantity of paper for one number may be
sent by the coach, and it is his intention to go to Penrith
next week to superintend the press.

Miss Hutchinson has told you that we are busy with
the cottage. I hope it will be a very nice place before
you come to it, though the poor laurels in the garden
have been so cruelly mauled by Atkinson that I fear they
will never look like anything but dismembered creatures.
John Fisher is very proud of his post; he is gardener
and steward, that is, overseer of the other workmen.

The weather is now very delightful, and it is quite a
pleasure to us to go down to the old spot and linger about
as if we were again at home there. Yesterday I sat half
an hour musing by myself in the moss-hut, and for the
first time this season I heard the cuckoos there. The
little birds too, our old companions, I could have half fancied were glad that we were come back again, for it seemed
I had never before seen them so joyous on the branches
of the naked apple trees. Pleasant indeed it is to think
of that little orchard which for one seven years at least

will be a secure covert for the birds, and undisturbed by
the woodman's ax. There is no other spot which we
may have prized year after year that we can ever look
upon without apprehension that next year, next month, or
even to-morrow it may be deformed and ravaged. You
have walked to Rydale under Nab Scar? Surely you
have? If not, it will be forever to be regretted, as there
is not anywhere in this country such a scene of ancient
trees and rocks as you might have there beheld — trees
of centuries' growth inrooted among and overhanging
the mighty crags. These trees you would have thought
could have had no enemy to contend with but the mountain winds, for they seemed to set all human avarice at
defiance; and indeed if the owners had had no other
passion but avarice they might have remained till the last
stump was mouldered away, but *malice* has done the work,
and the trees are levelled.

A hundred labourers — more or less — men, women,
and children, have been employed for more than a week
in hewing, peeling bark, gathering sticks, etc., etc., etc.,
and the mountain echoes with the riotous sound of their
voices. You must know that these trees upon Nab Scar
grow on unenclosed ground, and Mr. North claims the right
of *lopping* and *lopping* them, a right which Lady Fleming
as Lady of the Manor claims also. Now Mr. North allows
(with everybody else) that she has a right to fell the trees
themselves, and he only claims the boughs. Accordingly
he sent one or two workmen to lop some of the trees on
Nab Scar; Lady F.'s steward forbade him to go on; and
in consequence he offered £5 per day to any labourers
who would go and work for him. At the same time
Lady F.'s steward procured all the labourers he could
also at great wages, and the opposite parties have had a

sort of warfare upon the crags; Mr. North's men seizing the finest trees to lop off the branches, and drag them upon Mr. N.'s ground, and Lady Fleming's men being also in an equal hurry to choose the very finest, which *they* felled with the branches on their heads, to prevent Mr. N. from getting them; and, not content with this, they fell those also which Mr. N. has been beforehand with them in lopping, to prevent him from receiving any benefit from them in future. Oh, my dear Friend! is not this an impious strife? Can we call it by a milder name? I cannot express how deeply we have been affected by the loss of the trees (many and many a happy hour have we passed under their shade), but we have been more troubled to think that such wicked passions should have been let loose among them. The profits of the wood will not pay the expenses of the workmen on either side!!

A law-suit will no doubt be the consequence, and I hope that both parties will have to pay severely for their folly, malice, and other bad feelings. Mr. North is a native of Liverpool. I daresay you may have often heard us mention him as a man hated by all his neighbours. Mr. N. has taken an active part in the business. But to turn to pleasanter thoughts. You inquired after dear little Dorothy. She is now at Appleby with Miss Weir who keeps a boarding-school, and I have no doubt is as happy as the day is long. Her uncle Hutchinson, who has been here, saw her at Penrith, and he said she was very entertaining, very pretty, and the greatest chatterer in the world. She was very proud of the notion of going to Appleby and said she would travel in the coach by herself, "nobody should go with her." Accordingly she was to be entrusted to the guard, and Miss Weir would meet her at the inn. Her uncle says she spells very well, and will soon learn to read. She is not to come home till midsummer. I hope when she does come that it will be long before we part with her again, though I must say that Tom has almost supplied her place in the way of furnishing entertainment for the house.

My dear Friend, I am ashamed of this blotted letter. You will say I always write in a hurry, and indeed I plead guilty; but you must take it as a proof of affection that my penmanship is so bad, for in proportion as my friends have become more near and dear to me I have always been unable to keep my pen in such order as to make it write decently. When I wrote the first page of this letter Tom was plaguing me, and I hardly knew what I was doing. That is the cause of the superabundance of mistakes and blots; and latterly I have been expecting every moment to be called down to tea. After tea I shall walk to Ambleside with my letter. Mr. Jameson goes off to-morrow. William and I walked to A. last night, and were somewhat disappointed at not receiving a letter from you. Adieu. God bless you!

Believe me, ever your affectionate friend,

DOROTHY WORDSWORTH.

We have not seen the Proclamation, or Address, or whatever it is, of the Juntas respecting Saragossa. The carpet is not yet arrived.

CC

William Wordsworth and Sarah Hutchinson to Thomas De Quincey

GRASMERE.[1]

The other day I wrote to Mr. Stuart requesting him to look over the pamphlet, previous to publication, for the express purpose of ascertaining whether it contained matter which would expose me to a prosecution in any of the courts of law; and I pointed out to him a passage which I deemed the most objectionable of any that occurred to me, recommending, if he agreed with me, that the leaf should be cancelled. The passage is the one where I say, "What greater punishment could there be than to have brought upon themselves the *unremovable contempt and hatred* of their countrymen?" As Wellesley is now at the head of the army, it will be pleaded that it is very dangerous to circulate such opinions concerning men in such high stations. The blame, morally considered, belongs not to me for speaking thus of such a man, but to those who placed him in such high authority after his having given such flagrant proofs of unworthiness. But this I should derive no benefit from, if prosecuted. Therefore, though I left it to the discretion of Mr. Stuart to soften this passage or not, I am now decidedly of the opinion that it is much safer and more prudent to cancel the leaf, if the work be not already published. Let it stand something like this, just as it happens to suit: "What punishment could be greater than the unalterable

[1] These letters were undated, but the postmark was " May 8, 1809," and the postscript to the latter was written on Friday, May 5. — Ed.

sentence already passed on them by the voice of their countrymen?" or any words to that effect to fill up the space. Pray do also, previous to the publication, confer with Mr. Stuart upon this question in general, and beg him to exercise his most deliberate judgment upon it.

I must apologize for making this application so late and unseasonably after all the trouble you have had; but if "better late than never" be true in any sense, it is in a case like this. I am influenced chiefly by the consideration of Wellesley being now in so high a station, which makes it I think imprudent, and even improper, to be said now, though it might have been very justifiable, if the saying of it would have had any tendency to prevent his having so many precious interests confided to his care. Thus far I, William Wordsworth, have employed Miss H. as my amanuensis. She is now going to write a few words in her own person, and I retire from the field, begging leave only to say that we have not seen the decree of the Junta about Saragossa, and should be glad to see it. Neither have we seen the private accounts about Lord Cockrane, but my first feeling is that that noble hero would be greatly disappointed in the result; and I strongly suspected that, if the matter were investigated, heavy blame would be attached to Gambier for not having his ships where they could be brought up in time. Nothing effectual can be done in cases of this sort without considerable risk: excessive caution is cowardice. Farewell.

Your very affectionate friend,

W. WORDSWORTH.

P.S. — If the pamphlet is bound up, the leaf must be cancelled. — W. W.

The following was added by Miss Hutchinson : —

My dear Sir,

We females shall be very sorry to find that the pamphlet is not published, for we have not the least fear of Newgate — if there was but a garden to walk in, we think we should do very nicely — and a gaol in the country would be quite pleasant. But seriously, I hope that the passage may not be deemed objectionable, for another delay will be most provoking, and put Mr. Baldwin out of all patience with you both.

I am glad to tell you that the workmen have begun to-day in good earnest with your cottage; we have been down this morning superintending, and we expect that in less than a fortnight it will be ready for the painters. Ned Wilson is to make the shelves. The cabinetmaker said that mahogany would be very expensive, and of no use afterwards; for the *shelves* of bookcases were never made of anything but deal or common wood. We are sure that all will be finished long before you arrive, even if William does not call upon you to attend him into Ireland, of which scheme Miss W. must have told you; namely, that her brother is to attend me into Wales, and that Mr. Wilson is to follow us, and you join them at our house, and all proceed together.

Mr. Jameson is to be in London in a few days and Miss Wordsworth will write to you by him. We are all very well. Catherine improves, John grows a better scholar, and Thomas is quite the beauty, and much improved in his behaviour. One thing I forgot to say about your house, that if you leave it before your term, you must *offer it first to me*, in case I should wish to go to housekeeping, for it is going to be made so neat that I shall no longer prefer Mr. Gill's cottage, upon which I

had hitherto set my heart. Mr. and Miss W. are just
going to set off for Ambleside, where they expect to meet
with a letter from you.   God bless you !

Very sincerely yours,

S. H.

P.S. — Could you bring those books of Mr. Coleridge's
which were detained in London by Mr. Montagu ?   I ask
because I suspect that he may never think about them
himself, and I know that he wants Sir T. Browne's works
especially.   Mary desires her love to you, and advises
you to leave this disagreeable office entirely to Mr. S., as
you have had enough of the *unpleasant*.

CCI

William Wordsworth to Thomas De Quincey[1]

Wednesday Night.

My dear Friend,
    I have been much disappointed in not hearing either
from you or Mr. Stuart by this night's Post. I request
very much that you would procure an interview with Mr.
Stuart immediately, in order that, by your joint efforts,
everything may be done which is necessary. As the
pamphlet has been so long delayed, my anxiety to have
it out has much abated, and therefore, even on this
account, I request that Mr. Stuart would carefully cancel
every leaf that contains matter which he thinks, or any
person, if he cannot rely upon his own judgment, to whom
he may submit the work, thinks would render me liable
to a prosecution, either from the Government or the

---

[1] This letter, written a few days later, was addressed to De Quincey
at 82 Great Titchfield Street, Cavendish Square. — Ed.

individuals concerned. In fact, as far as relates to this country, as connected with the cause, my zeal is much abated as are my hopes. How can it be otherwise, when I see Lord Hawkesbury that was, declare in open Parliament that the establishment of a military Government in Portugal was justifiable in principle? and when I see, after such a commander as Moore, a disgraced man like Wellesley (and disgraced too in that manner) placed at the head of the British Army in the Peninsula? I mention this upon the present occasion as a reason for not being willing to incur any risk in directing the indignation of the public against such men; I therefore beg again, if there be any doubt concerning any passage, that it may be inexorably removed. I remember one which I requested some time ago, I believe when I parted from you at Ambleside, might be altered; where, speaking of the King's reproof of the city of London, I said, " They had been condemned under a sophism, insidiously or ignorantly applied." Pray, was that altered?[1] If not, surely it ought to be — some way in this manner, " As might be said if the words were not entitled to deference by having been put into his Majesty's mouth insidiously or ignorantly," etc. Another strong passage which I

[1] The above passage was modified to the following effect: "Now it was in the character of complainants and denunciators, that the petitioners of the City of London appeared before his Majesty's throne; and they have been reproached by his Majesty's Ministers under the cover of a sophism, which, if our anxiety to interpret favourably words sanctioned by the First Magistrate makes us unwilling to think it a deliberate artifice meant for the delusion of the people must, however (on the most charitable comment), be pronounced an evidence of no little heedlessness and self-delusion on the part of those who framed it " (see the *Prose Works of William Wordsworth* (Eversley edition), Vol. I, p. 200). — Ed.

recollect is, " In Sir Hew Dalrymple and his brethren we have generals who have a power of sight only for the strength of their enemies," etc.[1] I do not mention this last as particularly insisting upon it ; there may be many far worse. But I beg that this letter may be read to Mr. Stuart, whom I have already requested to exercise his best judgment — only interfering with it in that one instance about "*hatred* and *contempt*" — and this present of his Majesty's speech, if it is not already altered.

My first letter upon this subject to Mr. Stuart ought to have been received by him last Saturday, on which day he wrote a letter to me, manifestly not having at that time received mine, on which account I have had considerable anxiety.

I cannot conclude, my dear friend, without expressing my sincere and deep regret and sorrow that you should have had so much trouble and mortification in this business. I hope, however, you will soon be at Grasmere, when you may think of it in quiet as a traveller of a disagreeable journey which he has performed and will not have to repeat.

I am, most affectionately yours,

W. WORDSWORTH.

CCII

William Wordsworth to Thomas De Quincey

Wednesday, May 24.

My dear Friend,

Last night we received the pamphlet; I have not read the whole, but Miss Hutchinson will transcribe on the

---

[1] To this " and their own weakness" was originally added (see *Prose Works*, Vol. I, same edition, p. 157). — Ed.

opposite leaf the most material errors which I have
noticed; three of them are important, and the first, in the
motto from Bacon, exceedingly so, "zeal" for "hate";
the next "abuses" of the world for "abusers," in the
quotation from Sidney; and the next, "calenture" without the words "of fancy" following. These are much the
most important; and I dare say the fault has been in
the MS., either the words omitted, or written illegibly;
indeed I am surprised how you have been able to get it
done so correctly. I am quite satisfied with your note
upon Moore, which is very well done; but had I seen his
last letter before I entreated you to be so gentle with
him, I should not have been so earnest upon that point.
Could anything be more monstrous than his having made
that march, as he tells us, to satisfy the people of England
of a truth they were not otherwise to be convinced of,
viz. that the Spaniards had neither the ability nor the
inclination to do anything for themselves? that is to say,
he exposed his army to certain loss and to the probability of entire destruction, in order to prove thereby a
fact to the people of Great Britain which could not be
proved in this way at all, could scarcely have by this
measure any light thrown upon it; and further, a fact
which, if it were so, would soon show itself! But enough
of Sir J. Moore. He was one of the approvers of the
Cintra Convention, and I think you have great merit in
having treated him with such forbearance. It is now
time that I should congratulate you on your escape from
so irksome an employment and give you my sincere thanks
for all the trouble you have undergone. . . .

As to the passage about the Army, I hope and believe
it is no libel, but certainly Mr. Stuart's opinion (he having
had so long experience) it would have been safe to abide

by, because the passage was of no importance; but I hope he is satisfied. I cannot but think myself that there are several passages for which I may be prosecuted if they choose, but in this I have no certain guide to direct my judgment, as these things have nothing to do with morality or good sense, but merely depend upon the temper of the times, or of the people in power. I am much pleased with all the passages which you had altered. I am obliged to conclude in a great hurry, but I must beg to hear when you purpose to return to Grasmere. Your house is in great forwardness and very neat. We shall all be most happy to see you; but the beauties of this spring you cannot have, as a few days will carry them all away. John is getting by heart the ballad of *Chevy Chase* and promises himself great pleasure in repeating it to you.

Most affectionately your friend,

W. WORDSWORTH.

To this letter Miss Hutchinson, after giving a list of eleven *errata*, added the following: —

My dear Mr. De Quincey,

I give you free leave to laugh at my *blundering errata*, but I hope you will be able to make them out, though I do not suppose they will give you any pleasure, or be of much use, except for your own copy, unless a Second Edition should be called for, which is not likely. William has been in the house all day, so was in a hurry to get his walk before it was too late, and left me to this business, which I have not executed to my satisfaction. You must be so good as to send a pamphlet to Lord Lonsdale, Charles Street, Berkeley Square, from the Author — or rather desire Longman to send it —; but no, William bid me request you to correct, with your pen, the errors in it. I have found out that it is my *pen* that will not write, which makes me in a·*muddle*, for the hard labour my fingers are put to is quite enough to occupy my mind also ; and I am in too great a hurry to mend my pen. We are all very well, and wish most heartily that you could see your orchard just now, for it is the most beautiful spot upon earth, and a week ago it was still more so, for the blossom of the apple trees was in all its glory.

We hear not a word of *The Friend*. Mr. Southey has lost his youngest child but one, a sweet little girl; she died very unexpectedly, though she had been ill for some time. God bless you !

Yours very sincerely,

S. H.

You will understand that the second parcel is not arrived, which ought to have been here, according to your letter, at the time which the first reached us; namely, Tuesday night.

CCIII

William Wordsworth to Daniel Stuart

May 25, 1809.

. . . If we, who wish for a temperate reform, are utterly to reject all assistance from all those who do not think exactly as we do, how is it to be attained ? For my part I see no party with whom, in regard to this measure, I could act with entire approbation of their views, but I should be glad to receive assistance from any. . . . I do not think the reform will ever be effected, unless the people take it up; and if the people do stir, it can only be by public meetings. It is natural that in meetings of this kind the most violent men should be the most applauded, but I do not see that it necessarily follows that their words will be realised in action. The misfortune of this question of reform is that the one party sees nothing in it but dangers, the other nothing but hopes and promises. For my part, I think the dangers and difficulties great, but not insurmountable, whereas, if there be not a reform, the destruction of the liberties of the country is inevitable. . . .

CCIV

William Wordsworth to Daniel Stuart (?) [1]

My dear Sir, GRASMERE, May 25, 1809.

I suppose by this time the pamphlet is published, as I received two days ago some unstitched copies from Mr. De Quincey. I have no doubt that Mr. De Quincey was *the occasion ;* though I am at the same time assured that he neither was, nor could be, the necessary *cause* of the delay. The MSS. was transmitted to him, now nearly two months ago, nor has a single syllable of *the body of the work* been altered, either by him or me, since that time. It is now printed exactly as I sent it at that time, therefore, how could any alterations of his in the text have caused this long delay? The fact is that Mr. De Quincey must have insisted upon his punctuation being attended to, and the printer must have been put out of humour by this and therefore refused to go on with the work. But this is a matter of little consequence, the evil is done and cannot be amended. My inducement for placing it in Mr. De Quincey's hands was to save time

[1] This letter and the preceding one are printed as one letter in the *Letters of the Lake Poets.* — Ed.

and expense (our situation being so inconvenient for the post) and also to save you trouble. I shall say no more than that I am very sorry for what has happened and that you should have had vexation about it, thanking you at the same time for all the trouble you have taken.

I learned with great concern from Mr. De Quincey that a passage which you deemed libellous was not cancelled. This was in direct opposition to my earnest request conveyed in a letter which I desired him to read to you; in which letter I expressly said that (with the exception of two passages, one of which has been cancelled, and the other I find Mr. De Quincey had previously altered in the MS. agreeably to my request) I referred *to you entirely* to decide upon what was libellous, and what was not; adding that whenever there was a *doubt*, the passage should be cancelled without remorse. I am therefore very sorry that he should so resolutely have opposed his opinion to yours, but I hope that you were not overborne by his perseverance, or Mr. Baldwin's *authority;* but . . .

It is so late that I have little anxiety about the immediate effect of the pamphlet, but I hope that your exertions in its favour will do all that can be done to turn the few days of the Session which remain to a favourable account.

Affectionately yours,

W. WORDSWORTH.

Excuse this vile paper. I have taken it by accident. Should the pamphlet be republished when this reaches you, which I scarcely deem possible, I entreat that if there be any passage or passages which you think libellous they may yet be cancelled. . . .

CCV

William Wordsworth to Thomas De Quincey

[Postmark, May 30, 1809.]

My dear Friend,

I was reading yesterday to Mrs. Wordsworth your note on Moore's Letters with great pleasure, and expressing at the same time how well it was done : upon which she observed to me, "How, then, did not you use stronger language of approbation?" When you wrote to Mr. De Quincey you merely said you were "satisfied with it." I replied that this I considered as including everything; for said I, "Mr. De Quincey will do me the justice to believe that, as I knew he was completely master of the subject, my expectations would be high ; and if I told him that these were answered, what need I or could I say more?"

I am glad that you treated Moore with so much gentleness and respect. I could not have done so myself; my feelings would not have suffered me, nor would it have accorded with the sentiments I have expressed in the body of the work; for before the Board of Inquiry Dalrymple has taken especial pains to tell us that the Major-Generals approved of the Convention, and that Moore was of the number. I wish you could have contrived to say something handsome of Treir [1] — (how does he spell his name?) — for he has been infamously traduced, especially by the Opposition. . . . I am sadly

---

[1] Possibly General Bernardine de Friere, a Portuguese commander who had expressed a wish to Sir Arthur Wellesley that the British commissariat might supply his troops with British stores during the campaign. He made the refusal of this request an excuse for separating from the English army. This took place in August, 1808. — Ed.

grieved about that error in the press in the motto, *seal* for *hate*, as it utterly destroys the sole reason for presenting the passage so conspicuously to notice. I regret that I did not request the pamphlet to be sent down when the body of it was printed, as I might have reasonably concluded that there must have been blunders in the manuscript which could be known to nobody but myself. In spite of all this it is very correctly printed, and the punctuation pleases me much ; though there are here and there trifling errors in. it. I think, indeed, your plan of punctuation admirable.

Of Coleridge, or *The Friend*, we hear nothing ; he went to Keswick some time ago about it, but what he is doing he does not inform us.

Affectionately yours,

W. WORDSWORTH.

P.S. — The note on the Board of Inquiry is a clencher for that business.

W. W.

To the above letter Mrs. Wordsworth added the following : —

Friday, May 26.

My dear Sir,

I must take the advantage of this blank paper to express to you my congratulations upon your having at last reached the end of your labours, and to repeat at the same time what William has told you, how much pleasure your part of the pamphlet has given us. I will not say one word now about the vexations we have had in connection with the trouble it has caused you. That is all over, and I hate to repeat grievances.

We begin to wish very much that you were now amongst us again, but you have no chance of seeing Grasmere in its spring-tide beauty this year. Notwithstanding the most terrible ravages that have been made amongst the trees, I never remember to have seen the vale look more lovely than at this moment. Our weather is delightful; we now have gentle rains, after a long fit of most glorious dry summer weather. The workmen are very busy about your cottage, so we hope to have all ready for you in a short time. You can well conceive with what interest and pleasure we all (children and all) look forward to, and talk of, the visits we are to make to you, when we have you placed at the Town End. Johnny delights in the thought of it. He is learning to repeat *Chevy Chase*, and he tells me with great pride that he thinks he shall be able to "say it all, when Mr. De Quincey comes home." I hope you will find Catherine (your little pupil, as I often call her) much improved, but she is but a little creature yet. My sister will have told you that she was weaned a few weeks ago. Dorothy is still absent. I begin to feel motherly longings to have her at home again. We shall see great changes in her, but I am very doubtful whether for the better or worse. You will smile (and I confess I am half ashamed) at my simplicity for running on in this manner to you. However, the cause rests with yourself, for you have at all times taken so much interest about these children.

The latter parcel is not arrived. I fear there is still some further delay, particularly as the pamphlet is not advertised in the last *Courier* we have seen, namely, Saturday's. William wishes to see Lord Selkirk's letter to Major Cartwright; and, as the parcel must be sent off before you receive this, I suppose he means you to bring

it with you. My sister is going to walk to Rydale ; perhaps she may meet with the parcel or letter from you.
God bless you, my dear sir ! I hope you have gotten rid
of the toothache and all your complaints, as your last
letters do not speak of yourself. Believe me to be most
affectionately yours,   M. WORDSWORTH.

   I have written as though I were ambitious to out-do
William in blots and bad penmanship.
                                     M. W.

                       CCVI

          William Wordsworth to Daniel Stuart

                                   May 31, 1809.
My dear Sir,
   I learn from a letter received last night from Mr. De
Quincey that the book has been lying now ten days at
the printers', finished ; and is probably still unpublished.
With great sorrow I have perceived that this has been
owing to your not having been apprized that the printing
was done. Mr. De Quincey having been satisfied by the
printers' assurance made to him that you had been
informed when the sheets were going to be struck off ;
but at the same time he tells us that they did not wait for
your answer. Therefore when the printers had shown
themselves so inattentive to their promise to you, viz.,
that the sheets were not to be struck off till you had exam-
ined them, what proof had Mr. De Quincey that this message was sent ? Much less that you had received it ? But
it avails nothing to find fault, especially with one who has
taken such pains (according to the best of his judgment)
to forward this business. That he has failed is too clear,

and not without great blame on his own part (being a man of great abilities and the best feelings, but, as I have found, not fitted for smooth and speedy progress in business). I learn that the sheets, as I have said, were struck off without your having an opportunity to ascertain whether they contained anything libellous. This has angered me much, as it is an act of great disrespect to you, and may prove of most serious injury to me. In fact, if I were superstitious, I should deem that there was a fatality attending this my first essay in politics. I have kept my temper till last night, but I must say that Mr. De Quincey's letter of last night ruffled me not a little.

I hope you did not take ill my freedom with respect to the late conduct of the *Courier*. I spoke from the best motives. . . .

CCVII

William Wordsworth to Thomas Poole.

[About May, 1809. Postmark, KESWICK.] [1]

My dear Poole,

Before I wrote my last letter to you, the last sheet of my pamphlet was sent off to the printer, since which time I have not altered a word in it, or added one. Judge then, how I must have been used when I say that at that time a hundred pages were printed off! My patience is

[1] This letter was sent from Keswick in 1809. The date is uncertain. Mrs. Sandford wrote (*Thomas Poole and his Friends*, Vol. II, p. 229) that the date was March 31, 1809. Mr. J. Dykes Campbell thought it must have been earlier; for, on March 30, Wordsworth wrote to Poole that Coleridge had been about a month at Keswick.—Ed.

completely wearied out. I will explain to you the mystery
as far as I can. Mr. De Quincey, some time before the date
I mentioned, took his departure from my house to London;
and, in order to save time and expense, I begged that
instead of sending the sheets down to me to be corrected,
they should be transferred directly to him for that purpose ; and I determined to send the remaining portions
of the MS. to him as they were finished, to be by him
transmitted to the press. This was a most unfortunate
resolution ; for at the time the subject of punctuation in
prose was one to which I had never attended, and had of
course settled no scheme of it in my own mind. I deputed
that office to Mr. De Quincey. *Hinc illæ lacrymæ !*

He had been so scrupulous with the compositor, in
having *his own plan rigorously followed to an iota*, that the
man took the pet, and whole weeks elapsed without the
book advancing a step. And, as if there were some
fatality attending it, now that it has been entirely printed
off for full ten days, I have reason to believe it is not
published ! This is, I conceive, owing to the printer having neglected to inform Mr. Stuart that the printing was
finished ; Mr. Stuart having undertaken to advertise and
have it published. So that the pamphlet has been lying
ten days, and ten days at this season, and after so long
delay, makes it like a ship in a dry dock ! Now is not
this provoking? But I write the account to you not for
sympathy, but to clear myself from any imputation of
indolence and procrastination, which otherwise you would
be justified in throwing upon me. My hands in fact have
been completely tied. I should the less have regretted
the late appearance of the work, if I had been at liberty
to employ the time in adding to its value ; but in fact, as
I expected its appearance every day, I abandoned every

thought of the kind. I must take up with the old proverb, " What cannot be cured must be endured ! " — The pamphlet was sent off by me ten days ago, and the world may perhaps not see it for ten weeks !

I have yet another, and far more important, reason for writing to you ; connected, as no doubt you will guess, with Coleridge. I am sorry to say that nothing appears to me more desirable than that his periodical Essay should never commence. It is in fact *impossible* — utterly impossible — that he should carry it on; and, therefore, better never begin it; far better, and if begun, the sooner it stops, also the better. The less will be the loss, and not greater the disgrace. You will consider me as speaking to you now under a strong sense of duty, from a wish to save you from disappointment; and from a further, and still stronger, wish that — as one of Coleridge's nearest and dearest friends — you should take into most serious consideration his condition, above all with reference to his children. I give it to you as my deliberate opinion, formed upon proofs which have been strengthening for years, that he neither will nor can execute any thing of important benefit either to himself, his family, or mankind. Neither his talents nor his genius — mighty as they are — nor his vast information will avail him anything. They are all frustrated by a derangement in his intellectual and moral constitution. In fact he has no voluntary power of mind whatsoever, nor is he capable of acting under any *constraint* of duty or moral obligation. Do not suppose that I mean to say from this that *The Friend* may not appear. It may, but it cannot go on for any length of time. I am *sure* it cannot. C. I understand has been three weeks at Penrith, whither he went to superintend the publication, and has since never been heard of (save once, on his first arrival) though frequently written to. I shall say no more at present, but I do earnestly wish that you would come down hither this summer, in order that something may be arranged respecting his children, in case of his death, and also during his life-time.

I must add, however, that it answers no purpose to advise her [1] to remonstrate with him, or to represent to him the propriety of going on or desisting. The disease of his mind is that he perpetually looks out of himself for those obstacles to his utility which exist only in himself. I am sure that if any friend whom he values were, in consequence of such a conviction as I have expressed, to advise him to drop his work, he would immediately ascribe the failure to the damp thrown upon his spirits by this interference. Therefore in this way nothing can be done, nor by encouraging him to attempt anything else. He would catch eagerly perhaps at the advice, and would be involved in new plans, new procrastination, and new expenses.

I am, dear Poole, most sincerely yours,

W. WORDSWORTH.

CCVIII

William Wordsworth to Correspondent Unknown

Sunday Night, June 4, 1809.

My dear Sir,

Nothing but vexation seems to attend me in this affair of the pamphlet. Mr. De Quincey, according to my request, sent me down ten stitched pamphlets (he had

---

[1] His wife. — Ed.

previously sent four unstitched) and it was not till to-day
that I discovered that in two copies of these stitched the
page which was cancelled remains as it first stood, the
corrected leaf not having been substituted. Ten copies
have been sent me by this last parcel, two of them covered with green paper ; in one of these the corrected leaf
has been substituted. Of the other, I cannot speak, as it
is sent to a friend. The other eight copies were simply
stitched. Six have been sent off unexamined ; but the
two that remain are *both* wrong, both containing the passage only as it first stood, from which I conclude that it
is the same with all the others. This is most culpable
inattention on the part of some one ; the more noticeable,
as these copies that have not the corrected leaf contain
both of them the *errata*, which were printed on another
part of the same half sheet. I do earnestly entreat that
you would do all in your power to have this remedied.
It has mortified me more than I can express ; and after
so many disappointments, has robbed me of all wish to
make any alterations in a second edition if it should be
called for ; since I cannot think of saddling you with the
trouble of correcting the press, and therefore cannot have
the least hope but that such blunders and negligences
would not take place in inserting the alterations, as to
render the book utterly unintelligible. In fact nothing
can be more unfortunate for a work of this kind than a
residence so far from London and so unfavourable to
communication with the post.

I am much obliged to you for your kind suggestions
about an amended edition, and if I were in London, it
should be done; but, situated as I am, I must content
myself with requesting you, in case a second edition
should be called for, to put a copy into the hands of the

printer with the *errata* corrected — both those first printed and those since sent off — and to have it printed as rapidly as possible, which cannot be done with any effect without employing at least three presses; in which case it might be done in a week. . . .

Most truly yours,

W. WORDSWORTH.

I have addressed a letter to the same purpose to Mr. De Q., lest you should not be in the way, but do not let this prevent your looking to the business yourself, particularly as Mr. De Q. may have left town. I am grieved to impose this further trouble upon you. Many thanks for the newspapers. Schill is a fine fellow!

CCIX

Dorothy Wordsworth to Mrs. Clarkson

GRASMERE, Wednesday, 15th June, [1809.]

My dear Friend,

At ten o'clock yesterday morning Coleridge arrived. He had slept at Luff's, and came over the Hawes, and was not fatigued. This you will say is a proof of his bodily *strength*, but such proofs we do not need; for what human body but one of extraordinary strength could have stood out against the trials which he has put his to? You will have seen from his second number [1] that he intends to have one week's respite. His reason for this is that many orders have been sent in from booksellers,

[1] Of *The Friend.* — Ed.

and he wants to have the *names*, that the papers may be sent addressed to the respective persons. Whether it was absolutely necessary, or not, to wait a week I do not know. I am, however, convinced that it is a wise thing; for by this means — if he makes good use of his time — he may get beforehand, and I am assured that without that, it would be *impossible* that he should go on. He is in good spirits, and he tells us that he has left his third number with Brown, who is actually printing it. At all events, I am glad that he is here, for if he perseveres anywhere in well doing it will be at Grasmere; but there is one thing sadly in his way. The stamped paper must be paid for with ready money, and he has none. Now after the first twenty weeks — the time fixed for payment to him — this will be got over. He will then have money to command, but in the meantime I know not what is to be done. He has beforehand stamped paper only for two numbers. He has, however, ordered an additional supply, which I hope will come in due time for his fifth number.

There are a few passages in the two papers published which have given us pain; and which, if he had been at Grasmere, would never have appeared. One is where he speaks of the *one* poet of his own time. This passage cannot but have wounded Southey, and I think that it was unjust to S.; besides, it is a sort of praise that can do William no good. The other passages to which I allude are contained in the notes to the second number. I think it was beneath Coleridge to justify himself against the calumnies of the Anti-Jacobin Review,[1] foolish to bring to light a thing long forgotten, and still more foolish to talk

---

[1] *The Anti-Jacobin Review and Magazine; or Monthly Political and Literary Censor* (1798–1821). Edited by John Gifford (pseud. of John Richard Green). 61 volumes. London. — Ed.

of his home-sickness as a *husband*, or of anything relating
to his private and domestic concerns.   There are beautiful passages in both the Essays, and everywhere the
power of thought and the originality of the great mind are
visible, but then happiness of manner is awanting; and
the first number is certainly very obscure.   In short, it is
plainly shewn under what circumstances of constraint and
compulsion he wrote; and I cannot enough admire his
resolution in having written at all, or enough pity his sufferings before he began, though no doubt almost wholly
proceeding from weakness; an utter want of power to
govern his mind, either its wishes or its efforts.   He says
he rises at six o'clock in the morning; that is, he has done
so for more than a week, nay, I believe a fortnight; and
this morning, when I rung the bell to call the maid to
fetch Catherine away, he came all alive to my door to ask
if he could do anything for me.

A week's residence in Thomas Wilkinson's humble
cottage brought about this change, and I believe that
Thomas, even at the last, was the father of *The Friend.*
C. was happy in Thomas's quiet and simple way of life,
drank no spirits, and was comfortable all the time, and
Thomas urged him to the work.   This we heard from
Luff, and C. himself speaks with delight of the time he
spent under Thomas's roof. . . .

I hope that you have ere this seen my brother's pamphlet.   I cannot doubt but that you will have received
great delight from it.   What a pity that it did not come
out sooner!   It would have been then much plainer to
all readers (very few of whom will bear in mind *the time*
at which the tract was written).   What a true prophet he
has been!   C. has had an interesting letter from Charles
Lamb.   Poor Mary is again in confinement.   They have

changed their chambers, and the fatigue and novelty of removing were too much for her. Charles says that his new rooms are much better than the old, and the rent only £30; but he cannot take at once to anything that is new, and he looks forward to two or three months of melancholy separation. As he says, it is indeed a great cutting out from the short term of human life. . . .

Your child, Catherine,[1] is a sweet treasure — very fair, very bonny, but not beautiful in spite of her blue eyes. She is exceedingly mild tempered, and a very good sleeper. Mr. De Quincey has made us promise that he is to be her (Catherine's) sole tutor; so we shall not dare to show her a letter in a book, when she is old enough to have the wit to learn; and you may expect that she will be a very learned lady, for Mr. De Q. is an excellent scholar. If, however, he fails in inspiring her with a love of learning, I am sure he cannot fail in one thing. His gentle, sweet manners must lead her to sweetness and gentle thoughts. His conversation has been of very great use to John, who is certainly now the finest boy I ever saw. His countenance is delicious, and though not bright at his books, he is far from being dull in acquiring knowledge, and is very thoughtful: but what is most delightful is his tenderness of disposition, his joyous, benignant expression of countenance, and his exceeding modesty.

[1] The Wordsworths' daughter, Catherine, was named after Mrs. Clarkson. — Ed.

CCX

William Wordsworth to Correspondent Unknown

[Postmark, June 17, 1809.]

My dear Sir,

In order that you may not be puzzled with my bad penmanship, which I know must too often have been the case, I have begged Miss Hutchinson to be my amanuensis.

First, let me thank you for your kind exertions in favour of the pamphlet. I have some reason now for having better hopes concerning the sale than I ventured to encourage, notwithstanding your assurances. It has pleased much several persons who have read it in this neighbourhood, and I learn from Charles Lamb that everybody whom he has heard speak of it in town extols it highly. On this account, when I combine it with your confident expressions, I can scarcely doubt but, the edition being so small, a second will be called for. For the reasons which I assigned to you in my last, I am not disposed to make any other than trifling alterations and additions; but some I must make; and therefore I should be glad to hear from you, when a second edition is determined upon, should it be so; and will send you up, per coach immediately, a corrected copy to print from. I feel more strongly my obligations to you for the trouble you have taken in this business, when I consider your many occupations. . . .

I am, truly yours,

W. WORDSWORTH.

P. S. — If the pamphlet should have any sale I most *earnestly* entreat, nay *insist*, that you would reimburse yourself from the profits for all the expense incurred, especially the copies you have paid for and distributed.

W. W.

CCXI

Dorothy Wordsworth to Thomas De Quincey

GRASMERE, Thursday, I believe about the 25th June.

My dear Friend,

It is so long since we have heard from you that I cannot help writing to inquire after you, though I have only time to scribble a few lines. Mrs. Cookson of Kendal has been spending a week with us, and she is just going away, and will carry my letter to the post office. Sometimes we fancy that you are on the point of setting off to Grasmere, and therefore have delayed writing, and at times I, being of a fearful temper, fancy that you are ill; but I think it is most probable that you are so much engaged with your own family as not to have time to write a long letter, and that you do not think it worth while to send a short one; but whatever may have hitherto been the cause of your silence, do write, if but three lines, to tell us how you are, and when we are likely to see you again. We have been so long used to receive your letters regularly that we take very ill to this long privation of that pleasure. My brother is this morning gone out upon a fishing party with Mr. Wilson and his "Merry Men," as William calls them. They have a tent and large store of provisions, and they intend to travel from one town to another and lodge in their tent upon the mountains. Mr. Wilson intends to spend a week in this manner, but how long William will stay I know not — most likely he will be tired before the end of the week.

At all events Mr. Wilson is to be ready with his boats next Thursday, and we are to spend that day together on Windermere, the day of dear Dorothy's return. Miss Weir and D. and the Cooksons are to meet us at Bowness. We have had some wet weather; but it is now perfect summer again, and we have spent several happy days in the open air. On Monday we went to Coniston in a cart, and ate our dinner in a field near the lake. We wished for you.

Your cottage is painted, and I hope will be ready by the end of the next week or the beginning of the week after. It will be very beautiful next summer, but this year's roses have been almost all destroyed with repairing the rough-cast and whitewashing the outer walls. Ned Wilson has made deal bookcases, but in consideration of your having mentioned mahogany for the book-shelves, we have got all the rest of the furniture of mahogany. We were doubtful about it before, the native woods being at present so very dear, but your mention of mahogany, and the consideration that in case you should leave the country and have a sale, decided us; for no sort of wood sells so well at second-hand as mahogany. We advise you to purchase a stock of tea before you come, the tea sold here being very bad and very dear. We always get ours from London. You must also bring silver spoons.

Johnny improves daily; he is certainly the sweetest creature in the world; he is so very tender-hearted and affectionate. He longs for your return, and I think he will profit more than ever by your conversation, though great was the improvement that you wrought in him; indeed he owes more to you than to any one else for the softening of his manners. He is not famous for making extraordinary speeches, but I must tell you one pretty thing that he said the other day. His mother and he were walking in the lane, and, looking at the daisies upon the turf, he said, "Mother, the poor little daisies are forsaken now." "Forsaken, Johnny! What for?" "Well, because there are so many other pretty flowers." Now for a specimen of his logic, having given you one of his poetical fancy. He came running to me with "Aunt, may I tell you?" "What?" "Chips are water." "Water! how's that, Johnny?" "Well," he replied, "you know when chips are burnt in the fire, they go up into the clouds in smoke, and the clouds make rain, so chips are water, and I told Sally that she was washing me in chips." He was much entertained with this last original joke, but the other part of the process seemed to delight him as a *discovery*. Adieu, my dear friend. God bless you! You will be right welcome to Grasmere again.

Yours most affectionately,

D. W.

Coleridge has been with us nearly a fortnight. He is in good spirits, and going on with his work. Of course you have seen his second number; there were a few things in it which gave us pain, and we wished he had abided more closely to his promise. We have heard from several quarters that the pamphlet has made considerable impression, I mean among a few. Sometimes I have been afraid that the carrier lost my last letter to you. It was directed to Clifton. I should be sorry for this, as it was a long letter, though perhaps not very entertaining. Do write immediately.

Coleridge has desired me to open my letter to beg you to bring the Sanskrit MS. and his logical manuscripts.

CCXII

Dorothy Wordsworth to Thomas De Quincey

[No date given.]

My dear Sir,

I hope I am not too late in replying to your kind proposal of looking out for us in the collection of old books. I should have written immediately, but I was in hopes that my brother would make out a sort of catalogue of his wants or wishes; but the former include so much that the task seems to be altogether unnecessary. His library is in fact little more than a chance collection of odd volumes (setting aside the poets, and a few other books that are to be found everywhere). Therefore in general I may say that he wants all that is valuable and can be procured *very cheaply*. (Alas! if this last consideration could have been dispensed with, he would not now have had so small a stock of books.) Clarendon, Burnet, any of the older Histories, translations from the Classics chiefly historical, Plutarch's Lives, Thucydides, Tacitus (I think he said), (by the bye, he *has* a translation of Herodotus), Lord Bacon's Works, Milton's Prose Works; in short, any of the good elder writers. But (after having looked over your friend's books with this key) if you will send a list of such as you think may suit my brother, with the probable prices, he will make his choice among them. I write in great haste, not to lose the post, and my brother is not here to help my memory; but I hope I have said enough to give you a general notion of what we wish or want. In our walk last night we numbered over many books that we should like to have, but I took down no notes, and at this moment I cannot recall them.

I will not speak of our sorrow for your illness. You are recovered now, and we rejoice in thankfulness. At any time, and as soon as ever it suits you, we shall be most glad to see you. We are *settled* in our new house, where we have plenty of room and quietness for you. You may always have a sitting-room below stairs, and a bedroom above to yourself. All are well. The children delighted with the liberty and freedom of wandering up and down the green fields without fear of carriages or horses. With kind love from my brother and sister, I am, dear sir, your affectionate friend,

DOROTHY WORDSWORTH.

P.S. — My brother wishes very much to have Josephus's writings. Pray write and tell us when to expect you.

D. W.

CCXIII

Dorothy Wordsworth to Thomas De Quincey

GRASMERE, 1st August, 1809.

My dear Friend,

It is now my turn to cast reproaches upon myself for my long silence, and of these I have not been sparing, though a bustling, unsettled life for some weeks past has always furnished me with a present excuse, when the time came which I had beforehand fixed upon for writing to you. My last letter crossed *your* last but one upon the road. I have since received a very kind one from your mother's house. It is, I believe, a month ago, and you then talked of being at Grasmere in three weeks ; but we did not much expect you so soon, as no doubt your

mother and sisters will be unwilling to part with you. I
hope, however, that now the time of your coming draws
near. Your house is quite ready, or rather it will be so
in two or three days, for the bed-curtains are not yet put
up, but a woman is now making them, and I believe
before the end of the week all the furniture will be come.
The garden looks fresh and very pretty, in spite of the
cruel injury done to the trees by Atkinson's unruly axe.

We have had a delightful summer, and if you had not
lately been so happy in the enjoyment of a beautiful
country and the society of your own family, we should
have regretted that you were not here. We have had a
houseful of company; Southey, and some friends of his,
a succession of lakers, and Miss Weir and her niece,
and Mr. George Hutchinson have been with us more than
a month; and Mr. Clarkson, and his son and a friend of
his, have spent several days with us. This will explain
to you the nature of our-bustling life; and, besides, I
have been at Kendal, where I stayed twelve days, and
purchased all the articles of kitchen furniture and other
things which could be bought in shops ready-made for
your cottage. I carried your last letter with me, intending to answer it; but I never found leisure, and unluckily
I packed the letter in my trunk, which is not yet arrived,
and I have forgotten the address. So, as the carriers are
often slow in bringing goods from the warehouse, it may
yet be several days before I shall be able to send this
letter off; and this same unlucky contrivance of mine has
prevented my sister from writing to you, for, thinking
that I should probably not find time to write while I was
at Kendal, she would have written, but as I had your
letter with me, she could not, having also forgotten your
last address. . . . Coleridge has been very busy of late, and

his health and spirits are better; he has sent off the third and fourth numbers of *The Friend*, and is at work daily.

He desires me to say that he is exceedingly glad that you have got that book of Bruno. Can you have access to a series of any of the *Reviews?*—for instance, the *Edinburgh* from the first, or the *Monthly*. If you can, and if you have time, Coleridge would be very glad if you would look them through, and note down any gross blunders in logical or moral reasoning which you may detect, and any gross misapplication of praise or blame to names whose fame is already established. My brother has been much depressed by the Austrian defeat and the armistice, though he says he expected no better, that it was his wishes rather than his hopes that kept him alive to the cause before. He has not done anything of late; indeed we have had so much company that it was scarcely possible for him to feel sufficiently independent to devote himself to composition. I have not heard of the pamphlet having been reviewed, and I took the pains when I was at Kendal of going to the Book Club to look at the last Reviews. By the bye, have you seen the *Edinburgh Review* on Campbell's poem? I know not whether the extracts brought forward in illustration of the encomiums or the encomiums themselves are more absurd. There surely can be little sense left in the nation, or Master Jeffrey must very soon write himself into disgrace. The review of Miss Hannah More's work is equally as foolish, though in a different way.

The children are all well, your pupil as sweet as the best of them, though not quite so handsome. She wears no cap and has no hair — her father calls her his little Chinese maiden. She has the funniest laugh you ever saw peeping through her eyes; and she is as

good-tempered as ever.   Dorothy is beautiful, and a delightful creature when she behaves well; but I am sorry
to add that she is very wayward, and I fear we shall have
great trouble in subduing her.   She is quick at her
book, and quick at everything.   John is made up of good
and noble feelings; he is the delight of everybody who
knows him; all his playmates love him; he blushes and
looks pleased whenever your return is talked of.   Last
night, when he had finished his prayers, in which he
makes a petition for his " good friends," he said, " Mr.
De Quincey is one of my friends."   Little Tom has
been poorly and looks ill.   He often lisps out your name,
and will rejoice with the happiest at your return.   I must
remind you of a promise which you made to Johnny to
bring him a new hat.   I bought one for Tom at Kendal,
but remembering that you said you would bring John one,
I did not buy one for him.   Let it be a black hat, if you
have not already bought one of another colour.   Some
chests of books for you are arrived, also the smoke dis-
penser; but we have not yet got it put up.   It will be
done next week, when a workman from Liverpool is
coming to try his skill upon the chimneys.   If you
should come next week you will probably find your house
occupied, for we have offered it to Mr. and Mrs. Crump
for a week or ten days, they being desirous to look about
them at Grasmere.   We are well assured that you would
have done the same if you had been here, and that you
will feel glad in having had this opportunity of obliging
two worthy people.   If you should come while they are
here, you will think it no great evil, as we have plenty of
room for you at Allan Bank; but I fear there is no likelihood that you will come so very soon.   Only let me
entreat that you will not let the trees lose their leaves

before you see them again. Besides, you know you are to be of the party into Wales and Ireland. Miss H. still thinks of going. My brother will accompany her; and he and Mr. Wilson continue to talk of going into Ireland, and they hope that if they do go you will not draw back. They have not fixed a time, but I do not think it will be before September. Now, if you do not come soon, it will be hardly worth while to come at all till the Irish journey is over, and I am very sorry to think of that; but yet, for the sake of a week or two in this country, it would be a pity to come so far, when you could meet them so nicely in Wales. Do write and tell us all your plans; and if you now think of coming immediately, do not put off on account of this Welsh and Irish scheme, as the latter very *probably* may never be executed, and the former possibly. Adieu, my dear friend. God bless you!

D. WORDSWORTH.

Excuse scrawling. I have had a bad pen. Do write immediately. ˙Remember to bring spoons and tea. I have said nothing about the pony, for I think you will hardly prevail upon your brother to part with it, and it would be almost a pity that you should.

CCXIV

Mary Wordsworth to Thomas De Quincey

GRASMERE, Aug. 20th, [1809.]

My dear Sir,

. . . Catherine makes very little progress in talking, though she uses her tongue perpetually — a word of her own, that sounds like *Kisleca*, she is constantly repeating;

it is of universal use to her, for if she is angry it is
Kisleca, and if she is happy she goes singing about in
the archest, prettiest manner you can conceive, " Ah !
Kisleca ; ah ! Kisleca," for five or ten minutes together.
I often wish you could see her. And then she is the
nicest maker of a curtsey you ever beheld ! I hope she
will not have left off this practice when you come, for
you would be delighted to see her. She calls me mamma,
the first of them that ever used this word. She has never
been taught it, and I cannot make her say anything like
mother. She *could* say it distinctly at one time. There
is nothing entertains her so much as the form and
motion of a butterfly; she follows them about the room
(for we often have them in the study) with her eyes, and
almost exhausts herself with laughing at them. She is a
merry little creature, and, I think, grows prettier every
day. I will not tell you what a fine fellow your godson
is, as it was only an afterthought your inquiring for him.
All the rest will be delighted at your return. John was
in ecstasies when I read him from your letter that his
artillery was not forgotten. C. went through every room
in the cottage the other day to seek you.

Mrs. Wilson and her daughters, and Miss Jane Penny
and Mr. Wilson, were here last week ; they came in part
to see me, and in part to avail themselves of the privilege
which you had given them to use your cottage. After
drinking tea at Allan Bank we all repaired to the Town-
End, and drank your health in the little parlour. . . .

Our vale is now terribly infested by a horde of the
Astley tribe, part of which harbour in Robert Newton's
cottage. I am sadly frightened that some of these, or
other gentry of the like kind, may purchase Butterlip
How, which is advertised to be sold publicly some time

next month, or privately before that time by applying to Mr. Wilcock. I fear we shall be far *outbid*, if it comes to public sale, but Mary Dawson says that she "is sure you will buy it." It will be a grievous thing if it falls into bad hands. What do you think of Mr. Astley having made a stately gateway to his house, with a second road (this new one fitted for a carriage) up to the house?

. . . .

Mr. W. is now at Hindwell. I expect him home in less than a fortnight, and my sister is at Bury. I heard from her yesterday; both are well. I do not expect to see my sister before October. I think *your* sister will scarcely accompany you so late in the year, particularly as the weather is so unsettled. There is a great deal of hay to get yet in Grasmere. Ours was housed long before that of any of our neighbours. Mary tells me that Mr. H. begged his remembrances to you. I have not seen any of them lately. T. Southey and his wife have been staying at Brathy. Southey has got another daughter.

I am, my dear sir, your sincere friend,

M. W.

CCXV

Dorothy Wordsworth to Mrs. Clarkson

Sunday (I know not the day of the month)
26th or 27th August, [1809.]

My dear Friend,

. . . We have workmen all over the house, and shall have them yet for two months. The chimnies are all to be raised three feet, and a great deal is to be done in the inside of the rooms. We are putting out a recess with a bow window in the study, and going to alter the sideboard recess. . . . Mr. Crump and a part of his family are at the cottage, and very pleasant it is to see a cheering light there once again.   It is a very neat place, but I do not think, though the furniture is much better and more costly than in our time, that it is altogether so pretty as it was formerly, — I mean when it was in neat order, — for in latter days it was difficult to keep it so.   The garden is very much improved by being made merely a continuation of the turf of the orchard.   This looks very pretty, with the shrubs, etc.

The orchard is, of course, as it used to be, a perfect paradise.   But we have had showery weather ever since Mr. C. left us, and have not been able to sit there, when we have visited at the cottage.   We expect Mr. De Quincey in a few weeks.   As for ourselves, we have now but one year and a half in this house, for Mr. C. will certainly come to it. . . .   Coleridge is going on well at present. The fourth essay will come out next week, and I know that he has the fifth, and more, ready.   As to its future regularity, I dare not speak; only this I know, that he has no right to tax his customers with the stamp, unless he goes on differently from what he has hitherto done. At present he is full of hope, and has, I believe, made excellent resolutions.   Tell us what you think of William's book.[1]   All the judicious seem to admire it.   Many are astonished with the wisdom of it, but nobody buys! An edition of 500 is not yet sold. . . .

[1] Probably *The Convention of Cintra.* — Ed.

CCXVI

Mary Wordsworth to Thomas De Quincey

ELLERAY [September 12, 1809.]

My dear Sir,

I told my sister, when I parted from her at Ambleside, on my way hither, last Friday morning, that I should write to you before my return home. I then felt as if I should send you a very long letter; but, alas! the time has passed away and I have not written, and have perhaps, by my promise, prevented *her* writing. I must now merely content myself with adding a few words to the end of Mr. Wilson's letter to tell you that your last long and kind letter gave us all great pleasure, and that it deserved a more ready and worthy answer. I believe Dorothy would have written sooner had you not promised that we should hear from you again in four days. We have been looking for *that* letter — and since for your arrival. When are we to see you? All has been in readiness for you, and every one of us wishing to see you for a long, long time. I think William will not go into Wales; if my sister Sarah leaves us this autumn, she must be fetched by my brother. Mr. Wilson (as he has, I dare say, told you) is going into Spain, so he cannot be one of her attendants. Coleridge has been very busy lately. You have received the 4th No.,[1] and will be glad to hear that the 5th and 6th are in the printer's hand. He has, of course, been in more comfortable health. Heaven grant this may last!

Mr. W. is with me here, as is your friend John, who, being such a favourite with Mr., Mrs., and Miss Wilson,

[1] Of *The Friend*. — Ed.

and having so much of his own way and such a variety of good things to eat, is in such a state of happiness, that he appears in a character so different from his own, that, had you never seen him before, you might suppose him to be a sort of half-idiot; but in all humours he is glad to talk of his dear friend. William is in admirable health. I hope we shall hear a good account of yours. God bless you! I am writing while the family are sitting round me at supper. We go home in the morning, and shall perhaps meet with some intelligence from you. Believe me to be, with much love and esteem, your affectionate friend,

M. W.

CCXVII

Dorothy Wordsworth to Thomas De Quincey

ELLERAY, Sunday Evening, 18th Nov.

My dear Friend,

. . . William groans over the projected change in the Ministry. We have not yet received to-night's papers, therefore we have at present no later news than you have already got; but we shall have papers to-night, and if there be any news in them I will set it down for your amusement, keeping my letter open for that purpose; but, for my part, I am sick of expecting the great Battle.

. . . .

Your affectionate friend,

D. WORDSWORTH.

CCXVIII

Dorothy Wordsworth to Mrs. Clarkson

GRASMERE, November 18th, [1809.]

My dear Friend,

Sarah[1] has been kept almost constantly busy in transcribing for William, and for *The Friend;* therefore she has desired me to write to you. For William she has been transcribing the introduction to a collection of prints to be published by Mr. Wilkinson of Thetford[2] (of which I believe you know the history, as your husband's name is down among those of the subscribers). I hope you will be interested with William's part of the work (he has only finished the general introduction, being unable to do the rest till he has seen the prints). It is the only regular, and I may say *scientific*, account of the present and past state and appearance of the country that has yet appeared. I think, if he were to write a Guide to the Lakes and prefix this preface, it would sell better, and bring him more money, than any of his higher labours. He has some thoughts of doing this ; but do not mention it, as the above work should have its fair run. He mentioned his scheme to Mr. Wilkinson, to which I should think that Mr. W. will have no objection; as the Guide will, by calling Mr. W.'s publication to mind, after its first run, perhaps help to keep up the sale. . . .

Coleridge is pretty well, as you will judge by the regularity of his work. The tale of Maria Schöning[3] is

---

[1] Sarah Hutchinson. — Ed.

[2] Introduction to *Select Views in Cumberland, Westmoreland, and Lancashire, by the Reverend Joseph Wilkinson* (1810). — Ed.

[3] In Volume II of *The Friend*, after Essay XII is a new title-page with the inscription, " The Second Landing-Place, or Essays

beautifully told ; but I wish it had not been the first tale in *The Friend*, for there is something so horrid in it that I cannot bear to think of the story.   Sarah is grown quite strong.   Mr. De Quincey has been at Grasmere five weeks, and has taken possession of his cottage as a lodging-place. . . .

CCXIX

Dorothy Wordsworth to Mrs. Marshall

GRASMERE, November 19, 1809.

. . . As to ourselves we only want a roomy house to shelter us, with a few acres to feed a couple of cows, or without any land at all.   We know not whither we shall turn ; and, at all events, we must leave Grasmere, for there are only two houses besides our own that would hold us, and of these only one that is large enough.   The other to which I allude I daresay you may remember.   It is a neat white house, on that side of the lake opposite the highway.   It stands on the hill-side, with large coppice woods near it, and a green field, with a steep slope from it to the water.   This house belongs to a Mr. Benson, who has let it for ten years to Mr. Ashley of Dukinfield, near Manchester.   This Mr. Ashley has added a good dining-room to the comfortable but small house, and he is tired of the place, and has given it up to his younger brother.   Now, I think, that he too may soon be tired of the place, as he does not seem inclined to realise

interposed for Amusement, Retrospect, and Preparation. Miscellany the Second," etc.   The first essay in this section begins with an account of some of the free towns of Germany, and in the following paragraph the story of Maria Eleonora Schöning is told. — Ed.

a solitary life, being what the world calls a gay young man ; and, if this should happen, then we may possibly take the house ; but, as I said, it is hardly fit for us, being too small. . . . The winter storms have brought back winter smoke, and we are now forced to believe that we have only been less annoyed since the chimneys were altered. . . . If we could get any comfortable house within five or six miles of Grasmere, we would remove to it without a week's delay. Our friend, Mr. De Quincey, is come to the cottage,[1] rather I should say to Grasmere, (though we have already spent several comfortable evenings at the cottage), but he is with us at present, his servant having arrived only the day before yesterday, and she is now busied in preparing the cottage for his permanent residence. He has been above a month with us, and is like one of our own family ; so we have now almost a home still at the oldest and dearest spot of all. Mr. De Quincey has an excellent library, far too large indeed for the house, though he will have bookcases in every corner. You may judge of the number of his books when I tell you that he has already received nine or ten chests, and that nineteen more are on the road. Some of these books must be kept in chests, on account of the smallness of the house. . . . It is a great pleasure to us all to have access to such a library, and will be a solid advantage to my brother. You ask after our little folks. John is indeed a sweet creature. He is so thoroughly noble-minded, affectionate, and tender-hearted. Dorothy improves in mildness, and her countenance becomes more engaging, but she is not so richly endowed with a gracious nature as her brother. Perhaps it is that

[1] Dove Cottage.

she is more lively; and we see indeed that her waywardness is greatly subdued. She is at times very beautiful,
and *elegance* and *wildness* are mingled in her appearance,
more than I ever saw in any child.

CCXX

Dorothy Wordsworth to Thomas De Quincey [1]

George Green and his wife, our Sally's father and
mother, went to Langdale on Saturday to a sale; the
morning was very cold, and about noon it began to snow,
though not heavily, but enough to cover the ground.
They left Langdale between five and six o'clock in the
evening, and made their way right up the fells, intending to drop down just above their own cottage in Easedale (Blenkrigg Gill, under Miles Holmes's intack).
They came to the highest ridge upon the hill, that can
be seen from Langdale, in good time, for they were seen
there by some people in Langdale; but, alas! they never
reached home. They were probably bewildered by a mist
before daylight was gone; and may have either fallen
down a precipice, or perished with cold. Six children
had been left in the house, all younger than Sally, and
the youngest, an infant at the breast. Poor things! they
sat up till eleven o'clock on Saturday night, expecting
their parents; and then went to bed, satisfied that they
had stopped all night in Langdale on account of the bad
weather. The next day they felt no alarm, but stayed in
the house quietly, and saw none of the neighbours;
therefore it was not known that their father and mother
had not come back, till Monday at noon, when that pretty

[1] This undated letter belongs to the year 1808. The Greens were
lost on March 19 of that year. It should follow Letter CLXI at
p. 342. — Ed.

little girl, the eldest of the household (you will remember, having admired the exquisite simplicity and beauty of her figure one day when you were walking with Mary in Easedale) went to George Rowlandson's to borrow a cloak. They asked why, and she told them she was going to seek their folk, who were not come home.

George Rowlandson immediately concluded that they were lost, and many then went out to search upon the fells. Yesterday between fifty and sixty were out, and to-day almost as many, but all in vain. It is very unfortunate that there should be so much snow on the fells. Mary and I have been up at the house this morning; two of the elder daughters are come home, and all wait with trembling and fear, yet with most earnest wishes, the time when the poor creatures may be brought home and carried to their graves. It is a heart-rending sight, so many little, *little* creatures. The infant was sleeping in the cradle, a delicate creature, the image of Sara Coleridge. Poor Sally is in great distress. We have told her that we will keep her till we can find a nice place for her, and in the meantime instruct her in reading, sewing, etc. We hope she will continue to be a good girl. We do not intend her to have anything to do with the children after our new servant comes. We have hired little Mary, the young woman who lived at Miss Havill's, and who has long been so desirous to come to us. This very moment three, nay four, of the poor orphans (for Sally was with them) have left the room. The three had been at Mrs. North's, who has sent them here with a basket of provisions, and will visit them herself with clothes, all the younger being very ragged. That sweet girl looks so interesting, has such an intelligent, yet so innocent a countenance, that she would win any heart. She is a far nicer girl than Sally, and one that we could not but have pleasure from; but poor Sally has fallen to us, and we cannot cast her off for her sister; but we hope that Mrs. North will take *her*, or at least send her to school. Old Molly talks with cheerfulness of dying, except when she turns to poor John's desolate condition. I really think I have nothing more to say, for I have not heart to talk of our little concerns, all being well with us. We have been strangely unsettled for these three days. Pray bring Sally a New Testament. You can buy it at Kendal. The children are at school. . . .

Your affectionate friend,

DOROTHY WORDSWORTH.

GRASMERE, Wednesday.

I open my letter to tell you that we are at ease : the poor lost creatures are found. John Fisher has called at the window to tell us. He says they had rolled a great way, and were found just above Benson's. Where that is I cannot tell, but it must have been low down. She was near a wall, and he lying a little above her.

CCXXI

Dorothy Wordsworth to Lady Beaumont

GRASMERE, Thursday, December 28th, 1809.

My dear Friend,

Yesterday evening I returned with our whole family from the house of the very person whom you inquire after with so much anxiety. In our way thither on Christmas Day I received your letter, and wished to have answered it from that place, but I could not find leisure to take up my pen, and now I am at home again I am determined to make no further delay. Surely I have spoken to you (not by word of mouth, but by letter) of Mr. Wilson,[1] a young man of some fortune, who has built a house in a very fine situation [2] not far from Bowness. Miss Hutchinson, Johnny, and I spent a few days there last summer with his mother and sister, and I think I mentioned this to you. This same Mr. Wilson is the author of the letter signed Mathetes.[3] He has from his very boyhood been a passionate admirer of my brother's writings; and before he went to Oxford he ventured to write a long letter to my brother respecting some poems, and expressing his deep gratitude for the new joy and knowledge which his writings had opened out to him.

Several years after this he bought a small estate near Windermere, and began to build a house. In the meantime, however, he fitted up a room in a cottage near the new building, and by degrees made little improvements in the cottage, till it is become so comfortable that, though the large house is finished, he has no wish to remove; and seems, indeed, to have no motive, as the cottage is large enough to accommodate himself and his mother and sister and two or three friends, and as they are all pleased with the snugness and comfort of their present modest dwelling. Indeed, he often regrets that he built the larger house. If, however, he should marry (which is very likely) he will find it necessary. His mother and sister are at present at Edinburgh (where, in fact, their home is), but they are so much pleased with

---

[1] John Wilson, afterwards Professor in the University of Edinburgh, and the Christopher North of *Blackwood's Magazine*. See p. 474. — Ed.   [2] Elleray. — Ed.   [3] In *The Friend*. — Ed.

the country that for the last two years they have spent more than half their time here ; and we all, including Mr. De Quincey and Coleridge, have been to pay the bachelor a Christmas visit, and we enjoyed ourselves very much, in a pleasant mixture of merriment and thoughtful discourse.

He is a very interesting young man, of noble dispositions, and fine ingenuous feelings ; but, having lost his father in early youth, and having had a command of money to procure pleasures at a cheap rate, and having that yielding disposition of which he speaks — which makes him ready to discover virtues that do not really exist in minds greatly inferior to his own, which have yet a sufficient share of qualities in sympathy with his own to draw them to him at first — his time has often been idly spent in the pursuit of idle enjoyments ; and dissatisfaction with himself has followed. He had been more than a year in this neighbourhood before he could resolve to call upon my brother — this from modesty, and a fear of intruding upon him — but since that time we have had frequent intercourse with him, and are all most affectionately attached to him. He has the utmost reverence for my brother, and has no delight superior to that of conversing with him ; and he has often said that he is indebted to him for preserving the best part of his nature, and for the most valuable knowledge he possesses. He is now twenty-three years of age.

Probably before this letter reaches you, you will have received the nineteenth number of *The Friend*, which contains the continuation of my brother's reply to Mathetes' letter. Mr. Wilson sent the letter to Coleridge, and Coleridge requested my brother to reply to it, he being at leisure, and disposed at that time to write something for

The Friend. You will be glad to hear that he is going to finish the poem of *The White Doe*, and is resolved to publish it, when he has finished it to his satisfaction.

I should not have been so slow to thank you for the most interesting narrative of the life of "an English Hermit" if I had not been particularly engaged during the last fortnight. My sister has been at Kendal (we met her at Mr. Wilson's on her way home), and during her absence I was employed in arranging the books, and putting the house into order; we having only just got rid of workmen, who had been about the house ever since the month of July. I told you the history of the chimneys, and Mr. Crump has been throwing out a recess with a large bow window in my brother's study. This obliged us to have the books stowed in the lodging-rooms in heaps; and you will guess that it was no trifling labour to put them all in their places again upon the shelves. We have had much discomfort from the workmen; but, now that it is over, we think ourselves amply repaid, the room being so much improved. The new window looks towards the crags and wood behind the house, and a most interesting prospect it is; especially in the winter-time, when the goings-on of Nature are so various.

Coleridge has been very well of late, and very busy, as you will judge when I will tell you that he has published a series of essays in *The Courier*, on the Spanish affairs. We wish very much that you should see them. They have been published within the last fortnight. I do not recollect the date of the first; but you may easily, I should think, procure the papers by applying to any friend who takes them in; for, as Coleridge has signed his name, and as they have been so recently published, they will be easily collected together. In the nineteenth

or sixteenth number of *The Friend* Coleridge has desired
that the purchasers of that journal will pay their money
into the hands of Mr. Ward, bookseller, in Skinner Street.
I do not recollect the number — I mean of Mr. Ward's
shop — but you will easily find it by referring to *The
Friend*, or, if it be more convenient, the money may be
sent to Grasmere. We have received the books from
Coleorton. We were much affected by your account of
the good old Lady Beaumont's reception of you at Dunmow. What an affecting and instructive spectacle the
sight of such a woman at her years ! You have not mentioned Sir George's health lately. I trust he is pretty
well. May God grant you both many years of comfort
and happiness ! Believe me ever, with grateful affection,
your faithful friend,

D. WORDSWORTH.

I ought to have said more of the pleasure we received
from the interesting history of the Hermit, but I have not
room for it. Coleridge wishes it could be published in
The Friend, but perhaps this cannot be allowed. I was
mistaken. The answer to Mathetes' letter does not
come out in the next *Friend*, but the next but one.

D. W.

1810

CCXXII

Dorothy Wordsworth to Mrs. Marshall

February, 1810.

The essay of this week[1] is by my brother. He did not intend it to be published now; but Coleridge was in such bad spirits that when the time came he was utterly un-provided, and besides had been put out of his regular course by waiting for books to consult respecting Duty; so my brother's essay, being ready, was sent off. William requested Coleridge to proffer an apology for the breach of his promise; but he was, I believe, too languid even to make this exertion; . . . and here I must observe that we have often cautioned Coleridge against making prom-ises, which, even if performed, are of no service, and if broken must be of great dis-service.

CCXXIII

Dorothy Wordsworth to Mrs. Marshall

[Feb. 21, 1810.]

. . . We look forward to spending the next summer and winter in this delightful vale, I trust without further interference from workmen; and meanwhile I hope that

---

[1] In *The Friend.* — Ed.

some changes will take place by means of which we may be
suited with another house not far distant. . . . One point
we are determined not to give up.   We must be in the
neighbourhood of a grammar school, as we cannot afford
to send the boys out to be boarded, and indeed should
not wish it.   We should do well if we could get a place
near Ambleside, or near Hawkshead; but I do not know
of any good schools in any other part of this neighbourhood, and perhaps we may be obliged to remove many
miles off. . . . You do not mention *The Friend.*   I guess
that you join in the general complaint of obscurity.   I
allow that it almost always requires the whole power and
attention of the mind to understand the author, and that
probably that mode of publication is not the proper one
for matters so abstract as are frequently treated of; for
who can expect that people whose daily thoughts are
employed on business, and who read only for relaxation,
should be prepared for, or even be capable of, serious
thought, when they take up a periodical paper to read in
haste.   We expected that the number of subscribers
would be very much diminished at the twentieth number,
but it has not proved so, and there have been some new
ones.   The concluding part of the seventeenth, and the
twentieth number, were by my brother; and the essay of
this week upon *Epitaphs* is by him.   He has now published some sonnets in *The Friend,* which I think will
please your husband.   I now think the subjects of them
would interest him.   The translations of *Epitaphs from
Chiabrera* are also by my brother.   Have you seen my
brother Christopher's publication *Lives of Eminent Men
connected with Religion, from the Reformation to the Revolution?*   I am reading it with great interest.   The lives of
Cardinal Wolsey and Sir Thomas More are delightful. . . .

CCXXIV

Dorothy Wordsworth to Lady Beaumont

[ALLAN BANK,] February 28th.
[Postmark, March 5, 1810.]

My dear Friend,

. . . The children, each in a different way, are thriving, happy, and interesting creatures. John is bold and active, and gives daily proofs of a gracious and gentle disposition. Dorothy is a delightful girl, — clever, entertaining, and lively, — indeed so very lively that it is impossible for her not to satisfy the activity of her spirit with a little naughtiness at times, a waywardness of fancy rather than of temper. Thomas continues to be the most innocent of babies, a baby all over — in simplicity, in helplessness, in his fond love of those persons whom he has had about him, and in the guileless expression of his pretty face. Yet his eyes express *more* than innocence : there is a rich mildness in them, a kind of liquid softness which is most bewitching, they ought to have been the eyes of a girl. His little sister Catherine is a perfect contrast, to *him* especially ; but she is the only funny child in the family; the rest of the children are *lively*, but Catherine is comical in every look and motion. Thomas perpetually forces a tender smile by his simplicity, and Catherine makes you laugh outright, though she can hardly say half-a-dozen words, and she joins in the laugh, as if sensible of the drollery of her appearance. She is a plain child, has something peculiar in the cast of her face, which probably adds to the comic effect of her looks and gestures.

Miss Hutchinson does really intend to leave us in about a fortnight. Mr. Monkhouse, her brother's partner in the farming concerns in Wales, is here, and she is unwilling to let slip the opportunity of accompanying him when he returns. We shall find a great loss in her, as she has been with us more than four years; but Coleridge most of all will miss her, as she has transcribed almost every paper of *The Friend* for the press. You will be glad to hear that her health is, upon the whole, very good, though she is incapable of much bodily exertion. Mr. Monkhouse has been under the surgeon's hands ever since his arrival at Grasmere, about a fortnight ago. His horse struck him when he was driving him along at about the distance of a mile from our house. Fortunately some men saw him fall, otherwise, as the evening was cold and the daylight gone, the consequences might have been dreadful. He lay in a swoon some time, but at last by the assistance of the men he managed to walk to Allan Bank. He is however doing very well, and the apothecary says that he may travel safely in the course of a fortnight.

With Mr. Monkhouse we have also another gentleman from Wales ; Mr. Wilson also has been staying with us. These circumstances will partly account to you for my having been more than usually engaged in domestic employments. To which I may add another reason, that my sister, though in good health, is not able to go through much fatigue, and also that her chief employment of late has been transcribing for William.

Coleridge's spirits have been irregular of late. He was damped after the twentieth number by the slow arrival of payments, and half persuaded himself that he ought not to go on. We laboured against such a resolve, and he seems determined to fight onwards ; and indeed I do not think he had ever much reason to be discouraged, or *would have been* discouraged, if his spirits had not before been damped; for there have been many untoward circumstances and much mismanagement to hinder the regular remittance of the money, and many people have not yet paid, merely from thoughtlessness, who, no doubt, will pay ere long; and the work cannot but answer in a pecuniary point of view, if there is not in the end a very great failure in the payments.

By the great quantity of labour that he has performed since the commencement of *The Friend* you will judge that he has upon the whole been very industrious; and you will hardly believe me when I tell you that there have been weeks and weeks when he has not composed a line. The fact is that he either does a great deal or nothing at all; and that he composes with a rapidity truly astonishing, if one did not reflect upon the large stores of thought which he has laid up, and the quantity of knowledge which he is continually gaining from books. Add to this his habit of expressing his ideas in conversation in elegant language. He has written a whole *Friend* more than once in two days. They are never re-transcribed, and he generally has dictated to Miss Hutchinson, who takes the words down from his mouth. We truly rejoice in the satisfaction which *The Friend* has spread around your fireside, and there are many solitary individuals who have been proud to express their thankfulness to the author.

How have you liked the *Epitaphs from Chiabrera?* The essay of this week (No. 25) is by my brother. He did not intend it to be published now; but Coleridge was in such bad spirits that when the time came he was utterly unprovided, and besides had been put out of his regular course by waiting for books to consult respecting Duty; so my brother's essay, being ready, was sent off. William

requested Coleridge to proffer an apology for the breach
of his promise; but he was, I believe, too languid even to
make this exertion, and I fear that people would be disappointed, having framed their expectations for the conclusion of Sir Alexander's history; and here I must
observe that we have often cautioned Coleridge against
making promises, which even if performed are of no service, and if broken must be of great dis-service.

My brother's essay (as indeed most of the essays) is
sadly misprinted.   One or two of the chief mistakes you
will perhaps take the trouble to correct, as they render it
unintelligible.   For "Nestrian" in the Epitaph read
"Nestorian."   Page 406, after "pious duty" place a full
stop, and read, "And with regard to this latter."   Page
407, after "recurring to this twofold desire," add, "namely,
to guard the remains of the deceased, and to preserve
their memory, which has been deduced from the higher
feeling, the consciousness of immortality, it may be said,"
etc.   Page 408, for "an ingenious poet," read "*ingenuous
poet.*"   My brother has written two more essays on the
same subject, which will appear when there is need.   He
is deeply engaged in composition.

Before he turns to any other labour, I hope he will
have finished three books of *The Recluse.*   He seldom
writes less than fifty lines every day.   After this task is
finished he hopes to complete *The White Doe,* and proud
should we all be if it could be honoured by a frontispiece
from the pencil of Sir George Beaumont.   Perhaps this
is not impossible if you come into the north next summer,
and Sir George hinted at such an intention.   If you
should not come, we indulge the hope of seeing you at
Coleorton.   Do excuse this scrawl.   I wish I had taken
a larger sheet of paper, for I feel as if I had yet a great

deal to say to you. I am glad you are interested with my brother Christopher's work.[1] I am very much pleased with it. The lives of Sir Thomas More and Cardinal Wolsey are most exceedingly interesting. My brother and sister beg to be affectionately remembered to Mrs. Fermor; and may I present my best respects to her, though I have not the happiness of knowing her personally? Adieu, my dear Lady Beaumont. Believe me, your grateful and affectionate friend,

D. Wordsworth.

Coleridge bids me say he has received your letter, and has begun to write to Sir George several days ago. I am ashamed of this letter on looking it over. Can you read it?

CCXXV

Dorothy Wordsworth to Mrs. Clarkson

Thursday Night, I believe about the 12th of April.
[Postmark, Keswick, 17th April, 1810.]

My dear Friend,

. . . I need not tell you how sadly we miss Sara,[2] but I must add the truth that we are all glad she is gone. True it is she was the cause of the continuance of *The Friend* so long; but I am far from believing that it would have gone on if she had stayed. He was tired, and she had at last no power to drive him on; and now I really believe that *he* also is glad that she is not here, because he has nobody to seize him. His spirits have certainly

---

[1] His *Ecclesiastical Biography.* — Ed.
[2] Sarah Hutchinson. — Ed.

been more equable, and much better.   *Our* gladness proceeds from a different cause.   He harassed and agitated her mind continually, and we saw that he was doing her health perpetual injury.   I tell you this, that you may no longer lament her departure.   As to Coleridge, if I thought I should distress you, I would say nothing about him; but I hope that you are sufficiently prepared for the worst.   We have no hope of him.   None that he will ever do anything more than he has already done.   If he were not under our roof, he would be just as much the slave of stimulants as ever; and his whole time and thoughts, except when he is reading (and he reads a great deal), are employed in deceiving himself, and seeking to deceive others.   He will tell me that he has been writing, that he *has* written, half a *Friend;* when I *know* that he has not written a single line.   This habit pervades all his words and actions, and you feel perpetually new hollowness and emptiness.   I am loath to say this, but it is the truth.   He lies in bed, always till after 12 o'clock, sometimes much later; and never walks out. Even the finest spring day does not tempt him to seek the fresh air; and this beautiful valley seems a blank to him.   He never leaves his own parlour, except at dinner and tea, and sometimes supper, and then he always seems impatient to get back to his solitude.   He goes the moment his food is swallowed.   Sometimes he does not speak a word; and when he does talk it is always upon subjects as far aloof from himself, or his friends, as possible.   The boys come every week, and he talks to them, especially to Hartley, but he never examines them in their books.   He speaks of *The Friend* always as if it were going on, and would go on; therefore, of course, you will drop no hint of my opinion. . . .

CCXXVI

William Wordsworth and Dorothy Wordsworth to Lady Beaumont

GRASMERE, May 10th. [Postmark, May 16, 1810.]

My dear Lady Beaumont,

I am very happy that you have read the Introduction [1] with so much pleasure, and must thank you for your kindness in telling me of it. I thought the part about the cottages well done; and also liked a sentence where I transport the reader to the top of one of the mountains or, rather, to the cloud chosen for his station, and give a sketch of the impressions which the country might be supposed to make on a feeling mind contemplating its appearance before it was inhabited. But what I wished to accomplish was to give a model of the manner in which topographical descriptions ought to be executed, in order to their being either useful or intelligible, by evolving truly and distinctly one appearance from another. In this I think I have not wholly failed.

I shall prepare for coming to Coleorton as soon after your arrival as it will be grateful to you to be interrupted. I wish to have the summer by the forelock. Mrs. W. expects her little one every day; and should all go on well, and Catherine continue to advance as she has done, within six weeks from this time my sister, I hope, will also be at liberty, and we may take our departure together.

I assure you I long much to see you and Sir George, and the place also not a little. I feel also that I stand

---

[1] This Introduction (for which see p. 479) was afterwards expanded into Wordsworth's *Description of the Scenery of the Lakes in the North of England.* — Ed.

in need of some change; I cannot say that I am unwell, but I am not so strong as I have been. This I am sure of, though those about me will not hear of it, and I am not sorry that they will not.

The drawings, or etchings, or whatever they may be called, are, I know, such as to you and Sir George must be intolerable. You will receive from them that sort of disgust which I do from bad poetry, a disgust which can never be felt in its full strength but by those who are practised in an art, as well as amateurs of it. I took Sir George's subscription as a kindness done to myself; and Wilkinson, though not superabundant in good sense, told me that he saw it in that light. I do, however, sincerely hope that the author and his wife (who certainly, notwithstanding her faults and foibles, is no ordinary woman) may be spared any mortification from hearing them condemned severely by acknowledged judges. They will please many who in all the arts are most taken with what is most worthless. I do not mean that there is not in simple and unadulterated minds a sense of the beautiful and sublime in art; but into the hands of few such do prints or pictures fall.

Be so good, my dear Lady Beaumont, as to tell Sir George that I should have written to him long ago, but too much love, combined with a good deal of sadness, has kept me silent. I could not write without opening my heart; and that would have led to painful subjects, which, knowing his state of health and spirits, I thought it better to avoid. But I hope we shall soon meet, and such of these things as it is proper to say may then be said at a less price than when friends are separated.

I remain,   Your very affectionate friend,

W. WORDSWORTH.

P.S. — You said that Mr. Canning could not deny that I had spoken with the bone of truth. The misfortune is, with persons in Mr. Canning's situation, it is impossible to know when *they* speak with *sincerity*. But this I am assured of, that the events which have since taken place prove that I had at least some portion of the gift of pre-science. In fact, everything that has been done in Spain, right or wrong, is a comment upon the principles I have laid down.

W. W.

I cannot help adding a few words.

. . . .

You will be rejoiced to hear that we shall *not* be forced to leave Grasmere vale. We are to have the parsonage-house, which will be made a very comfortable dwelling before we enter upon it, which will be next year at this time. But oh! my dear friend, this place — the wood behind it and the rocks, the view of Easedale from them, the lake, and church, and village on the other side — is sweeter than paradise itself. For these two days we have again had sunshine, with westerly breezes.

. . . .

Adieu! God bless you, my dear friend.

D. W.

CCXXVII

Dorothy Wordsworth to Mrs. Clarkson

Friday, 11th May, [1810.]

My dear Friend,

. . . Coleridge went to Keswick above a week ago. As he said, to stay about ten days, but as he did not intend to return till our bustle with Mary should be over, it might probably be much longer, if his own irresolute habits had no influence in keeping him there, or preventing his return. . . .

Are not you glad? We do not leave Grasmere, but are going to the parsonage-house. Mr. Jackson, the present vicar, will make it quite comfortable for us, and it will have rooms enough. He will make us a good library out of a part of the barn, and there are already two parlours and four good bedrooms. The stair-case is roomy, and there is a lumber-room and servant's-room, a decent small kitchen, and Mr. J. is going to build a new back-kitchen. . . . William is not quite well. He has been deep in poetry for a long time, and has written most exquisitely, which has weakened him, and rendered him nervous, and at times low-spirited. . . .

CCXXVIII

[*Dorothy Wordsworth to Henry Crabb Robinson*][1]

GRASMERE, NEAR KENDAL, November 6th, 1810.

My dear Sir,

I am very proud of a commission which my brother has given me, as it affords me an opportunity of expressing the pleasure with which I think of you and of our long journey side by side in the pleasant sunshine, our splendid entrance into the great city, and our rambles

[1] Henry Crabb Robinson (1775-1867), barrister, literary man, friend, and correspondent of Goethe and Wieland, as well as of Wordsworth and Lamb, European traveller, war correspondent of *The Times* in Spain, one of the founders of the London University. Extracts from his extensive *Diary, Reminiscences, and Correspondence* were edited by Dr. Thomas Sadler in 1869. He travelled with the Wordsworths to Switzerland in 1820, and took the poet to Italy in 1837. — Ed.

together in the crowded streets. I assure you I am not ungrateful for even the least of your kind attentions, and shall be happy in return to be your guide amongst these mountains ; where, if you bring a mind free from care, I can promise you rich store of noble enjoyments. My brother and sister too will be exceedingly happy to see you ; and if you tell him stories from Spain of enthusiasm, patriotism, and detestation of the usurper, my brother will be a ready listener ; and in presence of these grand works of Nature you may feed each other's lofty hopes. We are waiting with the utmost anxiety for the issue of that battle which you arranged so nicely by Charles Lamb's fire-side. My brother goes to seek the newspapers whenever it is possible to get a sight of one, and he is almost out of patience that the tidings are delayed so long.

We had this morning a letter from Mrs. Montagu with alarming accounts of the state of the King's health. We are loyal subjects, wishing him a long life, and, if he die at this time, shall sincerely grieve for his death. No doubt you have heard that our friend Coleridge accompanied the Montagus to London, and possibly you may even have seen him. They and I were travelling at the same time ; but we took different roads ; otherwise we might have had a mortifying glimpse of each other's faces, or a three-minutes' talk at some inn ; for on your side of Manchester the people are never more than three minutes in changing horses for the mail. I am much afraid that Miss Lamb is very poorly. I have had a letter from Charles, written in miserably bad spirits. I had thoughtlessly (and you cannot imagine how bitterly I reproach myself for it), I had thoughtlessly requested her to execute some commissions for me ; and her brother writes

to beg that I will hold her excused from every office of
that sort at present, she being utterly unable to support
herself under any fatigue either of body or mind. Why
had not I the sense to perceive this truth in its full
extent? I have caused them great pain by forcing them
to a refusal, and myself many inward pangs. I feel as if
I *ought* to have perceived that every thing out of the common course of her own daily life caused excitement and
agitation equally injurious to her. Charles speaks of the
necessity of absolute quiet, and at the same time of sometimes being obliged to have company that they would be
better without.' Surely in such a case as theirs it would
be right to select whom they will admit, admit those only
when they are likely to be bettered by society, and to
exclude *all* others. They have not one true friend who
would not take it the more kindly of them to be so
treated. Pray, as you most likely see *Charles* at least
from time to time, tell me how they are going on. There
is nobody in the world out of our own house in whom I
am more deeply interested.

Our little ones are all going on well — the little delicate Catherine, the only one for whom we had any serious alarm, gains ground daily; yet it will be long before
she can be, or have the appearance of being, a stout
child. There was great joy in the house at my return,
which each showed in a different way. They are sweet,
wild creatures, and I think you would love them all.
John is thoughtful with his wildness, Dorothy alive, active,
and quick, Thomas innocent and simple as a new-born
babe. John had no feeling but of bursting joy when he
saw me. Dorothy's first question was, "Where is my
doll?" We had delightful weather when I first got
home; but on the fourth morning Dorothy roused me

from my sleep with, " It is time to get up, Aunt, it is a *blasty* morning, it *does blast* so "; and the next morning, not more encouraging to me, she says, " It is a *haily* morning, it hails so hard!" You must know our house [1] stands on a hill, exposed to all *hails* and *blasts*, and the cold seemed to cut me through and through. I did really think, with the good people of Bury who used to try to persuade me that we must be starved to death in the North among these mountains, that it really would be so in my case, and that Grasmere was colder than any place in the world; but it is time to deliver my brother's message. Can you procure any Spanish, Portuguese or French papers for Mr. Southey? He writes the historical part of the *Edinburgh Annual Register*, and they would be of great use to him. Pray let us know if you can, and how they may be sent, and upon what terms. My brother begs to be most kindly remembered to you. Pray make my respectful compliments to Mrs. Collier and believe me, my dear sir,

Your affectionate friend,

D. WORDSWORTH.

CCXXIX

Dorothy Wordsworth to Mrs. Clarkson

ELLERAY, Sunday Evening, 7 o'clock,
November 12th, 1810.

. . . Oh! these poets! (Mr. Wilson is a poet.) They have such pens! and such ink! and never a pen-knife! and the ink holder is a narrow-necked bottle which paints

---

[1] Allan Bank.— Ed.

my pen half an inch every time I dip for a little ink. I
should not much mind this if I were at liberty to scrawl
over my paper; but I have a great deal yet to say; though
the matter be not very important. I believe I wrote to you
last on the very day after we had left Hackett — where
we lodged for three nights — four children, and a maid,
William, Mary, and I! It is as poor a cottage as ever
you saw, standing upon a hill-top overlooking little Langdale Tilberthwaite, Colwith, and the vale of Brathay;
warm because it fronts the south, and sheltered behind
by crags, and on one side and in front by the barn and
garden wall, which exclude all prospect from the windows.
But at the door whether to the right or the left you
have mountains, hamlets, woods, cottages, and rocks.
The weather was heavenly, when we were there; and the
first morning we sat in hot sunshine on a crag, twenty
yards from the door, while William read part of the fifth
Book of *Paradise Lost* to us. He read *The Morning Hymn*,
while a stream of white vapour, which coursed the valley
of Brathay, ascended slowly and by degrees melted away.
It seemed as if we had never before felt deeply the power
of the poet " Ye mists and exhalations, etc., etc. ! "

That evening William left us, and I went a part of the
way with him. The darkness came on before I reached
the house, which stands at a great distance from the
road, and the way to it is over a peat moss and through
trackless fields. I lost myself, got into a wood, climbed
over high walls that I should have trembled at by day, at
last found myself again on the peat moss, and stumbled
on, often above the knees in mud, till I came to a cottage.
All this time I had been quite composed, and was planning what I should do if I were forced to stay out all
night; but, when I laid my hand upon the latch of that

cottage-door my heart overflowed, and when I entered I could not speak for weeping and sobbing. I sat a few minutes, put on a pair of the woman's stockings, and her husband guided me to Hackett; and I then perceived that it would have been utterly impossible for me ever to have got thither alone, after the daylight was gone. I found poor Mary in a wretched state with her bairns — Sarah and her father had gone out half distracted to seek me; and Mary was trembling from head to foot. The next day the woman of the house called to see me, and declared she was "never so *wae* for anybody in her life," I was in such wretched case the night before. Well! it is over, and this good is come of it, that I shall never again go alone in rough places, and on unknown ground, late in the evening.

Two days afterwards we returned. The day after we reached home was very fine, and we were out with the children as long as the sun shone; but the next morning Dorothy roused me from my sleep with "Aunt! it is time to get up, it is a *blasty* morning — it does blast so!" and the next morning with "It is a *haily* morning — it hails so hard!"[1] And this blasty and haily and snowy weather continued till last Friday, and during the first three or four days I was half killed by it; and I thought our house, with its plastered walls, half-carpeted floors, and half-furnished rooms, the coldest place in the world. I got used to it before the weather changed and bore it better; and, contriving to take a long walk every evening, I grew hardy and stout.

. . . Mr. Wilson was with us yesterday, and will come again to-morrow; but he is not very much at home in

[1] Compare her letter to Henry Crabb Robinson, November 6, 1810, p. 503. The repetition is characteristic. — Ed.

general, being actually, as it is said, engaged to Miss
Jane Perry whom he follows most assiduously. He
lodges in general at Wilcock's; but I am happy to say
he lives in a very orderly regular way, and has entirely
left off wine and many other follies. He has lodged at
home two nights since William and Mary came, I believe
entirely for the sake of William's company. . . . I wrote
so far last night after W. and M. were gone to bed;
in the evening Wm. employed me to compose a description or two for the finishing of his work for Wilkinson.[1]
It is a most irksome task to him, not being permitted to
follow his own course, and I daresay you will find this
latter part very flat. . . . Nothing can more clearly prove
the hurry in which I last wrote than that I never mentioned Coleridge's departure.

. . . The Montagus say he seems disposed to be
regular. For my part I am hopeless of him, and I dismiss him as much as possible from my thoughts. I have
recollected one debt that I left at Bury, and whenever I
have written to you I forgot to mention it, the altering of
my straw bonnet! pray, pay for it. The weather is
delightful. Oh could you see the glittering lake of
Windermere which lies before me — bays, islands, prom-
ontories. It is paradise itself, and if I go two yards
from the door I can behold Langdale pikes and the
Range of Grasmere and Rydal fells with the lake and
all the intermediate country. Oh! that I could see you
in this country once again my beloved friend. . . .

[1] The *Introduction* to Wilkinson's *Select Views in Cumberland*,
etc., see pp. 479 and 497. — Ed.

CCXXX

Dorothy Wordsworth to Mrs. Clarkson

GRASMERE, 30th December.

My dear Friend,

. . . We came home last Tuesday but are very sorry to change the snug cottage [1] for this large house,[2] with its long passages and clashing doors, and I am sorry to add smoky chimneys; for till within these two days, we have had stormy winds, and therefore smoky chimneys; our old sorrow, which we knew little of last winter, the weather having been remarkably calm. Commend me to a snug house under the shelter of a hill, with trees round about it; rooms plenty, but not over large. Yet when I speak ill of this house as a winter residence I ought to add that we have one sitting room fronting the South, which is absolutely cheering from its warmth. If the parsonage were ready to receive us — garden made, trees planted, etc., etc. — I should look forward with pleasure to the month of May, the time of our removal from Allan Bank. But alas! nothing is done, and the old parson is so ill that it seems absolutely inhuman to send workmen into his house. William has undertaken the whole charge of getting the business done, and you know how unfit he is for any task of this kind. Mary and I are, however, determined not to enter upon it, till it is finished completely; for we were thoroughly sickened of workmen when we first came hither.

I stayed ten days at Kendal, and walked to Elleray on the Saturday preceding our departure. It was a lovely evening when I reached Elleray, and the view from the

---

[1] Dove Cottage. — Ed.   [2] Allan Bank. — Ed.

cottage was perfectly enchanting. There never was a situation which was better calculated for invalids, for old people, or such as are much employed within doors, and cannot seek pleasure far from home. The view from our windows — except under accidental circumstances of mists and partial sunshine — is positively insipid, compared with it ; and then the cottage, though it stands high, is as snug as a wren's nest. But, on the other hand, for us who can walk abroad, and make that one of our daily pleasures, we are here much better situated. Which way soever we turn we find something more beautiful than what we see from our own windows, while the treasures of Easedale lie as it were at our door. . . . I have not yet read Southey's *Curse of Kehama;* but I believe, from William's account, that it has great merit. His English motto I dislike very much[1]; and, from what I gather in skimming the poem, it is not the kind of subject that will please me, though I daresay there will be much that I shall like scattered through the work.

I am going to prime you for an attack upon *The Lady of the Lake;* but let me first stipulate that you stoutly begin the battle. First, then, I will copy Mr. De Quincey's letter to Mary. "W. Scott's last novel, *The Lady of the Lake,* is the grand subject of prattle and chatter hereabouts. I have read it aloud to oblige my brother, and a more disgusting task I never had. I verily think that it is the completest magazine of all forms of the *falsetto* in feeling and diction that now exists; and the notes as usual, the most finished specimen of book-making. I have given great offence to some of Walter's idolaters by expressing these opinions with illustrations — and, in

---

[1] It was " Curses are like young chickens, they always come home to roost." — Ed.

particular, by calling it a *novel* (which indeed it is ; only a very dull one). Yesterday at a dinner party I had a hornet's nest upon me for only observing that the true solution of Walter's notoriety was to be found in this ; . . . that whereas, heretofore, if one *would* read novels, one must do it under the penalty thereunto annexed of being accredited for feeble-mindedness, and *missiness;* now (by favor of W. S.) one might read a novel, and have the credit of reading a poem. An excellent joke is, that all these good people think *The Lady of the Lake* infinitely superior to *Marmion;* and that it is possible to be even disgusted with the one, and enamoured of the other."

A still better joke is that the difference is ascribed to the criticisms of Mr. Jeffrey ! "Oh dear ! " a lady said to me, "the inferiority of *Marmion* is infinite, in my opinion — positively infinite ! " "Strange, Madam," I replied (to her unspeakable horror),

> Strange that such difference should be
> 'Twixt Tweedledum and Tweedledee.

Now I will turn to Coleridge's letter, but I have not room for half of it. I will only therefore give you the concluding paragraph. He says, " In short, my dear William, it is time to write a recipe for poems of this sort. I amused myself a day or two ago, on reading a romance in Mrs. Radcliffe's style, with making out a scheme which was to serve for all romances *a priori*, only varying the proportions. A baron, or baroness, ignorant of their birth and in some dependent situation ; a castle, on a rock ; a sepulchre, at some distance from the rock ; deserted rooms ; underground passages ; pictures ; a ghost, so believed ; or a written record, blood in it ; a wonderful cut-throat, etc. etc. Now to make out the component parts of the Scottish Minstrelsy. The first business must be a vast string of ——, and names of mountains, rivers, etc. The most commonplace imagery the bard 'gars luik amaist as weel's the new'[1] by the introduction of Benvoirlich:

> Uam-Var, copse wood gray
> Wept on Loch Achray,
> And mingled with the pine trees *blue*
> On the bold cliffs of Benvenue.

"Secondly, all the nomenclature of Gothic architecture, of heraldry, of arms, of hunting and falconry. These possess the power of reviving the *caput mortuum* and rust of old imagery. Besides, they will stand by themselves. Stout substantives, if only they are strung together, and some attention is paid to the sound of the words, for no one attempts to understand the meaning, which indeed would snap the charm. Some pathetic moralizing on old times, or anything else, for the head and tail pieces, with a bard — *that* is absolutely necessary — and songs of course. For the rest, whatever suits Mrs. Radcliffe, i.e. in the fable, and the *dramatis personae*, will do for the poem; with this advantage that, however threadbare in the romance shelves of the circulating library, it is to be taken as quite new so soon as it is told in rhyme. It need not be half as interesting, and the ghost may be a ghost or may be explained, or both may take place in the same poem. Then, the poet not only *may*, but *must*, mix all dialects of all ages; and all styles, from Dr. Robertson to the Babes in the Wood." . . .

---

[1] See Burns, *The Cotter's Saturday Night*, l. 44. "Gars auld claes look amaist as weel's the new." — Ed.

William has written fifteen fine political sonnets, which Mary and I would fain have him send to *The Courier*, both in order that they might be read, and that we might have a little profit from his industry. He is, however, so disgusted with critics, newspapers, readers, and the talking public, that we cannot prevail. The King of Sweden, Bonaparte, and the struggles of the Peninsula are the subjects of these sonnets.[1] . . .

CCXXXI

William Wordsworth to Robert Southey

My dear Southey,   [1810, or 1809.][2]

Colonel Campbell, our neighbour at Grasmere, has sent for your book; he served during the whole of the Peninsular war, and you shall hear what he says of it in due course. We are out of the way of all literary communication, so I can report nothing. I have read the whole

[1] See the poems belonging to the year 1810. — Ed.

[2] The year of this undated letter may have been either 1810 or 1809 or 1824. Evidence (which it is unnecessary to state) and the allusion to the pamphlet on *The Convention of Cintra* have led to its insertion where it stands, but Southey's book, the *History of the Peninsular War*, was published in 1823. The difficulty caused by this too common habit of literary men and women in not dating their letters is stupendous; and when no clue is obtainable from the contents or obliterated postmarks, conjecture must meanwhile take the place of knowledge. In the appendix to Vol. III some additional instances will be given; and letter CCCXXXVII, in Vol. II, p. 127, from William Wordsworth to Francis Wrangham, may belong to the year 1811. Its reference to his "five children," "three boys and two girls," in a passage not printed, seems to point to the year in which he lived in the parsonage at Grasmere, or it might have been written from Allan Bank in 1810; while Wrangham's poem, referred to in this letter, may have been *The Sufferings of the Primitive Martyrs* (1811). — Ed.

with great pleasure; the work will do you everlasting
honour. I have said the whole, forgetting, in that con-
templation, my feelings upon one part, where you have
tickled with a feather when you should have branded with
a red-hot iron. You will guess I mean the Convention of
Cintra. My detestation — I may say abhorrence — of
that event is not at all diminished by your account of it.
Bonaparte had committed a capital blunder in supposing
that when he had intimidated the Sovereigns of Europe
he had conquered the several nations. Yet it was natural for a wiser than he to have fallen into this mistake;
for the old despotisms had deprived the body of the
people of all practical knowledge in the management,
and, of necessity, of all interest, in the course of affairs.

The French themselves were astonished at the apathy
and ignorance of the people whom they had supposed they
had utterly subdued when they had taken their fortresses,
scattered their armies, entered their capital cities, and
struck their cabinets with dismay. There was no hope
for the deliverance of Europe till the nations had suffered
enough to be driven to a passionate recollection of all
that was honourable in their past history and to make
appeal to the principles of universal and everlasting justice. These sentiments the authors of that Convention
most unfeelingly violated; and as to the principles, they
seemed to be as little aware even of the existence of such
powers, for powers emphatically may they be called, as
the tyrant himself. As far, therefore, as these men
could, they put an extinguisher upon the star which was
then rising.

It is in vain to say that after the first burst of indignation was over the Portuguese themselves were reconciled
to the event, and rejoiced in their deliverance. We may

infer from that the horror which they must have felt in the presence of their oppressors; and we may see in it to what a state of helplessness their bad government had reduced them. Our duty was to have treated them with respect, as the representatives of suffering humanity, beyond what they were likely to look for themselves, and as deserving greatly, in common with their Spanish brethren, for having been the first to rise against the tremendous oppression and to show how, and how only, it could be put an end to.

WM. WORDSWORTH.

1811

CCXXXII

Dorothy Wordsworth to Mrs. Clarkson

Tuesday, 23rd February, [1811.]

. . . We have now not more than ten or eleven weeks to stay at Allan Bank, so that there seems to be nothing before us but bustle. . . . The Coleridges came to see me yesterday morning. Every time I see Hartley I admire him more. He is very thoughtful, often silent, and never talks as much as he used to do. Both he and Derwent far surpass their schoolfellows in quickness at their books, and both (especially Hartley) are beloved by their schoolfellows, not less than by Mr. Dawes, their master. It would pity anybody's heart to look at Hartley, when he enquires (as if hopelessly) if there has been any news of his father. I wish I had brought your last letter with me. I am sure there were several things in it to be replied to. I understand by the *falsetto* in music an affectation of an effort after beauties and ornaments, which are not founded upon just principles. In short, the false would be as good to my mind as the falsetto; only there is something of *glitter* conveyed to me by the word "falsetto!" In like manner I understand the word as applied to Scott's poetry; to the descriptions, to the language, to the passions, in which there is neither truth nor simplicity; a certain tinsel decoration, analogous to

the ill laboured and affected in music, which may dazzle
and surprise the ignorant, but never touches the natural
and feeling heart.   I wish William were here to give you
his notions. . . .

CCXXXIII

William Wordsworth to William Godwin [1]

GRASMERE, March 9, 1811.

Dear Sir,

I received your letter and the accompanying *booklet*
yesterday.   Some one recommended to Gainsborough
a subject for a picture.   It pleased him much, but he
immediately said, with a sigh, "What a pity I did not
think of it myself!"   Had I been as much delighted with
the story of *Beauty and the Beast* as you appear to have
been, and as much struck with its fitness for verse, still
your proposal would have occasioned in me a similar
regret.   I have ever had the same sort of perverseness.
I cannot work upon the suggestions of others, however
eagerly I might have addressed myself to the proposed
subject, if it had come to me of its own accord.   You
will therefore attribute my declining the task of versifying
the tale to this infirmity, rather than to an indisposition
to serve you.

Having stated this, it is unnecessary to add that it
could not, in my opinion, be ever decently done without
great labour, especially in our language.   Fontaine ac-
knowledges that he found "les narrations en vers très

---

[1] William Godwin (1756–1836), novelist, historian, philosophical
and political writer.   See *William Godwin : his friends and contemporaries.*   By C. Kegan Paul, Vol. II, pp. 218–220. — Ed.

mal-aisées," yet he allowed himself, in point of metre and versification, every kind of liberty ; and only chose such subjects as (to the disgrace of his country be it spoken) the French language is peculiarly fitted for. This tale — I judge from its name — is of French origin ; it is not, however, found in a little collection which I have in that tongue. Mine only includes Puss in Boots, Cinderella, Red Riding Hood, and two or three more. I think the shape in which it appears, in the little book you have sent me, has much injured the story ; and Mrs. Wordsworth and my sister have both an impression of its being told differently, and to them much more pleasantly, though they do not distinctly recollect the deviations. I confess there is to me something disgusting in the notion of a human being consenting to meet with a beast, however amiable his qualities of heart. There is a line and a half in *Paradise Lost* upon this subject, which always shocked me, —

> for which cause
> Among the beasts no mate for thee was found.[1]

These are objects to which the attention of the mind ought not to be turned even as things in possibility. I have never seen the tale in French ; but, as every one knows, the word "bête" in French conversation perpetually occurs, as applied to a stupid senseless half idiotic person. *Bêtise* in like manner stands for stupidity. With us, beast and bestial excite loathsome and disgusting ideas — I mean when applied in a metaphorical manner — and, consequently, something of the same hangs about the literal sense of the words. "Brute" is the word employed when we contrast the intellectual qualities of the

[1] See *Paradise Lost*, Book VIII, ll. 593–594. — Ed.

inferior animals with our own, "the brute creation," etc., "Ye of brutes human, we of human gods." Brute, metaphorically used, with us designates ill manners of a coarse kind, or insolent and ferocious cruelty. I make these remarks with a view to the difficulty attending the treatment of this story in our tongue, I mean in verse, where the utmost delicacy, that is, true, philosophic, permanent delicacy, is required.

Wm. Taylor of Norwich [1] took the trouble of versifying *Blue Beard* some years ago, and might perhaps not decline to assist you in the present case, if you are acquainted with him, or could get at him. He is a man personally unknown to me, and in his literary character doubtless an egregious coxcomb, but he is ingenious enough to do this, if he could be prevailed upon to undertake it.

Permit me to add one particular. You live, and have lived, long in London, and therefore may not know at what rate parcels are conveyed by coach. Judging from the size, you probably thought the expense of yours would be trifling. To be brief, I had to pay for your tiny parcel 4/9, and should have to pay no more if it had been twenty times as large. . . . I deem you, therefore, my debtor, and will put you in the way of being quits with me. If you can command a copy of your book upon burial, which I have never seen, let it be sent to Lamb's for my use, who in the course of this spring will be able to forward it to me.

Believe me to be, my dear sir, yours sincerely,

W. WORDSWORTH.

---

[1] The translator of Burger's *Leonora*, and *Iphigenia in Tauris*, Lessing's *Nathan der Weise*, etc. — Ed.

CCXXXIV

William Wordsworth to Francis Wrangham

GRASMERE, March 27th, [1811.]

My dear Wrangham,

. . . As to Coleridge, there is no accounting for his apparent neglect of anybody, except in the common way in which I have accounted for my own apparent neglect of you. He left this country in October for London, where he has since resided, and I have never heard *from* him since, though I have heard several times *of* him. . . .

You return to the Catholic Question. I am decidedly of opinion that no further concessions should be made. The Catholic Emancipation is a mere pretext of ambitious and discontented men. Are you prepared for the next step, a Catholic Established Church? I confess I dread the thought. As to the Bible Society; my view of the subject is as follows. First, distributing Bibles is a good thing. Secondly, more Bibles will be distributed in consequence of the existence of the Bible Society; therefore, so far as that goes, the existence of the Bible Society is good. But thirdly, as to the *indirect* benefits expected from it, in producing a golden age of unanimity among Christians, all that I think fume and emptiness, nay far worse. So deeply am I persuaded that discord and artifice, pride and ambition, would be fostered by such an approximation and unnatural alliance of sects, that I am inclined to think the evil thus produced would do more than outweigh the good done by dispersing the Bibles. . . .

I remain, with great truth,

Your affectionate friend,

W. WORDSWORTH.

CCXXXV

Dorothy Wordsworth to Mrs. Clarkson

Sunday, 16th June, 1811.

. . . I must tell you that we like our new house[1] very much. There are only three important objections to it. First, that it fronts the east, and has no sitting rooms looking westward, therefore we lose the sun very soon. Secondly, that it is too public; but this evil will wear away every year, for we shall plant abundance of shrubs in the autumn in addition to those already planted. Thirdly, that the field in which the house stands is very wet, and cannot be drained. It is no playing-place for the children, and being at present not divided from the road to the house, it leads them into continual temptation to wet themselves; but, when all other things are done, it is to be fenced off, and a plantation to be made all round the back part of the house. Mine is a large room, and a very large bookcase stands in it conveniently. Sarah's is smaller, but a very pretty room. The children's is a long cottage-like room with a coved ceiling. The parlours are small. We do not intend to have Hartley and Derwent for two days in the week, as at Allan Bank. The noise and confusion of so many children, for so long a time, in the house would be intolerable; but in fine weather they may always walk over on Saturday or Sunday morning, and spend the day with us. Hartley is here to-day. Below stairs we have two good kitchens, with a porch at the back door. William's parlour is but a little cabin; but it will be very snug and neat, when we have got the furniture put into it. It holds two small bookcases

---

[1] The parsonage at Grasmere, close to the church. — Ed.

conveniently. The larger parlour is considerably bigger
than the sitting room at Town-End, and all the rooms are
of a good height. We have a large store-room and dairy,
a wee cellar (big enough for us) and a good pantry. In
short there is no comfort wanting, and our furniture takes
to its places much better than at Allan Bank. At least
things look much more as if they were made for us and
the house, than at Allan Bank. . . . There is an oblong
four-cornered court before the door, surrounded by ugly
white walls. The kitchen garden lies prettily to the
river, but all is rough and desolate at present, and we
content ourselves with prophesying a speedy growth to
the shrubs. If they thrive, as at Town-End, we shall
soon be huddled up in a leafy nest. . . .

I am sorry to say (I would not say it but to you) that
poor Coleridge's late writings in *The Courier* have in general evinced the same sad weakness of moral constitution
to which you alluded in your last letter, as tainting his
intercourse with his private friends, and his casual acquaintances also. They are as much the work of a party-spirit,
as if he were writing for a place — servile adulations of
the Wellesleys.

I speak of the general character of his paragraphs
and short essays. No doubt there are amongst them
sentiments of a better kind. It has been misery enough,
God knows, to me, to see the truths which I now see.
Long did we hope against experience, and reason ; but
now I have no hope, if he continues as he is. Nothing
but Time — producing a total change in him — can ever
make him a being of much use to mankind in general, or
of the least comfort to his friends. I am sure I have no
personal feelings of pain or irritation connected with him.
An injury done to my brother, or me, or any of our family,

or dear friends, would not now hurt me more than an injury done to an indifferent person. I only grieve at the waste and prostitution of his fine genius, at the sullying and perverting of what is lovely and tender in human sympathies, and noble and generous; and I do grieve whenever I think of him. His resentment to my brother hardly ever comes into my thoughts. I feel perfectly indifferent about it. How absurd, how uncalculating of the feelings and opinions of others, to talk to your father and sister of dying in a fortnight, when his dress and everything proved that his thoughts were of other matters. Such talks will never more alarm me. Poor William went off to London, at our earnest request, *in consequence of his having solemnly assured Mrs. Coleridge that he could not live three months;* and, when William arrived, he had to wait daily for admittance to him, till four o'clock in the afternoon, and saw no appearance of disease which could not have been cured, or at least prevented by himself. But enough of this melancholy subject. Only I must add that I fear he slackens at *The Courier* Office, as there has been nothing of his for some days, and he has not written to Mrs. C. since the time I mentioned ; nor has he acknowledged the receipt of his MSS. which he was in a great hurry to receive, that he might publish them. By the bye he desired Charles Lamb to write to me about them; therefore, no doubt, he includes me in his resentments. I know not for what cause. . . .

I wrote so far on Sunday afternoon. In the evening I walked to Ambleside with William, and yesterday we were all employed in bearing the books out of the barn,[1]

---

[1] The small library of books (originally at Dove Cottage) had been stored in a " barn," and was now (in June 1811) taken to the parsonage. — Ed.

and arranging them; a most serious labour, as well as a very perplexing and troublesome job. We got the work accomplished and went to bed at ten o'clock completely wearied. This morning (Tuesday, before breakfast) is very delightful. The late wet weather has covered the vale, and the mountains, with greenness; and the growth and richness of the trees was never surpassed. . . .

CCXXXVI

Dorothy Wordsworth to Mrs. Clarkson[1]

KESWICK, August 15, 1811.

My dear Friend,

. . . In three days after she (Dorothy) was gone, i.e. on this day fortnight, William, Mary, Thomas, Catherine, and one of the maids left me to go to the sea-side. They are at a dreary place in the neighbourhood of Bootle, and I fear their accommodations, except in sea bathing, are very bad; but they are only five minutes' walk from the main sea. They first went to Duddon Bridge, where they were very comfortable, and the country thereabouts is enchanting; but the tide only served them for four or five days, and the water was hardly salt. I have not heard from them since their arrival at Bootle. . . . At Hackett[2] William and I walked about together in the rocky field before the house, which is scattered over with copses, and commands delightful and varied views; first, of the wild and simple valley of Little Langdale, with its mountainous head, a darling place of the clouds and mists;

[1] Compare the letter of November 6, 1810. — Ed.
[2] See Wordsworth's *Epistle to Sir George Beaumont*, and his description of Hackett in *The Excursion*, Book V, ll. 78-92. — Ed.

then we look into the green recesses of Tilberthwaite;
next comes Colwith, and then the valley of Brathay, as
far as Windermere, its fresh meadows inlaid with the
broad and glassy stream; next come the steeps of Elter-
water, and Loughrigg; and further to the north our own
mountains above Grasmere.   You cannot conceive a
more feeding spot for the mind than that hill top where
the cottage stands.   Within doors, — though we had no
luxuries but milk, butter, eggs, and bacon, and fresh
mutton provided for us, with plenty of peats for the fire, —
we wanted nothing for comfort. . . .

CCXXXVII

William Wordsworth to Sir George Beaumont

                              August 28, 1811.
                    Cottage 7 minutes' walk from the sea-side,
                              near Bootle, Cumberland.

My dear Sir George,
    How shall I appear before you again after so long an
interval?   It seems that now I ought rather to begin
with an apology for writing, than for not having written
during a space of almost twelve months.   I have blamed
myself not a little; yet not so much as I should have
done, had I not known that the main cause of my silence
has been the affection I feel for you; on which account
it is not so easy to me to write upon trifling or daily
occurrences to you, as it would be to write to another
whom I loved less.   Accordingly these have not had
power to tempt me to take up the pen; and in the meantime from my more intimate concerns I have abstained,
partly because I do not in many cases myself like to see

the reflection of these upon paper, and still more, because it is my wish at all times, when I think of the state in which your health and spirits may happen to be, that my letters should be wholly free from melancholy, and breathe nothing but cheerfulness and pleasure. Having made this avowal, I trust that what may be wanting to my justification will be made up by your kindness and forgiving disposition.

It was near about this time last year that we were employed in our pleasant tour to the Leasowes and Hagley. The twelve months that have elapsed have not impaired the impressions which those scenes made upon me, nor weakened my remembrance of the delight which the places and objects, and the conversations they led to, awakened in our minds. You perhaps will recollect that I mentioned in a letter a fine grove, or rather wood, of yew-trees at Hagley which we missed. I have since learned that there is in the village, in the possession of a gentleman whose name I have forgotten, a picture of exquisite beauty. My story is a large one, for I do not know what is the subject of the piece, nor whether it is by Rubens, or some Italian master. Mr. Sattesthwaite, rector of the parish of Bootle, where this is written, is my authority. Lady Beaumont well remembers to have met Mr. S. at Lord Lonsdale's; he has seen the picture, and, without affecting to be a judge, speaks of it in the highest terms. He adds that the owner is himself a great curiosity, in particular for his passionate attachment to the art of painting; not that he follows it himself, but as an amateur.

Mr. S. was particularly struck with one proof that he gave of his enthusiasm. It was about the height of the French Revolution when S—— visited him. He talked of a nephew of his, then abroad, and mentioned with infinite satisfaction the opportunity which the distracted state of the Continent would give him to pick up a picture of first-rate excellence. In fact, says S——, it was plain, from the good gentleman's words and looks and manner, that the French Revolution, with all its overthrow of Governments and desolation of countries, was by him looked upon as a happy event; inasmuch as it afforded the enterprising and the judicious an opportunity of laying hold of some inestimable work of art, which would otherwise have been unattainable, and have been locked up in a foreign convent or palace, till the canvas or tablet on which it was wrought mouldered, or its colours faded away. Under this aspect only did our connoisseur contemplate those awful acts of Providence, in which the French nation have been the chief instruments for the chastisement, instruction, and animation of mankind.

Thanks to the surrounding ocean with which this favoured land is guarded, and to our own excellent institutions and native valour, this innocent enthusiast of Hagley is still able to draw the green silk curtain from his single treasure when he likes, and congratulate himself upon his lot in possessing it. Happy England! where security allows such leisure to multitudes to indulge in dreams as harmless, each after his own fashion; and where national independence and civil liberty allow — or rather encourage — so many diverse humours in man, and mould individual character into such a variety of shapes.

The person who has led me to rhapsodise in this way was not a collector, nor wished his travelling nephew to become so. "A single piece," said he, "is enough, provided it be of a noble kind, and perfect in itself." He deemed himself the lord and owner of a star of the first magnitude, and provided his nephew should prove as fortunate, he did not seem to care what became of the inferior orbs; his family would then be set up for ever. I have been very prolix upon the subject of this old gentleman, and should not have mentioned him at all had it not been clear that in so small a village as Hagley he and his picture may easily be found; and Fortune perhaps may draw you thither at some time or other, though I well know that you are not a *pushing man*, and therefore all my information may be thrown away.

It is very late to mention that when in Wales last autumn I contrived to pass a day and a half with your friend Price at Foxley. He was very kind, and took due pains to show me all the beauties of his place. I should have been very-insensible not to be pleased with, and grateful for, his attentions; and certainly I was gratified by the sight of the scenes through which he conducted me. But to you I will say that, upon the whole, I was not in a kindly or genial state of mind while Mr. Price was taking so much friendly pains for my entertainment. His daughter put me out of tune by her strange speech, looks, and manners; and then, unluckily, Fitzpatrick was there, a torch that once may have burnt bright, but is now deplorably dim. It was to me odd to see a host and a guest who appeared to have so little satisfaction in each other's company, and full as odd to see a *hostess* and a guest so snugly and peaceably content with each other. But this looks like scandal, which is bad enough from the lip, but in a letter is intolerable. These things deranged me, and thereupon I was less able to do justice in my own mind to the scenery of Foxley.

You will perhaps think it is a strange fault that I am going to find with it, considering the acknowledged taste of the owner, viz. that, small as it is compared with hundreds of places, the domain is too extensive for the character of the country. Wanting both rock and water, it necessarily wants variety; and, in a district of this kind, the portion of a gentleman's estate which he keeps exclusively to himself, and which he devotes wholly or in part to ornament, may very easily exceed the proper bounds; not indeed as to the preservation of wood, but most easily as to everything else. A man by little and little becomes so delicate and fastidious with respect to forms in scenery, where he has a power to exercise a control over them, that if they do not exactly please him in all moods, and every point of view, his power becomes his law. He banishes one, and then rids himself of another, impoverishing and *monotonising* landscapes, which, if not originally distinguished by the bounty of Nature, must be ill able to spare the inspiriting varieties which Art, and the occupations and wants of life, in a country left more to itself never fail to produce. This relish of humanity Foxley wants, and is therefore to me, in spite of all its recommendations, a melancholy spot; I mean that part of it which the owner keeps to himself, and has taken so much pains with.

I heard the other day of two artists who thus expressed themselves upon the subject of a scene among our lakes: "Plague upon those vile enclosures!" said one; "they spoil everything." "Oh," said the other, "I never *see* them." Glover was the name of this last. Now, for my part, I should not wish to be either of these gentlemen, but to have in my own mind the power of turning to advantage, wherever it is possible, every object of Art and Nature as they appear before me. What a noble instance, as you have often pointed out to me, has Rubens given of this in that picture in your possession, where he has brought, as it were, a whole county into one land-scape, and made the most formal partitions of cultivation. Hedge-rows of pollard willows conduct the eye into the depths and distances of his picture; and thus, more than by any other means, has given it that appearance of immensity which is so striking!

As I have slipped into the subject of painting, I feel anxious to inquire whether your pencil has been busy last winter in the solitude and uninterrupted quiet of Dun-mow. Most likely you know that we have changed our residence in Grasmere, which, I hope, will be attended with a great overbalance of advantages. One we are cer-tain of — that we have at least one sitting-room clear of smoke, I trust, in all winds. It is a very small parlour, and in the winter will be exclusively my own. Over the chimney-piece is hung your little picture, from the neigh-bourhood of Coleorton. In our other house, on account of the frequent fits of smoke from the chimneys, both the pictures which I have from your hand were confined to bedrooms. A few days after I had enjoyed the pleasure of seeing, in different moods of mind, your Coleorton landscape from my fireside, it *suggested* to me the follow-ing sonnet, which, having walked out to the side of Gras-mere brook, where it murmurs through the meadows near the church, I composed immediately : —

> Praised be the Art whose subtle power could stay
> Yon cloud, and fix it in that glorious shape;
> Nor would permit the thin smoke to escape,
> Nor those bright sunbeams to forsake the day;
> Which stopped that band of travellers on their way,
> Ere they were lost within the shady wood;
> And showed the bark upon the glassy flood
> For ever anchored in her sheltering bay.

Soul-soothing Art ! which morning, noontide, even,
Do serve, with all their changeful pageantry ;
Thou, by ambition modest yet sublime,
Here, for the sight of mortal men, hast given
To one brief moment caught from fleeting time
The appropriate calm of blest Eternity !

The images of the smoke and the travellers are taken
from your picture; the rest were added, in order to place
the thought in a clear point of view, and for the sake of
variety.   I hope Coleorton continues to improve upon
you and Lady Beaumont; and that Mr. Taylor's new
laws and regulations are at least *peaceably* submitted to.

Mrs. Wordsworth and I return in a few days to Grasmere.   We cannot say that the child, for whose sake we
came down to the sea-side, has derived much benefit from
the bathing.   The weather has been very unfavourable : we
have, however, contrived to see everything that lies within
a reasonable walk of our present residence ; among other
places, Muncaster, — at least as much of it as can be seen
from the public road ; but the noble proprietor has contrived to shut himself up so with plantations and chained
gates and locks, that whatever prospects he may command
from his stately prison, or rather fortification, can only
be guessed at by the passing traveller.   In the state of
blindness and unprofitable peeping in which we were compelled to pursue our way up a long and steep hill, I could
not help observing to my companion that the Hibernian
peer had completely given the lie to the poet Thomson,
when, in a strain of profound enthusiasm, he boasts —

I care not, Fortune, what you me deny:
    You cannot rob me of free Nature's grace;
You cannot shut the windows of the sky,

> Through which Aurora shows her brightening face;
> You cannot bar my constant feet to trace
> The woods and lawns by living stream, etc.[1]

The *windows of the sky* were not *shut*, indeed, but the business was done more thoroughly; for the sky was nearly shut out altogether. This is, like most others, a bleak and treeless coast, but abounding in corn-fields, and with a noble beach, which is delightful either for walking or riding.

The Isle of Man is right opposite our window;[2] and though in this unsettled weather often invisible, its appearance has afforded us great amusement. One afternoon above the whole length of it was stretched a body of clouds, shaped and coloured like a magnificent grove in winter, whitened with snow, and illuminated by the morning sun, which — having melted the snow in part — intermingled black masses among the brightness. The whole sky was scattered over with fleecy dark clouds, such as any sunshiny day produces, and which were changing their shapes and position every moment. But this line of clouds immovably attached themselves to the island, and manifestly took their shape from the influence of its mountains. There appeared to be just enough span of sky to allow the hand to slide between the top of Snaefell, the highest peak on the island, and the base of this glorious forest, in which little change was noticeable for more than the space of half an hour.

We had another fine sight one evening, walking along a rising ground about two miles distant from the shore. It was about the hour of sunset, and the sea was perfectly

---

[1] See *The Castle of Indolence*, Canto II, 3. — Ed.

[2] See the *Epistle to Sir George Beaumont:* "Mona from our abode is daily seen." — Ed.

calm; and in a quarter where its surface was indistinguishable from the western sky, hazy and luminous with the setting sun, appeared a tall sloop-rigged vessel, magnified by the atmosphere through which it was viewed, and seeming rather to hang in the air than to float upon the waters. Milton compares the appearance of Satan to a *fleet* descried far off at sea. The visionary grandeur and beautiful form of this *single* vessel, could words have conveyed to the mind the picture which Nature presented to the eye, would have suited his purpose as well as the largest company of vessels that ever associated together, with the help of a trade wind, in the wide ocean. Yet not exactly so, and for this reason, that his image is a permanent one, not dependent upon accident.

    I have not left myself room to assure you how sincerely I remain

Your affectionate friend,

W. WORDSWORTH.

CCXXXVIII

William Wordsworth to Sir George Beaumont

[Probably from GRASMERE in Nov., 1811.]

My dear Sir George,

    Had there been room at the end of the small avenue of lime-trees[1] for planting a spacious circle of the same trees, the urn might have been placed in the centre, with the inscription thus altered:

> Ye lime-trees, ranged around this hallowed urn,
> Shoot forth with lively power at Spring's return!

· · · · · · · · ·

---

[1] At Coleorton. — Ed.

Here may some painter sit in future days,
Some future poet meditate his lays!
Not mindless of that distant age, renowned,
When inspiration hovered o'er this ground,
The haunt of him who sang, how spear and shield
In civil conflict met on Bosworth field,
And of that famous youth (full soon removed
From earth!) by mighty Shakespear's self approved,
Fletcher's associate, Jonson's friend beloved.

The first couplet of the above, as it before stood, would have appeared ludicrous, if the stone had remained after the tree might have gone. The couplet relating to the household virtues did not accord with the painter and the poet; the former being allegorical figures, the latter living men.

What follows I composed yesterday morning, thinking there might be no impropriety in placing it so as to be *visible only to a person sitting within the niche*, which we hollowed out of the sandstone in the winter garden. I am told that this is, in the present form of the niche, impossible; but I shall be most ready, when I come to Coleorton, to scoop out a place for it, if Lady Beaumont thinks it worth while.

INSCRIPTION [1]

Oft is the medal faithful to its trust
When temples, columns, towers, are laid in dust;
And 't is a common ordinance of fate
That things obscure and small outlive the great.
Hence, etc.

These inscriptions have all one fault, they are too long; but I was unable to do justice to the thoughts in less room. The second has brought Sir John Beaumont and his brother Francis so livelily to my mind, that I recur

[1] See *Poetical Works*, Eversley edition, Vol. IV, p. 77. — Ed.

to the plan of republishing the former's poems, perhaps in connection with those of Francis. Could any further search be made after the *Crown of Thorns?*[1] If I recollect right, Southey applied without effect to the numerous friends he has among the collectors. The best way, perhaps, of managing this republication would be to print it in a very elegant type and paper, and not many copies, to be sold high so that it might be prized by the collectors as a curiosity. Bearing in mind how many excellent things there are in Sir John Beaumont's little volume, I am somewhat mortified at this mode of honouring his memory; but in the present state of the taste of this country, I cannot flatter myself that poems of that character would win their way into general circulation. Should it appear advisable, another edition might afterwards be published, upon a plan which would place the book within the reach of those who have little money to spare. I remain, my dear Sir George, your affectionate friend,

W. WORDSWORTH.

CCXXXIX

William Wordsworth to Sir George Beaumont

GRASMERE, Saturday, Nov. 16, 1811.

My dear Sir George,

I have to thank you for two letters. Lady Beaumont also will accept my acknowledgments for the interesting letter with which she favoured me.

·   ·   ·   ·   ·   ·   ·   ·   ·   ·   ·

[1] The *Crown of Thorns, in eight books,* by Sir John Beaumont, has disappeared. It was printed; for the author says in his elegy on the Earl of Southampton, "He is the father to my crowne of thorns," and calls it (after his death) "an orphan booke." — Ed.

I learn from Mrs. Coleridge, who has lately heard from Coleridge, that Allston the painter [1] has arrived in London. Coleridge speaks of him as a most interesting person. He has brought with him a few pictures from his own pencil, among others a Cupid and Psyche, which, in Coleridge's opinion, has not, for colouring, been surpassed since Titian. Coleridge is about to deliver a course of lectures upon Poetry at some Institution in the City. He is well, and I learn that *The Friend* has been a good deal inquired after lately. For ourselves, we never hear from him.

I am glad that the *Inscriptions* please you. It did always appear to me that inscriptions, particularly those in verse, or in a dead language, were never supposed *necessarily* to be the composition of those in whose name they appeared. If a more striking or more dramatic effect could be produced, I have always thought that, in an epitaph or memorial of any kind, a father, or husband, etc., might be introduced, speaking, without any absolute deception being intended; that is, the reader is understood to be at liberty to say to himself, — these verses, or this Latin, may be the composition of some unknown person, and not that of the father, widow, or friend, from whose hand or voice they profess to proceed. If the composition be natural, affecting, or beautiful, it is all that is required. This, at least, was my view of the subject, or I should not have adopted that mode.

However, in respect to your scruples, which I feel are both delicate and reasonable, I have altered the verses; and I have only to regret that the alteration is not more

[1] Washington Allston, an American painter, began a portrait of Coleridge at Rome in 1806, and took another of him at Bristol in 1814. — Ed.

happily done. But I never found anything more difficult. I wished to preserve the expression *patrimonial grounds*, but I found this impossible on account of the awkwardness of the pronouns *he* and *his*, as applied to Reynolds and to yourself. This, even where it does not produce confusion, is always inelegant. I was therefore obliged to drop it; so that we must be content, I fear, with the inscription as it stands below. As you mention that the first copy was mislaid, I will transcribe the first part from that; but you can either choose the Dome or the Abbey as you like.

> Ye lime-trees, ranged before this hallowed urn,
> Shoot forth with lively power at Spring's return;
> And be not slow a stately growth to rear
> Of pillars, branching off from year to year,
> Till ye have framed, at length, a darksome aisle,
> Like a recess within that sacred pile
> Where Reynolds, 'mid our country's noblest dead,
> In the last sanctity of fame is laid, etc.[1]

I hope this will do; I tried a hundred different ways, but cannot hit upon anything better. I am sorry to learn from Lady Beaumont that there is reason to believe that our cedar is already perished. I am sorry for it. The verses upon that subject you and Lady Beaumont praise highly; and certainly, if they have merit, as I cannot but think they have, your discriminating praises have pointed it out. The alteration in the beginning, I think with you, is a great improvement, and the first line is, to my ear, very rich and grateful.

As to the "female and male," I know not how to get rid of it; for that circumstance gives the recess an

[1] See *Poetical Works*, Eversley edition, Vol. IV, p. 78. — Ed.

appropriate interest. I remember Mr. Bowles the poet objected to the word "ravishment" at the end of the sonnet to the winter garden; yet it has the authority of all the first-rate poets, for instance, Milton:

> In whose sight all things joy, with *ravishment*,
> Attracted by thy beauty still to gaze.

Objections upon these grounds merit more attention in regard to inscriptions than any other sort of composition; and on this account the lines (I mean those upon the niche) had better be suppressed, for it is not improbable that the altering of them might cost me more trouble than writing a hundred fresh ones.

We were happy to hear that your mother, Lady Beaumont, was so surprisingly well. You do not mention the school at Coleorton. Pray how is Wilkie in health, and also as to progress in his art? I do not doubt that I shall like Arnold's picture; but he would have been a better painter, if his genius had led him to *read* more in the early part of his life. Wilkie's style of painting does not require that the mind should be fed from books; but I do not think it possible to *excel* in *landscape* painting without a strong tincture of the poetic spirit. . . .

CCXL

William Wordsworth to Lady Beaumont

GRASMERE, Wednesday, Nov. 20, 1811.

My dear Lady Beaumont,

When you see this you will think I mean to overrun you with inscriptions: I do not mean to tax you with putting them up, only with reading them. The following

I composed yesterday morning, in a walk from Brathway, whither I had been to accompany my sister.

FOR A SEAT IN THE GROVES OF COLEORTON [1]

Beneath yon eastern ridge, the craggy bound
Rugged and high of Charnwood's forest-ground,
Stand yet, but, Stranger ! hidden from thy view,
The ivied ruins of forlorn Grace Dieu, etc.

I hope that neither you nor Sir George will think that the above takes from the effect of the mention of Francis Beaumont in the poem upon the cedar. Grace Dieu is itself so interesting a spot, and has naturally and historically such a connection with Coleorton, that I could not deny myself the pleasure of paying it this mark of attention. The thought of writing the inscription occurred to me many years ago. I took the liberty of transcribing for Sir George an alteration which I had made in the inscription for St. Herbert's Island. I was not then quite satisfied with it; I have since retouched it, and will trouble you to read him the following, which I hope will give you pleasure : —

This island, guarded from profane approach
By mountains high and waters widely spread,
Gave to St. Herbert a benign retreat, etc. [2]

I ought to mention that the line

And things of holy use unhallowed lie

is taken from the following of Daniel,

Straight all that holy was unhallowed lies.

[1] See *Poetical Works*, Eversley edition, Vol. IV, p. 80. — Ed.
[2] See *Poetical Works*, Eversley edition, Vol. II, p. 212. — Ed.

I will take this occasion of recommending to you (if you happen to have Daniel's poems) to read the epistle addressed to the Lady Margaret, Countess of Cumberland, beginning

He that of such a height hath built his mind.

The whole poem is composed in a strain of meditative morality more dignified and affecting than anything of the kind I ever read. It is, besides, strikingly applicable to the revolutions of the present times.

My dear Lady Beaumont, your letter and the accounts it contains of the winter garden, gave me great pleasure. I cannot but think, that under your care, it will grow up into one of the most beautiful and interesting spots in England. We all here have a longing desire to see it. I have mentioned the high opinion we have of it to a couple of my friends, persons of taste living in this country, who are determined, the first time they are called up to London, to turn aside to visit it ; which I said they might without scruple do, if they mentioned my name to the gardener. . . .

Do you see *The Courier* newspaper at Dunmow? I ask on account of a little poem upon the comet, which I have read in it to-day. Though with several defects, and some feeble and constrained expressions, it has great merit ; and is far superior to the run not merely of newspaper but of modern poetry in general. I half suspect it to be Coleridge's, for though it is, in parts, inferior to him, I know no other writer of the day who can do so well.[1] It consists of five stanzas, in the measure of *The Fairy Queen*. It is to be found in last Saturday's paper,

[1] It was by Coleridge. — Ed.

November 16th. If you don't see *The Courier*, we will transcribe it for you.

As so much of this letter is taken up with my verses, I will e'en trespass still further on your indulgence, and conclude with a sonnet, which I wrote some time ago upon the poet, John Dyer. If you have not read *The Fleece*, I would strongly recommend it to you. The character of Dyer, as a patriot, a citizen, and a tender-hearted friend of humanity, was, in some respects, injurious to him as a poet; and has induced him to dwell in his poem upon processes which, however important in themselves, were unsusceptible of being poetically treated. Accordingly, his poem is, in several places, dry and heavy; but its beauties are innumerable, and of a high order. In point of *imagination*, and purity of style, I am not sure that he is not superior to any writer in verse since the time of Milton.

SONNET [1]

Bard of the Fleece! whose skilful genius made
That work a living landscape fair and bright;
Nor hallowed less by musical delight
Than those soft scenes through which thy childhood strayed,
Those southern tracts of Cambria, deep embayed.

In the above is one whole line from *The Fleece*, and two other expressions. When you read *The Fleece* you will recognise them. I remain, my dear Lady Beaumont, your sincere friend,

W. WORDSWORTH.

[1] See *Poetical Works*, Eversley edition, Vol. IV, p. 273. — Ed.

CCXLI

Dorothy Wordsworth to Mrs. Clarkson

GRASMERE, December 27th, [1811.]

... I hope that she[1] will attend Coleridge's lectures, yet I cannot wish that she should see him; for I have little doubt that he would open out his sore afflictions to her, which could only distress her, whether she believed them justly so called or the delusions of his own self-deceiving heart. If you go to London, you will certainly see him, and the whole will be laid before you; and, for this reason, I do sincerely wish that you may not go thither; for I know so well the power of his presence that I should dread the effects upon your health. But perhaps, as I now trust he will, he may have triumphantly concluded his lectures; and in that case he will perhaps be too well satisfied with himself to delight in dwelling upon his supposed afflictions in the presence of one ready to rejoice with him in all good. As to the lectures themselves it is my opinion that it is a great pity that so many of his best thoughts, and of the thoughts of his friends, should be thus loosely scattered abroad; but that, if he does go through it, is well he *has* lectured, as he probably would have done nothing else; and, having completed one design, there is better ground to hope that he may hereafter complete others. He has promised to come down to Keswick immediately after the lectures. I wish he may; but I do not think he *can* resolve to come, if he does not at the same time lay aside his displeasure against William. Surely this one act of his mind out-does all the rest.

---

[1] Mrs. Clarkson's sister. — Ed.

William, for the most benevolent purposes, communicated to a friend a small part of what was known to the whole town of Penrith—sneered and laughed at there, to our great mortification—and we would have made any sacrifice to draw him away from Penrith. William communicated this to a friend, who, in three days travelling with C., saw the whole with his own eyes; and William is therefore treacherous ! ! He does not *deny* the truth of what William said, but William ought not to have said it; although in fact by so doing he believed that he was taking the best means of preventing the spreading further, and to fresh persons, what it was so distressing to him to know. But why do I return to this subject? William bears all with calm dignity, neither justifying himself nor complaining of C. If you go to London, you will, I hope, see something of the Lambs. *Much* it is not possible to see of anybody in that wide city. . . . When I described our house to you,[1] it was in summer; and we had no fires in the parlour. In winter we find the whole house cold, and — woeful to tell — our larger parlour smokes so much that we cannot light a fire there. Consequently we have no sitting-room but William's study, a *very* small parlour. . . .

Looking through the window, I see the moonlit mountains covered with new-fallen snow. But, to return to the smoke, we have been obliged thus far to submit to the inconvenience, and must endure it yet some weeks longer, on account of the parson's tithe-corn, which is lodged in the barn, and the chimney cannot be cured till that is removed. We hope however that it may be cured, but there are other inconveniences attending our

[1] See the letter to Mrs. Clarkson, dated June 16, 1811. — Ed.

situation, which in summer we did not fully perceive. The
field is a perfect bog; and our landlord is so dilatory
that we may wait yet another half-year before we are
clean and decent, even at our very doors. . . . We had
the finest Christmas day ever remembered, a cloudless
sky and glittering lake; the tops of the higher mountains
covered with snow. Instead of going to church I had a
pleasant walk with William in the morning. In the evening William and Mary walked by moonlight, and I played
cards with the children, a treat which is to be repeated
on New Year's day. . . .